Praise for Fifty Over Fifty

Women tell our stories to each other. We learn from them and we are encouraged by the honesty and goodwill behind them. Dr. Susan R. Meyer has taken this process one step further: not only has she found inspiring women who share their successes and failures, but she brings her own smart and experienced perspective to the challenges of taking risks and achieving your dreams. Suzanne Braun Levine, author,
Inventing the Rest of Our Lives: Women in Second Adulthood

I am blown away by Susan's ability to take the fifty interviews she conducted, and weave them into a fascinating book about resiliency, hope and finding happiness and fulfillment. There are great lessons here for all of us, but Susan takes them a step further with her helpful questions at the end of each chapter to get each of us thinking about how we can enhance our lives. Bravo Susan! Cheryl Benton, Chief Tomato, *The Three Tomatoes*

Fifty Over Fifty is a unique, inspiring book that speaks to every woman who wonders how she can lead a rich, full life ... both under and over fifty. The exercises and techniques provide a solid foundation for beginning to create your own wonderful life. The stories of these fifty women from different walks of life will make you feel like you know each of them, and perhaps even recognize yourself as one of them.

Speaking from personal experience, fifty is just the beginning! This book is for every woman who wants to make the most of this most creative, delicious stage of life. Donna Steinhorn, Executive Coach and Life Strategist,
TEDx Navesink Co-organizer

Fifty Over Fifty is a compelling insight into the underlying strength and magic of the human spirit. Dr Meyer shows us the qualities and foundation for modern women to 'own' and fully express their authentic power and leadership in a world in need of what women uniquely can offer any organization or community.

This book can bridge the generations and give all of us an insight into the wisdom that only living an authentic life can provide. My work has been about showing people that life gets better and better as we grow older—this book goes further to show us how we can also expect to become more loving, more adventurous, and more powerful every day.

At the end of the day, all I can say is THANK YOU for allowing me to share this insight into the power and wonder of women as they grow in wisdom. Jim Selman, The Eldering Institute

FIFTY OVER FIFTY

Wise and Wild Women
Creating Wonderful Lives
(And You Can Too!)

Dr. Susan R. Meyer

Dedication

THIS book is dedicated to Louise Lauro Meyer, my mother, and the first person to show me that writing about your life matters. And to Gloria, the first woman I ever interviewed, who set me on a path of discovery.

Acknowledgements

First, I will always be grateful to and delighted by the fifty women who generously shared their stories with me. They not only found the time for their interviews, but several of them, especially Corbette Doyle and Jan Babiak, introduced me to incredible women that I otherwise would never have met.

My editor, Bonnie McDermid, not only handled the delicacy of each story, but also did the interior design and served as project manager, handling the many details that so easily escape me and was a constant source of support and a shared laugh.

I am grateful to John Broughton and Mary Sue Richardson for opening up the world of adult development and women's studies to me and to Jack Mezirow for including me in his journey of discovery in the realm of transformative learning.

I'm grateful to friends, family, colleagues, and everyone who patiently listened to endless stories and supported me through bad transcriptions, missing files, writer's block, and all the other not-so-lovely parts of this journey of creation.

Finally, I am thankful for each person who picks up this book and shares my joy in exploring the wonderful life available at fifty and beyond.

Table of Contents

Introduction

HAVE you ever had a question that nagged at you and just wouldn't let go? It's that persistent type of question that led me to research and write this book.

For many years, I thought that being resilient—bouncing back—was everyone's natural response to life's twists and turns. I had certainly bounced back enough times myself. I thought everyone was persistent, curious, able to move past fear, able to think about the mark they would leave on the world.

But when I thought about the hundreds of clients I have coached and taught, I realized that, no, not everyone is born resilient. In my research, I found characteristics of resilience, such as curiosity and persistence, to be hallmarks of a special group of women who have been able to shape lives of significant depth and contribution, lives that are uniquely satisfying to them.

Upon further research, I came to realize that these are characteristics that can be described and, most importantly, can be developed. I know many women—from every socioeconomic level, ethnicity, heritage—who have learned them and used their power to build meaningful lives of their own choosing.

I developed these abilities, too, during a childhood that had all the characteristics of a scary fairy tale. My mother died shortly before I turned nine, and I began learning to take care of myself as best I could. We lived with relatives where my shy, introverted self couldn't keep up in a circle of extraverts, so I found ways to create little pockets of peace and escaped into books. My father remarried and his wife fit the stereotype of the wicked stepmother—she piled on the housework and was verbally and physically abusive. I, again, retreated into my books and schoolwork. Eventually, she sent me off to boarding school where I thrived.

Later, I was sent to live with my grandparents. Life with my alcoholic, verbally-abusive and physically-threatening grandfather was a huge challenge, as was the death of my father when I was thirteen. By then, I had learned that there would be no Prince Charming riding to the rescue—I needed to take care of myself.

The resilience I developed enabled me to look for reasons to be happy—and I found them. I got involved in school activities and the youth group at my church, made friends, and compartmentalized my home life.

That resilience has served me well. As an adult, I followed a few career paths—some disastrous, like math-phobic me as assistant to the comptroller of an employment agency. I taught at every level, from pre-school to graduate school, worked for employment agencies, and spent a couple of decades in organizational development, training, and training management. I discovered that the common theme in all my jobs is teaching and coaching and found the best ways to combine my strengths to create the work I love. Most important, I've built a happy life—wonderful friends and family, work, travel—and I'm still stretching and growing.

I just took it for granted that most people did the same; that everyone picked themselves up, dusted themselves off, and moved on. I assumed resilience was inborn, not learned.

Then, in the '80s, I became a cooperative education coordinator at Medgar Evers College, where the women I met gave me deeper insights into what it takes for a woman to pull herself out of poverty, bounce back from tragedy, and live her dream. I saw real strength in women who overcame abuse, loss, drugs, poverty, and neglect. They survived by learning to be resilient.

Their stories about developing self-esteem in spite of significant resistance were the focus of my doctoral dissertation. As they spoke about friends and family in their community opposing their dreams, it became clear that something distinguished my students from other women who simply gave up and settled into the multi-generational cycle of poverty.

How did they do it?

What made them want to beat seemingly insurmountable odds?

How did they change?

These are the questions that have intrigued me and nagged at me throughout my thirty years of working with women who want to change their lives. These are the questions that have driven me to research women's lives and the changes they have made and to use their life stories as a basis for teaching, coaching, and life planning. And these are the questions that drove me to interview dozens of women who have been especially successful at making major life changes—these women and their stories are the heart and soul of this book.

In these pages, you will hear from fifty women (The Fifty) who carved their own paths, found their own answers. Their spirit, courage, and life stories have deeply inspired me, and it is my hope they will inspire you, too. Whether you are happy and satisfied in your life and want to understand how you arrived at that place, or are feeling stuck and looking for motivation to make changes, there's something in this book for you.

Why This Book? Why Now?

I think that life should be an adventure. Every day holds possibilities and surprises, from making a new friend to mastering a new skill, from enjoying a magnificent sunset to cuddling a baby, from that trip around the world to exploring your own neighborhood, from enjoying live theater to curling up with a favorite book. Everything can be an adventure. Everything can create opportunities for joy.

What I see, what makes me sad, is that this feeling does not seem to be universal. You, your sister, your mother, or a close friend may be floundering, depressed, or just bored. You or they may be looking for a little bit of inspiration, or hoping to regain your optimism.

You are the reason this book exists; there is something valuable for each of you in these pages. To help you find the "nuggets" of wisdom and inspiration, or just to put yourself in a receptive frame of mind, read and think about the questions below.

Have you asked yourself some or all of these questions?

Is there more to life? Is there something else I could be doing? What's next for me?

Have you ever felt a niggling, underlying restlessness?

Do you just plain feel stuck and don't see why you should even try to change your life?

Have you embarked on a new journey "just because?"

Are you always looking to enrich your life with new challenges, new experiences?

Have you thought about how to create a better future?

If you are over forty, fifty is right around the corner. Why not start planning now? My grandmother charted a new course in her eighties.

Each chapter of this book contains examples of the paths women have taken. These stories are meant to give you ideas and to get you thinking about what might be possible. If you'd like to be better at change, you can use the exercises, tips, and tools in each chapter to help you learn how to develop the characteristics you're reading about and start on a new journey towards a more fulfilled life.

Looking for Meaning in Second Adulthood

Sometimes, it's easy to get stuck in our own lives. We move along, oblivious of how quickly time is going by, not focusing on what we really want to do. We become deadened by day-to-day events and we don't look more broadly at our situation. And, most importantly, we don't take time to develop a plan.

Some women experience dissatisfaction at midlife; they are ready to just give up. I imagine them with Peggy Lee singing in the background, "Is That All There Is?" Their answer to Ms. Lee's question is, "Yes," and they stop looking for satisfaction.

Other women, however, seem to have an innate sense of adventure, an ability to remain open to what might be available, to see how a new position will draw on old skills. They plan, rearrange, repurpose, and experiment.

What makes these two groups of women different? The first characteristic of The Fifty, the women who tell their stories in this book, is they have an innate sense of adventure. Some of them have had highly-visible, world-class successes; others have had equally valuable, but far less visible achievements. All have experimented and found ways to remain vibrant and active.

A second characteristic unique to The Fifty is they have chosen to be happy. They actively, persistently focus on the positives in their lives, even in the face of substantial difficulties. To paraphrase Lynn, "Yes, I've had a bad divorce, I've had cancer, and I've had financial hardships. But I've always chosen to be happy." No, she is not a Pollyanna or delusional. She simply chooses to find the happy moments, even in the hardest times.

In reading the stories of The Fifty in this book, you will learn the seven characteristics that contributed to their ability to change, to grow, to remain vibrant and active throughout their lives. What attitudes contribute to their buoyancy? Why are they resilient? This book addresses these questions.

To misquote Margo Channing (1950), "Buckle your seat belts. It's going to be a bumpy ride." And inspiring. And fun.

How This Book is Organized

The first section of this book offers context for the stories. It begins with a psychological description of midlife as a developmental phase followed by contrasting perspectives on midlife from a variety of experts plus a quick look at some relevant research. You will then meet the cast of characters—the fifty women whose stories and wisdom made this project possible. You will read excerpts from their life stories throughout the book, plus you will be able to read my complete interviews with all of the woman in a free e-book form or individual interviews on my website.

The second section of this book focuses on the seven characteristics that work together to create a fulfilling, satisfying, happy life, which I discovered through my interviews. One chapter is devoted to each characteristic, illustrated by stories of how several different women lived the core characteristics. Within each chapter, you will find exercises to help you look at that characteristic within your own life.

The third section of the book contains final notes, resources, and reference lists. If you would like to explore the seven characteristics further, that is where you'll find more information to help you.

The Seven Characteristics of Wise and Wild Women

Yes—you are a wise and wild woman. You have had so many experiences! You've learned so many lessons—how could you not be wise? Perhaps your wildness is subtle, but it's there.

A wild woman is simply one who continues to stretch and express herself. One friend of mine, in her '80s, expresses her wild side by participating in dance recitals. She still does a mean cartwheel, too. Another expresses her wild side by remaining a lifelong learner. This year, she is exploring spirituality. A third keeps improving her garden and trying—and posting—interesting recipes.

Wild means expressive. It doesn't necessarily mean headline-grabbingly flamboyant.

Below are the seven characteristics I identified in the women I interviewed, the traits that support creating a satisfying, wise, and wild life:

1. Resilience

Resilience is the power or ability to recover readily from adversity; elasticity; buoyancy. We will all face challenges in life—disappointment, disease, loss—all of these can stop us in our tracks. Sometimes, so much seems to be going wrong that it's hard to resist the urge to take to our beds ... forever. After all, it worked for Victorian ladies, didn't it?

However, if you are going to rise above your challenges and thrive, you will need the ability to bounce back and find alternate paths around them.

2. Persistence

Persistence is lasting or enduring tenacity; persevering in spite of obstacles, opposition, and discouragement. If something did not work the first time, The Fifty tried again, made adjustments, and tried again. They didn't give up or walk away from what they knew they wanted. Neither did they maintain a false optimism, chasing after something that could never become a reality. Instead, these persistent women identified the core elements of what they wanted and explored other paths to meet their needs.

3. Curiosity and Restlessness.

Curiosity involves, exploration, investigation, and learning. Curious people have a thirst for knowledge, and often, a sort of restlessness. They might be unable to resist either a new challenge or something different to explore. So many of The Fifty are lifelong learners. They are always exploring; some described themselves as easily bored.

4. Openness to New Things.

While this characteristic can be closely related to curiosity, it also includes a sense of adventure. Women who create their ideal lives are much more likely to say, "Why not?" than "Why?" If offered the opportunity to create a new business or move to Asia, they say, "Yes."

5. Scanning the Environment, Recombining and Synthesizing.

This characteristic has three elements. First, environmental scanning is the ability to look around, observe and see nuances and changes. When it is combined with synthesizing and recombining, it is a very powerful characteristic. Second, recombining is simply reorganizing; using skills and ideas in unusual or unexpected ways. Third, synthesizing is the ability to pull seemingly different ideas and skills together to create something original. These three elements work together to create one characteristic which is often present in conjunction with curiosity and openness to new things.

For example, many of the most successful women I spoke with were able to scan the horizon and see emerging trends and possibilities. This requires being able to take both a broad and narrow view. It is easier to create your ideal life when you see how everything you know and have done can be recombined and synthesized, reused in unexpected ways, or brought together in an unusual manner.

6. Dealing with Fear

We are all afraid sometimes. We are, in fact, hard-wired to sense danger and flee. Unfortunately, our brains often remain in cave-dweller mode, conditioned to revert immediately to flight or hiding as the only options.

Women who thrive learn how to handle fear differently. Yes, they feel fear, but they work through it. They face difficult situations head on. They separate unrealistic fears from realistic ones and then develop a plan to move beyond fear and into action.

7. *Creating a Legacy and Having Fun*

While it is easy to think of legacy as a financial issue, that definition is very narrow. Legacy can also be something transmitted by or received from an ancestor or predecessor. It could be a book you have written, an organization you have created, or that secret recipe handed down from your grandmother.

According to Jung, the second half of life is about making meaning—creating a personal legacy. The Fifty grappled with what their legacy would be. They thought about what they were contributing to the world and giving back.

In addition, I've added the notion of having fun to this chapter, since this seemed to be a key element in how these women thought about their lives. Having fun and giving back were inextricably linked for them.

As you move through this book, you may find that you have developed some of these seven characteristics fully and may want to increase your ability to incorporate the others into your life. Take notes. Write in the margins. Mark stories that speak strongly to you and come back to them.

This is a book that is meant to become dog-eared and well used. I have enjoyed every step of the journey that led to this book. I hope you enjoy it as well.

Chapter 1

What's All the Fuss About Midlife?

HAVE you ever wondered if there's more to life? Do you move from one new project or adventure to the next, still looking for the one that feels right? Have you simply stopped trying?

Some women have felt the exhilaration of doing something that felt so right, so powerful they could hardly believe it was happening. They might embark on a new journey "just because." They enrich their lives with new challenges, new experiences. Some women seem to have an innate sense of adventure—they remain open to new possibilities, what might be available; they plan, rearrange, repurpose, and experiment.

Yet other women find midlife difficult. They stick to what they know—and have always done. They don't see any space in their lives for new pursuits. Others feel just plain feel stuck and don't see why they should even try to change.

What makes these two groups of women different?

The stars of this book, the "fifty over fifty" (The Fifty), have an innate sense of adventure. Some of them have done really big things in the world; others have not. But all have experimented and found ways to remain vibrant and active. What they share is the ability to see life as something exciting, whether they are making preserves or scaling a mountain.

The Fifty have chosen to be happy. They want to enjoy their lives. To paraphrase Lynn: Yes, I've had a bad divorce, I've had cancer, I've had financial hardships—but I've always chosen to be happy. Lynn is not a Pollyanna or delusional; she simply chooses to find the happy moments even in the most difficult times.

In reading the stories of these fifty women, it is possible to identify common factors that contributed to their ability to change, to grow, to remain vibrant and active throughout their lives. What attitudes contribute to their buoyancy? Why are they resilient? These are the questions this book addresses.

I've been working with women who want to change their lives for over twenty years, and all of these questions have intrigued me. I also love stories—especially life stories. There's no one answer to life's big questions. In these pages, you will hear from fifty women who carved their own paths, found their own answers. They have inspired me, and it's my hope they will inspire you too. You'll also find some tools and tips to get you started if you want to take a closer look at your own life.

Embracing the Richness of Midlife

In spite of much evidence to the contrary, we Americans hold very negative perceptions of old age. One only has to go to the theatre or a movie to witness impressive examples of women who vibrantly alive, active, and busy well into their seventies. Think of Maggie Smith who is still acting in her late 70s and Jessica Tandy, whose career spanned six decades.

Vanessa Redgrave and Susan Sarandon have combined long and successful acting careers with political activism. Queen Elizabeth II, born in 1926, shows no intention of stepping down from the throne. Maya Angelou was a major literary and cultural influence until her death at age 86. Betsey Johnson continues to design. Gloria Steinham continues to be an active feminist and author. There are countless examples of women, famous and not-so-famous, who are leading rich, full lives.

So why aren't these the images that come immediately to mind when we think about growing older?

Youth Culture Erased the Mature Woman

Since the 1960s when young Americans rebelled against the status quo, youth has been glorified and maturity denigrated. As a result, attractive images and representations of mature women have been almost non-existent in advertising, movies, and the media, all which significantly influence American opinions and perceptions. Women talk about reaching "the age of invisibility," a time when they are no longer recognized as attractive or valuable by men, other women, or younger people in the broader American society.

Earlier generations of Americans revered and recognized elders as keepers of cultural knowledge and traditions. They held the wisdom of their culture and passed it on to the next generation, who sat with them, listened, and learned. In contrast, most of today's elders lead lives detached from their families, some alone, many in segregated retirement communities. The stereotypes we have aren't pretty or accurate—irrelevant old women shunting back and forth to activities or staring blankly into space. The wise crone—our elder—is no longer revered. She's hidden from public view.

The Numbers Game

The sheer number of women in their midlife years makes us significantly more influential than women have been in the past. According to U.S. Census data, there were 37 million midlife women in the United States in 1996. By 2011, that number was over 51 million. The current number of middle-aged people in society is unprecedented. Just a few generations ago, only ten percent of the population survived past age forty. (U. S. Census)

That's a pretty depressing statistic, perhaps, but it underscores how new this whole notion of midlife is. It wasn't something that was studied; it wasn't something we thought about too much.

According to Wikipedia, the life expectancy of women is eighty-two years. What this means for us is many midlife women will be able to reinvent their lives in ways that simply haven't been available to women in the past.

First, that generous life expectancy offers precious additional years for many women to reinvent their lives; the "bonus decades" as Abigail Trafford calls them. Second, much less social pressure to conform makes it easier for women to choose life paths that would have been frowned upon a few generations ago.

But this group of women has led and lived through significant social upheaval—working outside of the home, single parenting, medical advances and controversies, increased acceptance of lesbian relationships, the emergence of the women's movement, and increased cultural diversity—all which have broadened the opportunities and the choices midlife women can make today.

Many of my grandmother's friends (and most in my mother's generation too) either were homemakers and mothers their entire lives, active in the PTA and civic organizations, in gourmet cooking or square dancing clubs, and in their religious communities. Others worked, mostly in typically female occupations like teaching, nursing, or secretarial work and then retired to a relatively quiet life of gardening, mahjong, bridge or perhaps a book club. Maybe they traveled a little.

My grandmother was a bit different. Born in 1901, my grandmother worked as an executive secretary from age eighteen until she retired at sixty-five.

After my grandfather died, my grandmother went on cruises. She toured Europe. She moved in with her sister and brother-in-law, joined the local temple, and reestablished her religious roots. Boredom struck. Grandma moved into her apartment and, tired of visiting her grandchildren and great grandchildren, got a job taking care of an "old lady" when she was past eighty herself.

Today, more women are like my grandmother. A coach I know, now in her late seventies, moved to a new, more vibrant community a few years ago after decades in the same home where she had raised her family. "I love my old friends," she told me, "but I need to talk about more than lip gloss and grandchildren."

My own coach echoes that sentiment; she creates local and national events that allow her to spend more time with like-minded people. Another woman, also past seventy, created a salon to bring women together for serious discussions on a variety of current and important topics. Another discovered blogging and now has a thriving social media business.

As the country braces for the huge demographic shift—in 2014 there will be more older people than younger people—this is a good time to examine what this next phase (second adulthood, third act; take your pick of catchy attempts to name the phenomenon) really looks like for women and how best to create a successful agenda for what lies ahead.

Midlife Transition – Crisis or Adventure?

Being in the middle of life may be an impetus for change but is not necessarily grounds for a crisis. Midlife is a normal developmental life stage, and both men and women experience shifts at midlife. This transition can be a positive and mindful process of creating the whole person you will be for the second half of your life, or it can be dreary, scary and bleak. The choice is yours. It cannot be avoided. Live long enough, and it's as inevitable as was adolescence. You will experience loss and change and let go much of what you brought into midlife. Prepare now, pay attention, and you will be able to complete this journey with more joy and less struggle.

Shift of Focus in Midlife

Remember how important it was to win prizes, certificates, and awards to validate your successes during adolescence? We were real people pleasers who needed outward symbols to show the world who we were even as we were still trying to figure that out. For many of us, our happiness depended more on acceptance by others than acceptance by ourselves.

Some of us never let go of that need for external approval; for others, that need is replaced by inner satisfaction. We do more things to please ourselves and enrich our lives; that could be anything from creating CDs so our grandchildren have better music to creating an organization to promoting e-readers in our schools to working with the aging or ill who need our help.

At midlife, we focus on becoming who we were meant to be rather than who we think others want us to be. This second part of life often involves an intense, impassioned exploration and discovery of our inner world as well as reconfiguring our relationship to the outer world for a better fit.

Some authors call this time second adolescence or second adulthood. I call it *adultescence*. This term is more commonly used to describe adults who seem to be trapped in adolescence and is used in a negative way. I think we should flip it! I think of *adultescence* as a time to become wise and wild, to learn how to really enjoy life while finding deeper meaning and purpose.

Your Most Creative Years Could Be in Front of You

As with youthful looks and beauty, intellect and creativity are rumored to diminish with age. The skewed perception that midlife is the beginning of a long, downhill slide was influenced by Freud. Sigmund Freud was fifty-one years old when he wrote, "About the age of fifty, the elasticity of the mental processes on which treatment depends is, as a rule, lacking. Old people are no longer educable." And, in defiance of his own pronouncement, Freud went on to accomplish much of his best work past the age of sixty-five.

Early theories of intelligence insisted that intelligence peaks in a person's thirties. However, Gene Cohen's more current research reveals that, in fact, as we get older we have the potential to get better. He found that with age our brains "grow wiser and more flexible; they also tend toward greater equanimity." In addition, he found that "studies suggest that the brain's left and right hemispheres become better integrated during middle age, making way for greater creativity." (Gene Cohen, 2005)

Disturbing questions begin to bubble up: "Is this all there is? What's missing? What's next? Where do I go from here? Why haven't I found my passion by now? Is it too late for me?"

Most recommendations for those at midlife combine networking, self-exploration, and experimentation as ways of avoiding depression and decline. Researchers tell us that mental well-being is linked to life satisfaction. When women can't seem to figure out their lives, or can't seem to make the pieces fit, depression and lethargy may set in.

Many researchers focus on midlife as a period of loss, citing waning looks, reproductive capacity, physical strength, economic status, security, social network. For some at midlife, without warning, their rules for "the game of life" become invalid. They feel set adrift, unable to develop a new game plan for the rest of the journey.

Yet, it is just as easy to see midlife as a period of gain. Wisdom, freedom from putting the needs of others first, independence, new social networks, and great strength and capacity are all possibilities. Midlife does not need to mean the end of the line; retreat into retirement; being tossed to the side of the road. This is the opportunity for reinvention in unprecedented ways. Whether midlife signals the deepening and enrichment of the activities of adulthood or creating a whole new script, it is a time when women can shape their lives without all of the "shoulds" that may have constrained them earlier.

A Time for Reflection

According to Lachman & James (1997), midlife may be akin to mid-term or mid-semester at school. A midpoint is a good time to pause and reflect on what you have achieved and what you might still plan to do before moving on. Those who don't reflect are more likely to stagnate or become depressed.

For those who are goal-oriented, midlife is often a time for reflection. He says that in later life, achieving ego integrity involves accepting life for what it has been. That acceptance, though, does not necessarily result in passivity. The emphasis in midlife may be on what remains to be done.

Glass Half-Full or Half-Empty?

Whether you think midlife signifies that life is half over or there's half remaining could lead to different outcomes, according to optimism research by Isaacowitz. (Isaacowitz et. al., 2000).

"Baby Boomers at Midlife," a national survey by the American Association of Retired Persons, tracks baby boomers annually and compares them to younger and older groups. Baby boomers are generally optimistic about the future and expect things to keep getting better. Sixty-four percent of baby boomers said they were hopeful about the next five years and eighty percent were satisfied with the way their life was going. (AARP, 2013)

Optimism levels of baby boomers resembled those in young adulthood more than those of the older cohort. However, the two areas in which baby boomers felt they were not doing as well as they would like were finances and leisure time. They had expectations that things would get better in both of these areas, but were less optimistic they would reach all of their goals than other cohorts. (AARP, 2013)

Midlife offers opportunities to make new choices, to decide how you want to invest your time and resources, and to address areas that need change. Sometimes changes can be precipitated by "wake-up calls." A serious accident, loss, or illness in midlife often leads to a major restructuring of ways of looking at the world, or perspective transformation, a reassessment of priorities and a change of direction.

According to Maggi G. Saucier (2004), author of *Midlife and Beyond: Issues for Aging Women,* problems related to a woman's feeling that she no longer conforms to society's standards of youth and beauty may lead to low self-esteem, depression, and anxiety. As we see more role models active late in life, however, these norms are changing. The September, 2013 issue of *More* magazine had a four-page spread on coats modeled by Lauren Hutton, who was born in 1943.

Several of The Fifty didn't seem to hit their stride until past retirement. Some are creating new things in their seventies and eighties and show no signs of slowing down. As a woman over forty (perhaps well over forty), you too have much to contribute to the world and a lot of fun to have. Listen to the voices of the women in this book. Take away lessons from what they say. Be inspired to create your own wise and wild life.

Chapter 2

Cast of Characters

I was delighted to meet fifty wonderful, wise, and wild women on my journey to this book. Before you dive into the many things I've learned from them, I'd like to introduce each of them, so you have a glimpse of who you'll be listening to as their stories unfold. What follows are short introductions to the women who shared their stories with me. You can follow threads of each story throughout the book.

Debbie Ahl

Debbie Ahl, former President and CEO of Sterling Life Insurance Company and Olympic Health Management Systems, has enjoyed a career that has evolved serendipitously. Early on, she took a job in her local hospital's emergency room because it allowed her to complete her education. Thinking she would be heading off to a job in the media, she was offered a position as the hospital's Public Relations Coordinator. After nearly thirty years of experience in strategy development, business growth, and corporate leadership—including four corporate acquisitions—she is recognized as a perceptive leader with keen sensitivity to and awareness of organizational readiness, appropriate timeliness of new initiatives, and the dynamics of both individual and team interactions. She is also seen as a strategic leader and a skillful communicator, adept at intentionally building company culture, coaching and developing leaders, creating team alignment, and producing results. As she prepares for the next phase of her career, she continues her work in mentoring emerging leaders and start-up companies, continuing to apply the perspective and leadership skills she has sharpened through her work with a variety of organizations to make an impact on key issues that matter.

Jan Babiak

Jan Babiak started her first business before she was eight years old. While adventurous and flexible enough to embrace the unexpected, she is practical and a planner. She has combined the unexpected with the planned to create the life she wants, down to a home that accommodates her husband's need for long bike rides and their desire to create a retreat where friends are always welcome. Jan is an experienced business leader with more than thirty years in various global management and international board-level roles with Ernst & Young and other public companies. Her current focus is a full-time board portfolio focused on large global public companies. A current council member on the governing body of the Institute of Chartered Accountants in England and Wales (ICAEW), Jan is currently on the boards of Walgreens, Bank of Montreal, and Experian.

Cheryl Benton

Cheryl Benton planned to teach high school English until a shortage of full-time positions led her into a marketing position with a technology firm. She brings all the skills she developed in marketing and advertising to her current passion to improve the lives of women. Cheryl is the publisher of the *Three Tomatoes*, a newsletter focused on women over forty-five which she created because there were no resources for the seasoned, savvy women she knew who wanted to have a great life. Her career spans thirty years in the New York City advertising agency business. Today, in addition to publishing the *Three Tomatoes* she is at the helm of her own marketing consulting firm, 747 Marketing. Her desire to be involved with a broader agenda for women's rights worldwide led her to become active in the United States National Committee for United Nations Women.

Isora Bosch

Isora Bosch is a contradiction to any stereotype you might try to attach to her. She's a citizen of the world, detached from her country of origin and making space for herself in several cultures. She's a black Cuban, ex-Republican, clinical social worker who will bring out her guitar to play and sing flamenco at a moment's notice. Her educational background also includes organizational psychology and adult education. She fled Cuba with her parents when she was in her teens. Her career has spanned a variety of leadership positions in social work, training, post-traumatic stress disorder treatment, and mental health clinic management, wage and salary administration, mental health, education, and staff development. She says she's been trying to retire for the last five years now, but finds it impossible to turn her back on her clients.

Phyllis Campagna

Phyllis Lee Campagna meets life head on, with determination and a huge smile on her face. She credits her role model, Amelia Earhart, as the source of her conviction that she can do anything she put her energies into. Phyllis, a business and performance coach, is the owner of Excelsis Performance Strategies and has built her twenty-three year practice primarily from client referrals. Phyllis was the first business coach in the United States to be credentialed as a Chartered Business Coach™ (ChBC™) through the Worldwide Association of Business Coaches, and she has completed advanced mediation training through the Divorce Mediation Institute. She has served in more than twenty business and civic leadership positions including Rotary president and lieutenant governor, four years on the Community Unit School District 300 Board of Education, and volunteer mentor for Women Unlimited. Phyllis is the mother of two daughters and lives with her husband, Jerry, near Chicago.

Agenia Clark

Agenia Clark knows how to say, "Yes." Throughout her career, she's been offered mentoring and opportunities by some remarkable people, and she's made great use of every opportunity that came her way by working hard, remaining open, and continuing to learn.

Agenia is President and CEO of the Girls Scouts of Middle Tennessee. Following a career in broadcasting, she held executive positions at Northern Telecom, Vanderbilt University, and the Tennessee Education Lottery Corporation. Clark currently serves on the advisory council to the College of Business at the University of Tennessee, Knoxville and on the steering committee for Nashville's Agenda. She has served on countless community and state boards including the Nashville Area Chamber of Commerce, the Community Foundation of Middle Tennessee, Tennessee Board of Regents, and corporate boards including Avenue Bank. She is a committed volunteer for Leadership Nashville, the region's premiere executive leadership organization. She has also has been honored by the Corporate Board Walk of Fame and the Tennessee Economic Council on Women for her leadership and was inducted into the YWCA's Academy for Women of Achievement. One of her most cherished "Yeses"—accepting the invitation to be a guest coach for the famed Tennessee Lady Volunteers basketball coach, Pat Summit.

Nancy Colasurdo

Nancy is a journalist, blogger, life coach and the creator and founder of Unfettered50.com. She is commissioned to write for three blogs, including a weekly post called "Day Brake" for A Day Well Lived, a venture with over 250,000 social media followers. Nancy, who has been making a living as a writer since 1986, wrote a twice-weekly column called Game Plan for FoxBusiness.com for five years and has also been published on MarketWatch.com, Entrepreneur.com, CNBC.com, Beliefnet.com and in *Ladies Home Journal* and *Parents* magazines. While a sports writer/columnist at the *Trenton Times*, she won a national award for a series on knee injuries in female athletes, edging out competition from the *New York Times* and *Sports Illustrated*, and was a Knight-Wallace Journalism Fellow at the University of Michigan. She has also worked as a web producer (FoxSports.com, NHL.com) and a television producer (Oxygen Media). She has written her first book, a memoir.

Tish Davey

Tish Davey is a survivor. Her ability to buckle down, persevere, and do whatever she had to do—including accept the support of others—kept her alive. When Tish was pregnant with her third child, she started having extreme shortness of breath that her doctor attributed to her pregnancy. In June 1993, she met with a pulmonologist who finally diagnosed her with sporadic lymphangioleiomyomatosis (LAM). The only possible treatment, a double lung transplant, required her to move to St. Louis, where a tag team of friends cared for her during the wait. Six years later, she has been able to resume her career and her life.

Loretta Donovan

Loretta Donovan's natural curiosity and desire to play with new ideas keeps her vibrant, busy, and happy. Loretta is Chief Learning Officer and Director of Learning & Talent Development for the Health Quest System as well as the founder and president of the Worksmarts Group. She is the author of chapters and articles on appreciative transformative learning and coaching, and collective intelligence and social media. She has served as a member of the Global Council of Appreciative Inquiry Consulting. Loretta has been an Adjunct Instructor at New York University, where she taught courses in Appreciative Inquiry and e-Learning Assessment Theories and Strategies; she taught Strategic Learning in Organizations, Staff Development and Training, and Leading and Sustaining Web-Based Learning at Teachers College, Columbia University. She also contributed her time as the chair of the Career Grants Panel for AAUW Foundation, a member of the National Advisory Board, Stanford University Educational Leadership Institute, and a member of the Lifelong Learning Advisory Committee at Columbia University, Teachers College.

Corbette Doyle

Corbette Doyle's simple desire to return to school for an advanced degree led to a whole new career. Corbette is on the faculty at Vanderbilt University, where her areas of expertise include diversity in the workplace, women's leadership, risk financing, and the healthcare industry. She currently serves on the board of Martin Methodist College and the Professional Liability Underwriting Society. Formerly at Aon, she was responsible for leading the creation and execution of a global strategy to build a more diverse workforce and a more inclusive workplace. She consults with Fortune 500 companies and professional service firms on their diversity and inclusion strategies and is an external member of Nissan America's Executive Diversity Council. Prior board affiliations include Definity Healthcare, Sterling Insurance Company, the American Society of Healthcare Risk Managers, the CPCU Board of Governors, and the Owen Alumni Board.

Connie Duckworth

In retirement, Connie Duckworth is working as hard as she did at Goldman Sachs. Connie is a social entrepreneur who founded ARZU in 2004 to empower destitute women weavers in rural Afghanistan. ARZU, which means "hope" in Dari, started with thirty weavers and has transformed from a micro-business incubator into a learning laboratory for holistic grassroots economic development. Today, it employs some 500 women, providing access to education and basic healthcare; seeding multiple micro-business start-ups; building community centers, pre-schools, and parks; and creating award-winning fair-labor rugs—all in a country ranked as "the world's worst place to be a woman." She serves pro bono as ARZU's Chairman and CEO. Connie retired in 2001 from her position as Partner and Managing Director of Goldman Sachs, where she was the first woman to be named a sales and trading partner in the firm's history.

Nancy Fritsche Eagan

Nancy Eagan's experiences at Kent State influenced the direction of her life. Nancy is founder and president of People Potential and has provided consultation and training services to public and non-profit organizations since 1983. Nancy is a practitioner and steward of the Art of Hosting Meaningful Conversations and facilitates organizational and community development through the use of participatory and engagement tools. Nancy was part of the National Government Organization United Nations Commission on the Status of Women planning group in 2012 and 2014. She co-facilitated World Cafés with over 800 people at the 100th Ecumenical Gathering of the National Council of Churches and The Church World Service. Nancy serves on the board of Women's Initiatives for a Sustainable Earth, is a member of the New York City Center for Social Innovation, and works as a senior facilitator at Good Shepherd Services. She is a specialist in change strategies, relationship and community building, leadership development, and project management.

Sharon Fender

Sharon Fender is a woman who decides to do something and then lets nothing stand in her way. Sharon is a self-taught leader with over twenty-four years of experience as Principle of Baxter Industrial Services, Inc., a general contractor and project management company serving the food processing industry. Their projects include the construction and renovation of refrigerated food plants, cooler, and freezer rooms, and renovation of United States Department of Agriculture food plants. Previously, she was regional sales manager for West Personnel Services, Inc. a staffing company providing cerical placement and temporary employment services to small and large corporations. Her interest in travel, especially to Africa, keeps her active in the Association to Promote Tourism to Africa. She is also vice president of Ultimate Travel Adventures, Inc.

Sally Frissell

Sally used her long-time career as a flight attendant to explore the world and create an open schedule that allowed her to volunteer at an orphanage in Cambodia for extended periods of time. She most enjoyed the humanitarian flights that were part of her regular job, including reuniting members of the military with their families and escorting orphans to their adoptive families. Now, splitting her retirement time between New York City and Maine, Sally continues her volunteer work in Asia and is planning to volunteer at a preschool in Sri Lanka.

Charlotte Goldston

Charlotte has been in the financial services industry for more than three decades. She was the first woman stockbroker hired by J. C. Bradford & Company, then the largest regional brokerage firm in the southeast, for their Nashville office. She became a partner, in which position she remained until the firm was sold to Paine Webber and then to UBS Financial Services. She is Senior Vice President-Wealth Management with UBS where she is consistently one of their Club Level producers and continues to learn and get certifications in the financial industry. Her team, Goldston Financial Group, provides comprehensive financial and investment services for a select group of high net worth individuals.

She is well known in the Nashville investment community and wrote an investment column in the *Nashville Banner* for over fifteen years, contributed to other publications, and was a guest on local television and radio programs.

Charlotte is very active in the Community and has served on numerous boards, including those of Belmont University Massey School of Business, the Nashville Symphony Guild, Community Concerts, Rocketown, and the Fannie Battle Day Home. Life-long animal lovers, she and her husband, Michael, raise award-winning alpacas on their farm in the historic village of Leipers Fork; Charlotte served on the Southeastern Alpaca Association Board for eight years.

Kathy Gulrich

Kathy Gulrich has a wonderful way of combining and recombining her skills in a continuing experiment with the shape of her life. Kathy moved from teaching math and music to a twenty year career in advertising that included executive positions in Hong Kong, Singapore, and Milan. Her interest in art led to a career as an artist; then success in selling her artwork sparked a new business in coaching artists. In recent years, coaching requests from realtors led to a new career in Manhattan real estate. Most recently, she has relocated to Maine and has been considering coaching women at midlife and possibly continuing her adventures as The Cooking Coach. Currently, she's having a ball working as a disc jockey (lots of blues and jazz) at WMPG, Southern Maine Community Radio.

Robyn Hatcher

Robyn Hatcher turned a childhood disadvantage—extreme shyness—into the basis for a successful and joyous life. Robyn, an author and communication skills expert, is founder and principal of SpeakETC, a boutique communications and presentation-skills training company. She recently launched her first book, *Standing Ovation Presentations*. Prior to founding her own consultancy, Robyn worked as a professional actress. She appeared on stage in New York and in regional theatre productions as well as in television commercials and dramas. She is a voiceover talent for radio advertisements. Robyn served as a writer for two daytime dramas and is a contributor to American Express Open Forum.

Phyllis Haynes

Phyllis Haynes honed her skills as a great interviewer, fact-finder, and discoverer of what's best in people during her college and graduate years at New York University when she became active in politics and social causes. Phyllis is an award-winning television personality, producer, former ABC news correspondent, and former host of the long-running television show *Straight Talk* She has been motivating, training, and inspiring people around the world and across the United States for over twenty years.

Phyllis was invited to serve on the faculty at Emerson College in Boston and in the Netherlands; she was also invited by the European Union and the Hellenic Foundation to bring her knowledge of media and communications to the emerging broadcast markets of Central and Eastern Europe. She received the American Film Institute Award for a film with Susan Sarandon entitled *AIDS: The Facts of Life!* As the owner of Studio 1 Network, Phyllis produced the *Profiles in Wisdom* series. She continues her documentary work and interviews of thought leaders .

Susana Isaacson

Susana Isaacson learned a lot about diversity and living in a multicultural world when her family fled Romania. Prior to retirement in 2007, she served as Founding Director of Leadership Development, Organizational Learning, and Professional Coaching at the National Clandestine Service of the Central Intelligence Agency. In that capacity, she established a ground-breaking leadership development program which continues to thrive and serve the organization. Susana has traveled widely around the globe and lived in Europe and North and South America. Since retirement, she has built a robust practice as executive coach, consultant, and facilitator in a variety of organizations from government agencies to nonprofit institutions. She co-created the COPIA partnership in 2009. Right now, she's setting the stage for her next great adventure.

Marla Isackson

Marla Isackson is a senior marketing executive with over twenty years of experience, who has had a highly-successful career in growing and managing diverse businesses within the retail, Internet, and financial sectors. She is an expert in the development and expansion of consumer loyalty programs, strategic planning, and marketing development, and has created innovative and profitable marketing initiatives for some of the most famous names in business. She created Heart of Gold, an online community for teen girls. This evolved into LikeaBossGirls.com, the place to go to get the inspiration and information that Millennial girls need to make a living, make a difference, and make it big! The site gives young women the tools, information and inspiration they need to explore and connect with their goals including finding (or creating) their dream job, becoming entrepreneurs, social activists, leaders: basically pursuing success however they may define it.

Rita Henley Jensen

Rita Henley Jensen is Founder and Editor-in-Chief of *Women's eNews*, an independent, nonprofit daily news service which launched in 2000 to cover issues of particular concern to women. Jensen is a survivor of domestic violence and a former welfare mother of two who earned degrees from Ohio State University and Columbia Graduate School of Journalism. A former senior writer for the *National Law Journal* and columnist for the *New York Times* syndicate, Rita has more than thirty years of experience in journalism and journalism education. She has received numerous awards, as has *Women's eNews*, including the Casey Medal for Meritorious Reporting.

Bethene LeMahieu

A lifelong learner and teacher, Bethene has always experienced education as a setting in which to explore the human potential. Her seminal work in education—designing and implementing magnet schools to integrate a community by choice—has touched thousands of people and provided a framework of creativity and change.

As a Fulbright Scholar for study in India, Dr. LeMahieu has experienced profound realities in her work and personal life. As an Associate of The Actors Institute in New York City, Bethene has realized a new focus and a positive redirecting of her goals. In 2000, she created and led the course "Storying Our Lives" for The Actors Institute This offering was designed for cross-generational groups to come together to story their life experience; to discover themselves broadened, deepened, nourished, and known; and to experience the fullness of each other.

After 9/11, she co-authored an audio book, *Ground Zero & the Human Soul: The Search for the New Ordinary Life*. In 2006, she created Salon, a space where participants can take part in conversations that matter in a setting in which their opinions can be fully expressed, fully heard and responded to by others.

Bethene's most recent study has been a year-long exploration of women's spirituality as both verb and noun. This study began with the historical, a setting of context through time, moved to the personal and went on to the political. Now, it has become practical.

Deb Leon

Deb Leon began her career as an executive for a major retail chain and then became an artist whose original paintings sold for five figures. Her artwork was carried in over 300 galleries and shops worldwide and reproduced in prints, calendars, posters, cards, collector plates, and more. She used her entrepreneurial skills to build a 200+ employee call center that she sold to a client company in 2008. Her love of animals led to the creation of Whisker-Docs, the first 24/7 pet help line providing multi-channel access for pet parents to licensed veterinarians. She's currently working on two books, the first being *The Unlikely Millionaire: A Guide to Making Money on Your Own Terms*. Her second book, *The Little Book of Big Thoughts*, is a compilation of short, personal musings to inspire and motivate the reader.

Alice Aspen March

Alice Aspen March arrived in New York City four years ago to create the next phase of her life. Prior to her work with The Attention Factor®, Alice started and served as executive director of the non-profit group Focusing Awareness on Children and Television (FACT), which kept *Mr. Rogers' Neighborhood* on the air. In that role, she also sold the concept for and co-produced the Emmy-nominated documentary, *Latch-Key Kids*, starring Christopher Reeves. She was appointed to two different California State Commissions, to the White House Conference on the Family, and was recognized for her expertise at a national conference of 2,000 television executives in Las Vegas. Alice is a published author who has traveled internationally giving keynote addresses, staff trainings, workshops and seminars, and contributed to work and educational panels in New Zealand, Belgium, Greece, Mexico, and in various cities around the United States.

Lynn Meyer

Lynn Meyer's early career story sounds like a little Holly Golightly glamour mixed with a touch of Helen Gurley Brown's *Sex and the Single Girl*, living at the Barbizon Hotel for Women and prepping models in showrooms. Following a stint as a buyer at Bloomingdales, Lynn left the workforce to raise her children. After her divorce, she returned to work and has had a varied career, primarily in sales. She is the mother of four and grandmother of seven. After spending many years as a manufacturer's rep for clothing and novelty lines, she is recently retired and enjoying her grandchildren and volunteer work driving seniors to medical appointments.

Marcia Meyer

Marcia was a senior marketing executive at PetSmart who decided to take early retirement. She fell into the Be Kind People Project when she offered to host a crafts group for her sister. What started out as a small gathering of women who shared a commitment to learning, creating, helping, and supporting others in meaningful ways, turned into an annual event called Holiday Crafts, Cheers & Laughs®. The event now boasts over 400 attendees in Phoenix, Arizona and Kansas City, Missouri. Be Kind started out as a way to give back to teachers and has grown into a national movement promoting kindness in schools. You may spot Marcia's school bus parked in front of a school in your area.

Susan Meyer

Susan Meyer is curious and loves a good life story—exactly the combination she needed to create this book. Susan is President of Susan R. Meyer Coaching & Consulting and past president of the International Association for Coaching. She is a Master Masteries Coach with a doctorate in Adult Learning and Leadership and Master's degrees in Counseling and Educational Psychology. Susan introduced agency-wide coaching in New York City agencies when she created an executive coaching program for the Human Resources Administration. Her Women Living for Today and Tomorrow workshops were featured in the *New York Times* and her tele-class series, Mapping Midlife—Sensational at Sixty, has helped to energize the lives of many. Her books include: *Mapping Midlife–Sensational at Sixty* and *The Life Design Blueprint Playbook*.

Natalie Tucker Miller

Natalie Tucker Miller's childhood goal was to have fun. She has not only done that, but has also infused a spirit of fun into all her interactions. She is an internationally-recognized speaker, certified coach, instructor, and coach certifier. Natalie works with leaders in the elder care industry and provides training and coaching for executives and staff.

She is the founder of Ageless-Sages.com, a publishing company specializing in illustrated picture books for elders. She is also producing books on historic events of interest to elders and personal development books. From 2006-2008 she served as president for the International Association of Coaching (IAC) and currently serves as Lead Certifier for the IAC.

Louise Morman

Louise Morman brings determination and the ability to explore, learn, and create new things to all she does. Louise is an experienced management consultant and executive coach who has focused in the areas of strategic planning, marketing, energy efficiency, and sustainability. She served as a senior management executive for three major energy companies, including the New York Power Authority. Faced with the inability to get adequate care for her ailing parents, she turned their home into a first-class critical care facility. Currently, she is Executive Director of Miami University's Lockheed Martin Leadership Institute, a program that she developed in the College of Engineering and Computing.

Melinda Moses

Melinda has spent most of her career creating marketing and business development programs, producing content, and forging alliances that help emerging technology companies grow and prosper. Today, Melinda brings this expertise to her practice as a solo strategic marketing consultant and business coach. She helps independent, local, and artisanal businesses create marketing plans that create and expand audiences, build value, and enable the development of sustainable ecosystems that maximize their potential. The power of stories, content and techniques that engage her clients and their audiences is a fundamental element of her work. The planning always begins with life goals, resources, and maintaining a balance.

When not participating in the launch and ongoing color-commentary about important local ventures such as the Ashland, Massachusetts Farmers Market, Dragonfly Community Arts Festival, or STEM enrichment projects in local schools, Melinda can be found creating multifaceted social, digital, and community-building solutions that help her clients get found, get engaged, and get results. She dreams of creating rich, immersive experiences both online and offline that result in greater awareness of, investment in, and long-term viability of the locally made, the hand-crafted, and the magnificent people who are the creative economy.

Lynda Moss

Lynda has had a long career as an artist and in arts-related non-profit leadership. She is a working artist and devotes time to creating support for the arts. As a Democratic member of the Montana Senate, she represented District 26 from 2004 to 2012, working on policies ranging from historic preservation and social justice to planning and health care. She was a majority whip in the 2008-2010 session. Lynda served as executive director of the Foundation for Community Vitality for ten years and continues to create art and develop her consulting practice. Lynda has initiated regional and international cultural and economic development programs linking non-governmental organizations, foundations, and government agencies.

Valerie Olbrick

Valerie Olbrick decided that her bucket list couldn't wait any longer. She is an independent consultant who has been a high-impact business leader for more than thirty years with extensive experience in the global arena. Her specialties include global technology, operations, information security, knowledge management, social networking, business management, acquisitions, and divestitures. She is currently an information technology executive near Washington, D.C. A licensed boat captain, Val spends weekends and holidays on her boat. Her future may include a portfolio career, consulting, and/or operating her own sailing school for women.

Jeannette Paladino

After starting as a business reporter, Jeannette built a long and successful career in marketing and corporate communications, including positions as Senior Director of Citigate Communications, where she was responsible for managing the Deloitte Consulting account; Senior Vice President-Corporate Communications for Marsh & McLennan, the world's leading insurance brokerage firm; and Senior Vice President of Bowery Savings Bank. Jeannette is now a successful social media consultant.

Audrey Pellicano

Audrey Pellicano, RN, MS, has been in the health care industry for over thirty-five years as a registered nurse and case manager before becoming a certified grief recovery specialist. When she was widowed at the age of thirty-eight with four young children, Audrey discovered that available solutions did not work for her. Her studies in complimentary therapies, including guided imagery, yoga, meditation, nutrition, grief recovery, and thanatology, combined to create a unique set of skills to work with those challenged with panic and anxiety related to life and health challenges and to her program to provide relief and hope for those grieving a loss. Audrey is a contributing author to the Army Community Service's Survivor Outreach Services newsletter and is a volunteer bereavement counselor in New York City. She is also the host of New York City's first Death Cafe', where people come together in a relaxed and safe setting to discuss death, drink tea, and eat delicious cake.

Susan Perry

After some success as actress, Susan, her husband, and an agent friend created Actor's Information Project, an organization to support actors in being more productive and satisfied in their careers. This proved to be an early coaching initiative and started several now-prominent coaches on their career path. Susan also became involved with the Playwright Theater of New Jersey, a group that taught playwriting in juvenile facilities, leading her toearn a master's degree at Rutgers School of Criminal Justice and to her work as a probation officer in Newark, New Jersey. After moving to Charlottesville, she worked in a group home, then as a case management counselor at a women's prison. Wanting to make a lasting difference to women offenders, Susan is now involved in the establishment of a halfway house for women who have been recently released from prison.

Deb Roth

Deb spent thirteen years in the corporate world, followed by a stint as co-owner of a successful family-owned children's music business. She is now is a life and career transition coach, relationship coach, and interfaith minister. Her master's thesis was on the power of transformative ritual, and she loves creating unique, magical wedding ceremonies and baby blessings. Deb also leads monthly New Moon Sister Circles in New York City as well as "virtual" Full Moon tele-meditations. Deb sings in a women's chorus, is on the board of The Heart and Soul Fund (which supports community programs serving marginalized populations in New York City), and has produced six successful benefit productions of *The Vagina Monologues* to support VDay in their work to end violence against women.

Linda Schacht

For over thirty years, Linda has advised government, business, and non-profit leaders on communications and strategy. She is a veteran of the Carter White House press office and held the top communication position for a presidential campaign, the majority leader of the United States Senate, and the Senate Democratic policy committee. Schacht was the first public affairs director of *USA Today* and a member of that publication's launch team. She worked at the Coca-Cola Company in New York and Atlanta, serving three chairmen and retiring as Vice President-Global Communications and Public Affairs Strategy. In 2002, she returned to higher education as a senior fellow at the John F. Kennedy School of Government at Harvard University where she was affiliated with both the Center for Public Leadership and the Center for Business and Government. Schacht is also a former Woodrow Wilson Teaching Fellow and a board member of the International Women's Media Foundation.

Bunnie Schrober

After a career in data entry, customer service, and hospitality in the U.S. and Germany, Bunnie left work to raise her daughter. Just when she was ready to return to work, she became involved in caring for her ailing mother. After her mother's death, she realized that she needed to look for a new career direction. She was able to combine her prior experiences with everything she learned about health care to create a successful career in home health care.

Susan Schwartz

A Harvard graduate with a Ph.D. in Medieval Studies and a former university professor, Susan has over twenty-five years in financial services marketing and marketing communications, utilizing her powerful research skills and analytical processes that span a broad range of disciplines and lateral thinking. She is a published author of over thirty science fiction/

fantasy books. She has spoken at The U.S. Naval War College, The U.S. Military Academy, The U.S. Air Force Academy, Princeton University, Binghamton University, the National Securities Agency, Mount Holyoke College, Smith College, the Library of Congress, and was a participant in 2010 TRADOC Mad Scientists Conference.

Larraine Segil

Born in South Africa, Larraine immigrated to the USA in 1974. After practicing international corporate law, she co-founded a California thrift and loan company and a series of free-standing ambulatory care clinics. She is a regular commentator for CNN and CNBC and delivers keynote speeches on domestic and global alliances and mergers, and critical customer, supplier, channel, and outsourcing relationships. Larraine is the author of multiple business books, including *Intelligent Business Alliances, Fast Alliances: Power Your E-Business, Dynamic Leader, Adaptive Organization: Ten Essential Traits for Managers, and Partnering–The New Face of Leadership*. Her latest book, *Measuring the Value of Partnering*, is the first written on the topic of alliance metrics. Larraine has also written a novel, *Belonging*, and two cookbooks. A composer and lyricist, she has produced three compact discs under the label Rockin' Grandma. She also runs a small, family-held agricultural holding company, Little Farm Company.

Ivy Slater

Ivy Slater began her career as assistant to Lucille Roberts, the exercise center mogul. She then worked in a corporate event planning and catering firm before joining her father's printing business. After several years, she established her own successful printing business and spent fifteen years in the industry. She found herself giving advice to other women who wanted to start businesses. Persuaded by friends, she began to teach women how to create profitable businesses. Ivy has created a successful career coaching female entrepreneurs, speaking and facilitating workshops, and recently, has published her first book.

Donna Steinhorn

Donna's diverse background includes work in the fashion and training industries before she created her own coaching business. After years as a personal and executive coach, Executive Vice President of Coachville, and the Dean of Thomas Leonard School of Coaching, Donna partnered with Guy Stickney and Bobbette Reeder to create Conversation Among Masters, a high-level, invitation-only conference for coaches and The Coach Initiative, a non-profit organization which provides *pro bono* coaching to charitable organizations. Donna also serves on the board of the Transformational Leadership Council and was the co-organizer of a TED event.

Herta von Stiegel

Herta von Stiegel, J.D., is Founder and CEO of Ariya Capital Group, a Nairobi- and London-based financial services and project development firm focusing on clean energy and infrastructure investments in Africa. Previously, she held senior positions at Citibank and J.P. Morgan and, until 2005, was managing director at AIG Financial Products. A tax lawyer by training, she serves on the boards of several corporations and not-for-profit companies, as the first independent chair of CHAPS Clearing Company Ltd., the United Kingdom's primary wholesale clearer of sterling payments with a volume in excess of $100 trillion per annum, and Opportunity International, the second largest micro-finance organization in the world. For her fiftieth birthday, Herta organized a group of able and disabled individuals to climb Mount Kilimanjaro. She documented this experience in an award-winning film and in her book, *The Mountain Within*.

Carole Wehberg

Carole spent thirteen years in marketing, sales, and communications at Avon before starting her own consulting firm. After her marriage ended, she juggled consulting assignments so she had more time to support her son in dealing with the challenges of diabetes and blindness. As her son got older, she worked for the Girl Scouts and The Foundation Center. Her love of languages, travel, and the arts are combined in her newest careers, working with a French hospitality organization and as a tour guide at Lincoln Center.

Betsy Werley

After 25 years in the for-profit sector as a corporate lawyer and banker, Betsy became the first Executive Director of The Transition Network, an organization that provides support, networking, and activities for women over fifty who are planning the next phase of their lives. In July 2013, Betsy embarked on her own next phase—cross-country travel with her husband. Upon her return, she became an Encore.org Innovation Fellow, developing a network of encore organizations. Betsy has spoken about the encore stage of life and transitioning to the nonprofit sector for the American Society on Aging, the Positive Aging Conference, outplacement firms, alumni organizations, and networking groups. Her volunteer interests include mentoring and women's professional development. As president of the Financial Women's Association, Betsy launched a mentoring program for undergraduate women business majors at Baruch College, now in its thirteenth year. She was also a leader in J.P. Morgan Chase's women's network and launched its New Jersey branch.

Dina Wilcox

Dina was a successful editor at a publishing company when she became involved in political activism, leading her to become a lawyer. After the terminal illness of her husband, Dina left her law practice to become a spokeswoman and activist. She has published her first book, *Why Do I Feel This Way?* which describes how she learned to honor her feelings and build a new life after the death of her husband.

Barbara Woods

Barbara studied acting in college and landed her first acting job immediately after graduation. She has had a varied career as the first actress/model/DJ, including theater roles and parts in television series and commercials. She moved on to become a flight attendant and then worked for HBO, where she did production, promotion, and some marketing. She made an unusual shift into public service and currently handles special projects for the largest agency in New York City's municipal government.

Phoebe Woods

Phoebe is a principal of CompaniesWood, a consulting firm that specializes in advising and investing in early stage companies. She retired as Vice Chairman and Chief Financial Officer of Brown-Forman Corp. in 2008 with over thirty years of domestic and international finance and management experience in the energy, technology, and consumer products industries. Phoebe currently serves as a director of Coca-Cola Enterprises, Invesco, Ltd., Leggett & Platt Corp., and Pioneer Natural Resources. She is also a trustee of the University of Louisville, the Gheens Foundation, and the American Printing House for the Blind, and trustee emerita of Smith College, her alma mater. She has an Master's of Business Administration from University of California-Los Angeles and was named one of 100 Inspirational Alumni of the Anderson School of Management.

Victoria Zackheim

Victoria Zackheim is the author of the novel, *The Bone Weaver*, and editor of six anthologies: *He Said What?: Women Write About Moments When Everything Changed*; *The Other Woman: Twenty-one Wives, Lovers, and Others Talk Openly About Sex, Deception, Love, and Betrayal*; *For Keeps: Women Tell the Truth About Their Bodies, Growing Older, and Acceptance*; *The Face in the Mirror: Writers Reflect on Their Dreams of Youth and the Reality of Age*; *Exit Laughing: How Humor Takes the Sting Out of Death*, and *Faith: Twenty-Four Essays From Believers, Agnostics, and Atheists* (2015). Her play, *The Other Woman*, based on her first anthology, underwent development at the Berkeley Repertory Theatre. Her play, *Entangled*, is now in development at Z Space Theater in San Francisco. Victoria's first screenplay, *Maidstone*, is now in development. She is the story developer and writer of the documentary film *Tracing Thalidomide: The Frances Kelsey Story*, now in development, and writer of *Where Birds Never Sang: The Story of Ravensbruck and Sachsenhausen Concentration Camps*, which aired on PBS nationwide. She teaches Personal Essay in the UCLA Extension Writers' Program. Victoria was a 2010 San Francisco Library Laureate.

Shoya Zichy

Shoya is an internationally-recognized seminar leader, author, and coach. Shoya had a twenty-year career in marketing, management, and journalism at Citibank, Merrill Lynch, American Express, and *Institutional Investor* including a four-year expatriate assignment in Hong Kong. Creator of the award-winning Color Q Personalities system, she is the author of *Career Match: Connecting Who You Are With What You'll Love To Do* and *Women & The Leadership Q*. Past President of APTNY, the Myers-Briggs Association of New York, and former board member of the Financial Women's Association, she is an adjunct instructor at New York University. Shoya has recently collaborated on the creation of an online dating service based on her Color Q system

Chapter 3

Like a Rubber Ball – The Role of Resilience

Why do some women take "No" for an answer while other women successfully work around the obstacles between themselves and their goals? Why do some women keep going in the face of adversity? The answer is resilience.

Resilience is the power or ability to recover readily from adversity; elasticity; buoyancy. We all face challenges in life. What's important is having the ability to bounce back and to rise above or find an alternate path around those challenges.

Drive and Focus

Every woman in The Fifty has a strong drive to get what she wants out of life. She also accepts that setbacks, obstacles—even a certain amount of unhappiness—are part of life. In the face of adversity, rather than resist or give up, each woman finds and applies the lessons to make further progress toward her goal or to guide the creation of a new plan.

Creative and Flexible Thinking

Resilient women who negotiate change know how to figure things out. They have the ability to quickly survey the range of possibilities, evaluate them, and make a clear plan for their next steps. Even those creative and flexible thinkers who are not adept long-range planners tend to be great short-term planners, according to Shawn Achor, in *Before Happiness*. They have the valuable ability to select the most valuable reality—the view of circumstances that makes it most possible to move forward—out of a range of ideas. That also sounds like a good definition of resilience to me.

Realistic Perspective

Maintaining a realistic perspective is essential to resiliency. This includes both letting go of unrealistic dreams and accepting that life is a mixture of emotions and experiences. Comedian, singer, and workshop leader Beth Lapides asserts that in order to be fully happy 88% of the time, you must accept that you will be unhappy 12% of the time. (Lapides, presentation, August 16, 2013) She points out that being "fine" is as far from happiness as you can get, but that happiness and unhappiness are actually adjacent states. If emotions were represented as a circle or pie chart, they would be next to each other. Thus, she reasons, it is better to work through the unhappiness—change—than to pretend everything is fine and stagnate. Similarly, Martha Beck says, "Everything that happens to you—good or bad—is designed to wake you up and make you happy." It's all a matter of perspective. (Beck, presentation, August 16, 2013)

Resilience in the Lives of The Fifty

Both Cheryl and Phyllis C. showed early signs of resilience in the following stories from their college years. When Cheryl's initial approach to getting a job didn't work, she made a decision that redirected her life:

Cheryl: I actually started out, when I graduated, with thoughts of being a teacher and taught high school English for a very brief period of time. But I was substituting because in the early '70s, a lot of guys, in order to stay out of Vietnam, had actually gone into teaching. So, there were really no full-time teaching jobs. By this time, I was also going through a divorce, and I knew I was going to have to support myself and my daughter. I thought, *Well, let me just try and get some kind of summer job that pays decently and see what happens in the fall with teaching.*

I went to work for a technology firm, and I ended up getting into advertising and marketing which ended up being my career. So you never know where your life paths are actually going to lead you.

Seeing Opportunities Instead of Obstacles

Having an open attitude makes a huge difference in creating the life you want. Some women see nothing but obstacles, but these women saw opportunities. For Phyllis C., the opportunity to take a year off and travel around the country with her husband was not to be missed, so the obstacles of no income, living on savings, and family disapproval faded in comparison.

Phyllis C.: We [both] quit our jobs. Most of our family and friends were not supportive. We were both in promising careers and they felt that we were being extraordinarily foolish to interrupt those careers in what should be our career-climbing years. We took off and we had ... oh, my gosh, we had so many adventures.

Resourcefulness

Along the way, Phyllis and her husband were resourceful in finding ways to finance their travels and in the face of emergencies.

Phyllis C.: In Texas, we worked a rodeo with a family. In Missouri, in the Bible Belt, we ended up helping people fix cars. We lost the engine to our van in Salina, Kansas; had to have the engine replaced. Problem with that was it cut into the finances we [had] saved—we were really living on two to five dollars a day in order to be able to go for a year. So we stayed with some family of mine in Midland, Texas for a month. I had done some waitressing in college and I went into Denny's restaurant there and said, "You know, I'm here just for the holiday, and I know your system, and I'd like to earn some money." They hired me for a month. We replaced the money and went on.

John and I got to Phoenix. I believed with all my heart that the center of the universe for fun and joy and entertainment was Las Vegas. John and I had a little bit of a spat.

I said, "Well, why don't we leave for Las Vegas tomorrow morning?"

He said, "Well, you know, we could go to the Grand Canyon and then in a few days, we can go to Vegas."

I said, "The Grand Canyon? I mean, that's like a tourist trap, right? It's like a big hole in the ground, right?"

He said, "You know, it is one of the Seven Wonders of the Natural World, and we really should see it. I mean, we're traveling the entire country."

Reluctantly I said, "Okay, fine. Let's just get up there. We'll take a look at it. Maybe if we drive fast enough, we could still make it to Vegas tonight."

We got to Mather Point. I jumped out of the van. I thought, *Okay, we'll make short work of this*. I really was committed: I felt every fiber of my being pulling me to Las Vegas. We walked up to the Rim. I'm not sure what John was doing, but about thirty minutes later, he was at my side. This was one of those serendipitous moments of following my soul: I was stuttering.

I said, "Well, I don't know what we're going to do. I'm not leaving." There was no forethought, there was nothing; it was almost forced out of my mouth.

He was a little bit confused. He said, "Well, okay. There's a campground in the park. We could ..."

I said, "No, you're not hearing me. I am not leaving."

Once again, serendipity kicked in and every coincidence that could occur did. Within about three hours, we both had jobs in the park. We had made an agreement before we started traveling that we would never pick up a hitchhiker. But that day, we did pick up a hitchhiker in the park who had asked if he could have a ride to the dorms.

We said, "Dorms? Why are there dorms here?"

He said, "Well, people work here." (It hadn't occurred to me to think about that.)

We dropped him off and said, "How did you get to work here?"

He said, "The human resources office is over there."

We walked in and they said, "What can you do?"

We said, "We'll do anything. I'll make beds, I don't care. I just want to be here."

But once they went through our background, I was hired into the accounting department. John, who was a very good mechanic, was hired on the buses.

As fate would have it, in order to work on the buses, we had to agree that he would buy some tools. We either had to go back to Phoenix or we had to drive to Las Vegas [to buy the tools]. So, we had three days in Las Vegas. I discovered that, while it was a blast, it wasn't that much of a blast. That was another lesson.

We worked at the Grand Canyon for just about a year and then I was promoted from the accounts receivable department. I was specifically sought out to become the CFO of a new multi-functional resort hotel they had purchased in the National Forest,

Mokey Lodge. I wasn't needed for a few months, so I asked for a six-month sabbatical. We traveled six more months around the country, returned to the Grand Canyon, and worked there another year. I was part of a three-person executive team to open up this new unit of theirs.

We left to return to Illinois when I became pregnant with my older daughter. Part of why we came home was that auto-immune disease I had. One of the considerations I had was that I probably would have had a lot of trouble with the pregnancy; there was not much medical help up in the Canyon. Our families were back in Illinois, and I felt strongly that the children belonged with family. So, we resigned. I may have been about five months pregnant.

From the time we left the park to well past Flagstaff, I couldn't stop crying. I felt that I was leaving my soul, I really did. And what's funny about me—I'm not an outdoors girl. I can't imagine why people do picnics when there's a very lovely table inside the house. I just don't enjoy the outside, except for the Canyon. There, I want to be outside. I want to go to different places along the Rim and just be with it … for hours and hours. There wasn't a day in the two years I was there that I wasn't with it in some way. Maybe in a past life, maybe I was part of one of the tribes there.

Like Phyllis C., Susana used her ability to see opportunity in obstacles and turned her greatest challenges into her greatest successes:

Susana: There were challenges because the CIA infrastructure is mostly male. What I developed was the courage to speak truth and still be compassionate. I think a lot of people [both men and women] are willing to accept compassion from a woman.

What enabled me to "get across" is the fact that I am a woman doing what everybody called "touchy-feely work," which was more acceptable from a woman. So I started calling myself the Queen of Touchy-Feely because that was so contrary to what people were used to in that organization. So the fact that I am a woman, that I have a foreign accent, and that I am willing to show I care and open doors for women, opened doors for me. It gave me entry to places that I otherwise would not have had access. So yeah, it was challenging.

Never Take "No" for an Answer

Q. You mentioned challenges based on who you were: someone who had come to the United States. I'm curious if there were also challenges being a woman in all this?

Susana: It's an interesting question, Susan, because I think what I did with that challenge was to turn it around so it worked for me. If I learned anything in the first fourteen years of my life in Transylvania, it was to just keep going and to not take obstacles as walls, but to take them as, "Oh, let me see if I can look at this in a different way."

While some women may simply say, "Oh, well" when they come to an impasse, many of The Fifty saw "No" as an opportunity. Phyllis C. describes one of her college experiences this way:

Phyllis C.: I became a female DJ on the campus radio station, which was pretty unusual. In order to do that, I became a 3rd Class Engineer, so I could work at the radio station. I did the engineering side as well. And because I was a 3rd Class Engineer, I was recruited on a field trip to Chicago, to the studios of WGN.

This was about 1970. I remember standing in the engineering booth and being fascinated by what they were doing and saying, "I think I'd love to get my 1st Class Engineer license. I'd love to work in a place like this."

The engineers said, "They would never hire you, not ever."

I said, "Why?"

Well, because you're a girl."

I said, "What does that matter?"

They said, "Look. The men would be uncomfortable. What if they told a dirty joke or something? No, we just don't have women here."

What an impact that had on me, Susan. I didn't even know how to look at it other than to be outraged.

Along those same lines, when I was in high school, because of Amelia [Earhart] I became fascinated with aeronautics. The school I attended had an aeronautics class, so I applied. I was called down to the guidance counselor's office and they said, "We see you applied for this, and you're not going to be able to take this course. We're going to recommend that you take a home economics course."

I said, "Why? Is it full? What is your reason I can't attend?"

"You're a girl. Aeronautics is for boys."

I said, "Can you tell me what they're going to be doing in that course that I can't do, as a female? I mean, is there heavy lifting or what?"

"No, it's just that we feel it's better."

I negotiated my way into that class and got them to change the rule, so I was the first girl in my school to take the aeronautics course. The one thing I knew: I had to ace that course. I did. I got an A+ because I knew I was being watched, and if any girl after me wanted to take it, I HAD to open the door for her. So I did. Those are a couple early examples.

When Phyllis H. was faced with an obstacle she couldn't overcome, she simply changed direction and moved on. That decision led to an opportunity to host her own television show.

Phyllis H.: I had a dream of being a network news correspondent because I wanted to travel; I wanted to do what I did globally. I had tried to go into South Africa during the riots. I had gotten a South African diplomat to get papers to get me into South Africa, which had been very difficult for news bureaus to do. At the time I got permission to do it, NBC got in the way, objected to my going, and Garrick Utley got to take the spot

I had gotten. I was just flabbergasted. I was really upset. But that's because South Africa was letting in [only] a certain number.

I had requested permission. I needed a sponsor from an organization to go in. Because I had been familiar with NBC, I asked NBC, and Garrick was put in my place. So, I had done all the groundwork and that really hurt. That was the first thing that drove me to want to be a network news correspondent: I did not want that to happen ever again in my life. I wanted to go to the highest level. I started auditioning. Harrison Salisbury put in strong recommendation for me at ABC news and I did an audition.

"So What?" to Sexism

Sexism was the norm for many of The Fifty, especially early in their careers. But, as with Phyllis C., they didn't take "No" for an answer. Many of those who started careers in the financial sector experienced significant sexism. Their response was, "Yes. So what?" and then they did what they wanted to do anyway.

One woman was sent to an event at a club that did not admit women to the dining room. She ended up sitting on the floor outside the room, eavesdropping on the meeting she had been asked to attend. Several of The Fifty discussed similar experiences.

Q. I'm hearing it from a lot of women who started out in the financial industry, in particular, and what I'm hearing a lot is they said, "Yes. So what?"

Jeannette: Well, I have lots of examples. I'm going to give you one—a pretty grievous one. I was a contract employee, and we had to put in travel orders. Somebody in that organization was responsible for booking your plane flights, your hotel, and so forth.

We were going to have a big rum promotion for a new drink. We booked a two-week tour, doing rum tastings. We were also holding cocktail receptions for the trade, the stores, distributors, and so forth to introduce this new drink. I booked myself on TV [shows] to do demonstrations, so I had been looking forward to the tour. We hired a hot air balloon because we were going to around six to eight cities and we were going to give people at these parties hot air balloon rides. It was really a big deal and was going to be great fun.

Now, this is back in the era when everybody used to travel first class for business. In the third city, the head of Rums of Puerto Rico comes to my office with his deputy director. They said, "Look, we have to tell you something and we hate it, it's such an injustice, but the head of operations says you're going to go coach."

I said, "How come?"

"Well, because you're a woman. Women don't go first class."

There are eight of them sitting in first class, and I would have to go sit in coach.

They said, "We're telling you right now: if you don't want to go, you can cancel and you have our blessing."

I said, "Let me think about it."

I thought, *How can I cut off my nose to spite my face? This is going to be a fun trip for two weeks. I have all the dates of schedules with the television, radio. I'm going to swallow my pride and I'm going to go.*

Now, these decisions you make: do you want to stand on your principle, or do you want to do something you really want to do? These are the choices we have to make throughout our lives as individuals, personally and in business.

I told them, "Look, I want to go on this trip. I worked hard on this trip, so I'm going to go and I'll sit in coach."

The next day, an envelope comes with my tickets. I opened the envelope—and there are first-class tickets—somebody had forgotten. He hadn't told the people with the travel orders to change my tickets, and nobody ever cared to tell the travel department.

So, I went first class, but the obstacles for women were real. There were two kinds of obstacles: there were the blatant obstacles like, "You're going to go coach," and then there were the insidious obstacles which were [the things] you didn't know. At that time, in the *New York Times* they listed the job openings; on one side [of the paper were listed jobs for] women and on the other side, jobs for men. That immediately was a barrier.

One thing I want to say, with BBDO, which is really important: I worked with a general manager of this big agency, one of the big, glamorous, global ones. I worked on the agency's business; I worked on client work. I mean, come to think about, I worked like a horse.

The general manager was also the president of Capital Radio Television Advertising (CARTA). I was at his office every day, and I could see that the agency was going out of the public relations business. It was very apparent we were cutting back—we were shoved off to a corner up—way up—where nobody could see us.

So I went to him and said, "Mr. Schwall," (you didn't call him Jim in those days) "I'd like to move to the advertising side."

He responded, "We will never hire women executives. The clients would never accept it, and so you just stay here." He put his arm around my shoulder, "And we'll always take care of you, but you're never going to the account management side." I think that there was one copywriter, one woman copywriter.

Here's the other thing … it still happens, but it happens much less frequently, especially if a woman is running the meeting. Two meetings would be held for something. One meeting [that] everybody went to, men and women. [And the second meeting] was the circle of men who would talk among themselves, where decisions were made. You know what I'm talking about.

Q. *Yes, those decisions used to be made on the golf course, too.*

Jeannette: Yeah, the golf course. So breaking into the invisible ring, that invisible club at work is the toughest thing. Belonging to the Financial Women's Association, it's still quite prevalent. A lot of women made it big in financial services, but they still confront this invisible barrier of the men's club. It's still there to a great extent. I mean, not anything like it was when I was coming into the business, but it's still there and it's still a barrier to be overcome.

Sexism also showed up in the expectations of management, peers, and The Fifty themselves. Phoebe spoke about the difficulties faced by many women in management:

Q. Being able to set boundaries around work hours was practically unheard of for many, many years. You see more flexibility now in some places.

Phoebe: You see more of it now, but for many, many years, that was practically unheard of—actually being able to set some boundaries around work hours. I think it's very hard to do that. The demands are pretty intensive and you certainly don't do it in the middle of a deal. You've got to be smart about this, at all times.

I'm conscious of this [the demands] and who my competition is. I always think of them [my competition] as someone male who has a wife—a very capable wife who takes care of all of the parenting issues and all of the household issues. So, to the extent that the woman—I am involved in parenting—to the extent that I'm running my household, that takes time and energy from the workplace. No wonder we admire those employees, because they're terrific: male, female, it doesn't matter. If I think about it in a cultural context, I'm in the first wave of women who really had opportunities in the business world. I'm in the first five years, I think.

Before that, the [opportunities] just weren't there. Now I look back and ponder: it was just so highly irritating to me at the time. There's a club in Los Angeles and we had a banker's day presentation in this club. I'll never forget it: this is in the 1980s and women were not allowed in the front door. I was one of the hosts, and we were having all of our bankers there. I was not allowed in the front door; I had to go in the side door.

They also didn't think I was old enough to drink. I was twenty-nine at the time, and I remember having to go find someone to tell them, "Yes, I am old enough to drink," and get me served a drink.

It was very real. Now, when I tell my daughters, they don't even believe me. They think it actually is just impossible it actually happened. It's just not in their world, not in their world.

Q. Do you think that companies lose something, a richness and depth of understanding, with people who have a singular focus, being devoted 24/7 to their organizations, as opposed to someone like you who has multiple focal points in her life?

Phoebe: I think it depends upon the profession … I think that if you're an investment banker, it is different than if you are a surgeon. You can't do that intensive surgery; you'll become exhausted and you'll make mistakes. You might be able to do it in investment banking because the support system and the structure are set up around that. I think it's very career-specific.

I think you have to look long-term for culture, and say what it is that we're valuing here. The United States, in the moment, is highly valuing productivity. It changes with the mass movements that are going on, right? We experienced them in our century, last century, right?

To figure it out is hard; it is very hard for our society to figure that out. There's a wonderful woman who's been studying this, Laura Liswood. Laura Liswood ran the White House project for a while. She's been a consultant to Goldman Sachs and she's done a lot of research.

She did a video documentary interviewing all of the living female Prime Ministers, so she had Maggie Thatcher and Cory Aquino and Denise Rebuto, etcetera. She makes very interesting comments that have been very helpful to me just to understand this.

Jan and Connie also spoke about similar experiences of being one of the few women in their positions.

Jan said: That's the interesting thing. It's one of the lessons I learned: if you have women in leadership, it actually attracts other women. At the time, I was the managing partner of technology and security practice; there were nine business units. The average percentage of women partners was twelve percent. My practice had thirty percent. What was really noteworthy is that I had no women's programs at all.

My successor, a white male, had only reported to a woman (me) in the first fifteen years of his career. I tried not to be involved in the practice because it was his, but I wanted to be there for him if he ever needed to draw on my experience.

One day, he came to me and said, "I'm having a problem with recruiting because all of the headhunters are bringing me all-male slates of candidates. Did you have that problem before?"

I said, "Well, no, they never brought me only male candidates."

He also mentioned having higher levels of attrition among the women. Then, he said he thought he was going to have to start a women's program within the practice.

I looked at him and said, "That's strange, as we never had to do that before."

He was so insightful because he looked at me and said, "Jan, it's harder for me to help women understand that they can make it to the top than for you."

Knowing this is one of the most enlightened men I have ever known, I asked, "Why would that be?"

And he said, "All you have to do is show up and they know it's true. I have to actually do something to make it intentionally clear that women have an opportunity to progress."

That was a real eye-opener to me because I never thought about the fact that just being there actually showed women they can make it.

Q. That's interesting. Another woman said pretty much the same thing—that by being a woman in a high position, she attracted women.

Jan: That's exactly right. I sometimes tell the story about, in 2005, the Confederation of British Industry, the CBI, which is the biggest business group in the United Kingdom. It works with the U.K. government when the U.K. government wants to change laws. They represent business; they're the voice of business in the U.K.

They started these awards called First Women Awards because they felt they needed to do some things to raise the profile of women. There were something like seven awards—they would have the First Woman of Finance, and the First Woman of Science, etc. One category was the First Woman of Technology.

A colleague and I had organized the first-ever meeting of the women partners at Ernst & Young U.K. to talk about some issues experienced by the women in the firm. We were making some progress with the chairman and other leaders. Some of the women partners decided they wanted to recognize my effort by putting me up for the First Woman of Technology Award.

My initial reaction was, "No, I don't think so." It wasn't a good idea because it just seemed unseemly to be put up for an award. But they were quite insistent. So I finally agreed, thinking there would be a lot of people submitted, I wouldn't be selected, and it would go away.

Well, it turns out, they selected five finalists. It's kind of like the Academy Awards in that you … don't know who is going to win. I was shocked to be in the final five, especially when I read the list of nominees and saw that the other four women were absolutely incredible. Nominees were, of course, expected to "buy a table" for the night, which I did. So I put around the table only people I knew who were genuinely fond of me, and I didn't invite anybody who would take joy in me losing because I was certain I wasn't going to be chosen.

To my shock—and I do mean shock—they called my name. I hadn't even thought about what I would say on the stage. (Like the Academy Awards, the winner makes a speech.) These awards are so high profile, it was on the front page of the Times, me and the six other women who won. So the firm announced this in the global newsletter (with distribution of over 140,000).

While I heard from hundreds of my own team and people I knew, what was enlightening was more than fifty women that I never knew, that I had never met, wrote to me to say what an inspiration it was that there was a woman managing partner in Ernst & Young. And how it inspired them to try to be at the top of the business world because they knew that if one woman can do it, then they could do it too. As I was sitting reading all these emails, I realized that no matter how uncomfortable it is and how unseemly it is to be thrust into the limelight, sometimes you just have to do it, because if it inspires other women, it's a responsibility: "To whom much is given, much is expected."

Juggling Career and Family

Another high-level corporate executive, Connie's story shows resilience in meeting the demands of her career and her family.

Connie: I was perpetually pregnant for the next four years. I had three more children in four years all while being a partner at the firm. I was transferred, coincidental with the birth of my first child, who was born in L.A. My husband was a partner in a money management firm in Los Angeles. I was asked to transfer to run the Chicago Fixed-Income Bond Department. That was big, because it basically meant that either my husband or I would have to significantly change our career toward that path. And we had this newborn baby who was premature.

It wasn't obvious what the right outcome and answer to that would be. But interestingly, and I think this is so true of men vs. women, my husband's attitude was very much, "Well, if I stay," he was sort of the #2 person in his firm, "if I stay, you know I have the potential to run this firm. But if you decide you want to do this crazy thing and move to Chicago and leave L.A.—which we never thought we'd leave—to try to be a partner at Goldman Sachs, then that's fine because I can always run something else."

Whereas, my attitude, of course, from the woman's perspective was, *If I step off this track for one minute, then I'll be flipping burgers at McDonald's.* No. I think that it was probably an extreme outcome. But there was an element of truth in all of that.

Q. Yeah. Women in leadership roles were … certainly a small group and … we were doing the Ginger Rogers thing.

Connie: Oh, yeah—"Women do everything that men do, but backwards and in high heels." I love that quote. So we did take the move, and I was made partner. I was in the Chicago office until '97-ish, when I was asked to move to New York to co-head the Municipal Bond Department, which was public finance, sales training, underwriting, and derivatives. At that point, I had four children. When I was asked to relocate, my youngest was a year old and my oldest was seven.

It was honestly easier for me to commute Monday through Friday, than to de-camp this army and re-establish it in New York—a city we didn't really ever want to live in permanently. So, that's what I did. I commuted for those years. Then, I think the commuting—in combination with missing too much at home, and really wanting to be on the premises as my children hit their teens, having had a twenty-year great run—it just seemed like the right time for me to decide to retire and do something else.

Even for those of us who lived through these times, it's easy to forget how few women there were in leadership as recently as the '90s. To women in their twenties and thirties, even though we are still far from true equity, it may seem like a different universe. Connie was another woman who found herself in a unique position in the financial industry, as did Susana at the CIA.

Connie said: I became a partner at Goldman Sachs in 1990. At that time, Goldman was private and made partners every two years. I was the first woman sales and trading partner in the firm's history—the firm was founded in 1869. There had been one prior woman partner in the class of '86 who was in the investment banking area. There were three of us selected in the class of '90 (no one in '88), one who was really sort of a chief of staff to the senior partner, one who came from the municipal finance area, and then myself.

Dual-Career Couples

Several women discussed the resilience needed to be a dual-career couple. For Phoebe, this was especially challenging, as she and her husband worked for the same company:

Phoebe: At that point, I was thrilled I was going to be able to join the treasury group in corporate finance and implement some of the things I had been learning. I stayed there four years.

My husband graduated with his master's degree. There was an interesting time in there when he wanted to go to work for what he considered the best oil and gas training program, that was with Shell Oil in Houston. So we commuted between Los Angeles and Houston. I had just gotten my job in Treasury and was a brand-new MBA-type. I didn't wanted to give that up, and he didn't want to give up his opportunity to go and work for a great company that he knew had the best training program in the U.S. for geologists. We commuted for three years.

Q. That's pretty unusual …

Phoebe: Very unusual. We tried to not tell anybody about it because it was so unusual to live a life and not tell people that you're commuting, you know what I mean? We tried to see each other most weekends and at those times when we socialized.

I was in the financial development program: Atlantic Richfield had a very inspired financial development training program, where they believed you needed to have real experience in key areas in order to prepare for financial leadership positions. I became part of the system where I would be developed and moved around; so began a period of time where I was in financial roles in different locations.

It's interesting—this was triggered a little bit by the fact that my husband and I had been commuting for three years, and I didn't see an easy way for that to end, except for me leaving. I thought, *I'll just see if I can get a job with another oil and gas company in Houston.* So I sent out resumes.

It is a remarkably small industry, so it was not very long before they [my employer, Atlantic Richfield] called me in and said, "How about this? How about if Mark leaves Shell and joins Arco, and we manage you as a dual-career couple?"

So, we became one of many couples within Arco who were managed as a dual-career couple. They used this very well. They would sometimes have two engineers in China or England or a foreign location, which is much easier if you just have one household and two workers.

I would say that, at the end of the day, the senior women at Atlantic Richfield were married to men who worked at Arco, or they were single, because they did a very good job in that era of retaining women. I think that's how they came to distinguish themselves ahead of nearly all the other oil and gas companies.

So what happened then is we were both moved. I was moved from Los Angeles to Dallas, and Mark left Shell, came to Arco, and he moved to Dallas. So began a phase of moves—not always in perfect timing, not always ideal for either one, but okay for the partnership. Anyway, when I moved to Los Angeles, Mark soon followed.

When we were in Los Angeles, we were renovating a 1905 California Craftsman home in Pasadena. We got word that the International Oil and Gas Company was going to relocate to Dallas, Texas. So that meant that we would both be moved. I remember working our hearts out to get this house renovated in order to sell it.

Then we were asked to relocate to London, England as a couple. Big picture, if I look back on that a series of developmental moves for both of us, it was a series of financial management positions of increasing responsibilities, right? We moved to England in 1990, so if you think back, we've covered ten years. I graduated from UCLA in 1980 and started with Treasury, and by 1990, we're in England.

Q. *And this whole pattern is working for you.*

Phoebe: Remember, we had no children. We worked very hard, did volunteer work. I was an active member of Junior League and did things with Smith College alumnae groups, but it was a heavily career-focused period of our lives, very intensely.

So we moved to England. I guess I should add that in Bakersfield, we had this discussion about when we were going to have children. I had been in no particular hurry to have children at all, and at that point, I would have been happy if we didn't have children. But my husband really wanted to have at least one child. I couldn't get pregnant and started what ended up being five years of infertility work. I had surgery, which ultimately corrected the problem, and we then went to England. I had a child very soon after moving to England, so … our older daughter is a British citizen as well as an American.

So the '90s were really primarily two long stays. The first in England, where I was the Chief Financial Officer for the international division located in London, and my husband was a geologist for the same company. That was a great experience. Everybody should have the opportunity to live overseas and see what the United States looks like from across the pond, so to speak.

We were blessed with great British friends, we were blessed with great expat friends—one of them is Jan Babiak. That's how I know Jan. I think, between our little village and the fact that I had a baby there, I met other women who were in the same situation as I was. That was a tremendous experience.

We traveled extensively—I feel like I really took advantage of our time in there in a very meaningful way and, at the same time, I had great development opportunities in our companies.

I was, sort of, the representative of Arco to the banks in London. I didn't manage those relationships, but it was great to be part of it and I went to London frequently.

We were there about five years, and it was time to do something different. I think that repatriation is among the hardest challenges that companies have. They have not really seen the person who has been overseas for a while, so they don't know how much they've changed. We were lucky in that there was a position that opened up, a business development position in mergers and aquisitions (M&A) in one of our subsidiary companies in Houston, Texas.

We had this little child who spoke with a British accent and was quite cute and a brilliant nanny who had lived with us the whole time. We came back to Houston and worked on another home renovation until a great job opened up to be the chief financial officer for the largest subsidiary that Atlantic Richfield had—in Alaska.

We then moved to Anchorage, Alaska—again, a dual-career move—from January of 1996 to 2000. I would describe that as almost like living in a foreign country; it's remote, it has its own micro-economy, and it is a small place. But you play at a high competitive level because your competition is BP [British Petroleum] and Exxon. Also, because of the importance of state revenue from oil and gas, you developed a close relationship with the regulators and the government officials and the state. The combination was a great experience as a training ground and for government relations; a training ground for competitive play at a high level. It also was an interesting place for environmental issues and how to think about them, and how to embrace and work with them and resist all the same in an appropriate way.

The Gifts and Opportunities of Disruption

Often, disruptive life events in these women's lives led to reflection, and frequently, to a change of direction. Victoria's two triggers were divorce and her first trip to Paris.

Victoria: I stopped [working] and then I had children and was a full-time mother and wife. Then when I was divorced, I thought I needed a career. I didn't want to go into Speech Pathology [my field of study], so I got a job at an agency, as a copywriter.

When my children were both out of the area, off to university, I went to Paris for three months, thinking that I would study the language and just have that break and get away from the routine I had been living for years and years and years as a single mother. I ended up staying there for five years and created a whole new life for myself.

Q. Tell me more about Paris.

Victoria: That was the first real risk, I think, that I took. Well, actually, the second. The first real risk, I think, was the divorce; making the decision that I could actually survive on my own. In fact, I was telling somebody yesterday that I remember the first time I took off by myself on a holiday. I actually went to England for a friend's wedding. I rented a car in London and drove up to the Lake District.

As I was driving, I realized it was the first time I'd ever gone away all by myself, and the feeling of freedom was so extraordinary that I began to cry, just from a sheer joy of it, the excitement, the adventure—but the freedom. I cried because I felt free for the first time in my life. I had always been somebody's daughter or somebody's wife or somebody's mother, but I never figured out who I was, and that was really the first step for me.

Disruption

For some of The Fifty, forced relocation had a deep impact and shaped their lives. It played out differently, however, for each. Isora's family was forced to flee Cuba as Castro came into power. The disruption of living as a political refugee with her parents shaped Isora's gift and her drive to help others become resilient:

Q. So thinking back over all of this, what kind of threads do you see that run through all of the different things you have done?

Isora: I think it's always doing something for other people. It doesn't matter whether it was wage and salary administration or stress management. But, I think, serving others. That's how I see myself. I think that's my mission in life—to help others with those skills that God gave me.

I have to say that I feel very lucky because I had wonderful parents. I was able to learn a lot from them. They taught me it was important to have critical thinking, but they didn't teach me how to think. I had always these freedoms, freedoms to choose—even when they didn't agree—but they gave me a lot of freedom. I also learned a lot when I left Cuba at age fourteen as a political exile with nothing. That was a great experience.

My father was a banker, and when Castro took over he was asked to leave the country. So we left in 1962. We started a new life in Miami. During those times, it was very difficult because we did not have any relatives and had few friends. Those who left in 1961-1962, we didn't have a lot of support. So we were in Miami for only eight months. That's when I went to school. I went to ninth grade, but I didn't finish.

It was a difficult experience. I remember I used to go to an Italian bakery across the street from the school. I explained to them in my bad English that I was a political exile and I was hungry, and they gave me all the leftovers every day. I had a great experience in Miami I have to say. And my teachers really loved me. They gave me so much love that they helped me. My parents were tempted to leave me there with friends of theirs. But they said, "No, the three of us left [Cuba] together, we should be together." It was a very good experience. I think I would have adjusted if I had stayed in Miami.

Then we moved to Puerto Rico. I began working at age sixteen. At one point, I worked as a secretary for a law firm. I also worked for Monroe Sweda; they made those cash registers they don't use anymore. I had a great job. I remember I was the only woman, and they took care of me like a daughter. Then as I said, I stayed in Puerto Rico for ten years.

My father had to become a construction worker at age sixty-five, so he needed surgery for one of his arms. He wasn't used to that. My mother was lucky. She had been working as a teacher in a Catholic school. She got a job right away as a teacher in a Catholic school. They had a lot of friends from Cuba who were living there.

But as I say, I don't know what happened. I didn't have that many friends. It was difficult for me to get adjusted. Again, I acted on impulse. I said, "I'm moving to Spain," one day. And in less than a month, I moved to Spain. I didn't know anyone. I didn't have admission to any school. But when I arrived there, it was like "I'm home." For some reason, I still feel like that, like I'm home. Madrid and New York are my favorite cities. I feel at home both in New York and in Madrid. I sleep in Jersey, but I think I live in New York—that's how I feel my life is. And I still have the same friends I had in Spain forty years ago.

Life changed for Audrey, Dina, and Lynda when their husbands died. For Audrey, her world was turned upside down early in her marriage. Everything that her marriage was changed overnight when her husband was diagnosed with cancer. She spent the next seven years working to create the best possible life for herself, her husband, and her family.

Audrey: Six months after we were married, Joe got the flu, but he pushed through because he never missed a day at work. But then it never seemed to get better. We became very concerned. His office receptionist ... and I were really pushing him to see a doctor. "You know, this just isn't right. It has been two weeks now. It shouldn't be ... blah, blah."

So he didn't go rushing, but eventually did go to see someone. He was just completely lethargic. His white blood cell count was through the roof. He being a doctor and I being a nurse, we knew that wasn't a good sign. So I guess within the week—and we were pretty aggressive in the fact that we really had to determine what this was—he was diagnosed with CML, chronic myelogenous leukemia.

I think I started my grief then because I had been in love with the man of my dreams, truly. Six months into what we thought was the beginning of a wonderful forever together we found out, and we knew, ultimately, what the outcome would be when you're diagnosed with CML—we're talking twenty-nine years ago. There was very little [treatment] that was out there. I remember being at Columbus Hospital in Newark. We were trying to find the perfect match for Joe to have a bone marrow transplant, because he only had one brother (who was not a perfect match), and we just couldn't come up with anything. So that wasn't even an alternative for him.

We basically lived the next seven years of our marriage between my becoming pregnant—because I was determined to have a family and in the hope, too, that it would keep him alive—my running to my doctor's appointments and us running into New York City for his doctor appointments for his chemo. That was basically what we did. And we traveled.

Actually, I was pregnant with my third child, and we went out to the Midwest because there was some hopeful experimental drug. We also were looking at bone marrow transplant centers to see what the possibilities were of doing a non-perfect match. I was quite pregnant at that time. There was very little that could be done; it was basically having him going to his appointments, doing his chemo, hoping he wouldn't go into blast phase. I found out that I was pregnant with my last daughter, and a week later, Joe went into blast.

Q. How many children do you have, Audrey?

Audrey: I have four. So Joe went into blast phase and the doctors got together and got me a car service, so that every day I wanted to go in to see Joe, I had a car service take me in to Montefiore Hospital in the Bronx.

Jackie was born and she was two-and-a-half months old when Joe died. That was, I guess, the most unbelievable time. I've had so many people say to me—and doing grief work now, it's like knowing it when it happened—"Well, at least you had time to prepare." You don't prepare. The last thing my husband wanted to talk about was his death, you know. That was a taboo subject. We were going to beat this. We were going to have the miracle. So, left with four children and to add to it, you know, people were always saying when I told my story that it was unbelievable; and yet it was not to me. It was just something I lived.

Joe died on December twenty-first, and I buried him on Christmas Eve. Went home. Put the kids in their Christmas pajamas. Took their picture under the tree. Put them to bed. Put out the toys and went to bed and cried my eyes out. But my children—until, I would say, maybe seven to eight years ago—did not know that their father was buried on Christmas Eve because I swore I would never, ever let it interfere with Christmas for them. And it never did. It just all was wonderful. They knew that daddy died around that time, but there was no connection made. That wasn't easy, but it was something I was determined not to let them know while they were young … their father was buried on Christmas Eve. I didn't want to take anything else away from them that they would go through in the future. I'm very happy with the fact that my children didn't have the experience of connecting Christmas with the loss of their father until they were older.

I ran from my grief a lot in the first six months. I also needed to get out of the house we were in, although they say: "Don't make any major decisions." My husband died at home. I had hospice, so my oldest son and daughter wouldn't come into the bedroom, my bedroom. I knew this was not going to be a good thing, so I made the decision to move.

I moved into a totally new town, which is where my parents lived, because I also needed extra hands because I had a two-and-a-half month-old, a two-year-old, a four-year-old, and a six-year-old.

Q. *How soon did you go back to work?*

Audrey: I started working from home. I had gone for hypnotherapy certification years before because I was so intrigued by hypnosis. I was always into that—other, alternative side to healing—and I had gone and gotten certified as a hypnotherapist. I had worked with people for a very brief time for smoking cessation and weight loss. It was fun, but I wasn't making enough money. So when the kids were home—I only had my son in school; my daughter was in pre-school for a few hours—I started seeing clients. I did have life insurance, thank God, so I didn't have to go right back to work. But I was thirty-eight when Joe died and by the time I was forty, I knew I'd have to start looking for some serious job or something to support the kids. So, I actually made the decision that, in order for me to get a better job, I would have to go to grad school. I found an amazing babysitter two nights a week for two years. I went back to grad school. I remember sitting at the dining room table with my kids and we were all doing our homework together. But it was something that I personally wanted to do. It made me feel better about myself, and I felt I had more to offer in going out and looking for a job. I also didn't want anybody raising my children.

Q. *This degree was what?*

Audrey: I have a master's in Health Science. It was Jersey City State College. It was affordable. That's why I went there, and I could get there and back in less than forty-five minutes. Those were the things that were very important when I applied to grad school.

What I did after I got my degree: I still wanted to be there for my children, so what I started out, at first, was school nursing because that made sense, right? You work when your children are in school, you're home at 3:00 p.m., you had the vacations.

And I hated it. Oh, my God, the red tape! You couldn't put your arms around a child that was sad. You couldn't touch them. Like, *What is this? I'm a nurse.* I was doing paperwork and reprimanding kids for not having their clearance for gym. It was like, *This is the most bizarre and unfulfilling job.*

I lasted a year and said, "This isn't working. I have to do something else and it has to be something that is going to work with my children." My brother was facilitating a support group for people with panic and anxiety disorder. He didn't want to do the group anymore, and he asked if I was interested. I said "Okay. Well, maybe I could do the group." So I took on being a facilitator. I worked with people with anxiety and panic, whether it was ill health, or couldn't ride an elevator, or who couldn't fly in an airplane. Every fear you could think of, social phobias. I loved it.

It was so fulfilling to see people really making a difference in themselves. And working with, using meditation and guided imagery and having them utilize those tools to get them off of their medications and be more empowered. I knew this was definitely what I would have to do in some shape or form, but I didn't have any business acumen at all. You know, I was a caregiver. I was a counselor of sorts. I took care of people.

Q. Now somewhere in all of this, when did people start sending their widowed friends to you?

Audrey: When I was in Westfield and new to the neighborhood (which was the year after Joe died), I was kind of like an enigma because I was this thirty-eight-year-old young, attractive female with these four little kids. Everybody was interested in me. I was invited to all kinds of things; they wanted to hear my story.

Then I started getting calls from people, "Did you hear so-and-so's husband just dropped dead this weekend?"

"Okay, have her call me." I'd have them over to coffee with no thought at all of going into working with people in grief.

Now, my practice basically began with panic and anxiety disorder. I did work with people who were challenged with cancer and had a lot of anxiety in dealing with and grieving their loss of heath. I was able to do that for seven years. I just couldn't get to the point where I was earning enough money. I just couldn't figure out, other than putting an ad in the local paper, I didn't know what else to do to grow a business.

I actually had to move from my first house because I couldn't make ends meet. My children, I have to say, are extremely resilient today because they packed boxes more times in their childhood and moved. We literally moved four times. I had to sell the house.

My son was going off to college. I had no idea what it was going to cost. It just blew my mind, the cost of college. It still just is amazing. They wound up having to take out a lot of loans.

I sold the house. I did profit on the house, so I was able to carry me a little bit longer. I downsized because one child was out, so I didn't need as big a house. And because I wasn't able to make ends meet, I wound up having to go back and get a job. That was a very sad day, a very sad day.

I went back and started doing case management for an insurance company, and I hated that. Oh my God, it was terrible after being independent and having your own business. I said, "I've got to think of something else. Something else has got to be good for me." So I was always looking for something. "Okay, I have to build on what I already have, but I can't follow the whole traditional route." (All through what my husband went through, there was just so much lack in traditional healthcare.) Because I loved yoga at the time … I [decided] I was going to go and get certified as a yoga teacher. And I did. It took me a year, commuting back and forth on weekends to New York City. I got the yoga certification.

I started on the side, after my full-time job, taking private clients on because that was how I could make the most money; teaching one-on-one yoga. This only reinforced to me that I needed to get the hell out of that job, somehow.

I continued with it because of financial need, really. Joseph was the first one to go off to college and Laurie Ellen was the next. They didn't go to inexpensive schools. God forbid you go to Rutgers. My son, Joseph, went to the University of Delaware. My daughter, Laurie Ellen, went to Berkeley. So … I had to keep the job.

Then, let's see, we moved again because, again, I couldn't afford the house. Things weren't looking good. It was, "Okay guys, we're moving again. Pack it up." We did and I downsized again.

At that time, I had two children left at home and my third child, my son Patrick, was in high school, but going off to college the following year. He went to the New School. My youngest daughter, Jaclyn, followed him and is a senior now at the New School. Again, one of the most expensive schools in New York City. So they all have huge debt, huge debt, which is very sad.

But they stood by me. When mom was going for another job, seeking, searching— they were just so supportive. It was wonderful. It really, really was. They still, to this day, are just so supportive of everything I do.

So if nothing else, as I said, they are resilient kids. I've always told them to follow their dreams. I believe that's why my son lives in Beijing and my daughter stayed in California. It's been very interesting. I'm sure you've seen this too, where you look at your children and you say, "You know, they did listen … a little bit." They were paying attention.

So I started doing yoga one-on-one with clients. I was making decent extra income, but I still had to stay with case management because I had health insurance. I had children; I needed to have those benefits. So I stuck with that until I jumped ship about a year ago.

I have to backtrack, actually. I have had a house up in the Catskills that my husband and I bought the year before he died because he wanted to have a weekend home where we could go any season of the year with the kids. It's the one thing, THE one thing I have done everything to hold onto over all these years. It's the one place my children say that this is their home. It's a small little ski house, but it's home.

So when Jackie was actually packing off to college in August of 2009, I was packing up the house to move again. Only this time, I moved up to the Catskills. I was working telephonically, so that enabled me to come up here and have a year—actually fourteen months I lasted up here—to give a lot of thought to what I wanted to do, where I wanted to be.

It was a very interesting year. I'm not a Thoreau. This is a very secluded house in the woods, and I did really come to know myself far better, almost, than I think I wanted to.

I started going to these support groups. What I came to find out was that people were very good about attending the meetings—whether it was once a month or every few weeks—for years. I kept saying, "Look at this picture. You've come to work on your grief. Going to the support groups isn't working on your grief, it's telling your story, the same one every single month." *Hi, I'm Audrey. My husband, Joe, died when I was thirty-eight and twenty-two years later, I'm coming to this support group.*

That's the feeling I got and I kept saying, "This is not working. People don't know it's not working. I have to change this." What I came to realize—because I would go out there and talk about grief, go out for dinner with people and I'd want to talk about grief—is that people don't want to talk about grief. They only want to talk about pleasant things. They can talk about a death. They can talk about taxes. Nobody wants to talk about grief … which only inspired me more.

That's actually my mission … I am going to get people … people are going to learn about grief because it's about education. I actually started working with widows—telephonically again because I wanted to have the freedom, I did not want to be locked into an office. I knew if I came up to the Catskills I could work, I could be there for people, and I didn't have to be present in an office situation. It has actually worked out very well.

As I worked with widowed women. I was very comfortable with that. And all of a sudden, I had divorced women saying, "Well, what about us divorced women? We grieve too." I was like, *Oh, my. I have to rethink my niche now because divorced people are grieving.*

Then I began to look more and more into the whole concept of grief related to loss in general. I remember having read the book *The Grief Recovery Method* about six years after Joe died. It was eye-opening and it changed the way I looked at my grief: I understood it. I found the Grief Recovery Institute where the authors were [located]. I called them and I spoke with the founder. I was so connected with everything he said about grief: how society has really controlled how much we grieve, if we grieve at all, and how we have been conditioned since childhood how to grieve a loss or not, because typically it was not.

I spoke with him several times and then decided to go through their organization to get certification. I thought, *Okay, I'm going to go for the certification. I'll go to classes. That would be great. I can do that. School: done that.*

Little did I know that I had to go through it, the [grieving] process. The funny thing was because it had been twenty years since Joe died, I had definitely worked through my grief with Joe, every aspect of it and felt, *I guess I'll work on grief issues about Joe.*

I got there and—the program just blows me away every time I use it with somebody, it's just so impactful and life-changing—it came [to me] after the first day that my grief was related to another relationship, and that person was alive. But what I grieved was the *idea* of a relationship that couldn't exist. It totally changed my idea of the relationship. Just going through the process blew me away, it really did because that was the last thing I thought would [be an outcome]. That was really transformational for me because of the depth of the grief related to a non-death. I didn't physically lose anything, but there was a grief over not having had what I thought I should have had.

Q. *Makes perfect sense, though.*

Audrey: It does. It really does. I got my certification with them. It is a program that I use now. And talk about timing: It was a few weeks prior to [Hurricane] Sandy that I really made the commitment. I had people saying, "You really need a narrow niche. You really need a narrow niche." You know what? Grief is a narrow niche. Working with widowed women is a part of that. Yes, that is a sub-niche, but there are grieving people out there that need to know how to process that grief.

Audrey went through a lengthy process to discover the importance of support for women who are grieving. While only a few of The Fifty spoke of support in the context of grief, there are examples throughout this book of women developing strong support networks and individual friendships throughout their lives. Lynda was the second woman to describe the importance of friendships in helping her heal after the loss of her husband:

Q. Friendships, also, is another theme that I'm hearing here. It sounds like you've got a pretty large circle.

Lynda: Well, I've been on my own for ten years. I told you that my husband had died in a one-car accident—we still don't know exactly what happened. At the time, I had several dreams; I was haunted by dreams.

I was taken care of by friends for almost two years. I mean, at first, probably for six months, my sister provided a schedule for all my friends. Somebody would have me assigned to them every day. I traveled. I went with friends to Argentina, I went to the Outer Banks, I went to New York. That really showed me the importance of having friendships.

Having a very close marriage, we kind of did everything together—rode horseback, traveled, cooked, had two kids, but also had a circle of friends. In this period of my life, being on my own, I've really found the importance and beauty of friendships. Every day, I thank myself for the incredible friendships of people who have helped me through this very difficult period of my life.

Sometimes, what we think will be our dream job turns out to simply not be a good fit. Many of The Fifty were not afraid to move in an entirely different direction. Susan S. discovered that the career in academia she had spent years preparing for wasn't the right choice for her and needed to find other ways to use her research and writing skills.

Susan S.: I got a tenure-track position and discovered a few things: I had been trained and geared to do research, and I was teaching a great number of service courses. I had been used to working with some of the most brilliant students in the world, and these students, while they were lovely kids, some of them were quite troubled kids. I found out that I was going to be a suicide counselor, a drug counselor, an abortion counselor. Sometimes, they were heartbreaking. Then I realized that, financially, I was going to assume responsibility for my mother, and I wasn't going to be able to do it on a junior faculty member's salary.

I learned another important thing—that I was not a contemplative. Ordinarily, you'd say, "Big deal," but I was a Medieval scholar. And for a Medieval scholar to know that means she has to leave [the field] or accept being in bad faith. I was always a little too bouncy: you sort of think of Tigger with a Ph.D. I was teaching Chaucer and the kids were having a fit because I insisted on Middle English.

So I did what I wanted to do: I moved to New York. I pounded the pavements. I got jobs and I lost jobs. This was '80 to '82, the first recession after the Reagan administration. Finally, I got into finance.

Some of The Fifty had life-changing experiences that created a shift in perspective. Valerie was able to arrange her life to be with her sister throughout a terminal illness. As she observed how her sister lived, she was also able to reflect on her own life and came to a point, following the death of her sister, when she realized she needed a complete change. She also realized who she had been trying to make happy in the past and who she wanted to make happy moving forward.

Valerie: You know, it's funny. Two years ago, I woke up one morning and thought, *That list of things I always wanted to do isn't getting any shorter.*

I always wanted to get my captain's license, so I got my captain's license. I can now deliver boats and do charters. I got certified to teach sailing and, about a year-and-a half ago, I bought a boat. I'm living on the boat and renting out my house. I'm moving toward that whole different lifestyle which is really living in a marina. I'm living on a boat. I do some boat deliveries. I do some charters every now and then.

Every now and then I do some teaching. I'm not sure that's actually what I want to do full-time for a career because I really love technology. I love being able to help people and mentor people, you know, in that management role. But it helps balance the scale between work and life. And I've really enjoyed the culture and the community that you get in a marina. It's been a lot of fun.

So right now, I'm living on a boat and ... I've restarted my consulting company. I'm also looking at how to get more into board work. I have a lot of diverse experience in international [business] and technology at various levels of executive management, and it seems like I'd be able to share that in a way and help organizations grow. It seems that would be a really good way to do it. So I'm between consulting and throwing my hat in the ring on the board side and will see where things take me. In the meantime, I'm living on a boat and having a blast.

You know, that's a little bit different scenario. I so appreciate and value everything I've learned through those first two steps but ... it's been interesting to get to that third step: *Okay, I did it for my parents and my family. Then I did the work thing for me to prove I could do it. Now, I actually want to enjoy the fruits of my labor all of the time and do something a little bit different.*

I wouldn't have traded any of it [my past] for the world. Yeah, there are trigger points that actually made that [change] happen, but it was a fun path.

Q. What do you mean by "trigger points?"

Valerie: You know, my sister went to school and then she left (she was older). I was watching my parents react to what she was doing. I didn't want to disappoint them. So I did things because I saw how they reacted to what my sister did, which was absolutely right for her at the time. But I was watching *their* reaction, not *her* reaction. I didn't want to disappoint them, so I did a lot of the things I did because of them and to prove [myself] to them, and to make them happy and, I think, to make sure they knew how much I appreciated everything they gave me and everything they did for me. It was my way of paying them back. Does that make sense?

Q. It absolutely does.

Valerie: The reason I did a lot of that was because I was watching them react to my sister, and I internalized a lot of that. That's what drove me.

It was in my late thirties when I realized I really can't do this [for] my dad anymore because it was way too hard. If I was going to do this and I was going to move forward, I had to do it for me.

There was this other point—it was probably in my late thirties—[when I thought,] *If I'm going to keep moving forward at this kind of pace, at this breakneck speed, try to work ridiculous hours, and continue at this level of energy that I'm putting into it, I need to do it because I want to do it for me.*

I can remember it, almost as clear as day, just sitting in the living room thinking, *This is what I want to do for me, in the job world, in work.* Making that transition over from my parents to me.

Then, again, two years ago, waking up and thinking, *What are you doing? You're killing yourself. And you used to have this really long bucket list of things that you've always wanted to do. When are you going to do that? You're not getting any younger.*

I think when I turned fifty, it was kind of a major, *Oh, my gosh, I'm over fifty. It's time.* So there were three definite points where I could see that change happen.

Q. Yeah, but from a different vantage point. I mean, the vantage point where you are in life becomes so much more centered around creating meaning for yourself.

Valerie: Yes. That's exactly right.

Q. Yeah. And it's wonderful when it falls into place the way you've decided you want to make meaning in the world.

Valerie: It's really interesting because, sometimes, it's a matter of sitting back and waiting to figure that out. And sometimes, you've actually already got it, but you don't realize it. And sometimes, it takes other people to say, "Oooo, well, look what you've done!" It's been an interesting road.

Q. Val, you mentioned your sister and what an influence she was. So I'm wondering if you can tell me about your sister.

Valerie: Sure. My sister, gosh, she's an amazing woman. She passed away with brain cancer at fifty. But I have to tell you I was blessed to actually go through so much of that with her. I left my job at Ernst & Young and went out. A month later, she was diagnosed with brain cancer. I went out and actually went through chemo and radiation with her.

When you talk about amazing women and what people do and what they accomplish, my sister—she epitomized love. She did whatever she wanted to do. She would work to play. She had been down the Colorado a few times, rafting. You know, she just loved people. She loved being outside. She just exuded love.

When she was diagnosed with brain cancer, they gave her six months. She was incredible—she made it four years. We had so many opportunities to sit down and talk about life, what was important.

When I think about her, it has actually impacted my decision to get a boat and sail and be a captain. I would have to say, that has to be my sister ['s influence] because she is just smiling at the whole thing. She made me realize how important it is to actually play. And she was just such a big part of my life and still is. She passed a few years ago and she's still a big part of my life. I think about things that I do and I think about her as I do them.

Yeah, I am really … I am so fortunate to have been able to go through that experience with her. I hate the fact that she's gone, but it was a beautiful four years.

Q. What a wonderful relationship.

Valerie: Yeah. As I think about it, there are a lot of wonderful, beautiful people in my life that have impacted me—my sister probably the most. Jan has been an incredible, very powerful, very wonderful influence, adopting me as family because I'm a little short right now. Yeah. There are just so many beautiful people in the world. But my sister was absolutely my hero.

Often as we age and loved ones pass away, women pause to reassess their lives and their direction. Jan speaks of the loss of her mother and a number of other significant family members in a relatively short period of time. These losses caused her to revisit her own plans:

Q. Is there anything else that you'd like to add that occurred to you while you were talking?

Jan: Probably one more thing since you are focused on transformation after fifty. My mother passed away when she was fifty. Had a heart attack … big shock to everybody because we had never had a woman in our family die before the age of eighty. So it was quite a big thing when this happened.

Then in the last five years, I've lost both of my baby brothers, my father was killed in a car accident and then my grandmother, the aforementioned centurion, at one hundred years passed away. I have dealt with four estates and major attrition in my immediate family in less than five years. So the other thing that comes into play is all these things may come together to tell you it's time to make a change. My youngest brother was thirty-eight when he passed away, my other one was forty-nine, and Daddy was only sixty-nine.

You sit there and say, "Is what I'm doing joyful?" And joyful doesn't mean it's vacation every day or I'm sitting on a beach reading novels, but it does mean that I enjoy what I do. I could have continued in similar leadership roles until the mandatory retirement at sixty, another nine years. There's no doubt I would have made more money if I had done that. But the reality is I now have more choices.

I still make a very nice income because board work pays quite well if you're on the right boards and all. But I do think there is a point in time when you are fifty, maybe for some it's forty, I don't know, maybe it's sixty. But I do think you start to sit and say, "Am I really realizing all the joy that I can? Am I really taking all the gifts that God has given me and living to what He intended (or She) intended me to do with these gifts? And how do I fit into the bigger scene?"

So we haven't talked about that, but these were all things going through my head as I walked in one day and said, "Okay, I'm done." When you're in the Big 4, you're not allowed to sit on a corporate board so you can't start getting your board portfolio and then transition. Whereas, if you're a CEO, CFO, or a COO, you can do that. You really have to jump off the burning platform and hope there's water down there.

That meant my Plan A was to do a board portfolio, and I praise the Lord that worked out for me. But I also had a Plan B, C, and D in the event that it didn't. I think this isn't as binary as *I'm going to move from this job to that job*, and it's not all about the job. It's about your life and what's going on around you, so I think it's taking a holistic look at all of this.

Q. It's quite lovely, actually, and it makes me think: Jung talks about a sort of second adolescence in our forties or fifties when we focus on meaning. And it sounds like what you just said very much reflects that.

Jan: It does, but it's interesting because in that first phase, there are some very different motivators for people. There are some people who are trying really hard to prove to their parents they can be successful, or they're trying really hard because of a competitive nature or something. I think different things drive different people. There's absolutely no question for me what my driver was—that was financial stability.

When you come from the kind of background that I did … I don't think I have ever felt stable because I know you can lose it all. It's funny, because I have a friend that I'm talking to who has never really been without money. Now, she is experiencing some money problems and it frightens her.

I know what it's like to live in a trailer park and wait tables. I can do that again. In fact, when I was waiting tables, there were a lot of fifty and sixty-year old waitresses running around, and for the most part they seemed pretty happy. So it doesn't scare me that I could be back there at some point. But by the same token, I'm going to work really hard to make sure that Brian and I can live the life we chose.

A positive outlook is an integral part of resilience. Lynn faced many challenges that interrupted her career, including a husband who didn't want her to work, yet she maintained a positive attitude and persevered:

Lynn: He wouldn't let me work. I wanted to work especially as the children got older, when they were in school. There wasn't anyone around to play mahjong or canasta with. But anyway, we stayed there five years. It was the longest time we stayed anywhere. He was in the same company within H.I.S. and he got a new territory.

That's when we moved here, to Framingham. The kids were eleven, ten, and nine. We built our house here also. It was wonderful. We found many friends who liked the races and things that we liked. And he did well. Some things changed; some for the better, some for the worse. After a while, I started working with him at the trade centers. This was full of all the other salesmen, the clothing salesmen and the gift salesmen. I would work with him there; never on the road, but in the showroom and I learned.

Once I divorced him, I went to work for another rep, and I was a showroom rep. Then I worked for another rep after that. I was working on my own at that point, and I was earning a salary. It wasn't much, but it was a salary. And here I am after forty years, still very happy and not willing to give up my house.

I left the showroom [when] I stopped working for them. I worked for the phone company for a short time and, during that time, my mother was going through a lot of changes in her life. It wasn't quite dementia, but it was a little bit of dementia. Bonnie, my sister, couldn't stay with her in New Jersey, where my mother was living because she said her husband was depressed. So I had to go down there and stay there even though I had young children at home and bills to pay. I had to work.

But I stayed with my mother for a while and helped her out. You know, it was the kind of thing … she couldn't drive and she shouldn't drive. She would sneak out and drive in the parking lot every once in a while. Then my mother came up here and stayed with me, which scared the death out of me because at this point, she wasn't sure if she had taken her medicine. I didn't want her cooking because she didn't remember how to cook.

So we got through that and I picked up my own lines. I picked up some lines that I wanted to take throughout New England, and I started traveling on my own. I bought my first car by myself—owned it out and out—new car, all mine, a van. I traveled throughout all of New England. I did that for several years and then I started carrying lines, working for somebody else, a Calvin Klein rep who had a lot more force than I did in terms of getting customers. It was good. So again, I was working in a showroom and [doing] some traveling, mostly Massachusetts and Connecticut.

After twelve years, Jeff called me [to say he] decided to change the territory arrangements and that he had to let me go. He was sorry to do it and would help me out in anything else I wanted to do, but this was the way it had to be. This was two years ago. All the reps were my friends—we're a close group—and they all said the same thing: I was seventy-five. He put four other reps into the territory that I had. I don't know to this day if he made more money with four of them than he did with me. He probably did. And that was the end of my career.

I went to work for another sales rep—he called me. He said I shouldn't have been fired; I was too good a rep. He wanted me to work for him which I did for a while, but then I broke my arm and I couldn't drive. Since I couldn't bring in business, I resigned.

So here I am now, retired. I plan on going to Africa sometime next winter with Josh. I have always wanted to go to South Africa. Always. I adore the music, the color, everything about it. I said to myself, *What the hell? I might as well cash in a CD and do something I've always wanted to do.* So I am going to South Africa.

Q. *That is wonderful. Somewhere in the midst of all this, you had some health issues.*

Lynn: Yeah, I had lung cancer. I had half a lung removed. We lived in Framingham; George was out of the picture then. I had the lung removed and went back to work. All three kids were in college at the same time; I had to work. I had to help these kids out. Luckily, they were all good students, so they all got scholarship money as well as financial aid. Some of them are still paying it off.

Friends helped out—everybody was a big help when that happened. I wasn't laid up for that long; I remember being in the hospital for about three weeks. When I came home, my mother and my sister came to stay with me and all was well. I can't think of any other health issues that I had.

Q. *I'm curious about this: You said, "I did this, I did that, and just kept going." That's good, but in this, what kinds of things were a challenge?*

Lynn: A lot of things were a challenge, but, like a friend said to me, "I don't know how you do it." The only answer is, "You don't have a choice." Many things are a challenge, but you just have to work through them. You have to work to overcome them, or find a way to get around them. There's no choice; you can't give up. You can't just sit back and say, "My kids are in college and I have nothing to do with it."

I had to get rid of my husband because he was not the kind of man I wanted to be around, to put it mildly. He was a challenge. At that point, no one got along with him. But the divorce was messy. Being in court with him all the time was messy. He fought with his own lawyer—punched him out.

Like I said, many things were a challenge and yet, I don't remember being unhappy during any of it except when my mother was here. I was unhappy because of the condition she was in. But otherwise, I've always been in good spirits.

Q. That's the thing. What's interesting and unusual is how you managed to stay in good spirits.

Lynn: Well you have to or you stay in the doldrums. One of the things I missed telling you, one of the biggest challenges: I was working with a customer in Vermont one day, and I got a phone call telling me they discovered David had a tumor. David had cancer. I cried, I cried, I cried. I don't think I ever cried so hard in my life. I managed to drive myself home.

David started going through chemo and radiation all at the same time on a daily basis. It wasn't just once a week; it was every day. He lost all his hair and everything.

At the time, he had been living with his girlfriend, Annalisa. They had known each other for years and were totally devoted to each other, so she was with him. I went down to D.C. and spent some time there. It was hard to sit with him as he went through radiation. Josh, his older brother, just told his boss at work, "I'm taking my brother in every morning and I'm taking him home whenever he's finished. My work will get done." He took care of David and there's twelve years difference between them.

Just as he got finished with his chemo—they timed it—they got married. The wedding was planned, they got married—it was a beautiful wedding. David was bald, and all his groomsmen and the best man were bald—they all shaved their heads in honor of David's baldness. It was a nice tribute to David.

He had finished treatment the day before his wedding. Then he had a tumor removed a couple of years later from his back and, hopefully, they got all of it. Just a year ago, he had a brain tumor removed. He had cancerous things going on just before his wedding, and he had the tumor removed just after Sadie was born.

Q. He had some kind of health issue when he was growing up, right?

Lynn: Well he had neurofibromatosis (NF) which is tumors on the nerves. Ninety-five percent of the time, the tumors are not malignant. But David, unfortunately, fit into the smaller percentage where they were. There's still a lot of research on NF to determine what's causing it; there are different kinds they know about now.

That, probably, to me was the biggest challenge: trying to get my feelings in order and not breaking down because of his illnesses. I just walked around crying. I just could not stop crying. So I went to the doctor and she gave me an anti-depressant, and I suppose it helped. That's when I first started taking them. Other than that, most times have been good times, or as good as it gets. It's a wonderful world if you can keep everything going in a straight line and don't worry about things going off track, or going bad, or people getting ill, but you find ways to deal with it.

Q. I guess if I was asking you for advice it would be A. Don't worry and B. When things go wrong, figure them out.

Lynn: Uh, no, I worry a lot. [laughter] I worry a great deal. I worry about my grandsons now, getting their driver's licenses; one has a motorcycle. But even when my kids were away at college, I worried about them driving; I worried about them, whatever, the drinking, the drugs, and all that. You worry all the time. Sometimes you worry more, sometimes you worry less, sometimes you don't think of it as worrying, you think of it as, *Why can't I sleep? There's something keeping me awake!*

I think you do the best you can. You do what you can as much as you can. It's not that you don't worry about it and let it happen by itself.

I'm satisfied with my life. I'm unhappy about the wrinkles on my face, and I'm unhappy about little things—physical things, my weight, that sort of stuff—but all in all, in general, I would say life is good. If I had more money life would be much better, but that's the way it is and I'm going to have to get through it this way. If I have to be a bag lady, I will. I just hope I can stay mentally healthy enough to last as long as my money does.

Q. But you've got this great attitude and I love that because many women—not the women I'm interviewing—but women from my coaching practice just don't. They just lie down and give up.

Lynn: No, how can you give up? You can't give up! I have a house to maintain—I can't give up on it unless I'm ready to move, and I don't want to move. I have children who look up to me and want me around them—and I can't give up for that reason.

Q. You're a role model to them, and you have loving relationships with them.

Lynn: Yes, we have a very good life, a very strong family, and I think the kids get some of that from me.

Bouncing Back from Family Issues

Family circumstances often change and can reshape everything. This is increasingly true as women accept responsibility for multiple generations at home while immersed in their own careers. Louise was a busy executive and coach when the catastrophic illnesses of her parents caused her to change her entire life. Throughout this experience, she invented, created, pushed, and explored in order to create the situation she needed for her parents.

Louise: Okay. So I'm working in my senior vice president job at the New York Power Authority, and I'm on my way to a board meeting in the morning in Westchester. I'm headed on Metro North to a board meeting in the city, and I get an email from my cousin. The long and the short of it is: my mom is sick. What that ended up meaning was she had to have that valve replacement. And then the whole story of them being sick … blah, blah, blah for a long time. So anyway, in the process of living in a hospital for much of a year-and-a-half and starting a hospital at home and having sixteen critical care nurses and respiratory therapists work for me …

Q. Can you talk about that, because … you're the only person I know who has ever done this, and it's an important part of your story.

Louise: Yeah. So my mother had this valve replacement, which was not that unusual. But, unfortunately, she got something called Clostridium difficile (C-diff.), which is an incredibly common infection. She got dehydrated and ended up in the hospital for five months because she got all of the other hospital infections—the MRSA, staph, everything, almost the whole list—and was going to die from all of that stuff. She was on a ventilator. She had a feeding tube. She hadn't moved at all and she was in a quarter-of-a-million dollar bed.

So the nurses came to me at night (because I lived in the hospital, in her room). They said, "If you don't get her out of here, she's going to die for sure." In essence, it was not their fault. It was clean and everything, but the infections that you only can get in a hospital were killing her. There were two other people who helped me get it started—one was a respiratory therapist and one was a critical care nurse.

I said, "I'll try if you'll help me." So we made everything that's good from a hospital in their little house in Kalida, Ohio, and every bad bureaucratic stupid thing, we didn't do. Quite honestly—because it was not like an insurance company or somebody was paying for it—we could do it sort of the right way; what was right for us—put it that way.

We made a critical care hospital in this house and had everything because my mom was so sick. And when my dad got hit by the car, obviously, he was critically ill also. You needed a real critical care nurse … it wouldn't have been good enough just to have me because they were so sick.

We made a real live hospital in their regular house. So after that whole process, I sort of had no shame, and I would email people who were top in their field to ask for help in the various areas. It turned out they would respond in twenty-four hours. I got some amazing insights into elder care and things like delirium. I did a lot of speaking and things about it after that and became very close to someone who I consider to be the ultimate revolutionary and one of the most amazing thought leaders in the world, Dr. Bill Thomas and his wife, Jude. And there's another guy by the name of Dr. Peter Lichtenberg who is the head of the Institute of Gerontology at Wayne State in Detroit. I consider both of them to be the two most amazing people and, you know, caring about older people in the world. So it was an amazing learning experience and taught me a lot about leadership and organizations and priorities.

Realistic Optimism

In all these scenarios, it would have been easy to give up at the outset or after a few attempts. For these women, developing and maintaining a positive, yet realistic mindset differentiated blind optimism from realistic optimism as a key component of resilience. This realistic optimism helped these women bounce back, adapt, and move on.

How did they manage to keep a positive attitude? Shawn Achor writes about this in *Before Happiness: The 5 Hidden Keys to Achieving Success, Spreading Happiness, and Sustaining Positive Change.* He speaks about choosing a positive scenario from among multiple views of a situation, mapping out a plan for success, and blocking out all the naysayers.

Elements of Resilience

There are a number of elements of resilience illustrated in this chapter. They include drive and focus on the goal, creative and flexible thinking, the ability to maintain perspective, realistic optimism, and seeing opportunities rather than obstacles.

Phyllis C. demonstrated many of these elements in her cross-country adventure. She was able to figure out creative ways to finance their trip. Phyllis H., when thwarted in her efforts to go to South Africa as a reporter, had the flexibility to investigate other career options that led to her own talk show. Jeannette decided that travel arrangements would not keep her away from a wonderful work experience.

Several other women spoke about sexism in the workplace and the creativity needed to both combat sexism and to juggle work and family roles. Susana found ways to use sexism and her multicultural background to her advantage in carving out a role at the CIA. Valerie tried out a whole new lifestyle.

What we can learn from these women's stories is more than simply the importance of bouncing back. The skills they used are available to all of us. Each assessed her alternatives both in terms of realism and in terms of their overarching goals. Each examined available options and, if dissatisfied with those, created new ones. While they were optimistic, theirs was not a false optimism; they were not living in a fantasy world; they were clear about what was and what was not possible. Within that context, they had faith in their chosen course of action.

How You Can Develop Resilience

- Stop and assess your situation.
- Make a list of the options available to you.
- Outline possible outcomes for each option.
- Work with a coach or a trusted friend to assess each option.
- If one option doesn't work, go back to your list, possibly generate other options, and try them.

Below is an exercise to get you thinking through worst case scenarios.

Exercise

Catastrophizing

No, I'm not talking about obsessing about what could go wrong here: that type of thinking tends to stop us in our tracks permanently. One way to lose that "deer in the headlights" reaction and increase your ability to bounce back is to do a simple "What if…?" exercise.

Imagine a situation where something could (or does) go wrong. Ask yourself the same three questions five times:

1. **What's the worst that could happen?**
2. **What's the threat level? (How likely is this to actually happen?)**
   Rank the threat level from 1 to 10, with 1 being the least threat and 10 the greatest threat.
3. **What would I do?**
   Here's an example that uses a common fear among women:
   Situation: I'm going to lose all sources of income.

Round 1

1. **What's the worst that could happen?**
   I'll become a bag lady, living on the streets, and eating out of dumpsters.
2. **How likely is that to happen?**
   Threat level between 1 and 2
3. **What would I do?**
   I'd live off my savings while looking for a job.

Round 2

1. **What's the worst that could happen?**
   I'll never get another job, my savings will run out, and I'll become a bag lady, living on the streets and eating out of dumpsters.
2. **What's the threat level?**
   About 2
3. **What would I do?**
   I'd sell whatever I could, try to sublet my home, stay with friends or family, and widen the range of jobs I'm willing to look at.

Round 3

1. **What's the worst that could happen?**
   I'll sell everything and then run out of money. My friends and family will get tired of me staying with them, and I won't have the stamina for the kinds of jobs I can get. I'm too old to be on my feet all day.
2. **What's the threat level?**
   About 2

3. **What would I do?**

I'd apply for public assistance and move into a shelter if I had to. I'd work with whatever counseling I could get to explore other careers, and I'd brainstorm with my friends to see if they could think of unique things I can do. I'd keep applying for any job I can.

Round 4

1. **What's the worst that could happen?**

No one will hire me and I'll run out of options.

2. **What's the threat level?**

About 1

3. **What would I do?**

I'll start blogging about my experiences, using the computer in my local library. I'll put a contribution button on my blog, and I'll send contributors electronic copies of stories about my experiences that aren't on the blog as a thank you. I'll start putting the material together as a book.

Round 5

1. **What's the worst that could happen?**

I find out that I have absolutely no talent as a writer and can't make any money that way.

2. **What's the threat level?**

Between 5 and 7

3. **What would I do?**

I would apply for a job in the shelter and in any of the agencies I had gone to for services. I would ask everyone to refer me to other people who might have ideas for me. Absolute worst-case scenario: I'd wait for public assistance to find me work and suitable housing.

Okay, not necessarily a brilliantly happy ending, but not living in a refrigerator box either. You'll have much better examples in your own life. Look back over some of the stories in this chapter. Would you have done what these women did? What else might they have done?

Working through this exercise can help you learn how to cope well when things are going wrong. The women in this chapter faced a variety of obstacles, large and small. They came up with alternatives and kept trying until they found something that worked.

What made them different? Attitude seems to be the key. Women who believe firmly that there are always alternatives are better able to find those alternatives than those who believe they don't have choices.

Many years ago, when I worked with disenfranchised women, I had a client who was determined to beat the odds. When I met her, she was an unemployed ex-offender living in a shelter. She wanted out. She wanted a job and her own apartment. Every day, she got up, got out, and did as many things as she could to improve her situation. Some days, it seemed like nothing would work. She got turned down for jobs and turned down for apartments. Every day, she started over. She believed that she could turn her life around and she simply wouldn't give up. By the end of the nine-week program, she found a job with the Parks Department and moved into a subsidized studio apartment.

Part of what made this woman succeed was that her situation was so dire—the threat was palpable and inescapable. Still, she could have become numbed by the experience, she could have given up.

What we all need to beware of is what's called the "boiled frog syndrome." One symptom is that we tell ourselves things "aren't that bad." Beth Lapides says she came from a "fine" family; no matter what, they said everything was "fine," so there was no reason to change.

Consider what happens to the frog: if you put a frog in a pot of boiling hot water it will jump right out because it recognizes danger and the need to change. If you put a frog in tepid water and heat the water very gradually, the frog accepts the discomfort until it's too late. It boils.

If you're not happy with your life, don't wait until you're a boiled frog.

Chapter 4

The Little Engine That Could – Persistence

Persistence is enduring tenacity, especially despite opposition, obstacles, and discouragement. For these women, if something didn't work the first time, they tried again, or tried something slightly different: They didn't give up or walk away.

When trying something new, some women give up immediately if it doesn't work instantly or isn't easy. Other women keep trying until they figure it out—they find a way of living that's a good fit for them or find a way to make something happen that changes the previous outcome.

Active experimentation—using obstacles as learning experiences—is another trait these women have in common. For example, Herta's bad experience attempting to climb Mount Kilimanjaro at age forty shaped her successful climb at age fifty.

When Sharon decided to strike out on her own, she had no sales experience, knew nothing about construction or building components, or even about running a business. She simply set her mind on what she wanted and kept going. Sharon epitomizes that old sales adage that it takes ninety-nine "Nos" to get one "Yes:"

Sharon: I started calling on people, but it was the same thing, "Come back. Come back." I was down on State Street in Chicago where all the purveyors are. I walked in the door—for like the fourth time—and he said, "No. Come back."

I turned around and started to walk out, and I thought, *They are spending money somewhere.* So I turned around and said, "Is there anything I can help you with?"

He said, "Well, you see our storefront windows? Do you do those really nice aluminum ones?"

And I looked at those windows, and I looked at him. And I looked at those windows, and I turned around and said, "Yes. We do that. Yes, we certainly do."

I went back to my office, and I started calling window companies. I had no idea what the markup was. I had no idea what an invoice was. I had never seen any of those. I didn't know what percentage people mark things up. So I just put one on and I sold the job.

Victoria also didn't give up when something didn't work the first time. She demonstrated a form of persistence when she started paying better attention to those ideas that flashed through her mind:

Victoria: I teach Personal Essay in the [college] program. There are five or six different classes I teach, rotating around whatever they need at the time. I just got an email this morning asking me if I would teach the Advanced Personal Essay classes this summer. I said, "Sure, I will."

So, I [was] doing that and, of course, when I hit sixty, that's when everything changed. When I turned sixty, I made a promise to myself that any time I had one of those little flashes of creativity when I thought—*Oh, wouldn't that be a great book?* or *Wouldn't that be a great play?* or *Wouldn't that be a great movie?*—rather than just [letting it] slip across my brain and off with the wind, I promised myself I would pursue those ideas. If something came of it—wonderful. If nothing came of it, no problem.

People said to me, "Aren't you afraid of failing?"

I said, "For me now, the failure is not trying. If I try and it doesn't work, it's not a failure, it just didn't work."

Recently, I tried and my agent tried to sell an anthology. Everybody who was involved in it—there were some major, major authors involved—said, "This is a brilliant idea. It's going to be great." But none of them write on spec, so you have to sell the project [first].

Ivy worked in a variety of positions before she decided to go into her father's business. She describes her conversation with him as one of the most difficult negotiations she ever had. Persistence helped her win:

Ivy: After college, I worked in a few companies, two of them owned by women entrepreneurs. When I was about twenty-seven, I realized I wanted to start a family and needed an exit strategy from my job in a catering and corporate events business.

That's when I got into printing. I started researching printing franchises. At that young age and married, I was a quarter of a million dollars short with no credit to my name. So I spoke to my father, a business owner.

He said, "Well, I'm not going to lend you a quarter of a million dollars."

But I said, "You know, you get this. This [business] is based on advertising and printing—and you do printing.

He goes, "Well, I'll make a counter-offer: Come work for me for a year. If it doesn't work out, I won't fund your business, but I will help you find the funding."

So that was the beginning of a very challenging negotiation, because what my father offered me as a starting salary I was already making triple. You know, he looked at his daughter as being a young girl. Basically, he told me in no uncertain terms, "I pay my gals—G-A-L-S—$18,000."

I said, "Dad, I'm making close to triple [that]." And it was triple because I got a good portion of that in green [cash] at the time, in tips and gratuities from different events that I ran. I thought, *This just isn't going to work.*

That's when I really started learning about negotiating and being true to yourself. It was ... the first time I had to stand up for what I believed in, not just to [the person who] would eventually be my boss, so to speak, but to my own father, and negotiate based on principle and business, not based on relationship or age.

It was not fun. I have had only one other negotiation as difficult in the twenty-odd years since then. We ended up agreeing on a base salary, on benefits, and on a commission structure. At one point he said, "This is the amount I paid in the past."

To which I responded, "Yeah, but you're recruiting me. I didn't come and ask you for a job. I have a job. You're recruiting me to take your business and bring a whole new stream of business."

At the time, I was leading corporate events and was already connected to some very prominent people. I went to work and started making good money after the first several months I needed to really learn the business.. I went on to have my first child. I always worked. I was the person who, after I delivered, called my closest client who followed me through my pregnancy to tell them I delivered. That was how I always looked at a client relationship.

By the time my daughter was a year old, I went back into my father and I said, "I'd like a piece of the business."

And he, again, kind of chuckled and said, "Well, I have a junior partner."

I said, "No, no, no, no, no. I told you, I was going to be the leader of my own destiny, that I would be a business owner. At this point, my sales equal yours. That means we become partners. Or, I could take my book of business and do this on my own."

Interestingly enough, he had a junior partner with him who ran the inside for about twenty years. I became an equal partner to the junior partner and, in less than a year, the junior partner left because he didn't want to be in partnership with a woman.

Q. That was still a big deal.

Ivy: It was a very big deal around 1993-1994. My father wanted to find one of his old friends who would take me in. I said, "I don't want to be taken in. I'm going to build my own destiny." I found another firm that was equal in sales to ours and created a merger. The merger lasted about five years, which was a good run.

After that, I created Slater Graphics and went out completely on my own. I said to my dad, "You're getting older. You know, I will be happy to run any business through my company. I don't want any money. You'll always have a desk here and whatever you want; you always have a place to call your home. But I'm in business as of today."

Jeannette was always stretching barriers early in her career. She was always open to possibilities and took on as many projects as she could—maybe even a few more than she could handle:

Jeannette: My co-editor was graduating my first year of night school and, it turns out, he had been going to night school every semester for eleven straight years. He didn't take as many courses as I was taking and I thought, *I will never last eleven years doing this.*

I decided I would switch and quit my job, pursue the program, always working during those days, so that's what I did. I decided I wanted to become a journalist because that was my core competency. At that time, a journalism degree was very restricted—it was like getting a trade degree. I needed the flexibility so I could get through before my money ran out, so I decide to take an English degree. But I took all my journalism courses within that degree because we had more electives. I applied for a half scholarship from the Long Island Public Relations Association because I was still funding my own college because my parents didn't have any money.

In fact, the whole time I was at school I still had to pay board. That's the Italian tradition. This is not "poor me," it's just the way it is—even when you're in school. So I knew I was always going to work long hours and go to school.

Anyway, one of the members of the Long Island Public Relations Association turned out to be the editor of the *Daily Newspaper,* a business newspaper. He was really a visionary because he preceded all the Crain's publications and all the weekly and city business publications. I think he might even have been the first in the country.

He said, "Maybe, one day, we can hire you part-time."

The next morning, I called them up and said, "Is it possible that you might be able to hire me as a part-time writer?" And he did. For two years, I worked, I went to school, and then I was the reporter for the *Long Island Commercial Review.* It was a daily, sixteen pages, *Daily News*-size. Then when I graduated, he offered me a full-time job.

Early Roadblocks

Several of the Fifty were actively discouraged or blocked from their earliest career choices. Often, this was a sex-role bias; sometimes it was family pressure. Some reevaluated their options and switched to another track. A few persisted despite the roadblocks.

Alice's father made it very clear he didn't like women who stood out:

Alice: I do know that when I was about eight years old, my father was talking about a nurse at the clinic where he worked. He was a physician. He didn't like her. He called her a "ballsy babe," which was probably the worst expression he could call somebody.

At the time—this is very peculiar to me—I said to myself, "So, I won't be famous." I have no idea how that got into my head, where it came from, but that's what I said to myself. I realized that he did not like actualized women. He didn't like aggressive women. He didn't like women who showed up. Of course, he would not let my mother work. All of this influenced me a lot, but it was the culture of the time.

Q. It's really interesting that you were exactly the kind of woman your father didn't like. You were a "ballsy lady" from pretty early on but ...

Alice: I'll tell you the ramifications of what you just said: Along with telling me he didn't like ballsy women he also, so clearly, told me that his reason for being was to support his wife and his daughter. So I grew up thinking that if I ever earned a living it would kill him. So I've had major trouble making a living. Major. I'm getting better about it.

You hit something that is absolutely pivotal: those two things he told me, I've carried with me. And you know I know it. But it is so … I was an only child, and so I got all of the attention, but it wasn't the kind I needed. It was, like, under a microscope.

Betsy struggled with figuring out what she really wanted to do and ended up, more or less, falling into a career:

Betsy: The doctor piece fell by the wayside as I really struggled with math. So I decided that wasn't going to happen. Probably that was my mistake, but I didn't know how to get help [so I could] learn math. I had a brief period when I thought I wanted to be a teacher. Then I looked around and thought, *I think I only want to teach the smart kids who want to learn.* It seems like it doesn't really work that way; you've got to teach all the kids. So I moved on from that idea.

Then, I had the idea I wanted to become a lawyer; that was about age fifteen, sixteen. I went to college, and I went straight to law school … the University of Chicago. So, at age twenty-three, I had a law degree. One of the striking things, looking back, is that I had not really spent any time educating myself on what lawyers do. What are the different kinds of law? What is this work all about? And is this is something I would like to do? Again, as I got to my third year of law school, I was about to be launched on an unsuspecting world.

I realized I really had no idea what I wanted to do with this law degree, so I took the easy choice: accept a job offer with the biggest New York City firm that made an offer to me and figure it out then. Now, it was true that as a young lawyer, if you can make it in New York, you will make it anywhere. I figured out, basically, that it preserved a lot of options. So, my first career was going to a New York City law firm and starting to work as a corporate lawyer.

Phyllis H. contended with youth and gender as she built a name for herself as a broadcast journalist:

Phyllis H.: Even though I was young, I was still given positions of prominence in that anti-war endeavor. I was seen as a peacemaker between some very radical forces and some conservative forces. That just began everything; it began my career in television, and began my political view of the world, and what drove me to want to be a journalist. All I can say about WPIX is there was a lot of screaming.

The reporters—some were very supportive, some were very helpful to my career. Others—others were resentful. You know, it's a back-biting industry where people are waiting for you to fail. If you are on-air and you have a spot, somebody else wants that spot. But it was good. It toughened me up.

And what else can I say about WPIX? You know that any woman going into broadcasting at the time, which was in the '70s, found the presence of women to be a really rare thing. A lot of women were feature reporters at the time instead of hard news reporters. So it was a fight, always having to justify. WPIX-TV was a training ground for the toughening that I had to have for future work.

But after two years, I got tired of being the kid reporter in the group. There was an audition at WOR-TV. Carol Jenkins, who held that position at WOR-TV, let me know that she was leaving and I auditioned for her job. I was up against thirty other women—it was a co-anchor spot—but I did get it. And I think it surprised everyone.

I think it vindicated me with my parents because there was my father, hoping I would enter politics. I had gone to grad school while I was a reporter and had gotten my master's degree in political science, and he was still hoping that I would pursue politics. But when I got this talk show—which was a serious show, not the way talk shows are today, but an hour of serious talk six days a week—that, I think, gained his respect.

He then became one of my researchers. I could call him up and put him to work saying, "Dad, tell me what you think about this. Tell me what you think about that." So it was a little bit more respectable than the job of reporter, through his eyes.

It's called *Straight Talk*, and I was originally co-anchoring that with Elinor Guggenheimer. Then she left and we went to Mary Helen McPhillips. This was a very great opportunity: major world leaders coming through and major celebrities. It was a high-level talk show on channel nine and, in those days, the tone of talk shows had a commitment to serious content.

Q. What were some of the highlights of co-anchoring that show?

Phyllis H.: Well, first of all, I could express an opinion; it was not scripted. I think I got the job because I demonstrated some knowledge of the world and my political background. My knowledge of politics was substantial; I really had earned my master's degree.

My favorite interview was a guy named Harrison Salisbury. He was the managing editor of the *New York Times* and a very well-known and respected journalist that traveled the world. He was also a Russian expert. So I got a chance to really use what I had learned in the interview process. There were so many things that were special: I met people like Gore Vidal and B.F. Skinner.

I remember one of my favorite times with guests on the show was when you had them alone. Because we taped the show as if it were live, we would take a break every twenty minutes. So I had B.F. Skinner alone. B.F. Skinner, of course, was famous for his behavioral thinking and understanding of human behavior and had a whole theory about behavior and rewarding good behavior and ignoring bad.

I got him alone and I said, "Dr. Skinner, could you tell me how this applies to relationships and how you use your theories?" (You know, it was probably naïve asking this great man. He was innovative when I got to interview him.)

He looked at me over the top of his glasses and he said, "Reward the good. Ignore the bad." Which is easily done, by the way. But I do occasionally remember that and I thought that was great advice.

I co-anchored *Straight Talk* for thirteen years of my life, from the mid-seventies until 1984. Some of it overlapped—I also did a radio show called *The Matter of Money* on NBC Radio. Because I felt I wanted to know everything there was about economics and climates, I created a radio show that would give me a chance to interview anyone I wanted to—and I did.

But it did something else for me; I was on NBC when Howard Stern was on NBC Radio—and Howard Stern was always getting in trouble. Whenever he got into trouble, NBC would have to do a make-up program as an apology or to cover whatever it was he had done with guests he had insulted or whatever, so I would get to do this make-up show. I only saw him once in the hallway at NBC. He was very grumpy then. I do admire him. I think, you know, he's on the cutting edge of being outrageous, and he makes broadcasting today look very mild and very tame.

When you really want to talk truth with people, there are some people [for whom all you need to do] is "put your nickel in" and you get remarkable truth. Colleen Dewhurst was another one like that. Oh, it goes on. My life was so rich and so filled with thoughtful people that it drove me forward.

I have to say, however, that the most interesting person I ever, ever, interviewed was Woody Guthrie's widow, a not very well-known woman who came on and talked about the illness of her family, how their children had inherited this illness, and what it was like to be the wife of Woody Guthrie. I noticed that the same crew that normally didn't listen (only listened to Sophie Loren) they were all … their ears perked up. They were all paying deep attention to her. She had such a sincere and loving way of teaching. That also was a moment that altered my life because that said to me, "Okay, all these other shows are pursuing the celebrities. It's the thoughtful person that I'm after."

That set the tone for what I do now, that interview with Mrs. Woody Guthrie. There are people who people don't talk to all the time that could change the world.

I'm really glad that celebrities get involved in charity work and that they bring attention to charities and all that … but there [are] always these people in the background whose very presence causes a wave to happen. Right now, I find those people.

It may be self-serving to tell you that you're one of those people, because now you're interviewing me. But when you hit certain points in our first interview, there was a shift that I experienced—a shift in consciousness. There are people who do that. It's worth pursuing hundreds of interviews to get to the one that does that. It really, it just altered my whole way of thinking about celebrity. I could go on forever about the subject of celebrity.

Phyllis H. spoke further about her attempt to become a foreign correspondent and how that experience shifted her career: (see Chapter 3, page 27)

Phyllis H.: When I auditioned [to go to South Africa], the crew said, "My gosh. She did it in one take." I did my audition half in Russian and half in English. I talked about the politics of the fertile part of the Soviet Union (it was the Soviet Union then) and how the fights over land and food rights could affect the structure of the Soviet Union and the large population of Muslims. Much of … [what I spoke of] in my audition ultimately became true.

I talked about the challenges of the Soviet Union, and I also talked about a contrast between a Russian lullaby and an American lullaby. We talk about "the cradle falling down" in our most famous lullaby. In the Russian lullaby, it's "May there always be sunshine. May there always be love. May there always be Mama. Let there always be me." I did this in Russian and contrasted the lullabies.

I was really proud of that, but I did all that with the expectation that ABC would look at me as a Russian correspondent. Well, they had no intention of sending me. They did everything to discourage me. Once, I was so desperate to go, I volunteered to go on my vacation to Russia and pay for it myself. They said "Don't do that. It will hurt your career."

When you're young, you don't know when you are being treated badly. You don't always know that things aren't protocol. I was told it was too difficult for women to be there and that I shouldn't go. And now I feel cheated; I should have just ignored their comments and gone. But I still don't regret my journey to ABC because I had this wonderful conversation with Peter Jennings, who was very supportive of my decision, who really encouraged my reporting, and moved me forward. What caused the end of my career was that I was disappointed about not being utilized fully there. If you're not fully expressed in a given job, no matter how wonderful it is, you don't want to do it. So I went out of there very unhappy.

But, ultimately, I became a filmmaker because one of the things I wanted to do—which they would not sign off on—was a documentary on AIDS prevention. So I raised the money myself. I left ABC. I raised half million dollars to create a film called *AIDS: The Facts of Life* with Susan Sarandon and James Taylor.

I hired a director, a fantastic young director, and I put the film together. It was my idea. It was based on the idea that when the AIDS epidemic broke out, people were terrified. I kept thinking, "What would it would be like to be at your senior prom and wondering if you could even kiss your date?" I mean, that's how terrified people were when this hit. The *Daily News* called my film "a film you could see on a date."

That's what I wanted to make: I wanted to make something helpful for humanity, but it was too frank for television. Ultimately, it played in hospitals and colleges around the country. And it won the AFI Billboard Award.

Agenia, who also spent many years in television, started a career in communications primarily because she did well on an aptitude test. But persistence played a big part in growing her career:

Agenia: I went up there to do pre-med and stayed in the pre-med track for three years.

Over the summer, at the end of my third year, I had the privilege of working with a doctor, a woman who was starting her own obstetrics and gynecology practice. It was from working with Gretchen that I saw what doctors do. That was the first time I had ever witnessed that and I quickly learned I did not want to be a doctor and had no interest whatsoever in that kind of career or lifestyle. It was not what I wanted to do.

So, I spent more than a year—actually almost two years—working with her and helping to get her practice established. I went over to the university career assessment center and took a series of assessments. It was on one of those assessments that one of the counselors said, "You have put a lot of time into school; you've taken all these courses. The one college you can transfer all these courses to and still get out of here is the College of Communication. That may not be a career choice of yours, but it helps you graduate. Your aptitude skills test demonstrates you're capable, quite frankly, of doing whatever you set your mind to."

I transferred to communications which I knew absolutely nothing about. I learned that it required an internship to really make it in that area. So I ended up getting an internship at WIVK Radio, the country music radio station in Knoxville—the number one radio station in Knoxville, AM and FM. They were the only radio station that had a newsroom with a news director and reporters. I got an internship working there.

I was elated and excited; you can't imagine. That was the good news. The bad news was the radio station was located about three miles away—actually, it was about seven, maybe seven to ten miles away—from the university campus and I didn't own a car. So I would either have to ride my bike to work for my internship, or catch the bus to my internship. I did that and I had a fabulous experience.

During the local election for the mayor and the board, one of the reporters got sick and they needed me to step in. Although I was an intern, I was familiar with their processes and said I would work during the elections. But I had to tell them I didn't have a car.

I will never forget the news director looking at me and saying, "You've been riding your bike to the radio station?"

I said, "Yeah."

"So how do you get home?"

"On the bike."

He just sat there and he looked at me. Then he said, "Okay, I'm going to give you your assignment. And I'm also going to give you keys to a car," which was the news station's vehicle. "Here are the keys to the car; now let's get to work." And that was the beginning of my career in broadcasting at WIVK Radio as an intern.

Just a phenomenal experience. I worked really hard at that job, so much so that I got assigned several major news stories, a couple of which ended up being picked up by CBS Radio.

When all of that started happening for me, a local television station took interest in me. The one great thing about radio is that no one sees you, so you don't have to dress a certain way or look a certain way or have just the right makeup. I did not want to work in television for that reason.

But there was a woman that worked at this television station who was the hottest thing in television in East Tennessee. Everyone loved Edye Ellis. I remember seeing her on television and being, you know, quite smitten with her comfort and poise and her ability to deliver—she was just amazing. I ended up becoming a friend of hers due to a classroom assignment.

She said, "You really need to transition from radio to television. You should do this."

I kept telling her, "No. No, I don't want to be on television."

With her encouragement, I did transition from the radio station to the television station, but off-air. I worked as a newsroom assignment editor; this was at WBIR-TV Channel 10 in Knoxville. This television station, again, was a powerhouse in the community. It was rated number one from the minute it went on the air to the minute it went off the air—known for its news team and its newsroom. I had the privilege of working there and working off-air and it was magnificent.

Q. I see that a great many people offered you incredible opportunities along the way. Do you have any idea about how that came about?

Agenia: Hmm. No, I've never thought of it that way. They were just people that, you know, were in my life at a moment in time and still are. I mean, these are people who are still part of it—not as much today as they were then—but Edye is an interesting one because she was on television.

I had an assignment for a class at the University of Tennessee and I decided I wanted to interview her for that assignment. I'll never forget the instructor saying, "That's a waste of time; this lady is very busy. I would suggest you go after someone else."

I said, "No, I really want it to be with her."

So I kept calling the newsroom, leaving messages and, out of the blue, one day she literally called me back. I just remember being speechless and thinking, "I am on the phone with Edye Ellis." I explained to her what I was doing and why and how I'd like to meet with her.

She said, "Well, you know, I'm really, really busy during the weekdays, so I can't do it on a weekday. I just don't have the time."

I said, "Okay. What about Saturday or Sunday?"

So, we ended up meeting on a Sunday over brunch. I was smart enough to pick a restaurant I could walk to that wasn't far away from the university. We sat and talked for several hours while I did my classroom project and got the information from her that I needed. At the end of that, she made a comment about going to the theater on campus to see a play.

I said, "I'm getting ready to do the same thing this afternoon," so she and I went off to see the same play and that was just the beginning.

She said, "I'd like to see how your project turns out."

I followed up with her and that's how I got to know Edye. She ended up being the maid of honor in my wedding.

I've never forgotten—talk about people you can learn so much from—the lessons I learned from her are equally as important in my life and where I am today as the lessons I got from Father and Linda. When I think about the pivotal moments in my life, those three people are instrumental, instrumental in that.

Q. One of the things I'm hearing is that you're not afraid to try things and you don't easily take "no" for an answer.

Agenia: Yes, that's true. And … talk about not being afraid to try things. [laughter] That's just … that's happening in my life today. The reason I chuckled, thinking about it, is that I was in swim class again yesterday. If you saw me swim you'd ask, "Why are you doing this?" It's because it's something I'm not good enough at yet that I'm ready to give it up. But, when I get there, [laughter] I guess I'll move on to the next thing.

[So my brunch with Edye Ellis was] the start of a fabulous career in television. I loved working in that newsroom. I loved being in the newsroom because you sat there and—going back to Father and Linda—you kept up with all of the current news stories. All of them. You sat at a desk and then at the front of the newsroom, and you worked with the reporters and the photographers, helping them get their news assignments, what they were going to work on for today, what needed follow-up. You worked with the producer on how to stack the broadcast. You really, really understood what happened on the air between 6:00 and 6:30, or 5:00 and 5:30. [You needed an understanding of] every second of that broadcast: what happens to it, and what stories are important and relevant and why they are important. It was really exciting working, and I love, love, loved it.

Edye was the anchor along with Bill Williams, so I loved being a part of what they took to the community. It was really exciting. And sure enough, I was sitting in the newsroom one . There was a woman that did the community affairs program—I do not know to this day what happened, but she was let go.

Edye walked up to me and said, "Okay, here's the deal. This person is no longer here. I told the news director that you need to sit in the seat and do that community affairs program." I remember looking at her, absolutely petrified.

She said, "You can do this."

I said, "What will I wear? And who's going to do my makeup? I mean, how does this all work?" because I was quite happy where I was.

And she said, "Don't you worry about that; we will figure it out."

She coached me through doing this community affairs program. The news director was quite taken with the outcome. The next thing I knew, they were producing a show called *In Touch*, featuring me as the anchor. The purpose of that program was community affairs. They really spotlighted and highlighted what was going on in the African-American community of East Tennessee. It really took off and quickly became a huge hit. That's when the news director said, "Why don't we move you away from *In Touch* to anchor our early morning broadcast, because it's slipping in the ratings and we need to give it some new life?"

My broadcasting career really grew from there. The visibility of people knowing who you are all the time was extremely uncomfortable. After doing broadcasting, what I was doing in the newsroom as news assignment editor became dissatisfying; I just didn't like it as much anymore.

I had to do an interview one day with the dean of the business college at University of Tennessee. I wrapped up the interview, and he looked at me and said, "My wife and I love waking up with you in the morning. Oh, it's just such an honor to have you with us at our home."

I looked at him and said, "Well, that's nice to hear because this is not what I want to do." I just blurted it out to him.

He looked at me, astonished, "You've got to be joking."

"No, I'm not." I said, "I need to figure out how to transition from where I am to where I want to be."

He said, "Where do you want to be?"

I said, "I'd like to be in a business setting. I think that one thing I've learned from myself working in the newsroom—I like the management of things."

He said, "Well, I'm the Dean of the College of Business. You should apply."

I said, "Well, I will do that." And I did and I got accepted.

When that occurred, the television station came back to me and said, "Here's the deal—the ratings are too important to us. We will keep you on if you will come back in and do the early morning news broadcast every morning. You are free the rest of the day for business school or whatever else you want to do. But if we can get you to commit for the two years that it takes you to get your MBA that you will stay on-air with us, we will support you the whole way."

And that is exactly what they did. It was wonderful.

When Jan started her first accounting position, she had a plan and a history of hard work. Her attitude towards work, shaped by her childhood experiences, was different from her peers. She handled that by working hard, taking on any task, and maintaining a positive attitude:

Jan: I went off to Ernst & Whinney in Oklahoma City which, ultimately, became Ernst & Young when they merged with Arthur Young.

Q. What was that like?

Jan: It was great. It was an interesting experience. The company had very high standards; grade point averages had to be pretty high just to get an interview. It was very white collar and most employees seemed to be from white-collar families that encouraged them to be accountants, lawyers, etc. Whereas, I was kind of unusual in that I came from quite a blue-collar background. What was interesting was I often found that my peers—some had never worked before. Of course, I had been working since I was seven.

I remember sitting next to this one girl, and she was complaining because they were making us work late into the evening. She said we shouldn't have to work past five-thirty, and that we didn't make any money at all. She said her father paid her more when she was at the university than the firm paid her.

Now, I thought I was the luckiest person on the planet. I was so thrilled, and I didn't care what they asked me to do. I would stand at the copier for hours—this was before you had a computer on every desk—and make copies of hundreds and hundreds of client documents for the work paper files. I would make copies, work all hours, run errands, or just whatever had to happen.

I worked really hard and had a really good attitude. That really [served] me well, whereas a lot of people around me just complained a lot about the routine nature of the work or because of the late hours and things. For me, having worked full-time in law enforcement and full-time as a waitress before that; and having gone to school and carried a full load as well as having a social life as you do at that age; for me, it was a much better life than I had before. As a result of the fact that I worked hard and had a good attitude, I think I got better opportunities and faster promotions than my peers.

Q. I'm not hearing that you cared too much about what your peers thought of you.

Jan: Oh, no. I cared tremendously about what they thought of me. I was always quite sympathetic. I never joined in when they would sit there and whine. And I certainly didn't jump in and say things like, "You know, you should feel lucky to have this job." I just listened and watched. I've always cared a great deal about what people think and, you know, part of the things that drove me in my early years starting businesses was related to that.

All of the clothes I wore growing up were hand-me-downs. And it was always embarrassing to be wearing an outfit that the local kids had worn last year. You know, kids make fun of you and I think it's hard on you. It can make you really self-conscious about what people think.

Q. How did you deal with that?

Jan: I don't know. Persevered. I had no choice in these matters, you know? I guess, if anything, it probably drove me to make sure that in the future I wasn't in that situation. It's funny. My friends always joke with me because I won't wear three-quarters length sleeves or capri pants because they didn't exist when I was a kid. You would get these clothes that were perfectly good, but they didn't quite fit. The sleeves would be too short or the trousers would be too short or something. To this day, I can't wear a three-quarter-length sleeve shirt or capri pants without thinking that I'm wearing hand-me-downs that don't fit me.

I have friends, and we'll go shopping and they'll say, "Oh, this is a really cute jacket." I just look at it and say, "It has three-quarter length sleeves."

And they just roll their eyes at me and I say, "Sorry. If I don't feel confident in it and if I don't feel good about it in my own head, then I can't wear it." So you will never see me in three-quarter length sleeves or capri pants.

Q. So all of this was inside, but it sounds like you didn't let a lot of it seep outside? I'm curious as to whether other people had any idea about how you were feeling. It sounds like you were pretty good at kind of compartmentalizing.

Jan: I didn't talk about the fact that I grew up—much of my childhood, but not all of it—in a trailer park until very recently. I didn't want to be judged around that. Some of my closest friends would understand the three-quarter-length sleeve thing, but for the most part, I give the appearance of being quite confident.

But I don't think most people are truly confident. I mean, there are a few who are, but the highest performers, in my experience, are sometimes the least confident. The reason they are high performers is that they're trying very hard to fight their own insecurities. And so often, the most confident people are not the most successful, and the most successful are the ones who are least confident. But you wouldn't think that based on the facades we all wear.

Although Robyn experienced success as an actor and a writer, she felt she was forced by a changing market to reconsider her path. Once she set on a new course, she kept plugging away until she got the results she wanted:

Robyn: Opportunities, commercials, auditioning got less and less and less. Also, Internet advertising started to take a toll on how many commercials were being produced. All of that stuff really started to cut into my career as an actor which, inadvertently, gave me more time to focus on the business.

Then, I had to make a decision about the writing because I had been hired to write another screenplay. I loved doing that, but that's also extremely thankless because you can write and write and then the selling of the screenplay could take about twenty years, if ever. So about three years ago, I decided to listen to my husband and said, "I'm not going to stop doing anything, but I'm going to stop pursuing anything else other than my business."

I put in a lot of time, effort, and energy—joining more organizations, going to more networking things, doing more social network marketing, other types of marketing, just reaching out to people, emailing—to promote the business more. It really, almost immediately, started having an effect. I got more clients, more visibility, and more credibility. I would do presentations and from the presentations I would almost always get clients.

And as I did that and grew, I started to enjoy it much more because the more you do it, the more it feeds you. The more I started growing and continued to grow and expand the nature of what it was I did, the more I heard from clients how helpful I had been to them, the more I really started to cherish what I do.

I don't think I could be as good as I am without the trajectory that I went through, because I continually use almost all of the exercises I learned in college when I work with people on their vocal skills. When I work with people on their delivery skills, I use almost all of the acting exercises I know. When I help people create a presentation or a video script, I use all of my writing skills because I know what it is to engage and language and all of that. Especially in soap writing: I had to write for, in any given day, twelve different characters. So I had to know what their voices sounded like and how to get the outline information into the voice of this actor and not make it sound like exposition. So I use all of those skills now in coaching and helping people do what they do and do what I do. So that's my job trajectory!

Linda S. tells how just jumping in and not asking too many questions got her hired:

Linda S.: I got my foot in the door. I took the last $200 I had out of my bank account and bought a plane ticket to LaCrosse, Wisconsin, where I was supposed to interview with Jody. I got there, walked into the room, and he never turned around. He was at an IBM Selectric typewriter and was typing a news release and he never turned around.

The door opened and the person who had made the appointment walked in and said, "This is the person that Franklin Sutton asked you to interview. He knows her daddy." I walked in and stood behind the desk, and he never turned around. He jerked the news release out of the typewriter and passed it over his shoulder and said, "Edit this."

I was raised in the South. He was a Southern man. I was trying to figure out, "Did he mean for me to tell him how great it was, or did he mean for me to truly edit it?" I decided that I had not taken the last $200 out of my bank account to fly up there and not at least show that I had some sense about what I was doing.

So I edited it, and he kind of harrumphed and said, "That is better. Now, retype it."

The sad part of this story is that I had never learned how to type. It was a defensive mechanism—I did not want to know how to type because I would wind up being a secretary. At the time, that was one of the only things women could do, and it kept you out of the track of moving forward.

So it took me awhile. I had to hunt and peck and retype it. Then he said, "Take it to the filing center." I had no idea where the filing center was, but I walked outside and I ran into Ed Bradley, who had just come back from Vietnam, had been back a couple years, and was covering the campaign for CBS.

The first part of this story that I cite to young people is, "Don't be afraid to use your contacts." Second, "If you're showing up for an interview, show them you know what to do." In this case, edit the news piece. And the third piece is, "If you don't know something, ask." So I walked up to Ed Bradley and said, "Where's the filing center?"

I didn't tell him I didn't know what a filing center was. He walked me over to the filing center, talking to me, asking me about why I was there. I found out later that Jody hired me for two reasons: one, I had the confidence to make changes to the news release; the second reason was Ed had said he thought I would be a good addition to the staff. So I say, "Learn from this." It is something that shows that women at that particular time ... the choices we had to make about how we were going to respond to opportunities we were given.

Carole faced multiple obstacles as she was becoming established in the marketing world: being a minority woman at a time when development programs could offer as much stigma as support, going through a difficult divorce, and raising a child with physical challenges.

Carole: I was working in human resources, writing that book on benefits I told you about, and working as a trainer. One of the people who was in my class was the head of the placement office at New York University. He saw a job come across his desk where Avon was looking for professionals of the minority persuasion. Basically, he said, "You really ought to go up there." I had never thought of working corporate.
I'm like, "What am I going to do at Avon? My mother used certain Avon products."

He said, "No," and gave me a Harvard Business Review case study. Avon products had been written up in a case study. And in those days, Avon Products was a great place to go to work because they were doing really unique, interesting things there. He convinced me to go on the interview, and I got the job as a junior writer. And so my first corporate job was writing the Avon brochure.

I was one of, maybe, twenty writers and, maybe, thirty art directors. The only [company that] published more paper in the United States than Avon was *Reader's Digest*. The brochure went out every two weeks. We had three times as much material that went out to the local representatives. We always had 400,000 to 500,000 representatives. So by the end of the day, the amount of print material was voluminous, to say the least. It was one of the few places you could be creative and still get a lot of corporate work experience. That was really interesting.

That was back in, I want to say, 1977. I was already married, and my husband was kind of excited. He said, "Okay. You climbed up to the big time. Moving on up here." I remember I had no corporate work clothes, so we went to Bloomingdale's. I remember buying this beautiful wool cashmere coat and this angora hat and a whole bunch of things. I really never saw myself that way before—I had high heel shoes. "Wow, who are you, girl?"

Now, I was married. I had left NYU. I was working on something called a career, which, believe me, at no point when I was downtown trying on all these different things did I think I had one. Now it was like, "Okay. You're working for this company and you have a career. And you have to decide what you want to do." So that was the beginning of the career and, "Are you going to have a kid? Or, what are you going to do?" So, that was a lot to be thinking about.

Q. *How long were you with Avon?*

Carole: I was there thirteen years. I started as a writer, a brochure writer, and left as a director of communications.

Q. *That was kind of a heyday for women in minorities at Avon, right?*

Carole: Absolutely. There were a lot of women and minorities coming up the ranks. A friend of mine actually wound up being the first black female vice president at Avon and I wound up working for her at one point. We did a lot of things in what we called "special markets" back in the day, which were blacks and Latinos. We were trying to introduce new products and attract new customers. It was a very interesting time. I did relate, partially, because my mother used Avon products.

One of the things we all had to do—back in the day, if you worked in the New York headquarters—was we had to go out and sell Avon, because they wanted you to know what the representative experience was. So we actually were sent to Atlanta, Georgia and told to sell Avon. That was another of those life-changing experiences. I found out what it was like to be dropped off in one of those suburban Atlanta neighborhoods and go knock on doors. My friends in New York were like, "Are you serious?"

Q. *I had forgotten. Those were the "Avon calling" days.*

Carole: That's right—people still knocked on doors. It wasn't until years later that they became more of a workplace seller. Here in New York, the transition had already begun, but in the South? Oh, they were still at home. So that was kind of an interesting and new experience for me. Eventually, the fact that I spoke Spanish helped me in that job as well because we were opening the Latino market as well in other parts of the country.

But I was always torn, I think, between *Am I creative* or *Am I a corporate citizen?* In the long run, I think what I learned was I made some bad choices in my career because I somehow got convinced I had to become a director. I had to become a manager. I had to do this and this.

Actually, I remember the vice president sitting me down one day and saying, "I'd like you to take over a creative department." Now remember, I started writing brochures, but then I went off and did other things.

And I was like, "Oh, I don't know if I want to do that."

There was another job, a more corporate director's position, and I wound up taking that. And I hated it. Several months later, I had to move from there to director of communications, which they did for me because they didn't really want me to leave. I had paid my dues, you know.

And basically the vice president (who had, at that point, been promoted to president) took me into his office and said, "Now, try to learn a lesson. You're probably the most creative person I know. Why the hell did you take that stupid job in corporate?" And it was true. I had several people come back to me and say, "You had a couple of opportunities to go back to the creative work that you were so good at and you turned them down." And I don't know why. I think I would have wound up working there longer if I had actually taken the more creative work. But you don't know that at that point in time.

The other thing is, there was a lot of pressure in my life because I had already become a mom. I had discovered that my son had issues—physical—his vision was declining. I was really running scared, didn't know what was going to happen, even though my husband had a great job and whatnot. He wasn't making big dollars, but together we were doing well enough to buy a coop. So I figured, at that point in time, I just needed to move ahead in the corporation because I had a lot of expenses and a lot of things going on in my life. I really was afraid to go back to creative, you know?

Avon was the first time I was part of what they called the minority group. There were a bunch of us who were brought in at the same time, and we all knew what the expectations were and why we were there. There were constant questions about, "Are we being paid the same? Do we have promotional possibilities?" There were people who were working there who didn't believe we belonged there. So we were the first large group of minority professionals at Avon. And it was certainly an interesting ride.

Q. Say more about the experience of moving into corporations at a period of time when there was all this, "Why are you here?" from others and, "Why am I here?" from yourself.

Carole: I think for me, obviously, there was an opportunity to make some money and also to put my journalistic education to work. I had just come out of my internship at NYU. I got an internship at *Essence* magazine, and that was an amazing thing because *Essence* was so hot. It was new. There had never been such a hot fashion magazine for black women, and I was there as an intern. It was an exciting thing for me. The publisher liked me and basically offered me a job.

Back in those days, the salary she offered made me realize that the magazine world didn't pay. I was young and inexperienced and $9,000 a year might have seemed like a lot. But remember, I graduated late because I went back to Hunter [College] part-time, so by the time I was finishing graduate school at NYU, I was older than the other interns. And I was married and we were paying rent. So, when she offered me that salary, I wound up taking the job at Avon which paid me a lot more money.

But I wasn't there a week before there were conversations about, you know, "Are we really making the same as the other people who are working here?" My first experience with my first creative manager whom I worked for convinced me that we were not.

She paid as little attention to me as possible and constantly said, "I just hired MY writer. I need to go pay attention to my REAL writer." Her attitude was that she had hired her and someone gave me to her. So I was not "her" writer, really.

Clearly, I was a charity case. She really liked me, but she didn't trust me. She didn't know if I could write. Turns out, I had creative ideas. I remember going to a brochure conference the first year I was there, the conference for the fourth-quarter magazine. (The fourth quarter brochures are the biggest money makers of the year because the fourth quarter is Christmas. These are merchandizing vehicles.)

I went to my first conference, and my boss was just amazed that I actually did really well. I talked them into doing the first introductory brochure of the season. I came up with the theme of it. My boss's boss loved it. I began to get some recognition; people referred to me as the writer who came up with the Joy Book. They really liked the whole concept—visually and in terms of copy—to mark the introduction of the quarter. I got a huge raise the next month. (That was the whole chapter of … "Oh, so I was underpaid." That was like light bulbs going on every other day.)

So it was like, *Wow! How does this work*? I was introduced to politics in the corporate environment with an overlay of, you know, minority issues. How do you make it to the top when nobody up there looks like you? We were a human resources project that nobody wanted, you know? Eventually, some of us left. By the time two years passed, there were, maybe, half of us left. Those of us who stayed basically did okay. We wound up founding minority organizations for black, Hispanic, Asian, and women professionals.

One of the reasons this all came about was the senior vice president at that time was really very involved with human resources bringing minorities in. He wound up being chairman of the board before he left Avon. He basically was the one who saw what was going on with us and brought in a couple of consultants who really schooled everyone in the organization about minorities and how to lose bad, negative mindsets. And how positive mindsets were not only good for your soul, but were good for the business. So diversity was something that was going to boost our economy.

He developed a group of people—I was part of the group—and he basically said, "Hey. We're going to bring some people in, and we're going to give you all this developmental work." We went to conferences. Some people really hated them. They would go in—this was the old white boys' network—they would go in and they would smile and the minute they left the room they would go, "What a bunch of crap." That's what we lived through. And women, the same thing—women and minorities. Basically, the VP set up a women and minorities task force for us to make sure women and minorities became more involved in the business and were rewarded for contributions.

But it provided networking opportunities for those of us who were involved … with the people who were trying to make sure that Avon took risks, like Jim Preston and other people who worked there. He brought in a couple of really interesting people who became experts in the world of diversity. When I left Avon, I actually wound up working for one of them and doing a lot of work as a diversity consultant.

At that point, I decided I was going to have to go out on my own because Koert [my son] had gotten to the point where, not only was he was legally blind, but he [had] also developed Type I Diabetes. That was very, very difficult. He spent a couple of days in intensive care.

I decided, *There's no way I can go back to a full-time job. I'm just going to write and do consulting work.* So I did a little creative work in terms of writing. I also had another business—diversity work. That all started at Avon because I was networked into a bunch of people who were doing this [diversity work] not only at Avon, but at several other companies. That really was the key to my being able to spend the next six to seven years trying to support myself by doing that kind of work.

Toward the end, when I got divorced, there was really not enough work because the volume of work had decreased tremendously. So it was really tough, but I had really wonderful clients and it was only [due to the] economic downturn.

The actual economic downturn people remember as starting after 9/11. But it actually started before 9/11. [The year] 2001 was not a good year economically and my business almost dried up. And that was my son's first year of college. And my alimony had gone—I had no more alimony or child support. So I was on my own and could not survive. I wound up losing my apartment in 2001.

Q. I'm curious as to what happened to your political life once you started working at Avon and had a husband and a baby.

Carole: You know, it's a funny thing because I remember having girlfriends who wanted to get married and wanted to have kids. I never wanted to get married. I never wanted to have kids. And here I was with a husband, a kid, a job, and like, going a little crazy, you know? It was just like, *How did I get here?* kind of thing. I think all of us have those moments in our lives that we don't plan for and we have no idea how the things we are working on actually [will turn out]… *I started out to bake a cake and it turned out to be a loaf of bread.*

Q. So did you drop out of all the political stuff once you went corporate? Or were you still involved with the Republican Party?

Carole: I dropped all the political stuff once I was in grad school. I really was not doing any political work whatsoever. By the time I got to Avon, it was not so much about the political scene—it became, ultimately, about women and minorities in business. That was how I channeled a lot of my old political energies into the stuff that was happening at Avon at the time.

Q. So it re-emerged in a different way once you were at Avon?

Carole: I think so. I think basically all of these things that I learned from the elections, from all the organizing things that I had done, and the issues we had to deal with, came out in what happened to us at Avon. It was really interesting. I found that there were times when that was more interesting than the job I happened to have at the time. But you know, there were a lot of things. I wound up getting laid off and it was during a period when Amway was trying to take over Avon. It was huge—back in 1990, I think it was.

But by 1991, I was out of there. I spent a year at an executive placement firm—I got a year of career counseling and placement. All that was great. At the end of the year, I decided, *Okay. I can't go back to a full-time job. I'm just going to have to be a mom to this kid who is disabled and needs me. So I just can't be doing a nine-to-five gig.* So that was basically what turned my life around at that point.

Q. So you had your own business for a while….

Carole: Over 10 years; almost 12 years. I hated it. I hate freelancing. I hated … I am a security whore, okay? And I'm also the girl from Cheers: I don't like working alone; I like going someplace where people know my name. I remember being at the house and crying—literally, I had tears running down my face—and saying, "I'm going to have to work on my own."

The only thing that helped me survive was someone I had worked with at Avon. He produced events at Avon, and he was a producer on his own. He left Avon and he opened his own studio. It just so happened that I lived on 14th Street and his studio was on 19th Street. So I wound up working a lot of shows with him, mostly Avon, writing pitches, delivery pitches, writing speeches and scripts. The reason I loved that was because I got to go to an office. I got to go to his studio. I worked with him and another guy. And I had a really good time.

I didn't like working for myself. I'm a terrible marketer for myself. I hated receivables; I hated collecting money. So to me, the worst thing in the world was having to run my own business. I could never, I would never run my own business. I never did, really. I just got whatever work I got. Did the best I could and tried to survive.

That really was part of the downfall of my marriage: My husband married someone who worked full-time and, for most of the years we were married, made more than he did. He eventually overtook me, but he was not happy about the fact I was working on my own and not making as much money, and the fact that my son was … I didn't know if he was going to completely lose his sight, which he eventually did. I didn't know if he was going to survive the diabetes.

I was going through an emotional whirlwind; I was basically in full meltdown. I remember going to see my gynecologist. He said, "What's wrong with you? You're a mess." He sat down and did therapy with me for an hour and he said, "What is your husband doing?" And I realized he was doing next to nothing. I told him when I got home, "I just need some help. This is really a lot for me to do." That was really the beginning of the end of our marriage. He didn't get how seriously his son's issues were affecting both my life and his. He didn't get how seriously overstressed I was. It was only a couple years later that I saw my gynecologist again and he said, "You do realize you were going through a nervous breakdown?" He was the first person to tell me I was suffering from post-traumatic stress disorder. That was a big wake-up call.

I think the basic wake-up call was when Koert was ten. He started to lose weight, he was sleeping all day, and he couldn't go to school. I was thinking, "What is wrong with this kid?" One day, he was so weak I just picked him up and took him to the doctor. The doctor said, "I want you to go in a cab—I don't want you to wait for an ambulance. This child is probably having a diabetic seizure, and you've got to get him to the hospital very quickly."

I remember calling my ex—who was at the office because he was going to a business conference—I called him on the phone and I said, "This is what's happening: Koert is very sick. I have to take him to NYU Hospital. When are you going to come?"

He says, "Here's my medical insurance card number. Call me tonight and let me know how things are."

I decided, *I'm going to have to leave this jerk because if your son is on his way to a hospital and all you can give me is your medical insurance number, something is seriously wrong with you.* That was when I realized I would not be married to him much longer.

I wound up getting Koert to the hospital. He wound up in intensive care. I wound up sleeping in intensive care with my son for two nights because the doctor feared his blood sugar was so off the charts that he was going to have water on the brain, and that was going to be devastating.

He wound up okay, you know. But if I had post-traumatic stress disorder (PTSD) before that, I had big-time PTSD after that.

We had to transfer him from NYU to Mount Sinai because they had a pediatric diabetes program. He was on insulin and he's still on insulin. He's thirty-one. So you know, that was a really, really crucial time. Let's see, how old was he? He was ten and the divorce was when he was sixteen. I waited that long because we had a very tight three-person family and he loved being in this family. It was his main support.

I just didn't know how to handle this, you know? So I did, until I got to the point when he was fifteen. I decided to divorce, but I had to go through a whole bunch of stuff. You know, I grew up Catholic, so the idea of divorce was still huge for me, spiritually. It took me a year to come to the realization that this is what I really needed to do in my life. Financially, I didn't make the best arrangements. We didn't have a lawyer; we got a mediator. Even with alimony and some childcare for a couple of years, I should have asked for a lot more. So 1998 was one of the worst years of my life because, not only was I getting a divorce, but in February, the day after St. Valentine's Day, my mom died unexpectedly. And then we had to sell our coop; this was the only home that my child had ever known. We wound up staying in a hotel room until we could find apartments for the two of us, which we eventually had to do that summer.

I had to fight to get Koert into a special program at Columbia University that year because they didn't want to let him in. I don't remember the essence of the argument; it had to do with how he managed his diabetes. My son had already developed a characteristic that he has still has now, which is tremendous determination. If you disagreed with him, one, he knew he was right; and two, you knew you were going down. The counselor for the New York State Commission for the Blind said, "Well, we don't think Koert is ready to be on his own at Columbia this summer." I went wacko! And we got him in. He needed to be some place that summer because his family was falling apart. So that was really, really crucial; 1998 was a really bad year.

Q. Sounds it. So where did you go from there?

Carole: I wound up in this apartment in Gramercy Park with Koert on the East Side. We started to prepare him for college and for his major because, remember, Koert was blind. He basically went to three of the best schools in the New York City Public School System. He went to Public School 006 on the Upper East Side on Madison and 81st Street, which was considered a private school in the public system. People used to move to get their kids into that school. He was in the gifted and talented program there.

Then he went to middle school at the Chelsea School for Artists and Writers, a wonderful little school. That's where he lost the rest of his sight. But because it was a small school, the director took an interest. The Department of Education and the director got together and they got him through some basic Braille and some other survival skills, educational skills. They had a team working with him, so that three months after he started this program, he took the test for the Bronx High School of Science and got in. Then he went to the Bronx High School of Science for four years and wound up getting a partial scholarship to Hamilton College in upstate New York. And twelve years of free education.

Sometimes, failure to achieve a goal is the perfect reason to try again. Herta's initial failure to summit Mount Kilimanjaro prepared her to plan carefully for her second attempt. She couldn't arrange for better weather, but she could arrange better leadership and create a strong purpose and sense of team for her second attempt.

Q. First of all, what made you decide you needed to summit Mount Kilimanjaro? And second, I'm interested in how that group came together, the interesting people you had.

Herta: I write extensively about it [the second climb] in my book *The Mountain Within*. I attempted to summit Kilimanjaro for my fortieth birthday. That was one of those magic moments when I looked at Kilimanjaro and said to my husband, "I'm going to climb that for my fortieth birthday." He looked at me like I had two heads.

We climbed Mount Maru first, which is about 4,600 meters, in preparation for Kilimanjaro. Mount Maru is beautiful … it is such a beautiful mountain. Then we climbed Kili and from the moment we [began climbing], it started to rain. The weather was awful and we got to the Baranca Wall and decided this was just absolutely crazy. And we turned back. So, my first attempt to summit was really a dismal failure for three reasons: one is, I was not adequately prepared; second, the weather was definitely not in our favor; third, we had the lousiest leadership you could imagine. So it was really unfinished business, and the idea of summiting Kilimanjaro was kind of niggling at the back of my head, but it didn't shout with the megaphone ear—it was just niggling there.

Then a friend of mine—who was chairman of a disability charity—asked me to come on [her] board, so I joined the board of trustees as honorary treasurer. It became very obvious that this charity really needed to raise its profile. I'm not kidding, Susan: I was running on the treadmill in the gym and all of a sudden, it just came to me and I said, "I know how to raise it." I turned to my husband, who was running next to me, and I said, "I know how to raise the profile of Elemi: I want to climb Kilimanjaro for my fiftieth birthday, and we're going to take a group of disabled and non-disabled climbers. We're going to team them up in a buddy system and each disabled climber is going to have one or multiple non-disabled buddies and we'll make a documentary."

He just looked at me and said, "You're serious about this, aren't you?"

That was the beginning. It took us two years to really plan an expedition. It took on a dimension of its own and ended up, actually, as a much larger thing than I had envisioned initially. We had six U.K. [United Kingdom] non-disabled climbers and we had one from Saudi Arabia. We had a truly multinational, multi-ability team.

This, probably, was the first time something like this had happened, where you had disabled climbers supported by non-disabled buddies, where it wasn't all about one person. It was very much a collaborative effort. I wanted to do it that way because I feel that everybody is entitled to his or her own dreams, regardless of sex, race, gender, whatever, disability—you name it. Also, we can change so much more together than any one of us separately, and hence, the buddy system.

So the Kilimanjaro expedition became something really beautiful. The film we produced is a triumph of the human spirit. Normally, producing films is quite expensive. We were so humbled because we had people like Joe Brown, who is one of the top cinematographers in the world; he has at least three Emmys to his name. And we just paid him the expenses.

Michael Price, who is one of the top cinema composers, climbed with us and composed the music going up and down the mountain. Then the music was recorded at the Abbey Road studios. Abbey Road made the studio available, and we just paid the musicians. It was just unbelievable.

My husband and I had set up a small foundation, On the Road to Film, and it turned out to be such an amazing project that changed the life of everyone who was part of that project. It really had such far-reaching dimensions, far-reaching implications.

To this day, if something seems difficult, I give myself a good talking to: *Don't be a wimp. You climbed Kilimanjaro, you know, so just look at that perspective and get on with it.*

I wasn't thinking about writing a book, but the more I looked at the financial crisis and its aftermath, it seemed like we were emerging from one crisis [and going into another]. I felt very strongly that these things are, in the final analysis, a crisis of leadership and a crisis of values and principles, and not so much financial or political. At the core, we were experiencing a severe leadership crisis, and I felt I had something to say on the subject. And so, McGraw Hill published my book as the lead title for McGraw Hill Professional in the fall of 2011.

Q. I would almost say, "How could you not write a book?" when one of the three reasons you gave for the first climb failing was poor leadership. Clearly, there was so much thought leadership that went into the second climb, it was almost like you had to write this book.

Herta: You know, it's interesting you say that because yes, it was a lot of hard work, and I pretty much wrote every weekend for months, but it was a labor of love. It actually came fairly easily. When I was outlining the structure of the book, I wanted to be in conversation with people who, in my view, symbolized that particular leadership lesson.

As a young manager, Phoebe persisted in hiring handicapped workers—despite resistance— and her company became a leader in best hiring practices:

Phoebe: In my mid-twenties, I was running a group that was very large at a very young age. I had to have managers underneath me because I just couldn't have all of them reporting in to me. At the same time—remember, I'm getting my MBA from UCLA— there's a third part of this fun decade. That is: we were at some dinner party—I can't remember quite how it started—but we were talking about handicapped people. This was long before the Americans with Disabilities Act (ADA), right?

So we were talking about how it was such a problem, that nobody was doing anything about accommodation, people from Vietnam who were damaged, etc.

So somebody said, "Phoebe, what are you doing about it?"

And I thought, *Here I am, hiring all these people. What am I doing about it?* Right? So I thought I had better do something about it.

I think the first person I called was the Spinal Cord Injury Foundation. We didn't have the Internet in those days, and somehow we got associated with a group in Los Angeles that was in the placement of handicapped people.

I was thinking, *Well, I'll just go along,* and I was very proud of what I was doing.

I told my boss, the head of litigation, that we were doing it and he said, "Don't do this. You're going to get us into so much trouble; we do not have restrooms for [disabled] people, we do not have anything, we're just going to get sued. I want you to stop doing this."

I said, "I'm having this meeting with these people and they're going to my office." So when the people showed up, I had all the attorneys in my office because they were scared to death of what was going to happen if I hired someone who either needed a wheelchair or something else.

I thought, *Wow. But I'm going to keep it at this. I'm going to keep at it.*

I learned a huge amount about what it is to be handicapped; and that handicapped is also recovering alcoholics, and handicapped is someone who has any number of disabilities you might think of, not only paralysis. It turned out that they were terrific. The agency said, "Let us send you some people," and so they did. Then we began to hire.

I remember hiring the very first person who had cerebral palsy. I remember handling all these documents, right? At the beginning, my boss was not terribly happy about all of this until he mentioned it to a couple of lawyers from the liability point of view. It turned out that one of the senior executives at Atlantic Richfield had a handicapped child and was very supportive of everything that we were doing. All of a sudden, this became the priority for the company, and ARCO [Atlantic Richfield Company] became a leader in hiring the handicapped.

Similarly, Susan P. spent most of her career in Corrections, fighting for better conditions for her clients, not giving up—even when it became clear that she would be fired.

Susan P.: We moved down to Charlottesville ... I thought it wouldn't be hard for me to find a job, but it really was. The job I ended up getting was in a women's prison. When I originally applied, years ago, there was a state [hiring] freeze. I ended up working for an organization in a group home with juveniles for three years. Then, the last six-and-a-half years, I was a case management counselor at a women's prison.

Q. Tell me a little about that.

Susan P.: The big picture is, given my background, given a kid from Great Neck ... there was no [preparation for] working for a place like the Department of Corrections. That independent Jewish righteousness, that whole thing [that I was raised with], how do I say? ... it was really ... it was so against who I am.

When I was in graduate school I did extremely well. I had the opportunity—because I was the only one interested in criminal justice—to spend a year doing an evaluation for an aftercare program in Newark and actually got paid some to do it. It was basically from soup to nuts: at the beginning of the study, I had to do an extensive literature review. It ended up being an eighty-page report. I did the experiment myself. I created the instrument and did it—pre-test, post-test. It was a baby thesis. I mean, it was a thesis, but it was a baby dissertation.

I loved it! It was really, probably, what I was most suited for. But in my mind, I'm like, *Well, I need to work.* I think I needed to work. I wanted to be with the people, and my standards were incredibly high. I mean, I was an ADD mediocre student in Great Neck. I'm not Ph.D. material ... even though I thought about getting a Ph.D. for a very short time. Well, in hindsight, where I belonged was with the Ph.D. people because I was able to talk, in theory, not be angry, and actually be understood.

I'll give you an example: during the Bush Administration, there was a law passed called Prison Rape Elimination Act (PREA). It was designed to ameliorate rape in prison. They did some cool things, which were basically more cameras and things like that. Also, certain laws were passed [such that] if anyone in power—any security, any staff member—had sex with an inmate, they would be charged with rape. And they were going to be prosecuted.

The way they communicated this was when the women came into the facility, there was a movie that really was quite good. And you'd talk about that [rape is] not acceptable, and if you were accosted, either inmate-on-inmate or staff-on-inmate, what you needed to do.

My facility—Fluvanna Correctional Center for Women—was number two in the country for unwanted relationships between inmates and staff and inmates and inmates. Our head of security ended up going to prison for screwing around with inmates. The final report came out in April of 2012. If you just google "PREA April 2012" it comes right up; you can read the report and read about my facility. You can see how it's scathing. And the lack of integrity. I mean, it's just scathing. And the cover-ups. So I was one that didn't shut up; I was one that they talked about, that ended these practices.

I'd been trained brilliantly at Rutgers. And being brought up the way I was brought up, even though I'm not a heavy intellectual, part of my DNA is science and truth. So there's a respect for science, of course, good science over bad science, but there's a huge respect for it. I knew enough about evidence-based [science], as I had absolutely exhausted the literature on treatment.

And then they came in and they wanted to [claim] that … they're full of shit or people are lying. And then I'm e-mailing people above my chain of command and getting into huge amounts of trouble all the time. So, I ended up being fired.

It was very traumatic for me—the six-and-a-half years—because I couldn't be apathetic. I couldn't be … cynical. I was just me. Not only from that background, but I'm a performer, I'm out there, I'm expressive. I was an anomaly there; almost no Jews; it was very evangelical Christian. So I'm proud that I was acknowledged, and, certainly, the inmates loved me and I loved them. I mean, it's like a testament to me that I didn't change. I certainly gave it a go, but it was extremely difficult to have perspective and not be emotionally beaten up by that whole thing.

In the meantime, we—Jay and a colleague of mine—would talk about that we really needed to have some sort of place—a recovery halfway house, something for women—for when they come out of the prison. Jay was volunteering at the jail. They had a group—that was working on a recovery house or a halfway house for women—that was formed several years ago by the staff after a woman in Georgia had committed suicide in the jail, having struggled with alcoholism for many years.

Basically, the choice was either go home to her dysfunctional husband—who worked at our facility, by the way, so we knew him—or jail, so there was no place. We've been working on that for a while, so my mission, having left in January, is working on getting this house going. That's what I'm working on, but that's volunteer. It just feels like a way to complete my mission. If I can't work within the Department of Corrections in Virginia, it's still part of my mission in life: how to make a difference. So it seems like absolutely the right thing for me to commit to.

While some see obstacles as solid barriers, others learn that most barriers are permeable, and that with skill and persistence, it is possible to create a different scenario. Corbette learned from a mentor early in her career how to negotiate around obstacles:

Corbette: My husband wanted to move to Nashville because he's a songwriter. At this point, we lived in upstate New York and I'm like, *Oh my God, it's bad enough he talked me into moving here*, because I grew up near New York City.

So he finally convinced me to visit Nashville. At that time, I was working in the insurance industry, and I was in their research group. I had seen an ad for this consulting firm within a large insurance brokerage firm headquartered in Nashville. So I told them, "I'm coming to visit," set up an appointment with them, and bottom line, they ended up offering me a job and relocating us. I think I was twenty-eight.

It was a phenomenal opportunity for me. It was an amazing group. They were doing really interesting things. I ended up, like most consultants, living in an airplane, five days a week and travelling all over, including spending a lot of time in London and Bermuda and the Cayman Islands. I ended up getting my MBA, which they paid for, and graduated first in my MBA class at Vanderbilt when I was thirty-three. I ended up becoming the head of the alumni board and kept a long-term relationship with them.

I always thought that I was going to work in the insurance industry and then, ultimately, maybe when I was thirty-five, I would quit and go back to school and get my Ph.D. I kept getting promoted at the company where I worked and getting increased opportunity. I had an amazing boss at one point. He was possibly the most brilliant person I've ever had a chance to work with. He had a Ph.D. from the University of Pennsylvania and he was like Columbo; I mean, he was deceptive in terms of his brilliance. He was one of those people that always found ways around obstacles. I told him he was going to be a great criminal because he could always see the loopholes, and he knew how to close them, which was great in terms of consulting work.

He called me in one day and he said, "I need you to write a letter to me and this is what it needs to say." Bottom line, he told me what I needed to say in order to get a raise that he had been unable to get for me. I did get a raise, but more important, he taught me how to negotiate at work without alienating the organization, which so many people do when they try to negotiate more money. I never forgot.

I had my first child a year later, at thirty-three, and, after about a year balancing two jobs in the organization and being a young parent, I decided it was too much and management was not treated well. I was able to negotiate away all of my management responsibilities, a formal four-day work week, and I got a thirty percent compensation increase, all simultaneously. Instead of trying to do two different jobs, I focused on the healthcare practice, which was focused more on creating and leveraging expert knowledge than on managing individuals.

As a result of that, I was recruited by a company called Aon—which is now the largest broker and benefit consultant firm in the world—when I was seven months pregnant, refused to move to Chicago, which is where they were headquartered at the time and where the job was, and insisted on keeping my four-day work week. I was thirty-three and my plan at thirty-five was to retire from the insurance industry and go back and get a Ph.D.

I postponed that because the job was very exciting, the organization was very exciting, and they were paying me real well. They were a very innovative company, rapidly growing. When I joined them, they were under a billion dollars in revenue. They're now a twelve billion dollar revenue company. They were making up to thirty acquisitions a year while I was there, and I was able to make acquisitions and invest in different strategies and sit on boards and travel all over the world—it was just an amazing opportunity.

We discussed being a woman in this position and how her early upbringing exposed her to strong female role models:

Q. Let me just interrupt and ask you a question for a minute here: there can't have been that many women around. [laughter]

Corbette: No.

Q. So, can you talk a little bit about that and what that was like?

Corbette: I mentioned that my father was wonderful and took me to court with him, but my mother, when I was growing up, was global head of training for Estee Lauder. That was in the late '60s through the early '70s, and my mother travelled all over the world. I grew up with a very different role model at the time, and so you're right, there were very few women. I mean, there were few women in business in that era in particular. There were and still are very few women in the insurance industry.

I was blessed everywhere I worked. I worked for three corporations, one in New York, the one in Nashville, and then the Chicago one. I was blessed with amazing mentors every time. Same thing with college—amazing mentors in college and they were all men and they were all looking out for me and teaching me how to look out for myself. They were all very highly respected in the organizations where I worked, so that was my way into an amazing number of situations.

I would also say I have a good sense of humor. It's not difficult right now, but in the '80s, in the '90s, I'm sure you know a sense of humor went a long way.

Q. It did indeed and starting out with that kind of modeling at home had to go a long way to give you the confidence to say, "Yeah, they are all men. So?"

Corbette: Yeah, and I also think going to an all-girls high school—it was just a small school, I think there were ninety-eight in my graduating class and only two who didn't go to college. Lots of doctors, lawyers, who were really successful, amazing women, and that helped as well. It was not the high school I wanted to go to, but my mother basically gave me no choice.

Q. Really, such a wise decision. It made a big difference for so many women.

Corbette: So it was a very interesting time because they hired me when I was seven months pregnant. So I thought, *I've got two months. I could get all these things set up.* And my daughter came a month early, so I literally had a month to get things set up. But she went on her first business trip with me when she was six weeks old.

We have had the same nanny for nineteen years. She and her husband and her son and his family are all coming to our house for Christmas Eve dinner—they're like grandparents to my children. She and my daughter used to travel with me, up to eight times a year, especially when I only had one child. That, for me, made a huge difference, really cut down on some of my own feelings about being an ineffective parent. It was amazing: I spoke at a lot of conferences because of my role in the industry. And I think I became even more well-known than I might otherwise have in this industry because people knew I took my children.

It has been an interesting experience, but the person who recruited me gave me unbelievable opportunity as I tried to make investments, to run different businesses, all [related to] the healthcare industry. They had recruited me to help them get to the healthcare industry, and I did that for seven years (which, at that point, was the longest, by far, that I had ever done the same job). I was thinking again—OK, at this point, I guess I was early forties—and I was thinking of possibly leaving, going back to school and getting a Ph.D. So I went to him and I said, "I'm really tired of doing the same job. I'm really tired of travelling as much as I do."

When I took the job, I was trying to cut back on travel. He knew that and he always tried to help me cut back on travel, but it's hard to do the job well without it. Bottom line, I said to him, "Either I need to cut back to a three-day full-time week or I need to leave." I also told him I didn't think I could do my current job in only three days a week, so I said I really wanted a different job. He did give me a different job running a new financial institution strategy, allowed me to try the three-day work week, and that is what I did until I left eight years later.

I had turned over the healthcare strategy to my number two, but it was really struggling, so he asked me to come back, take it on, fix it, and promised me a major promotion in exchange for doing that. I told him I wasn't sure, that I was thinking about going back to grad school, and he convinced me to do it. I did get a promotion to executive vice president with a dozen industry practices reporting to me and was put on the executive board of that division of the company ... the largest division of the company. I did that for several years. That was probably the worst, it was one of the worst jobs I ever had and a big part of the reason was—there was one other woman in the room, so there were thirteen people reporting to her. The only other woman that came to the executive committee meetings was the woman who was the head of human resources for the U.S. and she didn't have vote, so I was the only woman with a vote.

This is a sales-driven organization. [I reported to a man who] used to run a different part of the company that was more business process-focused. When he was promoted and took me with him, I kept all my old responsibilities and picked up significantly [more]. So I went from being on an executive committee of a much smaller group that was very collegial, a very mixed group, to this much larger, multi-billion dollar group. I was the only woman with a vote and everyone there had a sales background.

It was not collegial. Even when you thought there was collegiality, people were stabbing each other in the back all the time. A number of them accepted me because I had been working with them for a long time, providing support to their businesses but, the way they would talk about other people behind their backs, I was shocked. I had never seen that up close before. It was a miserable experience. I mean, I have an electronic folder of resignation letters that I wrote because I kept saying, "This is not going to work out. I need to get out of this." I would come up with a strategy that I was going to go back to grad school; that was my fallback.

Actually, in 2003, one of my good friends and I started a research project. We both were thinking we wanted to go back to school and get our doctorates, so we surveyed about five hundred women and created a website (which is no longer active but we have it trademarked) "Where Have All the Women Gone?" What we were focusing on was the glass elevator—that idea that so many women were opting out—I thought that was a problem from an organizational standpoint.

I was focused on this idea that organizations could not be successful long-term if they couldn't figure out how to effectively keep all these female talents [they were] bringing in in their early career stages. We uncovered a lot of things such as a high percentage of women had turned down promotions that "asked too much of them." We were really invested in working to get that published; my plan was to go back to grad school, get my Ph.D., and use this research as the focus of the dissertation.

I was, let's see, late forties. I was going to do it at fifty because a certain amount of my executive benefits kicked in at fifty, and I thought, *That's when I'm going to do it.*

When I was forty-nine, we had a new CEO from McKinsey. He came in and looked around and [set up] his executive team—twelve white men from three countries, even though the company was in 110 countries.

He approached me because I had been very outspoken and I kept saying, "It's not about me; it's not about one person. You've got to come up with strategies to retain women: You can't wait until someone is successful and then do whatever it takes to keep them, or you'll never get enough women." He approached me about becoming their first global head of diversity and I said to him I was planning on retiring in six months and going back to school to get my Ph.D.

And finally, how a serendipitous event allowed her to return to school:

Corbette: He talked me out of it and he said, "Oh, you will have a much greater impact doing this." Anyway, he convinced me to do it, so I did it for three years and then, actually, after two-and-a-half years, I hosted a retirement dinner for the person who recruited me, who's my longtime mentor. I did all the table arrangements, so I was sitting at the table with two people who were retiring or had just retired, and we ended up having a conversation about retirement benefits. This woman from Human Resources said something about executive retirement that I had never heard about that kicked in at age fifty.

I said, "Excuse me, what did you just say?" Then she repeated it and I was thinking, *I have never heard this before.* I was an executive; I went home and researched everything I had. It was not in there anywhere, so I sent her an email and said, "I just want to confirm what you said." She confirmed it to me [that I was able to retire.]

This was early December. I guess it was ten days later [when] I'm on the Vanderbilt campus with the dean of the business school, who's a good friend of mine, telling him about my long-term dream to go back and get my Ph.D. and teach college. So he ended up setting up this series of interviews for me—he's the one who suggested that I try to look at doing something as a joint venture with the School of Business and Peabody, the School of Education. I'm like, "Why would I go to the school of education?" because I was not aware of the organizational leadership focus they had. So I ended up having this series of meetings with different individuals between the two schools about the Ph.D. They ended up at Peabody offering me a full-time faculty position without the Ph.D.

Charlotte was one of several women who discussed gender issues in the workplace. Her way of handling them was simply to stick to her attitude that there's no difference between men and women at work:

Charlotte: After a few years off, a friend said, "You should apply at J.C. Bradford," which was a financial institution, a stock brokerage firm. I interviewed, and I was the first woman they hired in the Nashville office; I was the first woman for a period of time. Interestingly enough, I had just returned from a conference in Atlanta ... it was a women's conference with UBS. It was a way to get my ego massaged because several people talked about the fact that I had mentored them; that now, a large number of women we have in this business, in J.C. Bradford to UBS, have come along because I broke the glass ceiling. That was a big compliment, and I appreciated it.

Q. Fantastic.

Charlotte: I always wanted to give back. I never felt it was gender-related. I didn't feel any discrimination, other than in 1978 when I started—the downtown Nashville dinner/lunch clubs were men-only. (When they said "men only" at the Cumberland Club and the City Club, women could not go into the main dining room.)

After I'd been with J.C. Bradford a year, there was an invitation from a money manager for some of the top producers to come to a dinner at the Cumberland Club. I guess they didn't realize I was a woman because when I got there, I was told I couldn't come in for the dinner. Finally, they let me sit outside on the carpet—but I couldn't come into the room. I didn't want anybody to make a fuss about it. I said, "Let's let it go this time, let's not worry about it." But I never pushed the women's lib part. I was going to be successful. I was going to do it—not in a woman's world, not just for women, but for men and women. They have the same needs.

I got called up to Jimmy Bradford's office one day, and there was Irbie Simpkins, who was, at that time, publisher of the *Nashville Banner*. Jimmy said, "Guess what? Irbie wants you to do a financial column for women in the *Nashville Banner*!"

I gave him the evil eye, and he kind of gave me a grin and I said, "Um ... I would love to do an investment column for individuals, but not just for women. If you'd let me do that, no problem." He agreed. I brought on a coworker, so I didn't do it every week and, I guess, well, it ran 'till the *Banner* closed, about fifteen years. There was so much response to it because we did it in a very elementary fashion; it was questions and answers.

Charlotte also had to contend with Southern "old boy" issues:

Charlotte: Another first client that happened to come to me at J. C. Bradford was a well-known attorney in town, my father's age, and they used to hunt together.

He called up and said, "I'm going to open up an account with you, baby girl."

I'd introduce him ... everybody knew who he was, but he'd come in and I'd say, "I want you to meet Mr. So-and-So."

He'd say, "I'm opening an account with baby girl!"

I'd say, "Quit calling me baby girl!"

But he'd say, "The reason I wanted to come open an account was, when she was just five or six years old, her daddy brought her fishing, and I took my little boy. He sat in the bottom of the boat and cried 'cause he was cold the whole time, and baby girl never whimpered. She stuck it out. She could go anywhere. I liked that." So I got one of my big clients from not crying, sitting in the bottom of a wet boat when I was a child. Because he felt that showed potential, I suppose.

When I started at J.C. Bradford, in the financial world, I was sitting in the part of the City Club where women could go, in the back room having cocktails with a friend. The J.C. Bradford manager was directly behind me and could not see me. I looked over and it was the Merrill Lynch manager who was sitting with him, whom I knew well. He and his wife—I had dinner with them occasionally.

He looked up and with this little evil wink said, "How's that female broker you hired doin'?"

The J.C. Bradford manager said, "Oh, she's fine. We had to hire a woman. It was time. As long as she dresses well, keeps her mouth shut, and shows us off well, that's all we expect."

I listened to that and I thought, *Well, you son of a gun! Dresses well, keeps her mouth shut, and just shows up?* I broke every record they had for new business, for new accounts opened, and I made their rewards trip … you have to produce a certain amount the first twelve months. I didn't understand. I was naive in a lot of ways. I used to think if somebody wore a coat and tie and went downtown and worked, that they were smart. I quickly learned that's not necessarily the case.

But I did keep my mouth shut a lot. The advice of my mom, many years ago: "When in doubt, just be quiet and let others wonder how bright you are on the subject. And don't open your mouth when you don't know and give them a reason to know that."

Susana's ability to keep trying seems, in part, to come from her early experiences, including a difficult relationship with her mother:

Susana: And then off we went to Paris where—this is, what, sixty-two years ago?—exactly at this time of year, we landed in Paris and the area in Paris, Montmartre. That was filled not only by East European Jews, but also with North African Jews who were expelled from Algeria, from Morocco, from Tunisia. So there was this cacophony of Jews living in Paris at the time, waiting for visas or waiting to be accepted into some country.

I remember Passover being a really confusing Seder because it was a large, large room filled with Ashkenazi and Sephardic Jews doing their own Seder. None of this made sense to me, but we were at the crossroads of human migration.

After two weeks in Paris, we went off to South America, to Columbia, to Bogota, where my father's brother had landed a couple of years before. There was another mental whiplash experience that, at the age of fourteen, we were in a culture that was completely different from anything we had previously known. I was in a Jewish school for the first time, surrounded by Jews who were free and who did not experience any kind of holding back or isolation.

There is something else that made me face these challenges head on and that was the fact that I had a really, really difficult relationship with my mother. No matter what I did, it just wasn't good enough, so hiding was what she taught me. She taught me to keep on hiding, and I got a lot, lot, lot of practice with this lady for whom I was just never good enough, never kind enough, never smart enough, never accomplished enough, and never anything. There was always something else that I needed to do in order to be acceptable. I never made it, actually, never made it to acceptability because she died last September, and I don't think I ever got there as far as she was concerned. There is a saying in Hungarian that if somebody spits in your eye, you wipe it, and you say, "Oops! It's raining again." I learned to say, "It's raining again," a lot, and just moved on.

Elements of Persistence

The elements of persistence include making repeated attempts; varying your approach to a goal; assessing whether further persistence is helpful; and learning from your attempts. Sharon learned that no one wanted to buy what she was originally selling, so she kept trying other products until she succeeded. Agenia kept trying until she finally connected with the reporter she wanted to interview. She got her interview, was hired by the network, and made a life-long friend as a result. When Robyn saw that it was getting harder to land roles, she shifter her acting skills to leading communications programs.

How You Can Develop Persistence

There are a few things that you can do to become more realistically persistent:

- Learn that lack of success is not a failure on your part. Sales trainers tell us that it takes a ninety-nine "Nos" to get to a "Yes."
- Study successful people in your field and make a list of things they are doing.
- Develop a range of possibilities to get what you want.
- Evaluate each attempt. What can you learn from it? Is there evidence that it is time to move on?
- Celebrate even small wins. That's what keeps you going.

When your goals are important enough, learn to see yourself as unstoppable. Even though it may take a while, your goals are not out of reach.

Exercise

All of the women in this chapter kept going despite obstacles and roadblocks. We all face obstacles in life; what makes the difference is how you decide to handle them. For this reason, I like to include planning for potential obstacles as part of the goal-setting process.

What is a big goal you would like to accomplish? Write that goal on a sheet of paper. Next, list three sub-goals that will get you to your big, overarching goal. Now, think about what might get in your way. For each of your sub-goals, identify one to three obstacles. Finally, create a plan to overcome each obstacle.

This is an example:

Within the next six months, repurpose, recombine, and expand current articles, exercises, and workshop materials to create one cohesive, two-day workshop, one two-hour promotional workshop, one six-part tele-class, and two four-part e-courses.

What are some obstacles to achieving this goal? What action planning is necessary to overcome each obstacle?

Obstacle 1: There might be time limitations.

Action plan?

Review schedule and create a number of short periods of time to devote to writing.

-OR-

Outsource the rewrites.

Obstacle 2: There might not be enough material.

Action plan?

Have guest authors contribute.

-OR-

Research additional material.

-OR-

Hire a researcher.

-OR-

Pilot the material and add contributions from the ensuing discussions.

-OR-

Use questionnaires or focus groups to generate content.

When you look at your goals from the broadest perspective, also hone in on them to understand what might get in your way and be prepared to address and eliminate obstacles.

Some people feel that anticipating obstacles is taking a negative outlook. I think that the opposite is true. When you can anticipate obstacles, you improve your chances of achieving success. Contrast Susan P. and Herta. Susan P. did not anticipate the obstacles she would face while working for the Department of Corrections. She would have behaved the same way—championing the rights of the inmates—but might have found ways to better protect herself. Herta anticipated the obstacles involved in summiting Kilimanjaro based on her initial experience. The lessons that she learned made a successful summit possible.

Chapter 5

What's Next? – Curiosity and Restlessness

CURIOSITY is the desire to learn or know anything, to figure out how things work. It is inquisitiveness and a lifelong quest for learning.

Restlessness, in the context of this chapter, is not necessarily constant activity or being adverse to quiet or inaction. Rather, it is an extension of curiosity, a desire to see what is next and an avoidance of boredom or feeling stuck in the same place.

Many of The Fifty are adept at balancing activity and relaxation and yet, are always open to what is next that might be interesting and fun. Most of them share a tendency to be easily bored and to not easily tolerate boredom.

One feature of a fulfilling life seems to be curiosity. Study after study tells us that remaining curious and being a lifelong learner keeps people young. For some women, curiosity is a drive to try new things. For others, it is more a matter of being open to possibilities as they appear. For still others, it's a conscious effort to add new things, to explore, to be a lifelong learner.

Reading to Fulfill Curiosity

Many of The Fifty are avid readers, conference attendees, and autodidacts (women who learn on their own). Agenia, speaking about her first mentors, said:

Agenia: One of the gifts I got from them is they were avid readers. If you ever had a conversation with either one of them you would have sworn they had travelled around the world fifty times or more. I mean, the conversations were always engaging, enlightening. They could speak, literally, on any topic. From being around them all the time I learned a lot because they read all the time.

So that's where my passion for reading came from—I learned it. You know, truly, the greatest gift I have is that I know how to read. Even today, that is an important part of my life. Between the *New York Times*, the *Wall Street Journal*, and my two book clubs, I feel like I'm constantly enlightened about something.

Q. *That's great. And it takes a lot to just keep up with it.*

Agenia: It does. It absolutely does, but I look at the relationships reading has helped me build over the years and the list is exhaustive. That was one of the gifts of many they gave me that I am forever grateful for.

I will never forget, one day Linda was explaining to me, "No matter where you live and what you do, you make sure you pick up that daily newspaper every day so you can better understand what's going on with the community." So I do have a subscription for the *Tennessean* and, no matter where I have ever lived, I've always had a newspaper subscription just 'cause I remember her saying that and it's true.

Moving On or Standing Still

We have all heard the axiom, "Bodies in motion tend to stay in motion; bodies at rest tend to stay at rest." This is true of women's lives as well as of objects. It is easy to fall into thought and behavior patterns and continue down the same old path unless something happens.

Some women whom I've met seem simply to shut down in the face of change. It's as if they have decided there is nothing they can do about their circumstances, so they just stop. In contrast, The Fifty choose to see change as a way to try something new. In the face of potentially deadly illness, divorce, death of a spouse, loss of a job, being forced out of their homeland, or simply boredom, they find ways to create new, satisfying lives.

What drives The Fifty to move from status quo to change falls into distinct categories:

Boredom

For some, the driver is simply boredom. Many of The Fifty are always looking for new challenges, always eager to learn, always ready to move on to the next great thing. Some easily recognized this driver as a governing influence in their lives. Others, like me, were a bit surprised by what drove us. Until I read my own [interview] transcript, I hadn't seen the pattern of needing a new challenge, of quitting a job primarily because I was bored.

Full Plate

While many of The Fifty moved from one enterprise to the next, and a few had two or three projects going at the same time, there were a few overachievers who seemed to have countless simultaneous projects. Loretta and Larraine had so many things going on at once, I felt like I needed a nap after interviewing them. Here are a few snippets that illustrate how some of The Fifty approach life:

Phyllis C.: I loved school and I still love school. In fact, I will be exploring going back to school sometime later this year to get my doctorate. But why do I want to do it? Because it's there and it's exciting.

Donna: I get bored easily, so the only way I can prevent myself from being bored is to have a variety of things that I'm doing. I have to say, since I became a coach I have not been bored!

Larraine: I get bored quite quickly, and I think that is probably the problem. I need to do new things, so it's really quite easy. Every now and then, I crash and I have to go to bed for the day. They send me off to have the grandchildren for two or three days.

I think that's the joy of life, to be a continuous learner. My whole career is based on reinventing myself on a continual basis —and I think my husband has done the same thing as well—so that's why people look at us and think we're successful. That's probably one of the criteria for success: the ability to evaluate the situation and see this need for change, and your need to learn again. To become an expert, you have to get up that learning curve as quick as possible, and when your expertise becomes irrelevant, you change and do it all over again. So that's the story of my life.

Agenia, speaking about her current position with the Girl Scouts:

Agenia: I think the most special part about it for me is it requires that I use such a wide range of skills and capabilities. No two days are the same. Every day calls upon you to use something in your tool kit that you may not have used the day before. The variation of the work day, the variation of the demand—as far as whether it's with the grassroots volunteers or a member of the board—the requirement to, sort of, represent the image and a future for girls in our community. It's just a very unique opportunity. You can explore that opportunity differently every day that you are in it. I think that is why I've been here nine years.

For Victoria, it is important to remain open to possibilities as they present themselves:

Victoria: I do have multiple projects going, not as many as I had six months ago, so that's good news. The other good news is I have these projects and I wrote a screenplay that has been optioned by Identity Films. We're just finalizing that now. And I'm working on a play based on a book that my director and I got the rights to, called *Entangled: Chronicle of Late Love*, which is a wonderful memoir that I am turning into a stage play. And I've done a couple of documentaries for On the Road Productions, basically about women and science.

So I don't want to take on projects that I find tedious or projects that don't fascinate me and don't compel me to move forward. I'm also very fortunate that I don't live lavishly, so I am able to say "No." I have friends who cannot say "No" because, financially, they can't afford to. I have other friends who have become wildly successful as novelists, as writers, as speakers, and they still don't know how to say "No" because they are always afraid all of that is going to disappear one day. So they are not looking in terms of what their lives are like now, they're looking in terms of protecting themselves in the future. And there's not much you can say to somebody—even a *New York Times* best seller who's afraid of having it all disappear—"It won't all disappear. Your work is too good; your fiction is too compelling."

But you have to have that sense of confidence too; there will always be something out there that will provide income, and it's wonderful. When I tell people how much I love what I am doing, some people look at me a little bit strangely because they see their lives and careers winding down, and I see my career as taking off. I figure I have another ten years, maybe twelve years of really strong, creative energy. Maybe not the physical stamina, but the creative energy, and I intend to maximize that.

As her story continues, it is clear that, although she doesn't take on every available project, Victoria is always open to at least looking at projects that come her way, and understands that she is in control of her own destiny:

Q. You're so excited by all these, so energized by all of these. I guess I'm wondering what made you suddenly say at sixty, "I'm going to say "Yes" to anything that comes along and see what happens."

Victoria: No, it's not that I say "Yes" to anything. In fact, I say "No" to a lot of projects. But what I am doing is I'm pursuing my own creative projects. When they come to mind, if they really engage me, I'm going to go for it.

The first thing I do is I call or email my agent, Jill Marshall at Marshall Lien, and I say, "Jill, I've got an idea. What do you think?"

And she'll say, "I don't think it will sell, but if you love it, I'm behind you," or "It's a great idea, let's pursue it." I have somebody there I trust and we're partners in everything I do, and I couldn't do it without her. She is a remarkable young woman, and having her in my life—my professional life and my private life, my friendship life—is extremely important to me and she knows it. I cannot tell her enough times how important she is because of her ethics and dignity and her great sense of the instincts for literature. It's wonderful; it is just wonderful.

I do turn down a lot of projects because after five anthologies and teaching my courses, I am contacted a lot. I would say, at least twice a month, people want me to edit a book. Unless it's something that I find very well written and totally engaging, I don't do it. Ten years ago, I wouldn't have thought twice about doing it—of course I would have done it. How can you say "No"? But at sixty-eight, you can say "No."

So it's the anthology, the first anthology, that opened a whole new world for me and I'm deeply grateful. I am very grateful for the way my life has moved over the last ten years.

Q. You don't take anything for granted but, at the same time, it just seems to me that you are very open to magical things happening in your life ...

Victoria: Magical, yes, but it is magical in a sense that it's a sense of wonder. I also—I'm not so quick to do what I used to when I was younger, which was kind of shortchange myself and say, "God, I'm so lucky because I've worked very hard to make a lot of this happen." This is something I talk about with women a lot. In studies done years ago they asked corporate executive men, "How did you get to this position?" They said, "I worked hard for it. I earned it. I deserved it."

And when they asked the same question of corporate executives who were women, many of them said, "I was at the right place at the right time, and I was lucky." I think that's a clear differentiation of the way we're brought up; that we feel we are lucky if something great happens.

I'm at a place in my life where some of it is luck, because you meet the right person at the right time and they want what you've got; but it's also that you've got it, and you recognize what you've got. I have learned to recognize where my skills are, where I'm strong, and where I'm not. If I know I'm strong there, then I go out and try to make something happen.

So, the majority of projects that I do are projects I've created on my own, hearing something, hearing a funny story about a prison breakout that I turned into a screenplay that was auctioned, or taking five of the essays from *The Other Woman* anthology and turning them into a play that was just developed at the Berkeley Rep.

Debbie's attitude is similar to Victoria's. Post-retirement, she became involved in volunteer work, went back to school, and is now looking for her next challenge:

Q. I am going to suggest that, with the decades of experience you have been synthesizing and blending, there is certainly a future somewhere in the creation of learning experiences for you.

Debbie: Yes, you know, I've always loved learning. One of the reasons I loved my job as a CEO—every day I learned something. Maybe it was something about the company. Maybe it was something about the market. Maybe it was something about how people worked together. Maybe it was something about my own skills and ability to inspire or guide or create direction within the company. But every day, I learned more than one thing. And I loved it.

Q. So, what's next?

Debbie: I don't know. I mean, I'm not really sure because one of the things I do know is that I have the capacity to keep myself really busy. So I'm actually taking the time to really try to sort that out in my own mind. I mean, there are days that I would love to just step back into running a company with the full force and effort of full-time commitment. I have the energy to do that, and I still have the desire to do that. I mean, I truly enjoyed that a great deal. That's a platform that can't be replicated by any other type of venture or any other path that I might take. So, there still is that. Thankfully, I really enjoyed the insurance market.

But I think a lot of my skills would translate pretty well to many companies. I'm a quick read in terms of understanding the market and products and environment. So, that's still something I toy with.

But, we like to travel a lot. I still want to have time with the kids—even though they are so grown up. And I'm hoping for grandkids. I don't think that is coming around the corner very soon, but I want to be available when that does happen.

I'm thinking of more of a portfolio career. I might do business consulting and, perhaps, a coaching kind of business for myself, something I could expand, because I truly do like working with other people and helping to develop other people. I very much would like to return to some level of national exposure. Our company was national in scope and I enjoyed my work back in Washington, D.C. I enjoyed the scope of our sales and distribution across the country and all the different markets and even the variations between state and federal regulations. I would like to be on a national board of some type so I would continue to grow and learn with that type of exposure.

Q. Sounds like you know very much what you want; the exact shape and form and location of it will emerge when it's ready.

Debbie: That's what I believe. I had a boss, at one point, who said, "We have to become comfortable living in the question." That phrase often returns to me now because I have to be comfortable living in this question, because right now it is not completely clear which way I want it to go. And a lot will depend on what kinds of opportunities arise.

Feeling the Need for Change

After several years abroad, Phoebe got restless and scanned the environment to see what was next for her.

Phoebe: We learned that British Petroleum (BP) was going to buy Arco … on April 1 of 1999. The federal government commission rejected the merger as planned. What they stated was that the company, that BP, would have to divest some of its Alaskan assets. So the Alaska subsidiary and its executives were held off on their own and had to be sold. So what we did, we basically had to put ourselves up for sale. It was ultimately sold to Phillips Petroleum. It actually took a long time. [We worked really hard to figure out], "How is this going to work?" That was complicated and intensive, but at the end of the day, you knew life was going to change pretty significantly. Those of us who were in Alaska were given a chance to stay with Phillips Petroleum or leave the company with the package.

Phillips, who I think highly of, offered me a position in Bartlesville, Oklahoma, which is where their headquarters was. By this time, by the way, I had a second child, born in Alaska. So we went there and it was pretty small and I was thinking, I don't know how I can raise a three-year old and a nine-year old, all of whom need soccer, piano, dance, etc., which you get in Tulsa, Oklahoma, a forty- to fifty-minute drive away.

So I declined to go to Phillips and instead, I left the company and I took the package. I then began the process of figuring out, What am I going to do, now that I have children? Leave this industry or leave this company?

I learned about an opening at Motorola. Motorola was going to spin off its business in which it owned parts of Verizon and AT&T in different countries. It turned out that Motorola, in order to sell its headsets, had created and started up and funded little companies that would actually do this. Think Verizon in Mexico or Israel or wherever—they had all kinds of minority (and some majority) … interests in telephone carriers. It began to be kind of a problem with their customers, so they decided to divest all that.

I was hired to come in and be the CFO for that new unit. We worked on the S1 [document for the SEC], preparing for the selling of the company, basically getting new investors into that spin-off. Then Motorola received an all-cash offer on this group from Telefonica, the national telecom company of Spain, and accepted it.

Here I was in Motorola and they said to me, "Phoebe, if you just take this job, I think you can be CFO next."

I thought, *I don't know about this,* because of course, I'm not stranded, right? I'm brand-new hired, but I'm not stranded.

Q. *Where was your husband at this point?*

Phoebe: Well, he had left Alaska to come and be with us in Chicago, so he was not working, he was taking care of babies, right? That's what he was doing before we figured out where we were going, what was going to happen here.

I accepted that role to be the Chief Financial Officer at Brown-Forman. Then we moved to Louisville, Kentucky—that was in February of 2001. So if you look back and think about the '90s, it was England and Alaska with a little bit of time in Houston, but mostly in England and Alaska, a five-year period of time. Then I came to Brown-Forman and their CFO position. Information Technology was added, we put in an investor relations function, and I was the CFO through 2008.

Q. *So, what kept you sane through all this?*

Phoebe: That's too funny. I don't know.

Q. *It's just who you are.*

Taking Life as it Comes

Although curiosity keeps The Fifty in a constant state of exploration, and restlessness makes them quicker to change than some women, those changes are often spontaneous.

Dina didn't necessarily plan; she remained open to whatever might come next:

Dina: This is my relationship with my work: I never had a plan. I always knew there were things that were very interesting to me in the world, and if I ever had a chance, I was going to take the opportunity. That was how I chose the jobs. I always, in retrospect, believed that the jobs chose me. I always think of myself, retrospectively, as someone who was always surprised to love the things I was doing, all the time, even though they were very different. But I think, because I had no particular plan other than to do the things I wanted to do, I was very happy with the choices that I made.
And so there I was, being [Peter Pan's] Wendy …

Q. *Can I stop you for just a second? Can you say a little bit more about this, loving what you were doing? What predisposed you to fall in love with each thing you took on?*

Dina: Well, I loved being an editor because I was literally editing books to prepare them for publication, and I was part of the publishing process, and that was very exciting to me. I really enjoyed it. I didn't work with any of the fancy publishers. I didn't work on novels, necessarily. I mostly worked on post-graduate-level science books. So that assured, pretty much, that I didn't have any idea what it was I was reading and editing, but reading and editing I was, nevertheless. It was always very challenging, and it was wonderful, and I loved it.

When I was working in politics, I discovered a side of myself that I had never seen before, the side that was very gregarious with people, and very able to engage people in conversations about what I needed to have happen, and how I needed something to go. I traveled all over the country doing that work. And I loved it. I loved that I was traveling around the country and really getting to know different parts of the country, and I loved the work. It always felt like it was something that was important in the world, and I was, therefore, making a contribution I felt was important in the world.

There were times when it was very exciting, as well. There were times that I would put together a strategy for an election day in a primary, for instance. We would be down to the minute, so we needed to know where our voters lived, so we could make sure that, as the evening went on and before the polls closed, we got to every neighborhood that we needed to get to.

I would be the person who would have the maps spread out all over the table, and was making the decisions about who went where, and how that worked, and who was offering rides, and who was on the phone bank, and all that stuff. It was very exciting to see all that come together. It's very different now, working on campaigns, because that was the height of going door-to-door.

The Multi-Taskers

Loretta, on the other hand, can't resist the challenge of a new project and sometimes has a few too many balls in the air although, somehow, she never seems to drop any.

Loretta: They announced a whole group of training opportunities, and they didn't have a trainer who was willing to deliver … and could anybody help? There was dead silence in the room and—you know me—I love a challenge.

So I said, "Okay. What do they need to have somebody trained in, and does it have something to do with communication skills? Do they have any resources?"

I was going to school, having my house renovated, doing a gifted and talented program for the children, and now, I had to go to Mount Holyoke College for the day and offer training for a bunch of Junior League people. I got to Mount Holyoke and, while I was doing the morning workshop, there were people wandering in and out of the back of the room, coming in, coming out, coming in, coming out. Who the hell are these people? They are not people in my class, but certainly seem to have a lot of interest, and what the heck is going on here?

Lunchtime came and I found out that they were people from the nominating committee for the national organization [of the Junior League]. They said, "Could you please sit and have lunch with us?" and "We think you should be nominated for Area Council to head the training for the Area One," which was the whole Eastern seaboard of the United States.

You know me—what the hell.

Before I gave that workshop, I got another phone call, "You know what? Since you're already working on that, this [other] workshop is already scheduled for New York City at the Junior League house. We need somebody for there—how about offering it in New York City?"

Now you have to know, up to that point, I had never given a whole day training by myself. I was thinking, *I'm not so sure I can stand on my feet without passing out.* It's a matter of physical stamina.

So I did actually offer it in New York City, and it was fine. I got through the entire day. What might have been part of the reason is that when I got to Mount Holyoke, they knew who I was. But anyway, I was offered the opportunity to be nominated, and I accepted it. That was at the end of November. Sometime before Christmas, I got a call one day from Chicago, with the nominating committee chair telling me that I had been nominated and would be on the national board slate, just waiting to be elected.

Q. *What year was this?*

Loretta: Fall of '85 until Spring of '86.

Q. *Your kids were how old?*

Loretta: Let's see, John was born in 1969, so he was sixteen, Ann was fourteen-and-a half, and Courtney was twelve.

Q. *So you had two teenagers and one almost there, and you were taking on this huge thing? Okay.*

Loretta: I was a very devoted Junior League member. I mean, we really made large-scale change in the region, and I'm very proud we did that. I don't think I recognized at the time what movers and shakers we were.

The election took place early in the New Year and then in May, I had to go to the national convention. I already had been to one national convention as a delegate from my own Junior League so I knew what it was, but it was the first time I was traveling across the country by air. I had to go to San Diego to meet all these fabulous people. I really had a wonderful year working with everybody, and I had an interesting setup at that point.

I would create the training materials, I would them put them in an envelope, I would mail them to New York City. We had somebody who was our office support, so they would do all my copying, put books together, ship materials for me. I traveled all around the Northeast and then I had a couple of other opportunities that were really nice. I got to go to Colorado for the first time. I was trained by the Coral Foundation there in community research. The first time I had done anything at the national convention with the Junior League, I was trained in change management.

Later in the interview, Loretta had this to say about a software company she worked for:

Loretta: I learned organizational skills—the idea that we could use software to help to solve a problem. I considered myself fortunate to be in a position where everything I was doing was new, and it was learning for me.

Donna also takes a multiple-project approach. She, like Larraine and Loretta, gains more energy from having simultaneous challenging projects and moving between them. I also fall into this category, as do Jeannette and Kathy.

Donna: It was not really intellectually challenging, so I went from there into advertising and worked for a direct mail advertising company with clients like Book of the Month Club and the U.S. Army. I was bored by about the third week. About the sixth week, I sat down with the head of the agency who looked at me and said, "You're not going to last here, because you belong in my job and I'm not leaving."

Q. So this is, sort of, a theme, being under-utilized and bored early in your career?

Donna: I would start a job. It would be challenging for anywhere up to a year. By the second year, I was coasting, and by the third year, I would be bored. Sometimes it came much quicker than that.

Then I stopped working to be a full-time mother, but of course, I couldn't just do that, so that's when I began to get involved with non-profits. I joined the Junior League, sat on the Red Cross board, and worked on the board of Family and Children's Services. At the Junior League, I became the head of training and did all the train-the-trainer programs as well as the direct training. That was really fun for me. At the Red Cross, one of the functions I did on the board was run their charity ball. That was where I really started getting involved with special events.

I had a part-time business during this time; I did marketing and copy editing. I would create brochures for people's businesses. I did some copy editing for a startup company, I did some marketing and public relations for companies, I did various things that made a little money here and there, but it was just mainly to keep my mind occupied. When my daughter entered high school, that meant my son was a senior and she was a freshman. It suddenly dawned on me that within a couple of years, I was going to have an empty nest and what was I going to do with myself?

That has been my pattern wherever I go. Rather than standing on the fringe, I get involved because you can get so much out of it. But more than even getting more out of it, you develop much deeper relationships with people doing it that way. So, whatever I've done, I think that's a thread throughout my life; that whatever it is I've joined or gotten involved with, I really put my all into it. I don't do that for unselfish reasons—I do that because I have always found I enjoy it more when I do that. It really always has been that I enjoy it more if I'm involved.

So I was there at CoachVille, and I kept getting more and more involved. Thomas started the International Association of Coaches (IAC), and I was one of the three people who wrote the first exam. But I was also involved in the International Coaching Federation (ICF) and, for a couple of years, ran the life coach track at the conferences. That is where I also had Judy Feld, who is the past president of the ICF, as one of my coaches.

I was getting really frustrated because half of the people weren't really getting things done, so I just kept taking on more and more responsibility. Eventually—probably four months into it—I became the executive vice president so I would have the authority to make the changes that needed to be made. I tried my best to hold CoachVille together as in Thomas's vision. I got the school organized, got some incredible content providers and teachers like Ivan Misner and some other people, and got the school ICF-accredited, and a whole bunch of things.

I had a vision at CoachVille, and Bobette had a vision at ICF for *pro bono* coaching or charitable arm. Neither CoachVille nor ICF were interested. We talked about wanting a conference where it was just for Master Coaches because the best parts of the ICF conference [involved] having conversations with other Master Coaches. We talked further at the ICF conference in Quebec, and out of those discussions The Coach Initiative and Conversation Among Masters (CAM) were born.

What also happened at that last conference in New Orleans is that Jack Canfield showed up. He had just started an organization called The Transformational Leadership Council (TLC) that, in its first iteration, for a year-and-a-half, had been for people who ran training and seminar organizations. He invited all of my speakers, plus Dave and I, to become members of this organization. A year later, I went to my first TLC meeting. It was a fairly small one in Tucson, but I offered to help run the program for the next one. So I did. A year-and-a-half later, I was running all of the programs, and six months after that, was asked to join the board.

I've left some things out during the time I was a stay-at-home mom, doing the editing and some other things. I started an organization called Home at the Shore, which was one of the first national networking groups for women. It was an organization of stay-at-home moms who had at-home businesses. We started out here at the Jersey Shore. [At the point when] I no longer had time for it and the woman who was working on it with me had moved, we had chapters in thirty states.

And now we have CAMelot [a CAM-related conference]. Yes, we felt there was a need for a smaller, more intimate, higher-level group that included people beyond just coaches.

Q. And you've created Association for Transformational Leaders (ATL), partially, I would guess, out of the desire to hang out with smaller groups of people?

Donna: That was created so I could have real conversations with local people who understand the transformational industry and personal development work. Whenever

I come across something and it makes interesting sense to me, I will throw myself into it in any way that I can, personally and professionally. I'm always open to what's next. I like cutting-edge.

Outgrowing the Job

From my own interview with Pam Ramsden:

Susan M.: I didn't like my office because I was in the Apparel Office, and you never really found anybody a job because it's seasonal work. So when everybody was laid off because the season was over they would show up to get their books stamped so they could receive their unemployment checks. They didn't want you to do anything for them. I got pretty tired of that.

I think it lasted less than a year … and I quit. I got tired of it, and I went back to school because what else could you do? I had been fascinated with this whole remedial reading thing, so I got a Master's in Education Psychology from NYU, specializing in remedial reading.

A roommate had been subbing in a daycare center, and he said they always needed people. I figured, "Okay, at least those kids are smaller than me. I'm going to do that."

I knew I wanted to be in charge of my own classroom, so I moved uptown to the Goddard Riverside Day Care Center on the Upper West Side. It was quite wonderful because I got my classroom organized so well that mostly my aide and assistant were running the classroom. I was out in the hallway, coaching the parents—so you could see where this was going.

I did that for a few years. By the time I left, I had instituted a reading program based on Sylvia Ashton Warner's work. The kids got to pick a word, they put it on a card, and if they remembered it the next day, then they kept the word card because it was significant to them. If not, then they just got a new word until they had a stack of cards, which was their sight vocabulary. Then you helped them write stories. These were old four- and young five-year-olds, and quite a few of them were reading by the end of the year. Also, I got the majority of the kids with psychological issues because I was very good with them.

About this time, I was getting bored with the whole thing anyway, so I decided, *Okay, I need to go back to school again.* So back I went to NYU and this time, I was going to get a Master's in Counseling because I was interested in that, I was doing all this work with parents, and I knew I was going to be good at it.

I did that [master's program] and got out of it with no idea what I was going to do. I couldn't get a job as a career counselor, and I couldn't get potential employers to take me seriously as someone who could work with adults. Because I had been working in day care for seven years, they assumed that all I knew was how to work with preschoolers.

Like several of the other women in this chapter, Susan M. would take on several projects at once to create a sense of fulfillment in a job. Unlike others in The Fifty, she was not as interested in a position of authority.

Susan M.: I think one of my issues was I liked being a generalist, so I never did say, "Okay, let me be in charge of this, so hire me full-time." I had to have several things going on to be amused and enjoy it. I enjoyed each piece of it, and I was getting energized by it. What would happen is they would keep giving me new programs that I really loved doing, and so I would stay a little longer.

I mean, for the managerial core program, we invented something called Transitville. We had somebody design for us a whole system based on the map of Brooklyn. We had four different depots and four different lines and they had to do some real-time problem solving with it. We had a lot of fun, we had a lot of really, really cool things.

It turned out I had thyroid problems. Somewhere, in the back of my mind, it was linked to stress. That was the beginning of the end for me with the Transit Authority because I realized there was a chance that job was going to kill me outright.

At the same time, the senior vice president of the Division of Subways came to us with an idea. He said, "I need for my General Superintendents to be better problem solvers, and I need them to think on their feet and do good presentations."

Okay, I was just burning to do an action learning program. I had fallen in love with the concept and I thought, *This is what we can do for the General Superintendents.*

We did some really interesting work [on this project] because it was not a culture where thinking was necessarily valued, and a lot of these people were blue-collar people. The senior vice president, in fact, went back and got his GED while we were doing this program.

So we bought them portfolios, and we put a pad and a new pen inside the portfolio so they would look like researchers. When they went out there, they could open up their portfolios and take notes. When we got to the point where we needed them to really start thinking, we actually said, "Now, we want you to all wear your thinking caps," and that's when we gave them their baseball caps.

They went out of there wonderfully empowered and really strutting their stuff. They did research and told people, "We're allowed to ask you these questions because Joe [the senior vice president] said we could." They came up with some wonderful ideas.

At the end of the first year, they put together a conference and all of the managers in the Department of Subways were allowed to attend. Each group presented the problem they had been working on and the solutions they came up with, and they actually facilitated the small [discussion] groups to come up with even more suggestions.

Q. So they had never been empowered, they had never been given a voice so they could have some say in making a difference.

Susan M.: Yeah, and most of them had never met the other people who were in their groups—they were voices on the phone. This alone was a huge thing, actually getting to meet their counterparts. The conferences were wonderful; they ran the whole thing, they made the whole thing work, and it was just beautiful.

I did that for two years. The second year, they actually opened it up to the supervisors and brought them out for conference as well. But by that time, I really realized that place was making me crazy. I knew what I liked doing was working with people more in the nature of problem solving and improving their lives.

When You Come to a Fork in the Road, Take It - YOGI BERRA

Jeannette talks about her openness to new things:

Jeanette: I was always interested in writing—I'm getting down to my core competency now—I always liked to write. When I went to night school, I always thought if I volunteered for a job, it always ended up that I was running the organization, right? That happened throughout my career. So I volunteered to write for the *Evening Standard*, I think it was, and I became a co-editor.

Kathy keeps trying new things and finds ways to incorporate skills from previous ventures into whatever she is trying next:

Kathy: I feel like I have a huge opportunity here in my life—I can do virtually whatever I want to do. What I don't want to do is waste it. I don't want to say twenty years from now, "Man, I had this great opportunity, and I just sat on the couch and watched TV and ate bonbons." I don't want to do that, so I do feel a little bit of pressure, like this week, but I don't want five years to go by and I'm still here sitting and thinking, *I don't know what to do with myself.*

I do want to use my life usefully in some manner—whether there is money involved or not is a little bit open at the moment. I don't know how or what is going to happen, but I'm thinking, probably, within the next three, six months I'm going to have a handle on it, because I never sat around not knowing for an extended length of time. I think, at some point, my spirit's going to be jumping up and down and saying, *Okay Kat, time for a decision.* I'll figure out something, but I do definitely think that … like my last few things, it's going to involve my teaching, my coaching—something very creative; something that involves writing because I love to do that; involves working with people, with groups maybe.

Sally always wanted to be doing more than one thing at any given time and supplemented her job with volunteer activities that lasted into her retirement. Her story demonstrates a deep need to give meaningful service:

Q. So what were some of your more exciting adventures that you remember from that period?

Sally: Of all the parts of the world, Asia became my very favorite place. I found the culture fascinating, and I met wonderful, wonderful people. Just about that time, Pan American offered us—all airline employees—an opportunity to join Young Wings, which was a group that helped around the world. Pan American sponsored us and would give us free passes.

My first experience was to go to India to escort orphans back to the United States. The children were already adopted. Many of them were handicapped, but the American parents could not go to get them. So I would bring another stewardess to India with me, and we would bring back anywhere from one to six children at a time, and they would be united with their new adoptive parents. I did this off and on when I had four of five days off [at a time], for about five years. I got so involved in this group that the gentleman who ran our organization sent two of us from Eastern Airlines to Hong Kong to work with the Vietnamese refugees. These refugees were coming to America and parts of Europe, but they didn't know anything about our culture. We would help teach English. At night, we would teach cultural orientation to the Vietnamese. This was very, very difficult, as most of them had never seen a telephone, a bathroom, a fork, knife ... but we did it.

I spent a month helping there. Then, about six months later, the same girl and I were sent to Phenat Nikhom Holding Center in Chonburi, Thailand. We did the same sort of work there, working with the Cambodians and the hill people. I learned so much because I had never heard of hill people, and I knew very little about Cambodians. But in a month's time, I certainly learned about the uprisings over in that part of the world, what these people had lost, and their excitement going to a new place.

These people would be held in these holding centers for weeks at a time, months. A lot of families were held for years at a time, living on one mattress, maybe six or eight people at a time. They were given rice each day and then mom and the kids would go out in the fields and pick whatever greens they could find.

I was very lucky; I could walk into town, and we actually had rice and boiled eggs and barbecued pork, which was a little piece of meat. I'm not sure what the meat was, but it was delicious. I would do this for a month, and those were my two experiences working with the refugees.

Later, I was hired by American Trans Air, a charter company, as a flight attendant. Most of the flying I did was military flights. We brought the troops and their dependents in and out of the bases throughout the world. I got to see and stay at some military bases that the average person cannot go to and definitely cannot stay at. This was during the Gulf War II. So I did a lot of that flying in and out of the Gulf, bringing the troops in and out of the war there. I also did the Somali uprising. When there were problems in Haiti, I was chosen to help fly the political leaders out of Haiti when they had to leave the country. That was probably one of the highlight trips of my charter career.

Q. Tell me a little more about that.

Sally: Our military had taken over the airport, and we had a little military base set up. So we went down in the morning, and there was another aircraft from another airline there. We did not know which aircraft would bring the political leaders out of the country. We sat from about eight o'clock in the morning. At three o'clock the following morning, we were told that we would be the ones to bring the political leaders to their destination, and the other aircraft would bring their family members to Florida. It was not announced before, because no one wanted the world to know where these political leaders were going. But I actually got to do that, which was very, very exciting. While I was at this charter company, I did several of the haj trips, where we brought the non-Christians on their once-in-a-lifetime pilgrimage to Mecca.

Q. Oh! What were those like?

Sally: The people had never, ever been on an aircraft before, so, of course, we had to teach them the ways of flying. Before each landing they would start chanting. The women would go to the back lavatory, and the men would go to the front lavatory, and wash their feet. So, consequently, the lavatories looked like little pools. But then they would come out, be seated, and start their chanting for the last few minutes of the flight.

What was really fascinating to me: each woman would have a white scarf on, shaped like a triangle, and each triangle was embroidered with a little edge. It just showed the wonderful handicraft work that these women did. The men would all have brand-new suits on. It was just something I had never seen or heard about before these trips into the land of Mecca.

Q. And tell me a little bit more about flying the military and their families. What was that like, what were some of the high points or difficult points in that?

Sally: We would fly them from base to base, and when the dependents were on, the children were just absolutely the most wonderfully-behaved children I have ever seen in my life. Whatever their parents told them to do—if they had to tell them to do anything—they wouldn't question. They would just sit down, get their games out, put their carry-on little bags underneath the seat, and sit there until we landed. The different bases in the world, the parents would tell me how wonderful the schools were, and they were all just happy, happy kids, and the parents were happy going to the bases.

One of the favorite bases, I remember, was up in Turkey. Everyone loved being based there. The school system was good. We also did a lot of flying in and out of different bases in Germany, as a lot of the troops went as far as Germany and then they were sent to different parts of the world. I think the hardest part was bringing the troops into the two Gulf Wars. They—a lot of them—showed me pictures of their kids, their girlfriends, their wives. A lot of them didn't think they would ever come home. A lot of them didn't come home.

But what was quite interesting: I brought them into the first Desert Storm, flying for Eastern Airlines and then Eastern went out of business. So a year later, I brought many of them back flying for the charter company. Quite a few recognized me, and a lot of them told me stories about their buddies not coming back, and that was really, really hard. But once we landed in the Unites State—it was usually Bangor, Maine—there would be so many Americans meeting these troops with American flags. We had hot dogs and beer for the fellows, because, of course, they were not allowed to drink on the aircraft. It was just a wonderful homecoming for them, the ones that did make it.

It was probably my favorite flying time because I did go to so many places—a lot of places I had never heard about before this. And it was great seeing our troops, taking our troops to their bases in the war zone and bringing them back.

I returned to Cambodia with a friend. While we were there, we took this boat ride down into Battambang, which is about a three-and-a-half hour boat trip from Siem Reap. Because of the low water it took us nine hours. But when we got to Battambang, we were only staying one night.

The next day, we met an Australian couple that helped start the orphanage in Battambang. I got to meet one of the gentlemen who helped start it and I told him I would be back to volunteer. I just loved the way the orphanage was set up, and I visited many, many orphanages in Asia. This orphanage was three kilometers out of town, and it had eight bungalows. In each bungalow there were sixteen kids, bunk beds with mats instead of sheets and mattresses, and one housemother. One of the bungalows had a little clinic where they had a nurse. There was one long building where there was a kitchen downstairs and the teenaged girls lived upstairs, and the other long building had offices downstairs and one classroom, and two classrooms upstairs.

I went back for the next five years, one or two times a year, staying from one week to a month. On a typical day while working at this orphanage, I would get up at six-thirty in the morning. I stayed in town in this very little boutique hotel, and up on the roof I would have my coffee and baguette. One of the boys who worked up there, in between spending time with their other customers, he would sit with me and I would help him with his English. I had a notebook, so he would play with my notebook and this young man learned English so well, he now owns his own tuk-tuk [motorbike taxi] and he takes tourists all around Battambang and around the province of Battambang. He did so well in life. I recently found out that he just got married. So the next time I go over, I'll have to meet his wife.

One of the boys from the hotel would take me on the back of a motorbike to the orphanage, after we finished breakfast. It was about three kilometers from town. At eight o'clock, I would see the older kids go off to school; they had to walk into the village. Then I went into the library and helped the preschool children play with puzzles. I would read to them—the library was very nicely stocked with English books from Australia and books written in Khmer. We would play with games, and I would help the children with whatever needed to be done. A couple of times the English teacher did not come to class, so I would help—one time with another volunteer—teach English to the grammar school children, who did not walk into town in the morning.

I can remember one time while in the library with the preschool children, one of the twins—who were two-and-a-half years old—was laying on the floor, crying. I ran over to him to see what was wrong. I picked him up, and he was so hot. I raced him to the clinic—and he had a hundred and two [degree] temperature. Over there, they don't have medical help like we do. They gave him a pill, and I brought him back to the library, where we made a bed out of pillows. The other small children would lie there and hold his hand, and by the afternoon, he was well. He was playing like he always did, making lots of noise. But this is the kind of medical attention that they had.

They were not ignored. The children that got really, really sick would go into town to the hospital, which was very, very rare. If they really needed help, they would have to take them up to Bangkok, which was about a three-and-a-half-hour bus trip to Siem Reap and then a forty-five minute flight to Bangkok. But all the times I was there, there was only one child who did not make it. She was a handicapped child, and she just was so sick and had so many problems that she was taken to the hospital in town, where she passed away. But the rest of the children were very, very healthy. Every now and then, they would have a dentist come in and work on all their teeth. They were just really wonderful kids. These kids were in this orphanage to learn English and school so they could go out in the world, and get jobs, and help rebuild Cambodia.

I did this each day. I worked mostly in the library while the children were on different shifts going into town, to school, and also taking classes right at the orphanage. At five o'clock, I would go back to town, and I would either take a cooking class or just have dinner and get ready for the next day, to go back. On Sundays, the children did not go to school, so a video player was brought in, and for about three or four hours in the afternoon, the kids would just sit on the library floor and watch the videos, mostly English cartoons. I have never seen a happier bunch of children, laughing, and—I never heard them cry. They were just very, very happy to have food, and ... most of these children did not have any family members. If they did, the family members had a lot of problems left over from the Pol Pot regime. It was just a wonderful, wonderful time and, as the children that I would spend time with got a little bit older, they were in school six days a week. So the last couple of times I have been back there I have visited the orphanage, but I have not done any work with them except to sit and hear what they are doing in school.

Q. Now, one of the things that you didn't talk about at all was that you did some work with Mother Theresa's organization.

Sally: Oh, yes! When I was at Eastern [Airlines], to go back to my Eastern days, this is when I started with Young Wings. We would go to India, and bring Mother Theresa's orphans back into the United States. I do believe I mentioned that a lot of them were handicapped. They were adopted here in the United States, but the parents could not go after them. We just looked out for their safety, and we took care of them; we were responsible for them from the time they were put on the aircraft in India, usually New Delhi, until we got into the United States.

If I brought them to New York, which was where they all came originally, it would take about twenty-four hours. We wore our passes, meaning we only flew if there was an extra seat for us. The children had seats, but we did not, so quite often we would get bumped off the flight in London. The Pan American ground staff would always help us out for the night, and we would continue on to the United States the next day. If the kids were going to some place besides New York, there would be another flight attendant to pick them up in New York and bring them to the various parts of the United States. I did this off and on for about five years.

I had a little time off from work. It wasn't vacation time; it was usually just building my days off into four or five days. It also gave me a wonderful time, during those four or five days, while I was waiting for the papers to be processed, to see the different parts of India. So I have really gotten to know India quite well. I just love it. After the children were adopted, I did hear from a lot of their adoptive parents. They were doing quite well here, and they got medical attention here, where they could not get … they could not get any in India, at the time.

Shifting Worldview

Some of The Fifty were always open to change. For others, a distinct event caused them to rethink their world. This process of rethinking and changing is called transformative learning. When a significant change in thinking results in a behavior change, it is called perspective transformation (Mezirow, 1991). One's whole way of thinking about the world changes through shifts in the thought patterns that lead to decisions and behavior. Following is a formal look at the process:

The Six Steps of Transformative Learning

1. Experiencing a disorienting dilemma

At some point, individuals realize that what they are doing is somehow out of sync with the rest of the world. Basically, this means finding out that your view of the world is different from that of others or that the world has thrown you a curve ball. This could be losing a job or getting divorced or simply finding yourself in a situation that is not what you had thought it would be.

2. Undergoing self-examination

After discovering a disconnect, the individual moves into a period of looking at what they are doing and believing. It often involves moving from the notion that something must be wrong with you—and therefore, you should just accept what is happening as what is supposed to happen in your life—to beginning to wonder if there's really something wrong outside of yourself.

3. **Conducting a critical assessment of role assumptions**

This next step involves looking at how you are functioning and examining the assumptions or deeply held beliefs underlying how you are living your life. Looking at what you have been led to accept that you should be doing—sort of an all (insert role) must do (insert behavior).

Examples: All widows must withdraw from the world, wear black, and never be happy again. All mothers must stay home with their children. People who accept public assistance will never go off it.

The key question here is, "Is that really true?"

4. **Recognizing that one's problem is shared**

Sometimes, if you are out of sync with the norms that are familiar to you, it is easy to think that you are all alone. It becomes easier to change when you realize that you are not alone.

5. **Exploring options for new ways of acting**

You begin to generate alternatives and plans, based on your revised assumptions about yourself and the world.

6. **Building competence and self-confidence in new roles**

Finally, the individual proceeds with changed behavior. Long-held habits of mind or perspective are examined. This results in the creation of new or altered perspectives. In order for this process to be transformative, both thinking and subsequent behavior must change.

This process of self-reflection has been thoroughly documented on the individual level: the beliefs that people hold about themselves, as key elements in determining how they will act. We set up filters based on what we believe to be true, and act in ways that are consistent with those filters—unless something turns our lives around. (Mezirow, 1991)

Experiences That Triggered Transformational Change

As described in Chapter Three, divorce and shifting relationships with her children were triggers for Victoria.

> **Victoria:** When I was divorced, I thought, *I need a career.* I didn't want to go into Speech Pathology, so I got a job at an agency as a copywriter.
>
> When my children were both out of the area and off to University, I went to Paris for three months … I ended up staying there for five years and created a whole new life for myself.

For some of The Fifty, like Audrey, the death of a loved one created a major shift in thinking and a subsequent transformation. Others realized that their thinking was out of sync with many people in their professional situation. Susan S. moved away from the professorate because she did not fit in:

> **Susan S.:** "I was always a little too bouncy. You sort of think of Tigger with a Ph.D."

Valerie realized that she was leading her life more to please her parents than herself:

Valerie: When I started out my career, going through school and going through college and making all those choices, I was doing it because it was what was expected of me by my family. Then it, somehow, turned into what was expected of me, for me, because I wanted to prove that I could do it myself. And then it's like, *Well, I've proven that. And now I really, actually want to do what I want to do.*

I did it for my parents and my family. Then I did it, I did the work thing, for me to prove that I could do it. You know, when I looked at going to school, it was never ... my sister kind of went to school and then she kind of left. I did things because, you know, I saw how they reacted to what my sister did, which was absolutely right for her at the time. But I was watching their reaction, not her reaction. I didn't want to disappoint them. So I did a lot of the things I did because of them, to prove [myself] to them, and to make them happy. And you know, basically, I think, to make sure that they knew how much I appreciated everything that they gave me and everything they did for me. It was my way of paying them back.

A big part of transformative change or perspective transformation goes beyond recognizing triggers to reflection—thinking about an old behavior pattern, deciding to keep the pattern or change it, and, if changing, experimenting with changing that pattern.

Edgar Schön introduced the concept of reflection-on-action (Schön, 1983, 1987) to describe the process of looking back on personal experiences to evaluate the reasoning that led to their behavior and build personal theories of action. Schön's discussion of reflection-in-action adds to the picture of learning from experience. (Schön, 1983)

Schön sees learning as occurring when a reflective conversation occurs, drawing on experience to understand a situation, framing and reframing, suggesting action, then reinterpreting the situation in light of possible outcomes.

Perhaps the stories in this chapter have sparked an interest in thinking about what events have been triggers in your own life. We all handle change differently. The exercise below will help you identify your own change pattern.

Exercise

Think about how you deal with change in your own life. What patterns do you notice? How do you react in action? Each of us handles life's challenges in our own unique way, but there are some general patterns that emerge when we look at different coping or problem-solving strategies. See which category seems to best fit the information you have uncovered about your own behavior. If none of these sounds like you, create your own. You are not trying to fit into someone else's boxes here; you are trying to understand how you have operated in the past so that you can make clearer decisions about which behaviors you want to maintain or strengthen and which you want to give up or modify.

Once you have actually named or labeled your coping strategy, it may be easier for you to understand it as a chosen set of behaviors rather than happenstance or dumb luck. Second, consider varying your strategy. If you have automatically or habitually used one strategy in the past and consider yourself to be unsuccessful, what else might you begin to try in the future?

The following change types may help you further define your pattern and offer optional strategies that you could adopt.

Planners have contingency plans for everything. They love to think ahead about what they might do in any situation and imagine that they are always ready for anything. Because they are in the habit of planning, when faced with the need to change, they use the habit of planning to face crises calmly and rationally. In the face of emergency, planners stop and make a plan; they research, they consult others. They may move slowly and deliberately, but they do move. They take their time and then take well-considered action.

Daredevils leap into the fray and never look back. These are the eternal optimists of change. They have great confidence and certainty that something will happen and everything will work out. Some of them are always in scrapes of some sort. They trust others to bail them out, if necessary, although they may have no idea who that somebody will be. They just move through life, sure that something will happen and everything will work out. They may have brilliant successes or dismal failures. In either case, they will still be ready for that next leap.

Chaos Creatures feel that, in life, most change arises out of chaos. They have great faith in their ability to thrive on chaos and come through it better and stronger than ever. They excel at on-the-spot planning, have good research skills, and can juggle multiple priorities. Multi-tasking is not just a computer term for these people—they usually have two or three projects going at once and a couple more on the back burner. A chaos creature is an excellent synthesizer, always looking for patterns and seeing possibilities. They love to hypothesize based on very little information.

Waiters just hold still until everything is over. If disaster strikes, they wait calmly, sort through the debris and then rebuild if necessary. If life brings them fame and fortune, they wait till the cheering dies down and then figure out how to make the best use of their good fortune. They are not prone to take action at the front end of change; rather, they let change roll over them and then make the best possible use of whatever happens. They may be calculating the odds during the change, or they may remain passive until everything settles down a bit. Like Chaos Creatures, they are excellent synthesizers; unlike them, they operate best from a position of calm when in possession of all the facts.

Which type are you? How can you use this information to help you handle future changes? Does your style make you more effective or get in your way?

We discussed varying your style. Sometimes, waiting makes sense, and you should go with your natural inclination. But sometimes a Waiter will wait too long, and action will no longer be possible. On the other hand, Daredevils may plunge in headlong and end up going over a cliff.

Single or Serial Career Path?

While some women are content with one life-long career or were serial career-changers, requiring a series of choices, some of The Fifty needed to have several things going on at once. Some had multiple income streams; some had careers and others had businesses that started as hobbies and grew. Generally, these women satisfied different needs through each venture. Donna, for example, wanted to travel and find a way to finance those travels. These needs led to coordinating two different event series that met regularly at resorts and spas.

Charlotte supplemented her high-powered banking career with what her husband presented as a relaxing hobby to fulfill her need to be surrounded by animals. She now breeds award-winning alpacas and is planning to start a store featuring products made from her alpaca wool.

Larraine simply has boundless energy and uses her many projects to meet her need for variety and to fulfill needs in her family and community.

Larraine: My son and daughter-in-law gave birth to a beautiful little boy, and honestly, it was just the happiest moment of my life. It was just such a beautiful thing to see this grandchild. And then, as he was growing a little bit, I started making up stories for him. He loved my stories; loved, loved, loved my stories. I would sing some songs for him and he loved my songs.

So I started to put together a series of songs. I decided I wanted to learn to play a guitar. I have always played the piano, very well in the beginning of my life and very badly in the latter years of my life. So I started to learn the guitar. My guitar teacher came in one day, heard me playing some things on the piano that I couldn't translate for the guitar, and he started to play along with me.

Eventually, I said to him, "This sounds really good." So out of that, we went to the studio and we recorded fourteen songs, things like "The Potty Song" and "The Birthday at School" song. I wrote all the lyrics.

Then I wrote three children's books that would go along with this mythical character called Sam, a broken robot who has a handicapped arm and yet, he manages to cope and find ways around his handicap.

My husband and I live on an urban farm. It's a property we bought thirty-four years ago. When I sold my company five or six years ago, my husband and I decided—we had chickens and quails already—we decided to get goats, and now we raise tilapia.

I make my own cheese, which I learned to do on the Internet. We have about 300 exotic poultries. I make all kinds of jams and relishes and I sell Camembert and ricotta and chevre, relishes and jams and cakes to a number of chefs who enjoy them and use them in their restaurants. I give it away, too, to friends and people who aren't friends who come by, and it's a lot of fun.

We really developed this little farm into a passion and a place for our grandchildren to come and enjoy, and also into the basis for these characters in my books and songs.

So I launched a website called RockingGrandmaMusic.com and started to sell products, which was a lot of fun.

But … I kept on saying to myself, *I don't want to build another business. I'm done, I'm done,* and all this time, I'm building another business. So at some point, a year into it, I said, "I'm done. I'm not going to build this business anymore." I just started to donate my inventory to children in children's hospitals around the country. The last month or two, I have given probably close to a thousand of Sam's little boxes with these three books and two compact discs to kids in the hospitals in Orlando and Dallas and northern California and Chicago and Atlanta. It has just giving me tremendous amount of pleasure.

I started blogging recipes because I always loved to cook, but didn't for many, many years because I wasn't here. Six years ago, I started cooking and now I have thousands of recipes. I blog a couple of times a week with different recipes, and I have a bunch of people who follow me on Twitter and Facebook and so on.

That has sort of been my passion. Going back to when I was at Vantage Partners, I joined the Committee of 200, a women's CEO organization. It was amazing for me because it was the first time in my life I found a group of women peers, whom I admired tremendously and whom I didn't need to mentor. It was just a relief and such a sense of joy, a feeling that has duplicated itself multiple, multiple times with the women whom I bring in as members or other people who bring in members.

That has been a remarkable addition to my life and, of course, because I can't help myself, I ended up recruiting new members on the West Coast and eventually became the region chair. Then I was put on the board of the C200 and became the chairperson of the C200 Foundation.

The foundation is my passion. I have donated a $25,000 scholarship, which will go to some of the young women we find in universities around the world. We go into what we call "reach-outs" where we give scholarships to women in MBA school.

My mission has been to bring medical schools, computer schools, and engineering schools along, so these young women can all develop their own networks early in life, which will help them become entrepreneurial businesswomen or corporate business-women. I really built up the foundation and expanded it significantly. It's a three-year term, so that is going to keep me quite busy.

Also, I met an amazing woman who became a very good friend through C200, who became CEO and chairman of the company now called Frontier Communications in Stamford, Connecticut. I joined her board close to eight years ago, and we have done some acquisitions. Since we were in the Fortune 300, I can truthfully say that has been and continues to be one of the highlights of my life.

I threw myself into education on corporate governance, attended a program at Stanford and became a member of the National Association of Corporate Directors (NACD). I became a speaker on corporate governance for the University of Southern

California Corporate Governance conference, and I am also now on the board of the NACD Southern California charity nominating committee. So that board experience has been fabulous.

The NACD Board is also very interesting. I actually launched a program with the Committee of 200 and NACD, where I brought in woman directors with male directors. I did a girl, boy, girl, boy seating chart for a hundred people to show the male directors who say, "I can't find a good woman director to come on my board." There were at least fifty superb woman directors with great experience in that room. So I am hoping to do my little bit to get more women on boards.

In the meantime, I have been on the Entrepreneur's Board of the Anderson School of Management at UCLA for twenty-three years now. I continue on that board and mentor Anderson's students—boys and girls, men and women—every year, taking them for dinner, talking to them, and advising them.

A funny thing happened: I got a call from the dean of Southwestern Law School, which I have not thought of since 1979 when I graduated, to say that he and the team would like to take me for lunch. I said it would be lovely and made that date. Then I put the phone down and I thought, *That's crazy!* So I called back and said, "You don't want to take me for lunch. I haven't practiced law since 1980, and I frankly hated it. Certainly, I hated being at Southwestern—it was the worst experience of my life—I'm trying to forget everything about that."

He laughed and said, "Yes, I know. Our graduates are extremely successful people, and they want to meet you for lunch." We went for lunch, and I ended up setting up a scholarship endowment to join forces with the School of Management to put a JD-MBA (Juris Doctor-Masters of Business Administration degree) together, which makes me very excited.

I put together an annual scholarship for women who are in that program, doing the JD-MBA, and I am now developing the little network of young women students whom I continue to mentor. Also, I went back to Pepperdine and created an endowment scholarship there for women students in the Presidents and Key Executives Program, because they don't get enough women residents to come into that program. My goal is to increase some sort of incentive. So, between my board work and what I'm doing with C200, my grandchildren—whom I absolutely need to see at least one day a week, and there are now four of them—I'm busy. My son has, they have a five-year old, a three-year old, and identical twins, two boys, who are fourteen months now.

Victoria spoke about women supporting each other and moving beyond the writer's fear that each project might be the last one:

Victoria: My friends are at the stage now where the ones who are not writers are retiring. The ones who are writers are taking the next project, like Barbara Abercrombie, who was here Friday night, spent the night. She came up from Los Angeles and then the next day I took her up to Marin. She was teaching a course at Book Passage, which is a phenomenal independent bookstore in Corte Madera.

We did a lot of talking. Barbara is a few years older than I am and has another book coming out. Her books come out quite frequently. She writes wonderful books on writing and memoir and personal essay. We were talking about that; we were talking about the fact that when you are a writer, you can work into your 80s or 90s; you don't think about retiring. I don't know any writers who said, "Okay that's my last book, I'm finished now. I'm going to retire." It's like, "Okay, that book is published. I can't wait now to get to the next project. I don't know what it's going to be, but it will be there sooner or later."

Audrey was one of several women who saw writing in their future. In this part of her interview, she is concerned with seeing her work both grow and continue beyond her:

Audrey: In the next ten years, where I would like to see it take me ... I'm actually working on my forthcoming book, so I'd like to have my book published within this year. I don't have much further to go for the first draft to be ready. So I would like to be a published author.

I would like to be known as a go-to person for grief recovery. And I really would like to see more education around the whole idea of allowing people to grieve their losses and feel better again. I'm going to take it to the corporate arena, because I think that returning employees, after a loss—when they are working forty hours a week (they spend more time there than in their homes)—have to stuff their grief, have to leave it at the door before they enter work.

So I think it's a lot of education, and I'm hoping my book provides some of that and certainly my outspokenness, and being a speaker on the subject. In addition, [I plan on] reaching as many people as I possibly can through the tele-seminars to understand the grieving process.

I will travel anywhere. I already told my husband before we got married, "By the way, if I have to travel to Paris, I have to go." It is very, very important to me to end this journey of my life over the course of the next, hopefully, twenty-to-thirty years, making a difference. And I think that's what most of us want to do—make some kind of a difference.

Tish underwent an unusual transformational experience when she received her double lung transplant. For someone who, although still fighting to live, is preparing to die, the return to a life without that constant threat required an enormous shift:

Tish: There was also kind of a mental switch, because as long as you were waiting for a transplant ... you were always waiting for something. In your mind, everything would be fine once you got it. Now you have it. And if something goes wrong, you have to deal with it. So it was kind of a mental switch.

For example, rejection is something that's, well, the enemy of all transplants. So the reality [is] I've got this now and if it rejects right away, I'm really in trouble. So it was kind of a different shift.

But I was very blessed. I did have a couple of challenges, but … I was well enough to come home after about three months and slowly start to build my life again. Let me tell you, it was so great to wash dishes again. It's going to sound so corny, but the first time I went to Costco and was standing in line I had tears in my eyes. This was great, you know. Just that semblance of everyday life that had been so closed off. It was great. I certainly loved every second being with my children again. And you know, I really took every moment I could to revel in that.

Q. That had to be a shift too, didn't it? That had to be a developmental shift, I imagine—to be a healthy person again.

Tish: Exactly. Yes. It did. To think of yourself in those terms and come to terms with the fact that I have been fortunate. Here is the reality: I'm going to take all these medications every day. I'm going to go four times a year [for a checkup], and I'm going to be petrified every time I'm there because you get the results right then. They can tell if some rejection is creeping in. But I am going to deal with it. I'm going to be strong enough to deal with it, and I'm going to try to have a normal life.

There are a lot of—particularly when you are first transplanted—there are a lot of precautions you need to take. Some people, I think, get stuck in that phase. They'll never go to a movie at night, or they'll avoid big crowds and be really reluctant to shake hands. I guess everyone comes to terms with that.

For me, I decided I had to live my life. I certainly took those precautions for as long as I needed to, but then I thought, *I'm not going to miss things because I want to be so careful that I'm not going to expose myself to something when—who knows?—the way life is, your child could be exposed to something and could bring it home.* So I made my peace with it: that I'm going to live my life and deal with the consequences of that.

I guess a hard thing was not knowing really how much "overtime" you have. Sometimes I refer to the fact that I'm really in overtime because I have had now, thirteen years I thought I never would have.

Initially there was … *Well, what do I do with my life if I know I'm not going to have a typical lifespan?* Because the reality is, there are a lot of risks of rejection. The medications are really toxic. So you accept all that. But what do I do? Do I just live every day? Or, thinking about going back to work—should I do that? Is that the right decision?

So there was a lot of coming to terms with *How do you go on with your life once you have been through something like this? When you don't know what the horizon is and have some sense it may not be the longest one, how do you make those decisions?*

I guess for me, it was probably a couple of different factors: I had always missed work and I had always thought I would go back some day. So, when my son was finishing middle school, I really thought, *It is time for me to start looking again.* I was fortunate enough that I had stayed in contact with people where I used to work. I heard of an opening there that people thought I would be a good fit for. So after fourteen years, I ended up going back to the place I had left when my son was born.

Q. So I'm wondering if there was a kind of a floundering and trying to figure out how to restart, now that you've had this whole new life given to you.

Tish: Right. Exactly. You know, because over time, you are very sick. You live from doctor's appointment to doctor's appointment. You don't have any real life. You are kind of defined by your illness. Once you get over that, it's kind of, *WOW.* Well, you know, *What is the real me underneath all that?* And getting stronger. And it's okay to go on with my life now.

Again, being mid-career, it was, *Well, what do I do now?* I think the best that has happened to me is—I guess when I was in my 20s, I had started an MBA program. I thought at the time, *Well, I don't think I really need it. I'm traveling, I'm doing really well.* So I just went for a semester or two and stopped it. It always bugged me in the back of my mind that I had done that. And so, a few years ago, I pursued having the bank sponsor me for an executive MBA program. They ended up nominating me. That was a great experience because I was certainly one of the oldest people there.

It was that sense of: *Look, it doesn't mean—because you didn't end up doing it back then—that the door is totally closed.*

So with that ... and the whole experience of being in a classroom again and also relating to a very eclectic class where there were lots of foreign students and younger students. Trying to navigate and figure out where could you add value? You know, what was your role in the study group, for example, was really a great, great opportunity and a great experience overall.

Q. Wow. So I guess that brings us up to—so what's next? What do you want to do next?

Tish: Well, I guess I go back to the idea that I wanted to be a writer. There are some times I think, "Oh, it was great to get my MBA." But maybe I should have really done something about writing because, even today, I find that it is easy for me to organize my thoughts by writing. I like to write. Some people have said, "Well, you should write your story. It's so interesting." I'm not so sure it is to others. I guess my true wish would be that I could find something to write about so that I could one day publish a book, publish a novel, maybe short stories. But if not that, an actual novel and just fulfill that wish, that destiny, I guess, that I had envisioned for myself way back when.

Q. Nice. That will be fun. And you know, maybe when you read this, you'll say, "Oh, well, maybe I do want to talk about this." Or maybe you'll just say, "Oh, well, no, here's the novel coming."

Tish: Right. Exactly.

Q. Yeah. So I guess I want to ask you—are there things you think other women should know if they come up against challenges or face decisions or move on with their lives? That was very broad.

Tish: That's okay. Well, I guess the biggest one was "You're stronger than you think," which is probably something a lot of people tell you. But I really fought hard to live long enough to get a transplant. I never really would have thought of myself as someone strong, you know, before this. So I think that is one thing to believe, that somehow, if you are faced with one of these challenges, you do have the wherewithal to do what you need to do.

And I think that the second would probably be related to this MBA program, because, I still think …we were in traditional roles in our marriage. For example, if we were going away on a trip, my husband would take care of all the logistics and the airport and all that. As part of the MBA program, we traveled to South America and we traveled to Asia. I traveled to Hong Kong by myself. So that experience, I think, really has been life-changing because, again, it forced me to do something that I never thought I had the capability to do. Now I really have, probably from both experiences, this conviction I can take it on—just about anything. Yeah. I can go to Asia, or I can go somewhere else, and I can do it on my own. That was really life-affirming, in that sense. I really encourage someone, I think, maybe for people who are looking to get back into the career world or resume something, that if they have an opportunity to go back to school, or be in a classroom again, or have that kind of opportunity, I think it's great.

Q. And the other thing that I am hearing in your story that women really ought to think about is: keep track of your support network. Keep that network strong.

Tish: Right. Well, all the things that you've heard about your friends, your girlfriends, as I have kind of described a scene where it was literally, "Okay. She's got to be out in St. Louis. Her family is staying here. She needs someone with her. How do we make this work?" It was amazing to me that they pulled this off.

"Okay. You're going on Saturday. And so-and-so's going next Saturday."

I never could have made it. We never could have made it without that. That was … one of the real blessings I have had in life, friends like that.

The other thing is when you go through something like this, you learn so much about the kindness of strangers. When I think about various incidents where I got myself into trouble—you know, thought I could do something and ended up totally out of breath somewhere—people were so kind, so willing to help. But the network—yes. Just that, in terms of taking care for me, taking care for my kids—people who were there and wanting to do something and then letting them do something—those were very important lessons.

Q. *Letting people do something. So many of us have a hard time accepting help.*

Tish: Right. It's true. And it was very hard, very hard for me to do, initially. And then, I look back and it's funny, but some of my friends will say, "We had the best time when we were out in St. Louis. We even took some crazy photos and blew them up." Again, it turned out to be a positive experience for them, too. It was, in some ways, a gift to them that they were able to help. And they felt good about it.

For Bunnie, it was her mother's illness that shifted her perspective and led her to work in home health care:

Bunnie: I'm trying to get hold of my mother and expecting a call at work, and she isn't picking up. Long story short, by Sunday, I still can't get hold of her. Now I'm starting to panic. I finally found a number for the neighbor: I'm going to have him go over there and see what's going on. I called her friend, George, from their church. He breaks into the house. And sure enough, my mom had fallen down the steps and laid there for two-and-a-half days. She was still alive, and that was the end of me working. I left Compaq to go up north and start emptying out her house. I was up there for six weeks and by March, we had to fly her down here. She was never able to walk again. So I oversaw her care in a nursing home environment.

Q. *And for how many years did you do this?*

Bunnie: Seven years. And believe me when I say I saw every issue imaginable.

Q. *I'm interested in a little bit more about working with your mother's issues and nursing home care.*

Bunnie: Okay. Bringing her down here was quite the adventure. We still had no idea why she fell. There were little hints, here and there. There was just so much wrong with her. They gave her blood transfusions. She had a dislocated knee that we found out about a year-and-a-half later. I really think the doctors just wrote her off. She was so dehydrated. Her skin had broken down, lying on a cold basement floor for two-and-a-half days.

I think there was something wrong with her right shoulder. They never x-rayed her shoulder. They x-rayed the wrong knee. But the fact that she was still alive was, to me, a wonderful thing. So, the merry-go-round started at the nursing home. It's still one of the best in my area, here in Georgia. I don't have a problem getting my hands dirty. She was incontinent and obviously not walking. Numerous hospital visits. So it became a learning curve.

At this point in my life, I don't trust any doctors or nurses in some of these places. You know, they have these rules and regulations. Even if they don't accept Medicare or Medicaid, it still falls under those rules. Some of them are stupid, like, you can't have a hotdog. One person in Georgia choked on it, that type of thing. So it's the same issues and I still think it has to do with the state regulations, so they won't get sued. Anyway, being bedridden for so long, she had a bedsore and that treatment went up and down like a yo-yo. I was fighting with them at the meetings once a month.

But after seven years, I would say it was really the last three months that it was just pitiful. I knew she was going to be passing away soon. After she passed away, I was home a year. My daughter, Jennifer, was getting married, so I was busy with that. And we were painting and doing all the catching up we should have been doing for seven years. Now it's, like, I have to find something to do. I didn't have a clue. I tried the data entry route. "No, you haven't worked in seven years." No one would ever call back.

Q. It had changed so much, right?

Bunnie: I don't think so. However you input it, it's data entry. If you're doing customer service on a computer, it's the same. No one would talk to me—and my age, too. By then I was fifty-eight, fifty-nine.

I saw an ad in the paper; they were looking for caregivers. I said, "Well, let me just call up. Either they want me or they don't want me." I went to the interview and they saw my background, you know, caring for mom all those years. And they hired me. The lady I was with was absolutely wonderful. I was with her for three years and she had Alzheimer's. I cooked for her and did laundry and helped her in the shower. We went out for lunch when she was "good."

Q. Weren't you also somehow involved with one of your neighbors when you were in Connecticut, who had medical issues or something like that?

Bunnie: Well, I drove them to go grocery shopping. I helped my grandmother, and yes, I helped my neighbor when she had hip replacement surgery. Back then, I just did it. I gravitate to seniors wherever I am.

Q. But it's pieces of the same skills. I'm just saying, you had done a lot of customer service by this time, plus you had been around this kind of care.

Bunnie: Yes, my mom always helped someone, and I was always dragged along, helping the sick. I just didn't think of it that way, but yeah. My neighbor up in Connecticut, she had hip replacement surgery. Her kids were out in California, so I was the one, when she had her surgery, who brought her home, brought her for doctor's appointments, cooked for her that first week, figured out how to get food from her kitchen to where she would eat and watch TV or whatever. I finally made her an apron so she could put her food in containers and get it into the living room to eat.

And then, my grandmother had ovarian cancer. Her blood count was, like, five and she needed a blood transfusion in the beginning and all that. Next thing, she was diagnosed with ovarian cancer. She ignored the letter that said, "Your biopsy wasn't good, so please come back." From January to June, I went up every day. Dropped Jen off at the bus stop or at a friend's house, and up to Meriden I went. And I'd be there on weekends. I didn't trust anyone to care for her as well as I could.

Then the following November, a friend from PTO got the news of ovarian cancer. I helped care for her. I had another old neighbor, and I would take her grocery shopping every Friday, you know, bring in the groceries, and [chat], or whatever. Went to Denny's for breakfast, too. I was taking her to see her husband in the hospital when he had a heart attack. So, yes I did caregiving, but didn't think of it that way.

Now I'm with Visiting Angels and I love it. My client is eighty-eight. Most of them are eighty-eight. She has her own home. A daughter-in-law is a nurse who cares for her during the day and just needs breathing room. She tried other companies, but they loved me and I loved them. And I've already been with them for two years.

Q. Tell me what you think about it. Tell me what you like about this work.

Bunnie: It's giving back for the loss of mom. I've always felt that way. I like helping, I guess. I just, you know, when Jen was little, I always had her friends over. We had a normal home life, where some of these kids didn't or the siblings were creeps. So they would hang out at our house. We always had her friends over. Even when Jen was in high school, the kids always came here. Not everybody has the knack for it. I'm very calm, cool, and collected. The bosses give me carte blanche.

Q. So it kind of sounds like you were born to this. You just didn't know it until pretty late in life.

Bunnie: Yeah. I just find my job so rewarding. Most of the clients are great. I have a fit when I go into some of these jobs and the family is only providing minimum, or they depend on Meals on Wheels, and some of those meals are disgusting. I had one client, his wife had leukemia, so he moved back home with the son. He was living at home. They had us eight hours a day. Meals on Wheels would show up and all he would have was the juice, and the bread, and maybe the fruit. There were so many other people that could have used this food instead of it sitting in his freezer. Don't you know this person can't get to the door and you're leaving the meal? It's a holiday weekend. So, that was one of my pet peeves: people not knowing their parent's health issues. So they're in the hospital, maybe out of state, but they are totally clueless in what to do. They trust everything the nurses and doctors are saying, where I don't.

Back to this one client: I was supposed to see her a week ago. I was supposed to take her to the dentist. She's a little bit of a cripple; she should have had hip surgery ten years ago. Never did. She had a urinary tract infection; it was very bad. She was in the hospital at least ten days and then they put her in a rehab. She was so weak and just couldn't get it going again. After three weeks, she finally got home. Now, I was talking to her about twice a week, just checking in on her. Verified the dental. She says, "I'm not up to it, and I'm still not right."

"Well," I said, "I want you to ask the nurse when she comes to check your blood pressure and everything." At two o'clock in the afternoon, the nurse still hadn't shown up. I said, "Well, call the office." She said she would. I said, "Ask them to do a culture again, maybe you still have a urinary tract infection." Anyway, the following Tuesday, Sue, she was dizzy, and fell, and fractured her left hip. And not the bad hip, her good hip. Now she can't walk. She just went into rehab yesterday. She'll be in there for four weeks. She's having a fit. She also had a bladder infection and that's why she was light-headed and still not right. So I gave her daughter a little bit of a wake-up call during that when she called me, frustrated.

So, it's stuff like that. That's the frustrating part. I'm sad that, when there is family, that they don't have home-cooked meals, nutritious meals. You have to sometimes coax them to eat. Some families are just wonderful. Give me carte blanche to cook whatever I want. Peggy, she forgets that she eats. You know, the Alzheimer's. She tells me she's starving half an hour after she ate. So I'll make her a snack, a fruit cup or whatever. There is always fresh fruit in that household, you know, and then you've got others who don't even have a banana in the house for the potassium that they might need. So, anyway, that's my life, but I just love it.

Louise, as an engineer, former manager, and executive coach, was able to combine her varied experiences and grow her long-time support of Miami University's School of Engineering into the opportunity to fulfill her vision to help engineering students understand the human side of business:

Q. Talk about your ties to Miami University and how that became an opportunity to contribute to the school.

Louise: I've been on the School of Engineering and Applied Science Dean's Advisory Council for, I don't know, twenty years. And the business people on the Business Advisory Council had been chatting, for [about] the last four years, that it was fine that our students knew things about physics and mathematics and thermodynamics, etc., but the world was so tough out there now—so much worse than when we graduated—that they weren't going to be successful in getting their ideas across unless they had the soft skills, too.

All of us come from this background, and we know that we never respected the soft skills. I mean, we just didn't. We know how we were; we thought we knew. Do you know what I mean? We all came from that background. We looked at each other and laughed and said, "Yeah. What could we do about that?"

There was this guy, Doug Troy, who's the associate dean, who had heard about career planning from one of his graduates. That's a different concept than higher education, you know. So somehow these two ideas merged.

We started talking about it. And the more I heard about it, I thought, *I would love to do that. I would really love to create something to help these students make a difference.*

My personal mission statement is to feel the rush from creating, developing, and leading something new that makes a difference. I thought, *If I can open their eyes to make a difference in the world that will do more than I can ever do, because there are whole bunches of them.*

Being one of them, you know, I can look them in the eye and, having worked for so long, it is like and "This is how it is out there." In higher education, all these guys, the professors and all, they are really smart. They do all this research, but they haven't lived in the regular, real working world. So it's just not possible for them to say what it is like, because that's not where they have spent their careers.

Anyway, I spent a lot of time before it actually got started, trying to help put the ideas together so we could get some funding. Lockheed Martin, which has, like, 60,000 engineers ... their chief technology officer at corporate got it in a second. He had no association—probably never heard of Miami University—but he got the issue. So that's how we started.

Q. *Well, you wrote the proposal for this whole thing. And you pulled this whole thing together.*

Louise: I did a lot, yeah.

Q. *You're being very modest here.*

Louise: Although I will say, in this world you really need everybody, especially in this industry. So we made it work for everybody. But I consider the small miracle: It is so fun to watch these students grow in front of your eyes. And it will make a difference to them. I tell them every day, "You're not going like me now. I don't really care. What I really care about is fifteen years from now: is it making a difference in your life?"

Q. *Well, it's going to make a difference in the world, isn't it?*

Louise: It will. They will make a difference in the world if we stress that it's not about playing with the robot, it is about changing the world. Broaden your perspective: you can make a wonderfully positive difference in this world.

They all do their own personal strategic plans. They have their mission statements. They talk about their dreams. They talk about how they want to change the world. They talk about strengths and weaknesses and Myers-Briggs and people and crucial conversations and all that stuff. So all the coaching stuff, I use more than I ever could have imagined. I don't coach them as students; I coach them as adults.

Q. *And as potential leaders.*

Louise: They will be leaders, right? I mean, they are leaders. It's how many people they have working for them that will be different. But they might have an idea, some of them that they'll be leading. They are all really different in their dreams, but you can see it. It's like exposing them to more than just the narrow black and white world. And sort of toughening them up a little bit because, you know, the world is ugly out there and nobody is going to give them a syllabus.

Q. *There is no "Life 101" course.*

Louise: No. And nobody is going to run after them if they didn't turn in an assignment. And if they just sit around and wait for the world to come to them, you know, life isn't going to be as good.

Q. *What is your absolute favorite part of what you're doing now?*

Louise: My favorite part? I think working one-on-one with the students. When they come in and talk about … we have the equivalent of coaching, sort of … how you do Purpose Coaching. We have those discussions, which I have with them one-on-one. I think that's my favorite.

The other favorite which I have is on the other end, in that we have many, many what I call seasoned leaders—not kids—who have a lot of wisdom from over the years. I thoroughly enjoy being with them. You know, everybody's different, right? We have all had different career things. We have all had different life things. So I like that too. And one thing I really love is [that] I'm creating now…we're creating…an Idea Kitchen.

Q. *Oh, how cool! Tell me.*

Louise: So we have an area. What I noticed with students is that, especially in the school of Applied Science … they are all working by themselves. And they've got these little ear things so that they don't hear things, and they're like looking down in their book or at their computer. It makes me crazy, right?

So we are creating an Idea Kitchen. It's got floor-to-ceiling white boards and it's painted bright colors and it's going to have bright-colored poufs that you can sit on. The clock is a gear clock and it's moving. It's going to have a big glass mobile hanging from the ceiling … it's just the idea that sometimes engineers don't see themselves as creative. I mean, they do in their own particular field, but not generally creative. So we're creating a space that's like for teens. And it is fun!

Q. *I know. I love hearing the excitement in your voice when you are talking about this.*

Louise: Yeah. It's really, really fun.

Q. *Yeah. So what is it like having a commuter life?*

Louise: Well, it's the airlines … first of all, I love airports, and I've spent a lot of time in airports. I'm really comfortable. However, I will not lie: I am sick of cancelled flights, I'm sick of delays. It's not easy, but when I think of all of my business friends who have to travel to Asia and all this stuff, and kind of helter-skelter, staying in hotels, I will say this—I have two homes and they both have toothbrushes and stuff in them. So it's not too bad.

Elements of Curiosity and Restlessness

Curiosity is a lifelong quest for learning. Agenia is an avid reader. Phyllis C. loves school. Curiosity is also a sense of exploration. It is what keeps Loretta taking on new projects, and keeps Victoria open to possibilities.

Restlessness can be seen as an extension of curiosity. Both Donna and Larraine spoke of being easily bored. There is also an element of needing challenges. Susan M. and Louise spoke of taking on new challenges.

Curiosity and restlessness show themselves in many ways. Every one of The Fifty enjoyed trying new things, whether new career paths or new recipes (which, for Larraine, became another business). Some, like Louise, had an idea forming many years before she put it into action. Others, like Kathy, often responded to new ideas as they appeared.

Quick to Google? You're curious. Remaining curious could be as simple as exploring websites or reading more about a subject that interests you. Creating a wise, wild, and wonderful life requires taking that curiosity to the next level.

How You Can Develop Curiosity and Restlessness

Curiosity and restlessness don't seem to be characteristics that can be easily developed. You can, however, take steps to keep an open mind and engage in exploration:

- When you see or read something surprising, explore it. Try to find out what is behind the initial impression.
- Remain open-minded about people. There is a quote, attributed to Oscar Wilde, which says something like, "I don't like that man. I must get to know him better."
- Experiment. Take a new route home from work. Try a different food. Try a new activity.
- Read. Read the newspaper. Read books. Read magazines. Just keep reading.
- If you are bored at work, explore why. Can you expand your job? Should you move on?

Exercise

Make a list of things you have always wanted to do or create a board on an online site like Pinterest. This is a collection of potential explorations, similar to a bucket list. Some might turn out to be worth further exploration; some you may drop after a bit of exploration. Now go try one! Not everything will be a great success.

When I finished my doctorate, I had two things I had promised myself. One was to go to Europe; the other was to learn to tap dance. The trip to Europe was wonderful. I explored places I returned to on later trips and I have many delightful memories. Tap dancing? Not so much. I bought the wrong shoes and had an impossible time keeping my balance.

I still can't manage to shuffle off to Buffalo, but at least I tried. And, more important, know I never want to try again. Failure can be fun, though. I have a lot of great stories about my failed experiments. Whether you cussed or not, with the right perspective on the experience you can still be the life of the party.

What small action could you take to enrich your life? Countless organizations need volunteers. You can help out almost anywhere—from the zoo or botanical garden to the library or a senior center or hospice. Most colleges participate in programs that allow seniors to audit courses at minimal or no cost. Museums and restorations need docents. There are a variety of organized long-term volunteer projects, from the Peace Corps to local groups working with recent immigrants. One woman I know volunteers with an organization that helps recent arrivals assimilate and learn English and, as a perk, gets free theater tickets. There are travel agencies that specialize in work experience vacations, where you can try out all kinds of jobs that interest you. You can start with a step as small as research and go as far as you want.

When you lose your sense of curiosity and wonder, you become stagnant. You become bored and stuck in your own life.

Chapter 6

I Can Do That – Openness to New Things

FOR vibrant women, boredom leads to trying new things or juggling a variety of activities, as described in Chapter 5, but there is also an element of thinking, "Why not?" The Fifty did not throw up barriers when presented with something new. Nor did they feel constrained by potential barriers that health, parental influences, or societal pressures tried to impose.

Openness to new things requires both self-knowledge and the ability to be introspective. This openness is not jumping at every new thing; rather, it is about knowing which pieces fit into the puzzle; which new directions make sense; which barriers are realistic and which are imaginary. Bethene described this well.

Q. So you finished this career and you reached retirement. From the outside, it looked like it was sudden, but it probably wasn't. You decided that you were going to create a very different life for yourself.

Bethene: Yes. The first part, though, was to recognize there were capabilities I had as an educator that I was going to call into play for my own life. So for retirement, the first thing I knew was I wanted to address those things that I hadn't been able to do so far—including fitness. I got into a situation with a trainer and did that several times a week.

I started art classes in life drawing at the Montclair Art Museum. I took that class several times over. I hadn't had any art classes throughout the whole of my life to that date. I had gone to a lot of museums, I looked at a lot of art, but I hadn't done any and so I loved those courses. Also, I started going to the Actor's Institute one day a week. This was the general structure I gave myself coming out of teaching and into retirement. I wanted some structure, but I also wanted to leave big chunks of time for more spontaneous kinds of choice-making and so on. The initial idea was to do those things that I had not had a chance to do heretofore. A few years later, my husband and I divorced and I began living on my own for the first time.

Q. I remember you talking about how you helped him get situated in what was going to be the ideal life he deserved.

Bethene: Right. Once again, I think of the educator coming to the fore. I had a real sense of the kind of setting or context in which he would flourish. I helped him find a place and set up his apartment. He began to flourish. Yes, indeed he has. That has been a very, very happy kind of development. And my own has been very like that, too. It has just been flourishing.

My first apartment on my own was in Jersey City. I rented a brownstone there for two-and-a-half years and then it was going to be sold. I needed to think about someplace to move. I recognized, during the time I was in Jersey City, there were weeks when I was in New York City five times. So I dared at that point to think about living here myself.

When I started looking for places to live, I looked in Jersey City again, but I also came into New York City. I like to say that I started out in Iowa and began moving east until finally, there was only the Hudson left to cross. And I decided to cross that, too. I'm living here very happily.

Q. Great. Great. So you had a lot of structure around this plan. One of the things that I loved about the first time you talked about your retirement to me was that you did not say, "Oh, I'm retiring and that's it." So I would like you to talk about how you structured this. I remember you telling me that you were going to do at least two new things a week, try different restaurants, and study different things.

Bethene: Oh, yes, I always have ideas about that kind of thing. The Artist's Way by Julia Cameron has been helpful as well. I've gone through it several times, on my own, in a meditative way with a leader and other seekers, and then on my own again. Some of the tools that are recommended in that book are morning pages, which I think are great. I write them every day; and an artist's date, which entails going to some place different on your own at least once a week, just to keep the creative juices going. In Walking in the World, Cameron adds walking to the tools that encourage creativity. I walk a lot.

But, yes, I do like to have these specific ideas about intentions, I call them. I don't have goals. I have intentions and then I like to be awake to the possibilities that show up. That is a process which, in itself, keeps us alert, I think.

Q. There are a couple of things that you have worked on consistently: the flower arranging, the whole art of conversation, and the salon. Could you talk about that up-close?

Bethene: Yes. You see, a part of these things grows out of saying "Yes." I got into flower arranging because a friend called and said, "There's this weekend offering of Ikebana; would you like to go?"

And I said, "Yes." [Laughter] I'm so glad I did because all of these years later, I am still practicing. I consider it to be my spiritual practice. Flower arranging for me is not just putting some flowers in a vase.

Q. There is also discipline, among other things, involved in Ikebana. True?

Bethene: Yes, right. I studied first with a sensei who had been trained in Japan prior to the war. After my weekend intro, I was told that that was the kind of teacher I should look for. It just so happened there was a woman in that weekend course who was studying with the sensei I eventually studied with. That woman and I are still practicing together; she was just here this week. We made our arrangements for the holiday season. We always start with meditation.

Each of us brings materials we share, then we do the meditation, and we make our arrangements. After we have completed our work and talked about it, we have tea or lunch, depending on the time of day. It is a wonderful, wonderful practice. The principles of Ikebana are something that just radiate through my life. This year as I thought about Christmas and decorating, I thought, *I really don't want to do it the way I usually do it. I want it to be different.* One of the things I have done is to take away a lot. That is one of the principles in Ikebana.

Similarly, Loretta spoke about learning from every experience and had this to say about one of her jobs:

Loretta: You take from a company what you can. I got a chance to introduce a program at Wharton. I got a chance to be able to introduce Appreciative Inquiry to a big organization. I mean, there were so many things to be proud of when I left there, despite the bittersweet experience. There were things about it that were really good, that whole notion of being able to meet people I would not have met in other circumstances—I had lunch alone with Frances Hesselbein. It's kind of interesting and cool, and I left there I guess with, probably a lot of pain, but also a tremendous understanding of how to be able to read what is going on in an organization.

I mean, I knew when my boss was let go that there was something wrong. I wasn't savvy enough to be able to understand what peril she was in. Now I would be able to tell you that. You see all that is going on around you, and you say, "I can see the birds are dancing in the sky in certain ways. I wonder what it means?" I think I'm better able, now, to see what certain things mean, and I think having been away from that gave me a chance to be able to say to myself, "What do I really want?"

[Between the time] I left there and wound up at Saint Francis Hospital—that whole episode of breast cancer, which I will go to my grave believing was an inherited opportunity from the Girl Scouts too—all those things put you in the spot where you become increasingly self-aware and circumspect about things that you might not have thought of otherwise.

Sometimes, openness means letting go of one dream and seeing what comes next. Victoria saw the barriers to her going into medicine as a probable blessing:

Victoria: Because I am a November child, I was always one of the youngest ones in my classes. So, when I started university, I was seventeen. I declared my major as pre-med, and my advisor talked me out of it. He said, "Oh no, no. It's very difficult for girls to do that, and that's not really a good choice for you." He really frightened me out of doing it. And of course I regretted it for many, many years because medicine is something that I really have a passion about. But I'm not sure I would have made it unless I had a burning passion and I was able to push everything else aside for that. I think at that age, I was too young to be able to do that. So, he probably did me a favor.

I majored in English and Speech, married very young, and ended up going on to getting my Master's in Speech Pathology, which I did not enjoy.

Valerie expressed an open attitude wonderfully:

Valerie: I have this thing where if the door opens and I'm not completely opposed to it, I walk through. Sometimes, I think that is how my whole career has been. *Well, that was kind of interesting—I think I'll go over there.* Yes, kind of one door after another.

Lynda made a similar comment:

Q. And it comes back to the same theme of openness and asking and expecting...

Lynda: Yeah. I have this little theme of, if someone else offers something, I always say, "Yes."

Sometimes, it was out of fearlessness and sometimes not, but there was an understanding that it is better to say "Yes" than to let things go. This somehow makes up for the fact that some of The Fifty, whom I would not necessarily characterize as fearless, said "Yes" to incredible things.

They also had the ability to be comfortable with the unknown and not having everything in black and white. Being able to deal with … being comfortable with … ambiguity was a big part of openness to new things.

Phoebe followed this pattern through her career, always remaining open and looking for her next challenge:

Phoebe: Big picture, I am unusual in that I was so old when I had my children because I had my first child at thirty-eight and my second at forty-four. So that's very unusual, I would say. I have done a real full thirty-year career in corporate America and have plenty of energy and plenty of curiosity and intellect left to carry on for much longer. I didn't necessarily seek this out; it was just so readily apparent that this was a very good thing to do.

We have redone eight houses. Every place we have moved—not every place, but most places—we have remodeled the home and done a lot of work ourselves, so that's kind of interesting too. I'm very good with tiling and wallpaper. It's funny.

I don't mean to offend you or anybody else who doesn't have children, but it has just worked out that way for me. Given that they are young, that's really fun because they can keep me up on technology in ways that otherwise, I just couldn't.

Who knows what is next? What is going to be there? I'm open and I read quite a bit to keep current and everything, so who knows? I will never be bored, this I know. I am not wired to be bored.

Well, I think that is one of the things that has been commonly seen in everyone I have spoken to, from people with big careers to people with what I would consider pretty dull careers. Each of The Fifty has the mindset, "Well, what else might be out there?" and, "Maybe I'll try this," or "What's the worst that could happen?" They don't want to be bored.

Kathy's career was comprised of a series of decisions to try new things:

Kathy: It was, probably, towards the end of the school year. I went to my principal and I said, "I'm not going to be back in September." I had no idea where I was going, but I knew that I wasn't coming back to teaching. What I did is, I think, I hired a career helper of sorts. And the recommendation, which happened to be a really good one, was to go interview with a billion companies where you don't even think you might want to work, but just go meet people, chat with them, figure out what the scoop is. And that is what I did.

I remember, after several interviews I landed in an ad agency. I was sitting, waiting for my appointment, and I liked the feel of the place; there was something about it that felt so different from the other places I had been. It felt open. It felt, in a way, more informal or something. I was meeting with the creative director there and he asked me some questions; we were sort of having our little nice … normal interview.

At one point, I said, "You know what? There's something about this place I really like. I think I would really like to work in an ad agency. How do I get a job in an ad agency?"

He asked me a really interesting question, "Are you a creative or an account person?"

I said, "I have no idea. I don't even know what these people do."

He said to me, "Well you don't want to be wearing a suit, so you shouldn't be an account person; so you're a creative. Can you draw?"

I said, "Oh no."

"Well, then, you're a writer."

I said, "Okay."

As it turned out, again, it's like the universe comes in and opens up when the time is right. He happened to be teaching a course for advertising copywriters with some advertising group in the city and he said, "Why don't you take my class?"

I said. "Okay." I took his class, I did great, and at the end of the class he sent me off to talk to two or three of his buddies. One of them hired me and that was it. Within two months, I figured out what was next, bumped into the right people, and landed myself a job and a totally new career.

Now, I took a huge pay cut—more than fifty percent—but it felt like what I wanted to do. I was in Boston at that time. People were telling me, "What the heck are you doing here? You should go to New York—that's where the advertising is." That sounded pretty good to me, so I moved to New York. I just moved down, and figured I would get a job.

I always have these things after I move; there's something wacky. There was a transit strike in Manhattan a couple of weeks after I moved there, so I was interviewing, walking all over Manhattan with my heavy portfolios and wearing heels, of course. I did get myself a job, and I was in advertising in New York. I was doing a bunch of different things, but doing very well and always on the creative side as a writer, assistant creative director, that kind of thing.

One of my friends, whom I had worked, called me and said, "Guess what? I'm moving to Hong Kong."

She was an account person and, as a joke, I said, "Hey, do you need a creative director?"

She said, "Why the hell do you think I'm calling you?"

I'm like, "Are you serious?"

She said, "Yeah. Come on over and work with me. It'll be fun."

I can remember getting out the atlas and looking, getting back on the phone with her and saying, "Are you out of your mind? It's like halfway around the world. You must be crazy." And then we talked and we caught up and stuff and that was the end of it.

Then the next day, I woke up and I thought, *Why not go to Hong Kong*? And within two months, I was living there and I was the creative director of an agency there. I ended up working in Hong Kong for over a year. Then I went down to Singapore and became managing director of the office for another three years and then moved to Milan, where I ran an office there for another couple of years before I came back to New York. So that was a really fun adventure.

It wasn't like I had planned my strategy for getting a job in an ad agency. Going to Hong Kong was the same thing. I had a friend who called me up and said, "Hey, want to come?" And I happened to be qualified and I happened to be at a time of my life when I wasn't encumbered by marriage and kids and schools and all sorts of things. There was no reason not to go.

Looking back, one of the things I can remember after I moved to Hong Kong is I don't know how many friends said to me, "You're so lucky. I never get exciting opportunities like that." Thinking about it, everybody says that, but nobody does it. People think they will move to Hong Kong, but if someone actually offered them a job, 99% of them are like, "Never mind."

I had the balls to do it. I did it and it was great. I got to see the world, I got to earn great salaries, I got to save a lot of money, I was able to buy my house when I moved back to New York, and I learned a lot.

Then the next big change seemed perfectly logical at the time, but looking back, it's like, *What*? I always wanted to do watercolors, and I decided to take a watercolor class. It was a figure drawing class as well. I can't draw people and my stuff was really terrible. I ended up getting into the perfect class for me. The instructor there had an incredible skill of taking students wherever they are and pushing them to the next level.

Within about six months, I decided that was it: I was going to do this full-time. I went to my advertising company and basically said to them that I wanted to take a two-year leave of absence to do this art thing. I arranged that with them; it was unpaid, but I knew that I could have a job after two years, which was a nice sort of fallback.

I left advertising to do art full-time and within a month, I knew I was never going back. It became clear this was not a leave of absence anymore. I had better figure things out because I wasn't going back to advertising and, sure enough, I didn't.

I began taking tons of classes and doing more work, selling my work, getting in shows all the time, making money from selling my work, and I really developed the business. What was happening was all of these artists that I was in process with and in studios with were asking, "How the heck do you do this?"

I started art at, like, fifty years old, so I was like the old lady in the class. A lot of people in my classes had been taking art classes their whole lives, trying to be successful artists and they hadn't sold a damn thing. Here I was, fifty years old, in my second class, and I was selling my work. They were saying, "What are you doing?"

I started telling them what I was doing and then I found out that there were coaches around. I joined CoachVille and I got my coaching credentials, and started coaching artists on how to be a successful artist, how to make money from your art. It developed into a whole business that I realized I was enjoying a whole lot more than selling my own work. I sort of transitioned from being a full-time artist to being a full-time artists' coach.

I then became an instructor at CoachVille. I was doing a lot of teleseminars at CoachVille and I loved it. I just really loved having students. It's terrific to be able to do it by phone; I can do it from home. I could work with people all over the country and all over the world. I really, really enjoyed it, and I did that, probably, for three or four years. I also did a lot of phone work with my own business, with the artists I worked with.

At some point, I got a call and, again, this is a serendipitous moment, like the universe opened and—maybe this stuff always happens all the time, but you just only notice it once in a while. I got a call from someone who was a real estate agent who asked me if I would coach them on building a real estate business. Well, all I knew about real estate was that I had bought my apartment.

I didn't know anything about the business and I thought, *Well, yeah, I could probably do that, but maybe I also have to take classes or something so that I have a little knowledge.* I knew how to coach people on reaching goals and that kind of thing—life, being happy, or reaching goals—but real estate—knew nothing. So, let me get some of that info in there so I can help this person better. I took the licensing course in New York State to learn more about real estate and, at some point, I said to myself, *Well, why am I going to help other people make money with this? Why don't I just do it?*

And I, again, talked to a few people and to a few companies, and moved into full-time real estate, probably seven years ago. And absolutely loved it. I kept on a couple of my coaching clients for a while until I realized that real estate was a twenty-four hour-a-day job, so I closed up my coaching business and did the real estate full time for a number of years.

Then, I come to where I am now and how I got here. Again, it was the universe sending me the right people. One other thing: over the last six, seven years, I lost over 100 pounds with Weight Watchers. In the process … I rediscovered—here's the creative again—my cooking skills.

I can cook anything and started developing recipes that were really delicious and really healthy. I was doing monthly cooking demos with Weight Watchers in Manhattan, fast and fabulous breakfasts, how to throw a party with lots of healthy food, Thanksgiving foods. For Valentine's Day, I did all these desserts that were healthy and good for weight loss.

That started developing into a cooking business where people were saying, "Can you help me with that?" more personally, and that was sort of getting back into the coaching skills, because there is a lot more to weight loss. It's helping people with everything from what costs do they have in the kitchen, to walking someone through their workplace cafeteria and talking about which foods are healthier, and why and that kind of stuff. So that's a whole business that started developing along with my real estate.

So what happened was that a Weight Watcher leader quit his job and moved to Portland, Maine. He opened a cookie shop. I had really considered him an absolute New Yorker who would never leave. He up and left to open this cookie shop in Portland. I can remember sitting with him, this was about a year ago now, talking about what he was doing.

While everybody else was saying things like, "My God, you must be out of your mind. What are you going to do without New York?"

I was sitting there saying, "I am so damn jealous that you got to go on this adventure and here I am, stuck. I'm working in Manhattan in a job I love. I've got to stay, but I'm working a million hours a day, I'm not becoming overly wealthy." It was not like I was socking away two million a year in my retirement fund. I was working hard, I was making a really good living, but I was also spending a pretty good living, living in Manhattan, and here he was all fun and adventure.

Next thing that happened: I had a friend in New Hampshire who came down and stayed with me for a week or so in Manhattan. I told her about my friend who moved to Maine to open a cookie shop, so I said, "I am just so damn jealous of his all fun and adventure and I'm not there."

And she said, "Why aren't you?"

That was really a good question. I would say, within two weeks, I decided that, you know what? I'm ready for a new adventure. The first thing I did, of course, is call my finance guy and say, "If I were thinking about making this move, what's the scoop?"

He basically said, "Well, yeah, you can do that."

"Holy cow." It really took someone I knew doing it and someone posing that question to get me to think about it, because it hadn't even occurred to me that I could stop working and go do something else or stop my real job and go do something else. It had not even occurred to me.

So here I am in Portland, Maine, in the snowiest winter of many, many years. I absolutely love it. I think the most interesting thing for me now is that I am not quite sure where this new adventure is leading me. I thought I was going to come up here and do my cooking business. Now that I'm here, it's not resonating for me, and I think that something else is going to happen—I'm just not sure what that is yet.

My gut is telling me that I am going to be working with other people, probably women, probably women in their forties, fifties, not youngsters, not oldsters; maybe people who are ready to jump off the cliff, and I'm going to be the person that pushes them off and is down at the bottom catching them. I think I want to help people have their next new adventure, in some fashion.

I'm also doing some volunteering, and I'm just getting out and about, learning the city and meeting people, so there is a whole lot going on in my life. I feel like it is, in some way, more in the coaching direction, but I'm not sure I'm going to be a coach, exactly. Teaching, I don't know.

Like Kathy, Loretta was always open to both new challenges and new ways to make connections, learn, and experiment:

Loretta: I learned organizational skills, the idea that we could use software to be able to help and solve a problem, all kinds of things. I considered myself fortunate to be in this position, where everything I was doing was new, and it was learning for me.

While I was at Teachers College, I had gotten acquainted with students who were taking some classes. My interest in self-directed learning had a good, natural connection to e-learning, which was still called distance learning, but the whole thing kind of came together, so I hung out with them. In fact, they introduced Marymount to the possibility of doing something with that, and I kept that interest.

They were pretty good in giving me money to be able to go to conferences. I had gone to Atlanta for one that was just for internal people who were doing some novel things for the first time in online learning. Nobody was allowed—that kind of thing. I made a lot of acquaintances, and we hung out with one another because it was good to know somebody else was trying to go down this road with you in the mid '90s.

We were going to roll out a software package where we had to train 800 people. I said, "This is ridiculous. If we look at all the travel and lodging together for 800 people, it's crazy, the logistics."

I had already gone through leading one software rollout ... at Walk for America. I hired somebody do the instructional design and put the program together for training people around the country. That way, we didn't have to train as many people, probably just four or five hundred. We had to put training centers together around the country and ship computers with software loaded on them.

It was just exhausting, so I said, "Let's take a look at what we can do." They gave me a quarter of a million dollars for the first e-learning program, and the people who were working with me were great.

Debbie was preparing to go in one direction when life presented other options. Rather than seeing her skills in a narrow way, she was open to possibilities and allowed her life to unfold:

Debbie: As I came into college, I found that one thing I really enjoyed was writing and communications skills. I was fascinated by the thought of journalism and being able to, basically, learn so much about the world while getting paid, writing articles on what was happening around the world and with different people and with different cultures. I remember having the sense of being able to turn over every rock and find out what was going on, and how things fit together throughout the world. That was how I ended up with a general focus, first on journalism and then what ended up being a degree in communications, because I was able to put everything together and create a communications degree through an interdisciplinary type of major. It was a great, really broad-based. I also had a minor in international relations.

I've always been fascinated by comparative politics. I started to think more about moving into international journalism or being an international correspondent. Of course, that was really intriguing and exciting back in my college days. But also, I like media; I like production. I liked the thought of taking the information I found as a journalist and doing documentaries to help other people understand the world and understand what was happening in different places and different cultures and different peoples.

Q. So how did that translate into finding a job when you got out of college?

Debbie: Ah, life happens. It never is quite as you intended. In fact, I think I might have told you this story on our first call, that at one point, I was back in Washington, D.C. to do some work on behalf of our company. One of my sons called and said, "I'm just really in a panic. I just don't know what to do."

I said, "What's the problem?"

He said, "I don't have a life plan."

I thought … *Well, when I was nineteen, there were two things I knew I would not do. I didn't know exactly what I was going to do, but I could tell you that I would never be in the insurance world, and I could tell you I never thought I would have kids, either.* And those two things—especially the kids—have been such an amazing part of my life.

How that translated into a job: as I said, I worked my way through university. Just after that first year of university, that summer, I ended up working full-time in the emergency room of a local hospital. And I loved it. It was great work. The physicians and nurses were great. The medics. I just loved the pace. It was a busy emergency ward—it was the trauma center. I really enjoyed it. Because of the schedule—the 3:00-11:00 p.m. shift or the 11:00 p.m.-7:00 a.m. (called the graveyard shift)—I was able to keep up on my schooling and not get a lot of sleep during those years.

But at the end of my schooling, when I graduated with my degree in communications, one of the administrators came down to the Emergency Room and said, "I hear that you have your degree in communications. And we've just lost our public relations person. Would you like to be our public relations coordinator?"

I said, "No, of course not." I was going on to the media market. I was at least heading to Seattle, if not abroad. I was going to be a correspondent of some sort. I was going to have an exotic life.

But I had also done my internship at a local television station and did truly enjoy that. It actually happened to be across the street from the hospital. I think I probably was a little bit conservative about taking off on my own. I thought I would work for a little bit, and earn some money and it wouldn't be a bad job and then I would take off and see the world and do great work.

So I started working. I did enjoy the work, but it wasn't overly challenging to me, I guess. But I enjoyed the work, and … what I was learning, and working with the hospital administration, the board of directors, the community, and designing a program. It did allow me to write.

Then they asked me to be on the administrative team and take a role in program development. That became more exciting for me. I enjoyed that because I liked putting all the pieces of the puzzle together.

So, this actually started to evolve into producing programs; how do we plan for it, and pull all the right stakeholders together, and create the right kind of programs, and ensure that the financial arrangements will be profitable for the program, sustainable. I enjoyed that sense of production, of putting all the pieces together, and making things work. It had a good mission. I mean, it was ultimately to help people and patients coming through the hospital.

One of the programs I ended up developing was a healthcare service contract in the state of Washington, which has the same license capacity as a Blue Cross Blue Shield. We started piloting PPO Medigap products, probably about 1984. The hospital was acquired by a multi-hospital system out of California; they wanted to test a lot of what they hoped to do in the senior market in a media market outside Los Angeles. That was a great deal of fun to be doing and working with the senior marketplace.

We started to take that concept and, beginning with member programs, to package and implement in hospitals around the state of Washington as well. That was called ElderMED of Washington. That's how my college actually translated into a job.

Then I became more involved in the community. I ended up getting married with a two-year-old stepson when I was twenty-four and so, had more responsibilities. I was really lucky enough to have my career evolve here in Bellingham, ultimately with different companies. The acquisition process always gave me the room for advancement and more challenge, while I got to stay in Bellingham, but had a broader perspective around the country.

Q. *OK. And so where did your career go from there?*

Debbie: Well, we continued to grow programs. A number of the programs were related to the Medicare market—The Centers for Rehabilitation and Physical Medicine, The Adult Day Health Program. We did start up the first employer-sponsored daycare in Bellingham, which was great. I had two of my kids go through that as well, which was nice. Then, of course, the healthcare service contractor, ElderMED of Washington, which was really focused on Medicare products, Medicare supplements, at the time. The hospital continued to expand those types of programs.

I was actually working with the ElderMED America Program—which was part of our parent organization, UniHealth America at the time, down in Los Angeles, was actually at a filming of the Golden Girls (you remember that show) when I got a call from the CEO of the hospital. He said the hospital was being sold to the parent corporation of the competitive hospital in town. So, I knew that my job was ended. I was on the administrative team, and this had been an acquisition. I took about three months to make sure that the employees were taken care of and the transition went smoothly. Then I found myself without a job.

I started my own company in marketing and communications, and thought a lot about buying a print shop at that time, to complement the communications side. But the CFO of the hospital had started a company called Olympic Health Management Systems. I started contracting my time; working with this company and helping hospitals around the country start PPO Medigap-type products, such as what we had done here in Bellingham.

Q. *Can I ask you—what got you so bought-into that? I mean, it's very far removed from your initial direction and yet, you had a pretty strong passion for this and kind of kept creating these kinds of programs.*

Debbie: Well, I think it really was the focus on how all the pieces worked together. Again, it was almost like putting all of the pieces of the puzzle together. I really enjoyed that. I loved the business side of it. Through the hospital, the focus was on program development, senior product lines, and on Medicare reimbursement. Those three themes kind of worked their way through, and these three elements were the basis for the start-up of the Olympic companies. All required a huge focus on communication and on pulling the pieces of the puzzle together.

We would go in and evaluate their marketplace, and evaluate their Medicare reimbursement, evaluate the market share, and then structure relationships with insurance companies to create these products and provide the hospital with data that would allow them to understand the best kinds of contracts to participate in the marketplace. It was also creating sales teams. Communication was the theme going through all of it and then, probably, my growing interest in this whole programmatic development and putting all the pieces of the puzzle together. I understand that it's not a solid, direct correlation, but yet the elements of it really are.

Q. Exactly. And that was what I was wondering. There almost always seem to be elements of something that intrigues us and kind of goes through us in life, even though how it appears is not the way we thought it might be.

Debbie: I had a friend, at one point, who was trying to figure out what he was doing in his life. And he said, "I got it figured out. I'm a driver." He was a fisherman, so he drove boats. And then he had heavy equipment, and so he drove the equipment. And so he said he was a driver.

I thought about that back at the time. I thought, *What am I?* I'm a writer. No matter what I do, I end up writing. That's kind of the core theme because, even as a CEO of the insurance company, I would so often write in terms of "these are the key messages" or "these are the key issues" or "these are the key challenges" or, in terms of the strategy, "here's what we don't know and here is what we need to find out." But to me, what pulled it all together for me was the writing.

Shoya took a chance when she moved into the financial industry and again when she left:

Shoya: So I got somebody to introduce me into Loeb, Rhoades. I was there for a couple of years and then got a job at *Institutional Investor*, which was a much better fit. *Institutional Investor* was a very creative place. You know the magazine—are you familiar with that?

Q. Yes I do. What in your background made you feel equipped to do this?

Shoya: I had no idea, except that I was interviewed there. I had a good introduction from somebody, and they just felt that I would be able to organize some good programs. So I worked in a conference department and also did some articles.

It was a wonderful place to work and then one of the people I interviewed once (this was the Senior Vice-President of Citibank) said to me, "When you're ready to leave, give me a call."

At some stage I said, "This is great work because you get a very nice overview, but I'd like to get some more in-depth knowledge of one area or another." So I got back to him and said, "Okay, I think I'm ready to be interviewed." That was the head of the private banking group at Citibank. Within two weeks, he said, "How would you like to go to Hong Kong for four years?"

I said, "Sure, why not?" I mean, I speak all these languages, but none of them is Chinese.

Q. And what was it like being in Hong Kong?

Shoya: It was a wonderful experience for a number of reasons. One, is our office was small. It was very creative. The relationships were very warm within the group itself and the clients were terrific. I covered four countries, and I got to know a lot of the people who run the societies. It enabled me to really understand those countries in depth and to form meaningful relationships with the leaders.

In some ways, I think it drew on my very best qualities. I didn't have to do investment decisions; there were always other people that could do that, the portfolio managers, etc. I just had to keep the relationships going. I am very good at understanding people and getting at what they are trying to accomplish. So that was [my] strength--it was never the investment side--and the clients trusted me. Outside of Hong Kong, I had the Philippines, and Singapore, and Malaysia. Every month I visited these countries, so I was really busy.

I loved my clients and they trusted me and they gave me a lot of money. That's where I began to study the personality differences. My whole system began when I was in Asia, where I picked up a book written by a Harvard professor, talking about these different personality styles.

I remember sitting in the Manila Airport, where I had found this book on the floor, and all of a sudden I said, "Now I understand why so and so—whom I had dinner with last night, he just threw a big dinner party to introduce me to all of his cousins—still has 80% of his assets at Chase. I talk in one way and he really prefers to absorb information in another way. So he likes me personally, but he doesn't always understand what I'm trying to talk about."

So I went back to the office and created a system that color-coded all the clients. It was very good for new business. I continued to use that over all of my next jobs. Okay? Then I came back from Hong Kong, and went to Merrill Lynch, and later went to American Express. For some reason, I can't remember why it wasn't quite as much fun as it was in Hong Kong.

I was really not meant to be on Wall Street—it's just not the best fit for me, even though I like the people on it because they're smart, and I like the creativity in it, but I'm not a numbers person, or not an investment person. So ultimately, I left the industry.

Q. Well, there is a little piece that's not in the bio but at some point or the other, you transitioned into art.

Shoya: Right after I left American Express, I suddenly said, "I'm going to take some time off to do something that I have been wanting to do since I was six years old, and I never had a chance to do it, because my life was so structured when I was little."

I went and studied, I studied at Rockport, Massachusetts for six months and then came back to NYC and I studied at the Arts Student League. Fortunately, I had a really nice Rolodex of friends from my activities with the financial community. So when I threw my first show, all these people turned up and bought paintings, so it was really nice, very nice. I had this wonderful mentor who had this beautiful townhouse that used to be owned by Jock Whitney; he gave me his townhouse for an evening.

So I had that show and, after selling some eighty paintings and continued painting for couple of years, then one day I woke up and said, "I really miss the business community." I began to look for ways in which I could have my own business and still connect with that business community. That is when I decided that what I had always, always loved to do is to teach, so why not train? I took my personality model and moved it into a training vehicle, and that's when the offer for the first book came, so I have written three books.

Cheryl was very successful in marketing. She also took a risk in trying to transition from marketing to advertising:

Cheryl: When I got close to that ten-year point, I was getting restless. I thought a career in the ad agency sounded so interesting and so much more exciting, so I actually went in and interviewed with some of the big New York City ad agencies. Even though I had ten years on the client side and was the director of marketing for a very large company, they all looked at me like, But you have no experience in the agency business. They all had these start-up programs they could put you through, but the pay was very low.

I thought, *I'm not ready to restart my career*, so I said, "The heck with this, I'm just going to start my own advertising agency," which I did. I took my technology company that I was working for; it actually became my first client.

I owned an ad agency on Long Island for ten years. We had a lot of high-tech companies. And then, very close to the ten-year mark, my agency got acquired by a big ad agency in New York City. It actually happened to be one of the agencies who did not want to hire me or who would have to put me through one of the training programs. I always thought, you know, *Revenge is sweet*.

So I joined them. That's how I got into the advertising agency world. I really love that side of the business, and that was where I spent the next ten years of my career, before leaving [advertising] about five or six years ago…starting a marketing consulting firm, and then starting the *Three Tomatoes*.

When I stepped out of that world and into the world of the *Three Tomatoes*, it just opened up these amazing opportunities and amazing chances to meet so many people whom I just would never have met had I stayed in that little circle, opportunities to get involved in other organizations. For example, I am very involved with UN Women. It was really through a Three Tomatoes subscriber who reached out to me and said, "I love what you're doing, and how you're focusing on women giving back, and women supporting groups. I'd like to tell you about this group."

I ended up being invited to join the board and the last three years, I have been president of that organization, which has been great. But that would not have happened had I stayed in that other little world. I always like to say to people—in fact I was at a conference last week addressing some women—I think it is really about just being open to new possibilities and new opportunities, and keeping your mind open, and not being afraid to jump in and try things, and say, "Hmm. I wonder where that's going to go."

Q. That's fantastic. Let me ask you about the UN women. Tell me a little bit about how you got involved and tell me how that has evolved and become a big piece of your life.

Cheryl: I have to say, all the years I was involved in what I was doing, I was never really involved actively in women's issues. But really, over recent years, I think my awareness and my consciousness-raising has been around women's global issues. We are so privileged to live in this country. Sure, there are still issues we need to address here for women. We still make less money than men on average; we are still not represented on corporate boards in political leadership, even though there are more women in Congress. But we don't live in dire danger and dire circumstances every day.

The more I became aware of how really a majority of women in this world live and are still living in the Dark Ages, we privileged women in civilized countries have a moral obligation to do something and speak up and lend our voices, because we really can change that.

The great thing about getting involved with the *Three Tomatoes* is starting to meet other women through other organizations. I now have this great appreciation for the power of women when they work together. What they can do that raises issues is so critical, because I think we really can change the world. When we empower 80% of the women in this world, then that will start to create change.

So the United Nations Women opportunity came along just as this was starting to seed itself within me. And I'm like, "Wow, here's an organization that is on the ground in so many of these places, has the power of the UN behind it, is the voice within the UN to all of the different organizations to make sure these issues are on the agenda, and is actually doing concrete things."

I knew that was something that just made sense and I could be passionate about.

Like you, like many of us, we have been invited on other boards, and sometimes you will say "Yes" because it seems like a nice honor, but you get on and suddenly, it is not something you feel passionate about. I have served on boards and left and said, "You know, this just doesn't feel right for me." So this is something that does feel right and that I am very passionate about and I love having the opportunity to do that. We have a very active chapter in New York, so what I have been able to bring to it is the marketing expertise, so that more people are finding out about what we are doing, what UN Women is doing, and what the issues are.

Impetus to Change Direction

Victoria credits her move to a different format to something she heard on the radio:

Victoria: It was kind of an accident. I never read anthologies. I knew they existed but they were never a form of literature that really appealed to me. Occasionally, I read a book of short stories, but the personal essay was totally an alien concept to me. I had no idea what it meant, but I was in a car one day listening to National Public Radio (NPR) and I heard somebody say the expression "the other woman." And for some reason, I thought, *Wouldn't that be interesting to get bunch of writers together, writing about their experiences with infidelity?*

Betsy summed up what it meant to her to be open to new things:

Q. So what haven't I asked you that you think is important for women over forty who are thinking about their lives?

Betsy: Well, I think that some of the important things are: [First,] to find ways to get comfortable with taking risks. That will give you many opportunities to see what you like and you don't like. Second is, certainly, don't think so much about failure. I mean, my own feeling is, as long as I learn something from an experience, it is not a failure. So try things, see if they work. If they don't work, figure out why they didn't work and dwell on those lessons. I think the more open people can be to new experiences, to putting themselves in different situations, the better.

And I think the other thing is, of course, in my role in The Transition Network. I talk to a lot of people who say, "I loved working in the non-profit sector. I'm thinking about a change and I really could do so many different things. I have so many interests, I could do so many different things."

So, one of my more tactical pieces of advice is, "That's great, but pick two things, and walk around and tell people you're interested in those two things." If you say, "I'm interested in different things; I could do anything," nobody can help you. So you need to help people to help you by getting specific.

As it happens for me over and over again, give people that "velcro," so that when they hear something, your name sticks to whatever they heard. And they can help you, because people want to help each other; they just need you to make it simple.

Q. That's wonderful; that is terrific advice. One of the things I often do with a client is have them do a skills sort: they need to look at the things that they love and are good at; the things that they don't love but would not mind doing in support of the things they want to do; the things that they have to do; and then there are a whole bunch of things that—it doesn't matter how good you are—you have to put them on the trash sheet. You just have to let go of them, because that stops people from doing that "all-over-the-place" thing and gets them to exactly what you're talking about: "Here are one or two things that I know I can do, that I'm really good at, and I'm going to go with that." I love hearing that from other people. [Laughter]

Betsy: I do think this is a period for experimentation, where you can try lots of different things. I'm all in favor of that. I want to find more activities that have meaning. That is, something that enhances my life powerfully, whether it is paid work, unpaid work. Then,

I think you need [to do] some hard work and get focused and then use your network. I mean, that is actually the other piece of advice I have for people: A wonderful benefit of being our age is that you know a ton of people, and people in dimensions that you never even thought about.

So as soon as you can get clear on what you are looking for, start talking to people. Talk to your dentist, talk to your hairdresser, certainly talk to your college classmates, talk to your bridesmaids, talk to your family and their friends, and you will be absolutely amazed at what comes back to you.

Most of us have an idea now and then that we might do something different, but can't seem to muster up the strength or energy to make the change. Self-confidence was an important factor for The Fifty, in the ability to remain open to new things. These women were sure enough about themselves to experiment with no guarantee or expectation of a particular outcome.

Victoria: All of these things and having the experience of that play gave me the confidence to move forward. I am working on a play that I dearly love and you know what will happen? I have no idea. Will the film be made? I don't know. Identity Films optioned the screenplay and they have been at my side every single step of the way, no matter what I have asked; they have been there to give me the guidance I needed. So they are excited about the project and, I think, if the movie has the merit, they will be able to sell it. But who knows? I don't know.

As my granddaughter said when she was eighteen months old, "I no-oh." I no-oh either. We just don't know. But you don't know and you won't know until you try, and that is the difference between who I was fifteen or even ten years ago and who I am today. I am willing to try it all. If it's ethical, if it's fun, if it's creative, if it's exciting, if it's energizes me, I'm for it. I'll give it a try; I'll give it a shot. If it doesn't work, okay. Those things happen.

That's what my life's about; taking risks, and pushing myself, and pushing myself to new areas, and challenging myself, and then seeing what happens. As it happens now, because of the energy that I have created around what I'm doing, I get invited now to speak to women's organizations about taking risks, and the issues and the non-issues of age and creativity and women.

Charlotte got into an unexpected new venture because she needed to reduce her property taxes:

Charlotte: We had gotten our property taxes. We lived, at the time, on Old Hickory Boulevard with forty-eight acres. When we got the property taxes ... they tripled that year. And [my husband said] "Oh, my gosh. Oh, my gosh. We've got to green belt [make changes that create a green environment] ... we've got to do something."

So I thought, *Okay, good! I'll grow pumpkins and sell them. That's green belting!*

He saw an ad about the benefits of raising alpacas, not just the ability to have these cute, wonderful animals, but there were tax benefits. You could green belt, but then the alpacas themselves, you can insure them. They multiply, so you know, it increases the value. So he thought this would be a grand idea.

At the time, we had horses and donkeys. One donkey I had rescued—they were putting her to sleep, and she was pregnant. Petunia came to live with us. And then we had Applesauce. One night after Petunia got loose and got in the apple orchard and just made herself sick, she just popped out Applesauce the next morning.

So he said, "We could have another barn, we've got the space."

I kept telling people, "Do not make eye contact with him; you know what'll happen if..." He is the most fun person, loves animals, loves doing this, but let's just say that when push comes to shove, knowing animals, he's never lived on a farm, he never had livestock that was sizable, and I was like, "I don't want to do this ... I don't want to."

One day, he came in and said, "Let me ask you one question: do you not care about my blood pressure?"

I said, "Of course I care about your blood pressure."

He said, "But what you're saying is I can't have alpacas; we're not going to do it because it will lower my blood pressure. It will make me happy and make me live longer, and you're saying "No.""

So we got eighteen alpacas, first go-round, and built a barn. We were having so much fun with it; it wasn't just having animals there. We got into the high-end breeding of animals. I got into looking at, you know, if you breed this way or that way, you're breeding all the time because you want their fleece to be better.

So Michael would go out and say, "I just bought such-and-such bloodline." He came home early one day. Everybody realized this was his deal, you know, I was just kind of going along. A truck pulls up and he says, "What's that?"

I said, "I don't know. Go in the house; you're not supposed to be home."

I was thinking, *Get him out of here, quickly.*

The truck pulls up and downloads twenty-one alpacas. I had decided that I wanted blacks because most of the ones we were seeing were whites. I thought, *There is a big market for the yarn; it's all-natural, it's all organic.* I also thought, *I want blacks. I want some blacks in there, to be well known for grays and blacks.* So I went out and I got every black female that was pregnant, every black girl that was capable of throwing a black, gray or black.

I was kind of sheepish and said, "This is what I just did."

He said, "Well, when you have that gut instinct ..."

I said, "I do have this gut instinct," which was great because we became well-known for our colors. We had blacks and grays, which are a little more rare than your whites and your fawns.

We decided that we loved what we were doing. We built a second barn, and then we had to fight Forest Hills, as it was in the middle of a Nashville neighborhood.

So we asked ourselves, "Do we want to keep the number we have and have fifty, sixty alpacas … or would we like to really get involved more in this business and have more alpacas?" We decided we did want the latter, and we … looked for farms for several years.

When this one came open in Leiper's Fork, we knew that was it. So we bought the farm, moved our farm manager and the animals out there for a couple of years before we moved.

They have a National Alpaca Association meeting every year, and, for a number of years, it has been in Louisville. He came in, like a little kid with a new toy, and said, "I have the biggest surprise for you!"

I said, "What?" with, you know, that tone kind of like "beware of the wolf in sheep's clothing."

He said, "I got you the last slot in our class at the national convention. They only take eleven, and you got the eleventh slot!"

I said, "What is it?"

He said, "Birthing!"

"Birthing?"

"You know; come on!"

I said, "Well, what are you going to do?"

And he said, "I'm going to marketing."

So I went to my first class. You have to stick your hand in a … a simulated place and it has a real dead cria—a cria is an alpaca baby. You have to turn it, remove it, and figure out how to get around it, and I was, *Oh my gosh. I don't know if I can do this.* But, you know, I got in there and started sitting and listening, and Michael came over to have lunch with me, brought his little box lunch, and I was watching the film, the optional film, and he had to get up and leave.

So he can birth … every time there's a camera, Michael is showing his abilities. You know, he will be picking up the baby and carrying it, but never shows that Jake and I were in the background, getting this baby taken care of, cleaning it up, and helping the mother.

So I have birthed babies, I have turned breech babies around, I can give shots. When we do the ultrasound for the babies, if they are huge and have ribs, I can see them. But if they are just thirteen, fourteen days, when everybody else is going, "Oh, look at that! Look at that!" I'll be going, "Yeah, isn't that great!" and I'm thinking, *I don't see anything.* But that's why we have a farm manager and have somebody else to run the day-to-day.

Q. But you still seem to have a lot of hands-on with these alpacas. I'm curious as to how you manage to do that and still maintain your career the way it is and, in fact, have it get bigger.

Charlotte: Well, two years ago, I decided I wanted to grow my businesses even more with UBS and what I really love. I had a manager for our home that was just my right hand, and I thought I could just turn more of the things at home over to Marilyn.

At the shows, I would be the one that sent them into the show ring. We have won; we have hundreds of blue ribbons and purple banners for championships from all over the country. We have a staff of three people now. We have decreased the number of animals we have; we were getting too big.

I guess luck has a lot to do with ... you know, you can be successful, and you can do it by working hard, being smart, and there's always a little smidgen of luck that, I think, comes into it, too. But from the first alpaca national convention that we went to, I sat next to somebody, just by happenstance; it turned out she was the retailer of the year, for a number of years, for alpaca products. She has them manufactured and then has her own company she sells them through. I thought, *Okay, I'll do this.*

On Farm Day, we always have alpaca socks, alpaca sweaters, and things. We opened a winter arts store in the middle of Leiper's Fork, and Ann gets fine arts in there, the gallery, and a woman who is running it now for me, did jewelry. After it was over, it had done so well that they said, "Let's keep it open."

I said, "As long as I don't have to be involved, and as long as you don't expect me to be at the store, I'll order merchandise, and pick it up and get it to you, but we'll do it." So we have been open for about a month and a half, and are already showing profit.

I have the contacts in ordering. A lot of it is American-made; a lot of it is made in Peru, from the Fair Trade. I am actually having some things made specifically for High Meadow Alpacas. We are doing some throws using silk and alpaca. We had a line of alpaca sock monkeys, all hypoallergenic, all stuffed with alpaca—they are such adorable things. I am going to take them over to Children's Hospital and see if they have an interest in buying some of our alpaca monkeys.

I just have fun, and I can't sit still. When I am sitting still, I'm still thinking of ways to do other things.

Natalie was open to adventures and growth experiences and drew several themes through different professional experiences:

Q. There were some themes, weren't there? I mean, looking back, do you see some themes with these things?

Natalie: Absolutely. Themes and definitely ... patterns. But [I was not thinking], *I think I will do that.* It was more, *I think I'll do that in the future.* [Something] would show up and I would think, *I'll do that now.* I am not suggesting this as a route for anybody or everybody because it definitely has its downside; there is not a lot of stability there. If you were somebody that really needs a lot of stability and assurance, this would not be a path for you.

There have been times that I questioned it myself because it has to have, obviously, its ups and downs and struggles. But when I look back, I realize I could not live any other way.

I started getting more involved in my parents' and in-laws' care as they were getting older, and there was something about this age group. There was something about the elders that drew me, really drew me in. I do see a correlation with young children also. Oftentimes, the young children and elders do not get the focus that really is required for them to move through life in a way where they can get their needs met.

As we grow from early childhood, we start to develop some of the self-care, self-reliance models that [tell us] we can take care of ourselves. I still think there's vast room for improvement in … people learning what their needs are and how to get them met, but we're more apt to be able to do that when we're of a certain age.

Then, once you reach the other end of the spectrum—I define elders as eighty and above—there's a really wide range there, because obviously, we're all humans and we're all different—there is brain research that does support that after the age eighty, the brain make some significant changes, but we haven't really focused that much on what happens after eighty.

It is a very different developmental stage of life in seniors. I found it really fascinating they were faced with a lot of the same frustrations as young children have when they are not being heard … not being listened to, and resented for the knowledge that they have. I know young children have a vast amount of wisdom and knowledge that we can learn from. The same is true with elders, yet somehow, we have lost sight of that. Without being too negative, this is the side of eldercare that really concerns me.

I am working in a field and, hopefully, making some changes, even if it is throwing a pebble in the pond and letting it ripple. I hope that is what I am doing already … because it seems like an incredibly big task.

The reason I chose to homeschool my kids had a lot to do with … feeling this frustration of: You're not looking at the individual and helping them grow to get their needs met so they can be happy and have fun. It all comes down to, What do I want in life? I want to have fun. Now, I don't believe everybody else just wants to have fun in life, but for people who do, there's not a whole lot of guidance. So that is my job—to provide that guidance. How do you like that?

Q. I love that. Let's go back to where you are becoming more and more involved with elder care within your own family circle.

Natalie: That's how it began, yes. I started noticing some of those parallels and also some of the distinct issues that were showing up with elders that were not really being addressed. It's really common for family members to make the assumption that, My parents probably can't process the way they used to, so I have to come and just do everything. It is true they don't process the same way they once did, but that doesn't mean that the most appropriate approach is going and doing everything.

There are ways you can learn to relate to people in this stage of life in a way that preserves their dignity, respects them, and really elicits their answers. We have this assumption that they don't have the answers anymore, so now I have to take care of them. There are certain things, some custodial care that's going to need to be done, but I'm finding that in cases of dementia, that is not always true. I think it surprises people sometimes. I have had some pretty wild and pretty remarkable experiences. I can choke up just thinking about it.

The other thing that I do in that sphere, I do reflexology. Actually, that interest began in high school as well, but there is also a healing modality called entrainment. What entrainment reminds me of is Bucky [Buckminster] Fuller's philosophy around tetrahedrons being the strongest structure in the universe. Okay, stay with me; it ties together. So entrainment actually [requires] you putting your attention in three places at once. It's not multitasking; that's not what multitasking is. This is putting your conscious attention three places at once, which creates this energy shield. So I have decided that I want to experiment a bit with tetrahedron reflexology. It doesn't exist, mind you. That's my own thing, but I wanted to play with that and see. So I was practicing reflexology on another friend of mine who has dementia. It was so beautiful because, as we got further and further into the massage piece and as I energetically was there with her, she looked at me at one point. I could see a shift in her body and she said, "You're going to think this is silly, but I felt that in my heart." That is a pretty powerful statement, and this was from someone with dementia. I knew exactly what she meant. It was so powerful, and it is so important to me.

Q. I think it shows how these different pieces are connected to each other and how you move back and forth between different things. What are you doing to generate income since you left the pre-school?

Natalie: Well, the coaching piece, in general, informs my way of life. It informs everything that I do, it informs every conversation, every decision that I make; it is very much ingrained in me. Part of the reason it is ingrained in me is because once I started coaching, I followed that path, actively working in the coaching community. So that's part of the income I get through coaching individual clients as well as working for a professional coach organization.

Q. You were also teaching coaching for a while for a coaching school.

Natalie: Yes. I taught coaching for a while and that is one of the reasons I think it's just so much a part of me now. It's who I am and, in so many ways, as corny as it sounds, it is really what I was born to be. I always knew that's what it was.

In fact, after I had been coaching for a few years, I found an old journal of mine I had written in '94, '95. There was entry in the journal that pretty much describes coaching, "…if I could do this, this is what I would do for a living". I almost forgot about it; I put it away. I thought, *Look what I manifested.* I think I manifested coaching in my life; isn't that wonderful? So when I found that journal entry, I laughed and thought, *Wow, that's what I'm doing.*

The other piece is my private coaching clients, because I could never do just one thing at once. I have created a couple of projects around elder care. One is a business, but I created the Ageless Sages books for elders. That started in 2007 and now, I'm also on a board with people who are interested in changing the face of elder care—particularly for people with dementia—who have a philosophy that doesn't include pharmaceuticals. That's a challenge for group residences, assisted living, and memory care units because, quite honestly, there is a reliance on medication. Not so much because it's going to reverse any effects or even reduce any effects, but it does create easier behavior management.

Some of The Fifty moved into fields that were more clearly related to earlier employment. Herta was open to trying something that was very new, yet still drew on her past professional experience:

Herta: When I left AIG I was, okay, that was in 2005, so I was forty-seven. So I started to look at, What do I do now? In 2005 and 2006, I took multiple trips to Africa, and I became fascinated with microfinance. Up to that point, Africa was always a place where my husband and I would go on vacation.

It would literally take me forever to unwind when on vacation. But, for some reason, when we went to Africa, being in the Serengeti or the Ngorongoro Crater or places that were so magical, if you will—to me, so magical—I completely unwound. During my investment banking days, Africa became this wonderful destination of respite, of something so magical and so different.

But I was not oblivious to the incredible poverty and so forth. And so, in 2005, 2006, I took several trips to Africa, and I kept asking the question, "What are the consumer industries that are at the core of poverty alleviation?" We have probably dumped over a trillion dollars of aid into Africa with limited, limited success. I said, "There's got to be more to it," and I started to look at microfinance. I started to very much think as a banker, as an investor. I said, "What can I do here?" It took me a while to figure this out.

Because I looked at trends, I looked at demographics, and I said, "You know, the world we're living in is just not sustainable," because in Europe, the population is shrinking. In the U.S, it's maybe growing by a hundred million by 2050, but you are looking at emerging markets and you are looking at a continent like Africa where the population is going to double by 2050. So you know it's going to be a continent with two billion people at the time when China is blossoming, when India continues to grow, etc. If we look at demographics, we need to start thinking about, How do we invest and how do we capitalize on these very favorable demographics?

Then on the other side, the whole climate change debate. I became very, very interested in climate change and, more broadly, the whole energy security issue; because it is very clear there is a direct correlation between energy consumption and standard of living. The more energy people consume, the higher the standard of living. It is not a coincidence that the energy consumption in the States and Western Europe, etc. is as high as it is and the standard of living is correlatively high. So I looked at the energy security issue globally and basically felt that really Africa was becoming a very, very interesting destination for investment.

So I set up Ariya. I capitalized it; I set up my own company. This was in 2008. I was fifty years old. In 2008, I had climbed Kilimanjaro for my fiftieth birthday. That's a whole other story. I set up Ariya just before the crash.

Q. We are going to circle back to Kilimanjaro, but let's get Ariya set up first.

Herta: Yes, so I set it up with the verbal backing of two major financial institutions. Then, within weeks afterward, we have the crash in September, and this was a shock. This was really my third career, but this is really a calling, in a sense, because Ariya, to me, is just a vehicle that brings out some of the best in who I am. It's also the most difficult thing I have ever done because, after the crash in 2008, there was practically no risk type for Africa; certainly, no capital type for what I would want to do.

So, I invested my own money and put a lot into the company. I am delighted to be at the point where we are now: we have become a good developer of clean, renewable infrastructure projects in Africa. It has taken a long time to get the trust of heads of state because what we are doing is addressing the fundamental energy security issues and infrastructure issues in these countries. One of the flagship projects we are working on right now is an airport in Uganda.

I will be in Kampala again next week to meet with President Museveni, to get the land lease. We will be getting four thousand hectares of land, over twelve thousand acres of land, to build a cargo terminal or passenger terminal. It will be the first solar-powered airport in Africa. We put together a consortium to do a large eco-industrial processing center and then to build a solar panel assembly plant. So that is a flagship project for us.

It has taken a long time, literally under the scrutiny of people like President Museveni. And then, after months and months, he basically decides, *This is the person I want to deal with.* So that has been a major, major breakthrough for us.

We are working in Uganda, in Tanzania, in Kenya. We are going into Rwanda and Utopia. It has been a long haul and a painful process at times. I have made the transition from a high-flying corporate executive to entrepreneur, where you are chief cook and bottle-washer.

I mean, I have always been entrepreneurial, but all of a sudden, having your own company and it's your name and it's your money and it's your reputation. And you have no safety net to fall back on, and you don't have a stipulated company behind you. You don't have anything. Every mistake that you make is glaring.

To me, that transition has been one of the most challenging, and I feel like I had the most growth during this time. I made plenty of mistakes, but I also wouldn't change it for anything. But that would be a completely separate book, "How to Become an Entrepreneur After a High-Life Corporate Career," you know, for all the women out there who are looking at what they are going to do when they are after fifty.

Openness in All Aspects of Life

Openness to new things is not simply a professional issue; that characteristic carries over to other aspects of life. It's the trait that allowed Larraine to expand her farm products to include a line of preserves and cookbooks. Openness is what led Kathy to take her first art class. And for Sharon, openness created interesting life changes. Sharon speaks about opening up to finding love:

Sharon: I was not married. I was single for a long time, and I wanted to marry. This is a story I really love because … it is a major one in my whole life. I was separated, and my first husband, with my kids, was killed. So I had been alone for a very long time.

I started deciding that I really would like to meet somebody. Actually, it was Phyllis; thanks to Phyllis pushing me, I put an ad in the paper, a little local paper where I lived, which was Palatine, Illinois. It wasn't like today with the computers; this was in the '90s. At the same time, I was seeing a counselor, just for some life support and direction.

Simultaneously, I had this vision, this incredible vision of me on the back of a motorcycle; I had never ridden a motorcycle in my whole life. I'm on the back of this motorcycle and there is a guy and I can't see his face. We are going over this low, one-car bridge with flagstone on the sides. It is a real pretty little bridge and it opens to a massive green meadow with flowers and trees all around the perimeter. I never see his face; I'm just holding on in the back. I told my counselor this, and she went numb. She went, "Sharon! That is a very powerful dream!"

Well, I met a man shortly after that whom I married. We lived an absolutely incredible life and wound up traveling to sixty-some countries, one of which was Africa. That was another dream I had as a little kid. I mean, I was in the fifth grade, and I decided to go to Africa.

I wound up going to Africa, of course. Anything I really wanted [in life], I think I just never lost sight of. I went to Africa by myself because nobody else would go. I sat on the side of a lake at five in the morning and watched a panorama of all these animals coming in. Fantastic! Stupid, but fantastic. I thought, *God, if I were only here with somebody I loved.*

Several years later, Doug and I were in Africa. We were driving in a Land Rover by ourselves, with our driver, and all of a sudden, I see this lake.

I go, "Stop! Stop, stop, stop! Let me out! Let me out!" And I said, "Doug! This is where I told you! You are here with me! And this is where the elephants came in. This is where the baboons were. This is where the mongooses were. This is where the buffalo got killed and the panorama unfolded." It was just the most amazing moment.

We traveled together. My little ad that I wrote for the local paper, he found it because his daughter wrote for the little local paper. I said that I was looking for someone who loved adventure travel, photography, was honest, and had a zest for life. And he showed up, and that is what we did for the rest of our life [together], until he died on December 20, 2012.

We have a big family, and my husband instituted many, many wonderful things to bring all the family together in a fun and energetic way. So he is going to be terribly missed. He added so much to our lives.

Now, Sharon is looking for her next projects:

Sharon: I think I am only starting to look at where I go from here. Three things I look at: purpose, self, and health, probably first, because without your health, you're kidding yourself if you think you aren't going to be limited in doing the things that you want. Then, I really do believe having satisfying, interesting pursuits—whether you call that work, or volunteer work, or something—is going to be essential.

One of the ideas I came up with because I have a granddaughter that has four kids and they are having a hard time making healthy meals on a budget. I thought if I could take a low budget and figure out how to make healthy, good meals do-able, I could open a practice and charge for coming into a home and working with a family to develop a real plan for eating smart on a budget. I like the one-on-one.

Working with the elderly was another [idea]. I think they get ignored: If they aren't able to run a marathon, they aren't worth talking to. I think there is an unfortunate gap in our society when it comes to the elderly; they are sort of put on a shelf instead of integrated. If I could be inspirational, to help ignite any interests that they may still have ... I don't know how I would go about it, but to give them a sense of possibilities.

Q. So, I am just going to ask ... is there anything else you can think of in the moment that we haven't talked about?

Sharon: I do have one thing else that you may find of interest ... this was after my husband died. Two things happened: one, I took over his phone and he had his Kindle on his phone. I started looking at all his books, and I realized what a story it told about him. Then I see he has an office full of books.

I started thinking about when a person dies, how they fade into ... like they have never existed. I thought, *I'm not going to let this happen.* I decided to make a list of all the books he read, that he really liked—and they were so diverse.

I am telling you, Susan, how that affected me; I felt like he was with me. I was elated, like he was walking with me for all that day and the next day ... I felt like I could turn around and talk to him. That is how present he felt . Everybody that I have given it to, so far, loves it.

I think phase two of this process is going to be a book called *Pop-Pop.* I get choked up about it. I want these kids to know who their "pop-pop" was. They can read it and know him. They will know him through the stories. They will know him through his books. They will know who that person was, in a deep and real sense, and in an interesting sense. Not just a picture, or not just, you know, oral conversations once every three years when they are sitting at a table. They can sit by themselves and digest it. So I want him to be real forever, in the lives of the people related to him.

While some women were clear early in life about what they wanted to do, others came more slowly into a realization of their purpose. Deb R. spoke about realizing exactly what she was called to do:

Deb R.: At that point, I was really clear. The boys were little and so I left there in '88. Peter took me to my first astrology reading, and I went to my first channeling things with him. He was, kind of, the catalyst for all the woo-woo stuff that is such a big and wonderful part of my life and work now.

My affirmation, that I would say every day on my way to work when I was looking to leave TIAA-CREF, was, "I have interesting, challenging part-time work that pays well and gives me more time with the boys."

I ended up, for two years, as the VP of administration for this small employee benefits consulting firm (that had been one of my brokers, one of the people I worked with at Union Mutual) for three-and–a-half days a week, which was terrific. I left there in 1990. Peter had started his kid celebration personalized cassette tape business at that point. I worked with him and helped him with that for a couple years. I had the flexibility to bring the boys to school and pick them up and that kind of thing, but it did not feed my soul in any way.

And '92 was one of those real pivotal years when this bunch of things happened within months of each other. I went with a good friend, who is a therapist, when she went to get a tarot reading by a woman who was also a therapist who did tarot, Ellen Goldberg. I was blown away by what she told my friend. So I went back and had my own session, and that blew me away. I ended up studying both tarot and palmistry for a couple years. At the same time, I was shopping Unitarian churches in the city, having really just found out about them, and walked into 4th U [4th Unitarian Universalist Church], and basically never left.

I was introduced to the whole notion of the divine feminine by the minister at that point, Darrell Berger, one of the founders of the Covenant of Unitarian Universalist Pagans, which is a denomination-wide organization to support the pagan community and the earth lovers and goddess lovers in Unitarian Universalism. For me, that just cracked things open. It was like, *Oh, my God! This is what has been missing in my own personal connection to the divine, this whole notion of the goddess.*

I went to my first women's ritual there, heard Phyllis Curott speak. She is the reformed lawyer who ended up taking on the helm of one of the major pagan organizations of the city and fought, and probably still does, for legal rights, religious rights, and religious tolerance for pagans. Margot Adler, who is still a broadcaster on public radio, wrote a wonderful book called *Drawing Down the Moon*. She came to talk at 4th

U. You know, all this stuff happened within, literally, six months.

I started, at that point, just inhaling everything I could find about astrology, tarot, women's spirituality, the goddess. Somewhere, Jung kept showing up. I remember thinking, God, where was Jung when I was a Psych major? I felt like I was in school.

At some point, after about two years of this—inhaling everything and going to courses at the Jung Institute and whatever I could find, checking out different women's spirituality groups—I answered an ad in one of the big astrology magazines for a counseling training program that was taught all by therapists who were also astrologers.

It was very cool. It was all this psychology stuff and all the different models of counseling, but then, with all the archetypes of astrology brought in, and art and science. The director of this program—Joseph Crane—was also on the faculty of Lesley, College.

In '96, I enrolled in the Astrology Institute's counseling program. That became one of the key foundations of my master's program because you had to present a proposal of what coursework you were going to do. The other big component of my proposal for my master's program was this two-year counseling training program. The other was that I would start facilitating my own women's circles and each month, would critique it.

Oh, the other common thread that I was seeing between all the things I was studying was the archetypes of the four elements: fire, water, air, and earth. I was fascinated. Jung did a lot of work with the four elements. They show up—big time—in astrology, tarot and palmistry, and when you are creating rituals, earth-centered ritual.

My master's thesis was, "Weaving a Path of Wholeness Through Women's Ritual and the Four Elements." It was, basically, getting credit for doing what I loved the most. I did all this research about women's ritual and women's spirituality and feminist psychology, and offered a one-day workshop with the same title that became the major case study in my thesis.

So, as I was just getting into writing the thesis at the end of '97, the wife part of the team handed me an article in *Money* magazine about coaching, because I kept saying to them, "You know I know I don't want to be a straight astrologer. I know I don't want to be a straight therapist. What do I do?"

She said, "I think you're a coach."

And she was right. So, I basically, I never did an introductory course. I just … it was like, *Oh, my God,* you know? Like so many of us—*That's what I am! I never knew what to call it.*

Q. *Oh, my goodness—it has a name!*

Deb R.: Yeah. Exactly. Exactly. I interviewed a bunch of mentor coaches, and Harriet Salinger was the one I chose. She has been part of my life ever since then. We actively coached together for three years when I first started coaching. We are still friends. Everything just started to fall into place after that. I was doing the women's circles already; I started doing them in conjunction with my master's thesis and coaching, and it just evolved. I knew—because of my love of ritual—that the most obvious, societally-celebrated rituals are weddings.

I could not quite handle going to a seminary because I had just finished this program. But I wanted to do more than something like the Universal Life thing. So I found this wonderful ministry called Sanctuary of the Beloved where their ministry is traveling around the country to ordain people who are already counselors and healers. I got ordained through them and started doing weddings. I think my first wedding was around 2000. Then somewhere, maybe '03, I had married maybe ten or fifteen.

A couple of them came to me and said that they were not on the rocks, but they would like some couple's coaching, if I did that. I wasn't trained in that, but I thought, *Okay, so I'll do the coaching that I do with a couple instead of just individually.*

Then another couple—actually two other couples that I was about to marry—asked if I did pre-marital coaching. Right at that moment, Coach U put out something about their connection with the Relationship Coaching Institute. So I started training and ended up getting certified in both singles and couples coaching with them.

Then, I got a call from Pam Richard from Coach U who was working with Laura Berman Fortgang to launch her *Now What? 90 Days to a New Life Direction* book and program, asking me if I would be on the training team. When I first started coaching, Laura had a scholarship program for people who had read her books but could not afford her higher coaching fees. So there were maybe two or three of us who came on … we were WINGS coaches. (I can't remember what that stood for.)

I got to know her through that. That was pretty cool, to be one of her senior trainers for four or five years. I got the call from her [and then] literally within a month, I got a call from *Modern Bride* magazine asking me if I wanted to be one of their Top 25 Trendsetters in the wedding industry.

I said, "That sounds great! How much do I have to pay for it?

They said, "No, no, no. This is a new thing we are doing. And we want you on our advisory board." So that was pretty cool.

In my own story, as told to my interviewer, Pam Ramsden, I discussed feeling at loose ends about what I really wanted to do.

Susan M.: When I got bored with the State Employment Service and went back to school to get my master's degree, I had no idea what I would do next. My brief experience with high school students made it clear that I would not be teaching high school English, but I knew that I enjoyed teaching.

Q. How do you think that came about? Where did you get that skill that you were good with children with psych problems?

Susan M.: I don't really know. I mean, I had a lot of empathy for them, as I had had a messy childhood myself. Maybe that helped, but it was just one of those things where

I was really good with them. I could handle the violent kids just fine up until the point where I got a kid who was taller than me. Two of the boys in their family suffered from gigantism; he was 5'4, 5'5 when he was four years old. He was very difficult because we expected him to act his height, not his age.

When I did my Master's in Counseling Psychology, I had done an internship at the school's counseling center, and imagined I was going to be a school counselor some place. I couldn't get a job; I just somehow could not get a job. I didn't want to leave New York City—I think was part of it—and there just wasn't much going on.

One of the things that did happen was one of my friends had wanted to get on the *$20,000 Pyramid* television show. I got picked to be on the show, and I won $10,000 in less than three minutes. I was able to live on that, and I moved to my second apartment in Chelsea. But it was right next to a supermarket where they were doing deliveries all night, so I got tired of the noise and ended up moving out to Brooklyn. I was able to do nothing for a time while I was thinking about what I was going to do next. In those days, you could live a long time on $10,000.

Alice didn't have any clear sense of calling but, as a single mother, needed to support herself. She spent many years as a weaver before she, more or less, fell into her life's work:

Alice: Mark [my son], was, at that time, very active and went to Washington to work. Subsequently, he met a man on the Federal Communications Commission, Nicholas Johnson. He had been very active in Washington and Mark worked for him.

One day he called me up and said, "Alice, I would like you to give a lunch for the Media Reform people in Los Angeles. And I'll pay you. You do it, and I'll pay you."

So I did. Afterwards, I was sitting around the table. All the people who realized that they weren't visible on television were there. Women were there. Hispanics were there. I think there were some gays there. Blacks were there. It was very interesting.

During the discussion, a lady from San Francisco said, "Well, I've changed the face of children's programming in the Bay Area using all volunteers. I thought that was very interesting because at the time—this was 1977, so I had a ten-year-old and two other ones—I was very concerned about Jonathan's excessive TV viewing. And nobody was doing anything about it, that I knew. I mean, there was no conversation.

I said, "Sally, if you ever come back to Los Angeles, I'd like to talk to you."

She said, "OK."

So Sally was back in about a month and called me up and said, "I'm having lunch with the Media Reform people at UCLA because we want to go after the licenses of the stations because they're not doing any quality programming for kids."

So I thought, *Okay, I'll go.* And I went.

There was a law professor and a media professor and a communications commission professor. There were about ten of us. The professor at UCLA turned to me and said, "Well, Alice, you aren't doing anything. Why don't you run a conference for us at

UCLA?" I had never run a conference. I didn't know very much, but I knew how to do things. So I signed up.

A man who was a writer for the *Los Angeles Times* found out about me and what I was doing. He interviewed me about what was going on. When that happened, people called me up and asked if they could come to this conference. They were very interested. Amongst them was Natalie Friendly, whose husband was Ed Friendly, who did *Backstairs at the White House* and *Little House on the Prairie*.

So I planned it. We had about fifty people in the morning—they were community people, people from social work, people from preschools—anybody who acted on the life of a child. We did a needs assessment about what television stations have to do for their audiences, and we came up with what kids—young kids—needed on television. I knew very little at that point, very little. I was interested because of my son, but I didn't know the impact of TV on kids—this was an entirely new thing. I was inviting all these people, I was welcoming them, and I could hardly talk.

Anyway, the morning was very successful, and then we had lunch. We invited the broadcasters in and we talked about what we had done in the morning—but we gave them cheese and wine. Of course, they were very excited with us.

I said, "Okay. I'm through. We did it."

And Sally said to me, "Oh, no. You're not through. I want you to come up to San Francisco and work with us because I want you to go to every station in Los Angeles and talk about kids' programming and see what they're doing."

I said, "I don't know anything."

She said, "You will after you come to San Francisco."

So I did.

She said, "Now, you've got to join some of the people who were there at your conference, and you've got to visit every station."

I said, "I'm not doing that."

And she said, "It'll just take a week."

So, I did that.

I remember standing at a street corner with my group after we had come out of one of the stations. I said to the group, "These people are evil." I had an internal transformation because I knew I had to decide. They didn't care how many or what kind of commercials were on children's programming, and some of them were very impactful and damaging to kids.

So that really was the beginning of my career. I spent the next four-and-a-half years learning everything I could about the impact of TV viewing on children. I started a group that was not directly linked to San Francisco, but was sort of an attachment … but we were doing it differently. We were talking to anybody who impacted on the life of a child, where Sally and her group were trying to change television, which never worked.

I was very successful. We had one hundred and twenty-five people in our group. Peggy Charren, president of a group called Action for Children's Television in Boston—who was the most widely-known and respected in the country—came and said, "How did you get all these people?"

I said, "Well, we live in the production capital of the world."

We never got any money. Every time we wrote a grant, the people said that they had already given to Action for Children's Television and so they thought we were covered. We were not covered. It was very hard. We did get some money from one grantor in Los Angeles, but we were all volunteers, and we worked very hard. And I put in a lot of my own money.

Q. What was your group called?

Alice: FACT—Focusing Awareness on Children and Television. I spoke all over California because people were really eager to hear. While I was working as executive director, I had some "deep throats" who were in careers in television.

One of them called me up one day and said, "You've got to do something. KCET is not going to buy *Mr. Rogers [Neighborhood television show]*.

I said, "Okay."

At that time, I was on the Community Advisory Board of KCET, which was an appointed position. They thought they were going to co-opt me, but they never did. I wrote them a letter on our stationery and I said, "Okay, if you're not going to buy *Mr. Rogers*, who are you going to buy for that age group?" And they had nobody else. So they had to buy Fred Rogers, which kept him on the air for twenty-five years.

I also, during that time, commissioned a play. I thought we would do a satire—that ultimately went through the Los Angeles public school system—to teach teachers and kids what was the effect of TV viewing on them. This came out of the conference that we had.

The play was shown at the conference. I was standing at the door of the museum—that's where the conference was—and a man rushed out, put his hand on the door and said, "I have to go right home. That's my family."

It was a satire and it worked. It was about aliens coming down and looking at people watching television with these ears, these TV ears, and not understanding why all these people were watching a box.

And the teenager character comes home one day and says, "Mom," (she's sitting in front of a TV), "Mom, I've got to talk to you right away."

"Honey, I'm watching TV."

"But I've got to talk to you right away. Johnny says he's going to commit suicide."

And the mother says, "That's nice dear. I'll talk to you later."

That's when the father ran out.

I was also appointed two times by the California State Senate, once to be on the Conference for the Family that was under Carter. That was the first time I really got an inkling of the right wing, because they wanted two and-a-half children, white, on TV. That was what they were fighting for.

First of all, they targeted the Media Group; I was in the Media Group. At first, they started [out feeling and sounding] like me. They wanted kids … parents to watch television, and television would have this and this and this. The more they talked, the more weird they got. By the end of our particular group, I said, "My God. I have to do something." These women all had nametags on with all kinds of stickers. They were right-wing, and they were prepared.

I took no lunch. I sat with another person from the media. We drew up a proposition or a proposal. It said that television had to include more than two-and-a-half parents with two-and-a-half children and they had to be diverse. Well, they so voted that down. It was unbelievable.

Anyway, when we voted on this, they put on black armbands and tore up their ballots. A lovely young man who was nineteen and going to college and black got up and said, "If this is what results in no parent education, I think we have to start all over again." He got applause from everybody.

I couldn't speak to enough people. I mean, everybody wanted me to speak and we just burned out. But we burned out at the same time when I realized that my youngest son—who was probably the reason I did this, because he was watching a lot of television—went from being a television addict to a drug user. I was terrified because I thought—and this was about 1977, I think—I could lose him. So I changed my lifestyle.

A Chance Moment

Sometimes, something as simple as a phone call or exposure to something new created a whole different career direction. Phoebe spoke about how serendipity led her into angel investing and board work:

Phoebe: So, it's 2001 and here is what is so funny. Remember, I have been twenty-three years in the same company, right? Different divisions, different subsidiaries, but with the same company. The oil and gas industry was given two primary functions, the engineering function and the finance function. They are very analytical, they're process-oriented, they are structured; it's capital allocation, it's quantitative, right?

So I moved then to consumer products. Within the first week, I remember someone showing me bottles and saying, "Look at the shoulders on that bottle. Isn't that a beautiful bottle?"

And I'm looking at it and I'm thinking, *I don't even know what you're talking about because the idea of "shoulders on a bottle and it is beautiful" just doesn't compute with my analytical, process-oriented, low-cost environment, right? Where have I landed?*

I would say that I thoroughly enjoyed learning the consumer products industry and everything about building a brand, issues on distribution, issues on incentives and motivation. This time, we are not allocating capital, this time we're allocating advertising dollars—that's what it is.

I had a great experience there. I was hired by Owsley Brown II, who is the fourth generation of Brown-Forman, and a wonderful, wonderful human being, who just died in the last year. He died way too young. That was a very good relationship, a very well run, family-controlled, publicly-traded company.

Owsley Brown II was reaching his sixty-fifth year and retirement. The successor, whose name is Paul Varga, wanted his own team and deserved it. There were many of us who all left around the same time.

I was fifty-five, and I retired and didn't really know what I was going to do next. I played with the idea of going and taking another full-time job, but the jobs that were being offered to me were generally either serious problem companies or in an industry which I thought was inappropriate—I just didn't want to do that. So I said to those people, "Give me a little time here to figure this out."

Then a very funny thing happened. When I was in England in 1991, I got a call from a friend of mine who graduated from Mount Holyoke.

She said, "Phoebe, we have a classmate of ours from Mount Holyoke who's got a company. It needs capital; it needs help. We want to put our money [into it], but we don't know how to do this. Could you help us please? Could you help us figure out how to do this?" In other words, "Could you do recapitalization of the company?"

I said, "Okay, I can help you. I can do it." So I got all the information, I figured out what to do, and we ended up putting money into the company. Anyway, long story short, I ended up with a small equity position in a company, and I didn't really do too much more with it.

I remember telling Mark at that time, "Consider this a charitable contribution because we may never get our money back from this investment." I didn't join the board. I didn't do anything. I just funded it and then we had our equity position and we got information on it.

Fast forward to 2000, when I called up the president, Susan Brown. I said, "Susan, I don't know you, but you have done a beautiful job with this company. If I were you, I'd think about selling this company."

She said, "I think you're right, but it's a little too soon."

I said, "Okay I'm just telling you, if I were you, I'd think about selling it."

So I got a call from her, this is in 2008, and she goes, "Phoebe, I'm really trying to sell the company, but we're having a hard time and the board is divided. Could you just come back and join the board and help us figure it out?"

I said, "Well, as it turns out, I'm going to be retiring at the end of April. So why don't I come back and help you do this?"

I didn't even stop. All I did was stop a little, stop working in one location and pick up working in another location. And I'm doing a big deal to see if we can get the company sold in May of 2008 and we did. We closed it at the end of May 2008, which is before it crashed in September.

That company is Boppy. Boppy is a product that you would use while breastfeeding a baby. It's like a neck ring that you wrap around your waist and it holds the baby as you breastfeed. It's very popular; it's used all the time. It's available in Target and Walmart and Toys R Us and on the Internet and it's a very, very successful consumer brand.

So I'm having lunch with people who asked, "What are you doing?"

I said, "Well, it's not like I even stopped working. I went from one job into the next job."

They said, "Wow. Do you know what's that called?"

I said, "No."

"That's called angel investing."

"Really?"

They said, "Oh yeah, there are a lot of people doing this professionally. They just look for companies that they can invest in and help, and see if they can grow these little companies."

I said, "That's really interesting to me." That is, indeed, what I did on Boppy.

I started attending meetings and reading books and kind of getting into all of this angel investing and its possibilities. At the same time, I'm trying, figuring out, *Am I going to join [boards] because I joined a corporate board in 2002?* It's the first board I joined—OshKosh B'Gosh. I had joined their corporate board in 2002, and I was on the board until we sold them to Carter's in 2005. I was thinking, *Shall I join another one? Would there be a conflict?*

I did talk to a headhunter about joining the board of Invesco which is a mutual fund company. They have 270 mutual funds or so and manage about $700 billion of assets. I ultimately joined their board on January 1, 2010. I didn't really [want to] be a CFO. I really had been there, done that. I joined the board of Invesco and two days later, I got a phone call from the same recruiter saying, "We are very interested in having you join the board of Coca-Cola Enterprises."

I thought, *Well, if I take this role, I'm kind of committed, then, to board work.* So I did talk to them and thought, *What a great way to use to use my beverage company experience in a non-alcoholic beverage category. That's a perfect fit for me.* So, it's interesting.

So anyway, I decided to join Coca-Cola Enterprises and their board. That put me on three boards. At that point, I was committed to not going back to the corporate world but instead, creating a world of work and enjoyment and life outside of the corporate world. So I have done that.

Since that time, I have thoroughly enjoyed my time on those corporate boards and have supplemented that with work and investing in startup companies. The startup company work is sort of working with non-profits, so I work with them as much as I can. I'm kind of like an incubator and accelerator for several of them. Then I do my corporate work and I have three non-profits.

I have always been interested in non-profit work and have always supplemented my life with those activities, so I was really pleased to be on the board of trustees at Smith College for ten years. I am now on the board of trustees for the University of Louisville. I'm in my fourth year there, appointed by the governor. I serve also the American Printing House of the Blind, which is a federal agency that produces books for those who are blind and vision-impaired in America. Very interesting group of companies. I do one more, I sit on a foundation of about a hundred million in assets, where we give away one grant each year.

I have not talked a lot about my non-profit work, but I try to do as much as I can. I have done everything from Boys and Girls Club to being a trustee where my children have gone to school, etc.

I don't think that's terribly important for the scope of your work except it adds richness to life; I think that's important.

I don't want to denigrate the work I have done parenting, which is important and very satisfying to me. I sort of struck a bargain in my career. I said, "Look. I will work really hard from Monday morning to Friday evening, and I'll travel as much as I have to, and I'll work as much as I have to. But I'd like two days per week for my family, with the exception of, maybe, some Sunday nights." I really kept that bargain and so that meant that I was able to spend time with, especially, my daughters as they were growing up.

Sudden inspiration created a shift for Deb L., who was quickly moving up the corporate ladder when she went to an art show that changed her direction entirely:

Deb L.: So I was promoted, three times in two-and-a-half years, to bigger and bigger departments. And then they sent me to the Sears Tower. That's when I started to see more about the bones of what they did. The place that they put me was really boring. I mean, half the time, people were in there, making paper airplanes all day. I was ready to conquer the world. You know, I did not want to sit there making paper airplanes and having long, extended lunches every day.

After about six months, I attended an art show. There was a woman I knew who was an artist. My family has a lot of artistic ability; my sister was an artist, my Mom was an artist, lots of musicians, etc., in my background. So, I met this artist, and she told me about her life, and how she traveled around the world. I went, "Oh, travel! I'm feeling the itch!" I thought about it for probably a month, and I walked in, and resigned my job at Sears to go become an artist.

I can remember my parents going, "What are you doing?"

I said, "I'm bored! I just ... I'm bored!"

They said, "But you've never taken any art lessons in your life!"

I said, "But haven't you noticed I could always draw?" People who have a high math ability often are artistic; it's the same side of the brain.

They said, "Well, yeah, but making a living as an artist is hard."

I said, "I'm bored! Did I tell you, I'm bored?"

So, for the next ten years, I learned on the job. I learned how to paint. I started in malls doing portraits, and then moved to art fairs. At the ten-year mark, I was very good at it, but I was bored again! So, it was like, *Okay, this is not enough.* Art should be more inspiring.

A fellow I met at an art show, a lawyer, liked some of my pieces. By then, I was painting more than portraits, painting Native American images ... all sorts of interesting things.

He loved those and said, "You know, you're a wonderful artist; I can see it. But until you paint from the heart, you're never going really make it." Then he said, "What do you love most about what you do?"

I said, "The Native Americans, especially the Lakota Sioux. My whole insides vibrate when I paint them."

He said, "You need to paint those, then."

And you know how that is: you're at a point in your life where something in you knows it's time to move, and someone says just the right thing that triggers you, and everything in you says, "Yup. It's time." That was one of those defining moments.

So I said "All right!"

He said, "I'll tell you what: I'm going to commission a painting, but you have to promise me that you'll paint it from the heart."

I said, "Okay!" I remember coming home from that meeting with him and thinking, *How do I get into my heart?* I had always painted what I saw externally; now I had to go inside.

I remember thinking of my son, who was three months old at the time, because that always got into my heart right away. And I started to cry. I am driving; it's the Kennedy expressway in Chicago. I'm driving and all of a sudden, I start crying and I saw a painting completed in front of my eyes. The title was printed below it in gold letters. It was on a black background, and it was called *Grandfather, Teller of Tales.* It was an old Lakota Sioux grandfather talking with his grandson in front of a fire. And the fire was shedding an orange light on the grandson's face. The grandson was looking up at the grandfather, and behind the grandfather was the moon, shining a silver light on the grandfather's ... the back of his head. Behind the boy, in the smoke from the fire, was the shape of a hawk.

I pulled off the road and I thought, *Oh my God!* It was one of those goose bump-body things. I just sat with it, let the tears run down for a while, and said, "Okay." I had never painted anything without something like a model, or pictures, or something to look at, so it was a bit challenging to get it done. But I did and the man fell in love with it.

We took it to print, a limited edition lithograph. It sold out almost immediately. It was a huge success. The painting and my artwork just started to skyrocket after that. It ended up being part of a whole series, telling the whole life story of that boy. That ended up getting published: collector plates, prints, note cards, calendars. I mean, everything just took off after that. Within a couple of years, my originals were going for, well, within the first year, they were going for over a thousand dollars. Within two years, they were going for over ten thousand dollars apiece. By the end of my career as an artist, I had two hundred galleries carrying my work.

It was because I painted from the heart; that was the only difference. You know, the skill level, you always get better. But after ten years of painting portraits, you are either really good or you're not.

So that was that section [of my life]. And for me, when I talk about these things, I always think that these are distinct lifetimes within one. This was one of them.
World events and emerging industries

Serendipity and disaster both had a role in Nancy C.'s transition into coaching:

Nancy C.: I had been loosely following this new adventure called Oxygen. I have a particular interest in what women are doing in the world. Geraldine Laybourne ... she was on the front page of everything. I was just so enamored with Oxygen [Media] and I had been reading it every morning.

They had an ad, one day, on the front of their website that said We're hiring. And I clicked on it. They were looking for a Sports.com producer to marry TV content to the web. They wanted someone who had some print experience, some web experience, some management experience, some knowledge of women's sports. It was custom-made to my entire resume, so I applied for it.

I was in Florida on vacation when I got a phone call from Lynn. She said, "You know, I read your resume and thought this is just fake; it's made up." She was laughing. "Too perfect." And she said, "Would you mind doing an initial interview on the phone?"

I said, "Not at all. I'm actually on vacation, but I'll be happy to speak to you." So, I sat in the hotel room and did an interview with her.

She said, "I'd really like you to meet the next two people."

So when I came home, I went in to interview with the executive producer of Oxygen Sports, whom I had never heard of. I sat down in a chair in her office.

She said, "I know your name."

I said, "Well, I don't know from where."

So we talked for a few minutes and she said, "Wait a minute!" (She was looking at my resume.) "You won an award for a knee series you did on injuries to women."

I said, "Yeah—The Women's Sports Foundation."

She said, "Oh, my God. I was a judge."

Small world.

So, yes, Lydia hired me and Oxygen was pretty dreamy. I liked so much about it.

So this is now ... the web stuff is still hot at this point, Okay, keep in mind, so this is the year, either 1999 or 2000. I started working there and I just loved it. I had one person working for me, but that was the time when you started to see that everybody probably had been a little too enthused on their hiring of web staff. So the web staffs throughout Oxygen were getting cut. We were seeing layoffs, and it was really demoralizing.

I was called in one day. Lydia said, "Look. I think I'm going to lose you if I don't do something, because web staffs are going. And I've seen what you can do. You clearly can tell a story editorially. I think I can develop your eye. Would you be willing to be in training and become a TV producer?"

I thought, *Who the hell in New York ever gets this opportunity*? I mean, there are people clamoring, coming out of school, to be TV producers. "Would you mind if we taught you?" No! I would not mind.

So, that became my next job. I became a TV producer for Oxygen and was in the very unique position of having associate producers and production assistants who knew more about TV producing than I did. I had a lot of respect already there, thankfully, and friends. So I started producing. But I was shadowing—it was her idea that I shadow experienced producers on a few shows and then do my own. She gave me some of the strongest assistants, so they would be holding my hand a bit as we went along and think of details that I might not think of.

There were aspects of it that I was really good at. You know, you had to write a studio lead-in for a host; I loved doing that. I don't think I really had the eye, ultimately. I was getting a little discouraged with it, I mean, I was definitely sticking with it, but ultimately, it didn't matter because they canceled Oxygen Sports Show and we were all laid off in 2002.

Q. So, it folded and then you did what?

Nancy C.: In the fall after 9/11, I was called in and told that TV producers apparently were making less money than web producers, so they cut my salary pretty significantly. That was probably five to six months before we all got laid off, so that was probably part of what prompted me to pay more attention than I had, because it was post 9/11.

They had a volunteer fair where, during lunch hour, we could just go talk to these various non-profits that were set up in a room at tables. The last one I talked to was Future Possibilities. Basically, they were pairing an adult coach with an under-served child in New York. (They had a format and a program to follow.)

I didn't know what this whole coaching thing was about. It was the first I had heard of it that did not involve sports. But I knew immediately that was what I wanted to do out of all the volunteer opportunities that were there. So, I started volunteering to coach a nine-year-old boy in Harlem.

Of course, they're not just going to say, "Hi, stranger, here's a child." They screen you and then they take you through an all-day orientation in New York. As I was going through the training, the person running the training was a life coach. And I was like, *Huh?* No clue what that was.

It was a very rigorous, rigorous training day. I mean, it was role-play; it was breaking into groups; it was, "Now come back to the whole group and show us what you learned." And I'm like, coaching somebody in front a group of people. This was really … this was the training. This was the first time.

At the end of the day, this life coach came up to me and she said, "I don't know you. I just met you today, but I'm telling you that you have a knack for this, and you're a natural, and you should pursue it."

I didn't even know what that meant. I thanked her politely, with my plate very full, and left, and continued my volunteer thing. But then I saw, weeks later, an ad in the *New York Times* that said Become a Life Coach. And I was like, *Hmm. Now somebody's talking to me. This is a little weird.* So I called her.

It was for a training program, Results Coaching, and they had an information session in January. I signed up for it because I thought, you know, *This might be good to supplement my income, now that my income has been cut.*

I went to the information session and I was like, *Ooo, boy. Do I want to spend money right now on this kind of thing?* I just wasn't sure. And I didn't really think I was going to be laid off the following month.

In retrospect, I'm glad I didn't know. So I just grabbed some cash and threw it at the situation and decided to do this training. In three months, partly in-person and partly through tele-classes, I became a certified coach. In the middle of training, I was laid off. I was the first person in my class to get an actual paying client, probably motivated by poverty. And that started it. And wow.…

Q. This was mostly personal coaching, initially? So, you started the coaching. You liked the coaching. And somewhere there you got back into the writing as well.

Nancy C.: Yes. You know, I started doing a lot of networking. The people I trained with, I stayed in touch with. We did some information sharing about how to network and promote ourselves. I'm not a business person and don't really naturally gravitate to that. I was kind of feeling I didn't know what to do.

I thought I could probably freelance. So you know, I picked up some magazine assignments. I did some pieces for the *Ladies Home Journal.* I did a piece for *Parents* magazine (ironically, since I have never been a parent and didn't want to be). They were very well-paying. So that was helping, but I was really unemployed and trying to put together some kind of business without any business training or savvy.

So I started hitting the ground running. I live in a very flyer-friendly town. I created flyers with pull-off tabs and I became a pro at where I could hang them, from grocery stores to the Arts Center building here that has all kinds of studios in it and has bulletin boards on every floor. So I constantly carried flyers with me to freshen and replenish the supply. I became very good at flyer karma—when somebody would cover my flyer with theirs, I would move it and try to make room so that both of them were visible. It was like this dog-eat-dog flyer world for a while.

I became much more involved in my community. I spoke at some Rotary events. Did Chamber of Commerce networking things here. Did Business Network International (BNI) for a year. I got involved with a local bookstore here, a used bookstore which also did community events. I started teaching the *Artist's Way* through there. He let me charge without having to having to pay him for the space because I would use it after hours. By getting a core group of people who started coaching with me, or who started taking the *Artist's Way* classes with me, I then was able to get a bit of a local following. I was teaching a writing class at the high school in the adult education program and then the people would sign up for that because they knew me from the *Artist's Way*. It all kind of just started to happen that way, a lot of word of mouth.

But at this point, I was generating almost nothing on writing as far as income goes. I had nothing happening on that front, so I had to take a money job for a while, you know? Not the thing you want to do, but you need a bring-in-the-cash kind of job. That was working for a real estate company in New York, thirty hours a week, just putting in my time and leaving there at two-thirty and then coaching people. I built all my coaching sessions after two-thirty in the afternoon with people so I could build that up simultaneously.

Remaining Open to New Things

It is so easy to find reasons not to do something different or new that we often forget it is equally easy to be open to new things. We can talk ourselves out of anything. We can come up with hundreds of reasons to say "No." We can keep our blinders on so we don't see all the possibilities around us.

But why? There are possibilities that present themselves every day. These women were open to trying new things. This trait is similar to curiosity and restlessness (Chapter 5), yet not exactly the same thing. While curious and restless women tend to move from one thing to another or keep adding more to already-busy lives, openness to new things has more to do with a woman's attitude.

The Fifty have a mindset that allows them to react to life in a particular way as it unfolds. They are a little like kids in a candy store. While the curious and restless are generally in a constant state of flux and active experimentation, women who are open to new things expect and accept surprises; they tend to approach life in a state of wonder. They may not be seeking something new, but when it presents itself, they are open to saying "Yes." When they get up in the morning, consciously or unconsciously, they wonder what the day will bring. Little things can be exciting. Suggestions can become possibilities.

Natalie created a publishing company because, when presented with the realization that elders would respond to a different kind of reading experience, she said, "Why not?" Bunnie didn't see any reason why she couldn't be successful in elder care, so she moved into a new career. Kathy learned about real estate so she could help coaching clients make more sales, then asked, "Why not do real estate myself?"

Elements of Openness to New Things

Openness to new things includes the following elements:
- Having a "Why not?" attitude
- Seeing potential gains
- Evaluating potential obstacles
- Knowing oneself
- Taking considered action (i.e. being spontaneous but not recklessly impulsive).

Bethene and Loretta were both open to what they could learn from each new situation in their lives. Part of the excitement in Kathy's life has always been trying new things. Shoya got good introductions into different fields and was open to whatever possibilities appeared. Victoria feels that life is about taking calculated, informed risks.

How You Can Develop Openness to New Things

- Try to let situations unfold fully before rushing to judgment.
- Envision scenarios for new possibilities that come your way. What would your life look like if you said, "Why not"?
- When you think that an obstacle will hold you back, check to see if the obstacle is real or if it is your own self-talk.
- When encountering real obstacles, develop an action plan to overcome them.
- Try something new at least once a month. It can be as small as a new ice cream flavor or as large as a career move.

Exercise

Are you open to possibilities? Here are two ways to expand your horizons:

Narrow your focus
1. Practice looking for specific things.
2. Look for red cars. How many do you see in a single hour?
3. Pick a specific animal. Until I started looking for them, I had never realized how many doves were out there among the pigeons.
4. Feel that little jolt of pleasure in discovery.
5. Move on to looking for something else—maybe something a little more unexpected.

Broaden your focus
1. Try looking at your world through a different lens and discover what you see. For the next week, look at your world as if you were a stranger:
2. What do you see that you haven't seen before?

3. Is there something that you have never noticed and never tried that looks appealing? Start as small as a different coffee blend or a different route to work.
4. You can expand as far as you would like: spend time with someone new, try a new activity, attend an event that you have never considered, or sign up for a class.

Enjoy the surprises!

Chapter 7

Puzzles – Scanning the Environment, Recombining, and Synthesizing Skills

SCANNING the environment is the art of carefully looking around, observing everything. Synthesis or recombining involves taking both similar and seemingly very different concepts, ideas, and skills and putting them together in a unique way to create something new.

Many vibrant women have the ability to recombine skills in new and interesting ways. They can see how mathematical ability can inform music and art. They understand how an ability to make people feel comfortable can be as useful in restaurant work as in home care. They move through life, scanning their environment and making decisions about how different things can be useful, what to keep, what to let go.

As Bethene said,

> **Bethene:** You create spaces and you touch the spaces, but your aim is not to build in all of them. So I'm always conscious of, "What can I take away? How can I simplify here? How can I open up some space for new kinds of possibilities?"

Early Aspirations

Another thing I wondered about was how many women had childhood dreams that involved being a leader or taking a strong role of some type. How were childhood dreams, school experiences, and early employment folded into later aspirations and choices?

Many of The Fifty reminded me of Bettina Aptheker's descriptions of constructed lives in *Tapestries of Life*. She speaks of women keeping scraps, bits, and pieces, working them together to construct something greater: "patchwork lives." The truth of this was reflected by The Fifty in their stories.

When I was a child, galloping through the neighborhood on my imaginary horse, I was always the leader of the gang. I started organizing people and taking charge before I was five. Even when I moved on from wanting to be Gene Autry to wanting to be a teacher, those organizing and leadership skills stayed with me and served me well.

Several of The Fifty wanted to be actresses or dancers or cowgirls. One patterned herself after Amelia Earhart, honing in on her determination. These were strong role models. Even though none of the women followed through on any of these roles, the early identification with their role models' characteristics stayed with them throughout their lives.

Phyllis C. says this best:

> **Phyllis C.:** When I was nine, I absolutely became captivated by Amelia Earhart. I read her biography. I don't know how much you know about her, but she was certainly ahead of her time in just about every way. She was determined to do what she wanted, how

she wanted, and that really caught my imagination. I thought, *Well, gosh, if she could do anything, I think I can too.*

Phoebe saw herself as a Western hero at one point. She never thought about it again, but perhaps that streak of adventuresome spirit influenced her work in mergers and acquisitions and her relocation to Alaska. Perhaps that early desire for freedom and risk factored into her later decision to become an angel investor.

Phoebe: In my boxes of memorabilia, I have a drawing from the fourth grade of what I wanted to be when I grew up—it's a picture of a cowgirl. It's very funny to me now that it was I thought I wanted to be. I don't have any recollection of it other than that particular document … that my mother saved. That didn't seem to last very long—it was probably in the same category as when a boy wants to be a fireman or a policeman.

The first real recollection I have was when I did my application to Smith College. One had to write what you were interested in doing, and I wrote down that I wanted to be a family counselor. I now know and look back at that as being highly reflective of my parents. My father is a minister and became, in his older years, a chaplain at a hospital. My mother was a social worker and worked part-time as a social worker into her 80s. So I came from a social service, serving-people family and think that was very influential in … what I wanted to do as well. So I majored in Psychology at Smith College and was on that path, but while there was introduced to a whole other world—economics and the world of business, just a different world.

For Deb L., a variety of childhood experiences created an outlook of openness to new experiences:

Deb L.: I was so immersed in school; I loved going to school, I loved learning, I loved reading, I loved math. Those are my two favorites—I loved reading and math.

We moved around a lot. We moved to Japan for three years, so I spoke fluent Japanese at three years old. One of the things that has never changed, that came from that, [is] I yearn to travel. It's interesting: if I don't travel somewhere in a year's time, I get a sense of longing about going, seeing more things, and learning more things when I travel. We lived all over the United States. My dad was in the military, and we were transferred almost every year for a while. So more of my attention was on learning what the kids were doing, learning how everybody talked, learning how everybody was, learning the local culture. Even today when I travel, that's how I travel; I want to get into the culture.

I don't so much care about the hotel we're in or the restaurants we're going to eat in—although I love food—but I care about the villages we're going to see, the people, how they think, how they interact, how they are with their families, what they do for a living and why they do it and how much do they like it, and how happy they are. So those kinds of things were, I would say, more on my mind as a kid than anything else.

Q. That's delightful. You went on to college, I'm assuming?

Deb L.: I knew you were going to ask that next, too. College was a grand experiment for me. I thought that when I went to college, I wanted to go into politics. I studied political science, I studied philosophy, and a lot of courses like that.

It was the tail-end of the sixties, so I think I had some disillusionment, based on a great deal of naïveté as a college kid; a lot of idealism and naïveté. I was really impacted during school—emotionally, spiritually, everything—by the civil rights movement, the assassinations of Martin Luther King and Bobby Kennedy and John Kennedy, the deaths of some wonderfully-talented musicians and artists. Also, like so many of my generation, the whole hiding under your desk for a nuclear bomb …

Q. Oh, "Duck and cover!"

Deb L.: Yes—under our desks in fifth grade, hiding under our desks for a nuclear war. For many of us of this age, I think it was a unique phenomenon, because we grew up in a world that felt very shaky all the time; the Cuban missile crisis. We were bombarded with news and, if you think about our parents, they grew up in a time when they weren't so bombarded with news. They had their rough times, but they didn't have television that they sat in front of all night. So I don't think our parents had the numbness we have today. They were panicked—I remember seeing it on my parents' faces, like, *What is going on in the world?*

As a kid, I think I wanted to make that different. So that idealism, as I got to college and then when I studied political science and philosophy and metaphysics and all of those things, everything I studied was more centered around trying to explain why things work the way they work. Why is it this way, and can we make it different?

Of course, I went to a liberal, liberal arts college and, at the end of four years, I don't think I really understood much more about why things were the way they were, but I understood more about why I was the way I was. That's really the question that is more important anyway. I came out of college more interested in me and my journey and why I chose the things I did. So, I came out of college not knowing, still, what I wanted to be when I grew up, but having a better sense of who I wanted to be.

Q. In many ways, this is the first generation, I think, that asked that question at such a young age.

Deb L.: I think that is one of the huge gifts, because we questioned everything. I can remember, in my college environment, people making fun of people who knew what they wanted to do or who weren't doing something with their hands. That was when it was nobler to be a carpenter or a plumber than it was to be a lawyer or a professional or a doctor. That was confusing because a lot of the students were really bright. We were like, "What do we do with this now? What is the noble thing to do?" In one sense, it set us all back a little bit. But in another other sense, as I broaden my perspective and look back, it actually gave me a really interesting journey.

Q. That was college.

Deb L.: A lot of experimenting. I studied a lot of things outside of school as well, like I studied with some folks that were spiritualists and psychics. I went to a lot of existential kinds of retreats. The college that I went to was a really intense think-tank about things like that. There was some exposure to some very interesting philosophical systems and I think it opened my mind. I don't think it directed it; it opened it.

Q. So ... with that as a backdrop, what did you decide to do with yourself when you did finish school?

Deb L.: It did become clear that I was going to have to make money to survive, and I wanted to live on my own, did not want to live at my parents', and I really still had no clue what I wanted to do. My parents knew someone who was the director of human resources for Sears Roebuck in Chicago, 'cause I'm from Chicago.

They said, "Why don't you go? They have a whole battery of tests that they give to people they are hiring ... just to see where they fit. Your personality profile, your strengths." Probably was a Myers-Briggs or something.

I said, "Sure, that sounds like that would be helpful."

So I went and I had the test, and the fellow called me into his office. I think he was senior vice-president of human resources. He said, "Okay, so here's the interesting thing: Your profile is identical to mine. I've never seen that before, and you're perfect for management." He also said, "You would be a great leader, a great executive. You have tons of potential. We'd like to have you come and work in our management training program."

So I said, "Okay! That sounds interesting. Let's do that."

Kathy's high school interests led her into a teaching career, but then developed into a skill set that supported her success in selling her art and becoming successful in real estate:

Kathy: When I was in high school in the early to mid-1960s, I wanted to work at NASA (the space company), and I was going to be a mathematician there. I took advanced math in high school and I was math major in college. So I was on that track until I flunked all my classes because I learned to play bridge and instead, became the dorm bridge champion. I was on academic probation my first two years.

Phoebe recognized her parents' influence on her initial choice of college major. Still, she was scanning the horizon to see what else was out there and remained open to other possibilities:

Phoebe: The chief investment officer of Smith College ran a seminar for people who were interested in business on Wall Street. I took it. We learned all kinds of things. We went to Wall Street and I thought, *This is really a lot more "me" than just being a social worker or in a service profession.*

I finished up Psychology, which I surely enjoyed, but added economics, government, and liberal arts, and also was encouraged by professors to go to law school. So in the course of a very fine education, which I did on a scholarship at Smith College,

I was introduced to a new world, new worlds of, maybe, being an attorney, a new world of, maybe, business. So that was transformational, frankly, just having that world open up to me.

Charlotte also spoke about her parents' influence:

Charlotte: When I was growing up, I was fortunate to have supportive parents who wanted me to have more confidence than possible. They made sure I knew I could be anything I wanted to be; there were no limitations for any reason, be it gender or anything else. If [there was] something I wanted to do, I could do it.

My mother had a secret desire for me to grow up and be Miss America and marry Elvis Presley; those were her goals. My father was thinking I might grow up to be President. So, totally different goals but they did a very good job of instilling in me that I could do anything I wanted. And I grew up with a great deal of confidence.

I can remember—as a very young child, maybe eight or nine years old—a trip with my mother and her favorite cousin. Mother was saying (I was supposed to be napping) she wanted to make sure I grew up with all the confidence she didn't have because her mother wasn't supportive.

I grew up with a father who took me everywhere with him. I learned to hunt and fish and do the tomboyish things. With my mother and grandmothers, I learned how to be the proper little girl.

I was allowed to say I didn't want to do something, but before I said, "I don't want to learn to sew" or "I don't want to do this, I don't want to do that," I had to try. I had to prove I could do it and then I could say I didn't want to do it.

I never wanted ... I didn't want to take home economics because I didn't really want to sew. I could do embroidery and do needlework—I could do beautiful needlework— but I didn't want to sit down, take a pattern, cut it, and put it on the sewing machine. So I grew up having modeling lessons, fencing lessons, dance lessons—everything that was available to children to widen their horizons.

My parents traveled a lot, and they traveled with me, so I was very fortunate to have a wider view of what was going on in the world than simply growing up in a small town and never leaving. So ... as far as what I wanted to be? For years, I thought I'd be a forest ranger, just simply because I love animals and nature. I love everything about it.

Then I fell in love with the financial world as a teenager. I can remember, in one of my economics classes, the professor—who had a great influence on me—decided we all were going to have a [fictional] amount of money, and we were going to put together a stock portfolio. We did put together a stock portfolio, went through the papers, took care of what we had, and I thought that was wonderful.

So, in the back of my mind, I had always thought that would be a wonderful career. But growing up in the age we did, when I graduated from college, I had a degree in Elementary Education which I didn't really want. I had changed routes during college, so I also had a degree in business and economics.

Robyn was a shy child whose mother enrolled her in an acting class as a way to help her move beyond that.

Robyn: I thought I wanted to be a pediatrician, and I don't remember where that came from. And then, to get out of my shyness, I started acting classes that my mother put me in. That didn't work. However, when I was in high school and I really wanted to get out of being shy and get more friends, I decided to go back and try acting ... and I became good at it. I was being recognized as an actor, and everybody thought I had talent, and I decided I would go to school for acting.

Several of The Fifty were not aware what their skills were early in their careers. This is not uncommon and, for many women, their twenties are a period of exploration. They may move among very different career options or try out several choices as they figure out what their talents are, what skills they prefer using, and what their overall lifestyle might be. Some will choose to be in the workplace. Others may decide on marriage and child-rearing with outside work postponed. Still others will decide on dual-track futures, combining family and career. These initial decisions often remain fixed until midlife, when a second period of exploration occurs. Nancy C. expressed that early lack of clarity:

Nancy C: I never really understood what my specific gifts were back then. I knew I had something, and it definitely was not a mind for stats, as a lot of sportswriters have. I wasn't one to sit and memorize that kind of stuff, like a lot of the guys on the staff. I was very good at getting to people and the issue. Do you really need to know every goal that was scored? Not really. What you want to know is—did somebody dominate? And ... maybe you could interview them about why they had such a strong day. I really learned what people will do to compete and push through injury and play to your level of competition. You know, I just witnessed so much and, not having been an athlete myself, I was just enamored with all these athletes.

Q. It sounds like you were writing about people; you were writing more people stories.

Nancy C.: Yes. I was a writer that writes about sports. I would do occasional pieces if something was going on that interested me in the world, like when Frank Sinatra died, I did a piece for the op-ed page. When I went to London and I saw all kinds of quirky fashions, I took some pictures and did a piece for the fashion page. I would speak up on occasion. I did book reviews, so my reach was definitely beyond sports.

Agenia's early influences were shaped by finding mentors who broadened her horizons far beyond anything she could have imagined:

Agenia: You know, it's so funny to think about that because my childhood was not one that focused on what we would do when we grew up. My mom and my dad divorced right before I went off to college. I remember my mother being astonished that, not only had I picked the school to go to, but we lived in Mobile, Alabama and the university was in Knoxville, Tennessee, which was more than 500 miles away. That was just such a foreign concept, not only to my mother, but to my friends and everyone else. So I was not one of those who grew up thinking about being anything other than what was perceived, at that time, to be the only professional careers for African-Americans, and that was—it was okay to be a doctor, it was okay to be a school teacher.

Those were, sort of, the professional careers you heard about, but something happened for me that was really unique and extremely special. My mom took me, my sister, and my brother to church at a little Episcopal church that was there in the urban community of Mobile, Alabama. It was a wonderful little Episcopal church.

The priest at that church, Father Malcolm Prouty, and his wife, Linda, took an interest in helping the youth in that church set a vision for themselves as to what they saw themselves doing next. That was the first time I ever heard about the importance of going to college and, more important than that, how it could help you transcend where you are today, as far as where you live and how you live to whatever you envision it being tomorrow. They were really the absolute, most instrumental in my life at helping me realize that I could [do] just about anything I decided I wanted to do.

Victoria's early aspirations didn't lead to a career on stage, but they did lead to a very public career as an author, playwright, and movie producer:

Victoria: When I was very small, because I loved music, I think I wanted to be a singer; I wanted to do musical comedy. Oh, and my parents took us to see Mary Martin in "Peter Pan" when I was a little girl. I remember her flying out on the wire and thinking I wanted to be able to do that as well, and sing the way she sang, and dress the way she dressed. I actually pursued that for quite a while and enjoyed music, but I was a terrible, terrible actress. Then I realized I had better go into some other field.

Phyllis C. got more than determination from her interest in Amelia Earhart. She also learned how to research:

Phyllis C.: So Amelia Earhart truly because a major catalyst for me; she stayed with me on the journey. During that time then, I also got into wanting to know the answers to things. We know that Amelia was lost at sea; I decided that I was going to try to find her.

During fourth, fifth, and sixth grades, I researched everything I could. My mom took me on the train down to Chicago to the public library, and I looked up all the microfiche and that sort of thing. I was about ten then. That really served me well later in life because I am an amateur genealogist and I do a lot of that work now; that's one of my hobbies. I learned a great deal about how to do that back then. Well, I didn't find Amelia but I did have a lot of fun, and I did make some friends along the way doing that.

Bunnie has often been in jobs that called on well-developed social skills and service to others, both of which parallel her early desire to become a hairdresser:

Bunnie: I actually wanted to be a hairdresser.

Q. Okay, interesting. You never did that, though, did you?

Bunnie: My mother wouldn't let me go to beautician school. That had to do with her mother, my grandmother, owning two beauty parlors and my mother working in them. My mother always said if you do that, you're going to have varicose veins and I don't want you doing that. She was adamant about it.

So I did every hairstyle during the '50s and '60s. I used to find friends, their parents, whomever, to create the latest and greatest hairstyle. When we had our dances or parties, I would do all the girls' hair and then I would have to actually go to the beauty parlor to have mine done. I never had time to do my own.

Much later, I cut my father's hair. My mother always said that I probably inherited the gene from her father—he was a barber at one time.

Betsy gained confidence from her parents' support:

Betsy: Growing up, I always thought about being a doctor. That's partly because I come from a family of doctors, including my great grandfather, my grandfather, my father, and my uncle. So it was pretty clear to me that was a great career path, and I had a lot of support from my parents.

I'm the oldest child and my father—in an age where I think people had, perhaps, lower expectations of women—my father paid me one of the greatest compliments he could pay any woman by saying, "You're so smart. I think you could be the first woman Vice President of the United States." So hey, that was good enough for me. So again, I was raised with a lot of support and self-confidence.

Phyllis H. also gained confidence from her parents' aspirations for her, but following her father's hopes that she would become involved in politics, actually led her to move in the opposite direction:

Phyllis H.: Well, when I grew up, it was in the era following integration reform. My father was an activist, politically. He felt, you know, he was American. He believed in voting rights and fought very hard to make sure that people could have the right to vote. He was part of the civil rights movement. In that time, girls were led towards what their parents wanted. So my father was very interested in my holding public office. I think he believed the teachers who told him that I could be the President of the United States, which I thought was kind of funny.

I think he really believed that I should have a political future, so I grew up believing that I would probably become a lawyer and some level of politician. Worst case scenario: I was going to become a political science professor … or do some diplomatic work; it was always in the area of government or politics. My life as a student reflected that; I always ran for public office in school and won. That continued in high school and college at NYU. I was very active in the anti-war effort and that gained me some prominence at NYU.

I was a young college student, but very involved in the anti-war movement. So politics, to answer to your question, I grew up thinking I would be something like Julian Bond, or any of the major political black leaders you can think of. That's what my father wanted for me.

But lo and behold, I disappointed him greatly because what happened in my college years is that I fell in love with broadcasting, working at the college radio station. Then, the kids at the college radio station were also working part-time at a local television station which, in our case, was WPIX-TV.

I went to the Republican Convention, and I wound up on TV every night of that convention because the delegates did not want to go until the final night of the voting. So I wound up in the front row. Since, at that time, there were not a lot of black people present, CBS-TV was constantly showing me. We were there to support Nelson Rockefeller, who was anti-war at that time, and he lost that convention. This was really an experience … but it was seeing behind the curtain, I think, that made me move more towards being a journalist. That the delegates did not want to go—even though it gave me a seat—was shocking to me.

Q. Tell me more.

Phyllis H.: I think that changed my mind about the purity of politics. There was a lot of other stuff I saw. I was the person who believed in merit and high standards, and I didn't see that in the political realm when I got to take a close look. Also, being a student reporter, I would go to press conferences when I was on the college radio station. I remember getting booed by all the reporters in the room because I asked a question that caused the local politician to answer, at least.

The reporters really weren't interested in anything other than the quick photo ops. So, my asking questions that went into depth and their reaction just really shocked me. That also kind of turned me off on reporting, so I decided I wanted to be an excellent reporter. That just moved me further, to work harder.

Audrey was caught up in prevalent sexist attitudes and lowered her expectations:

Audrey: What I wanted to be when I grew up was a doctor, a medical doctor. I did not become a doctor. I went to a private girls' Catholic high school in Brooklyn. Of course, the nuns were the primary teachers. A classmate and I went to the advisor and I said, "Okay, this is what we want to do." She wanted to be a lawyer and I wanted to be a doctor, and we wanted to know what would be the best course for us. She actually laughed at us; it was just so devastating to me.

My parents are typical Irish Catholic. You basically became a nurse, a teacher, or a nun. The nun thing wasn't going to work for me. Teaching didn't do anything. And I thought, *Well, if everyone says I shouldn't be a doctor, I'll be a nurse.* I went to nursing school and got my Bachelor's degree in Nursing. That was as close as I got.

Larraine's roadblock was much closer to home:

Larraine: I wanted to become a doctor—which my father was—but my dad was adamant that I was too young and, being a woman, I needed to go and become a teacher and get married and have children. Since he was on the admissions committee of the medical school, that was that, basically.

It is easy to see the roots of Susan S.'s eclectic career when we look at the range of her childhood aspirations:

Susan S.: What I wanted to be? I wanted to be a lot of things. I wanted to be a writer. I wanted to be out of my hometown. At one point, I thought I wanted to be a nuclear physicist, but then there was this little question of the mathematics. I just wanted things to be interesting.

Q. That left a lot of possibilities open, didn't it?

Susan S.: Yes, it did. There were many possibilities in my life. I had an art teacher who wanted me to go into that. I had a piano teacher who wanted me to go into that. If I have a talent, it's for recognizing ability. [What I recognized about my own talent was] it said writing. It said criticism. It said … actually, when I was a child, my goal was to get the best education I could.

Q. And did you?

Susan S.: No. Not in my junior high and in high school. I was fortunate to have some of the last survivors of the very old-fashioned teachers. So I got the English. I got the Latin. I got some history. It was well-taught, but it was an inner-city junior high and high school. What I subsequently learned was the best thing I got out of those schools: I learned a certain amount of courage because some of my fellow students were not too friendly. If they thought you were a snob they'd wait for you after school.

I got enough education to get me into the sort of school I wanted. I remember getting in and crying because I knew I was being released into the larger world I knew was out there. When I was eight, my goal was to go to Harvard and join a fraternity. And everybody laughed. But I did go to Harvard for my Ph.D. I was one of the first two woman graduate students to join the Hasty Pudding. So I guess I did it, after all.

Natalie's early aspirations shaped a lifestyle more than a specific career. Natalie said:

Natalie: What did I think I was going to be? I remember playing around a lot, just as kids do, trying on different hats. Nurse—I remember as a young girl wanting to be Nurse Natalie. That didn't last, though. And, of course, teacher and housewife—all those things that little girls in that era tried on. But when it comes to me … I always just wanted to have fun. I didn't know what that might look like; I just knew that when I was an adult, I was darn sure going to have fun.

So I reluctantly started college, and I was really glad that I did because it was completely a different experience. I started at a very small college. I had graduated high school with hundreds and hundreds of other students and then I found this quaint little college. There really was individual instruction, and you got to know your instructor. So college was really a lovely experience.

The difficulty I had was declaring a major. Because I wanted to have fun, I wanted to try everything. I'm a doer, so just sitting down and having these classes—this track of the classes you have to take and this is what you have to do—I ignored that for as long as I could and just got a little bit of a taste of everything. I was involved in theater and then I started taking premed classes because I really got into alternative health therapies. I was just all over the place and I was having fun.

Early Difficulties Shaping Life Choices

Several of The Fifty had childhood challenges that moved them towards or away from certain careers. In some cases, these challenges provided opportunities to develop useful skills; in others, they created determination and a clear path away from a particular lifestyle.

Jan decided, early on, that she wanted a life different from her parents', and ran her first business when she was seven years old. The management and planning skills she developed then—she hired, supervised, and fired employees—served her well throughout her career:

Jan: My earliest recollection of wanting to be anything would probably be in my teens. I don't remember younger than that, other than I knew that I didn't want to be a mother. When I was eight—apparently, there's a legendary story in the family about me being given a baby doll, Betsy Wetsy or something like that. I declined the doll, suggesting that it would be better for my sister, because I preferred to have a Barbie because she had high heels and a car.

My mother, who had three children by the age of twenty-two and a fourth by thirty asked, "Don't you want to learn how to take care of a baby?"

I said, "That work was way too hard," which was based on watching mother work every waking hour, compared to Daddy "only" working six days a week from dawn to dusk on bridge construction, which seemed a better deal since he got to rest in the evening. When mother pointed out that shoes and cars costs money, I said, "Well, I'll get a job."

So I was eight when I decided what wasn't in my future, but I hadn't concluded what I wanted to do. In my teens, there were two things that were of interest to me: One was computers, because they were becoming new and the thing to do and I knew my father was interested in them. He saw them as a way out of his blue collar existence. While he never made it out, some of his thoughts around computers being the wave of the future influenced me.

The other thing I thought about was journalism because in high school I did some writing … I think I was an assistant editor or something for the high school band newsletter or something like that. So those were two things I thought about, but by the time I had gotten into high school and was about to go to university, I had begun to change my thinking.

Q. *So what directions were you thinking about by the time you got to college?*

Jan: Well, I was beginning to really understand the implications of poverty, and it was very, very clear that I had no desire to deal with the poverty and discrimination that my parents had dealt with. This wasn't the first time I realized it, though. I went into my first business endeavor at seven to earn the money needed to buy my school pictures—not that I really wanted the pictures, but I certainly didn't want the embarrassment of being the only one who couldn't pay for their pictures.

I guess I always knew that having a job was quite different than having a career. So my first job: I was seven when I first started selling flower seeds. I would pick up pop bottles to build up capital for my inventory, because five packets of seeds cost a quarter and each packet sold for ten cents, so I would collect pop bottles to buy my starter capital. Then I reinvested the capital by buying ten packets and then twenty and then forty, etc.

By the time I was eight, I had saturated my market (since I wasn't allowed to leave my neighborhood). Since no one was going to be buying any more flowers, I would sell my services to plant the flowers, since I noticed they had bought but not planted the flowers. Then it expanded to lawn moving, babysitting, and stuff like that.

I quickly had more work than I could do myself, so I would hire other kids to work for me and I would sell their work. I would take a ten percent agent fee but make sure they showed up and were doing a quality job, or else I wouldn't use them again.

Q. *You understood the principals of business ownership and entrepreneurship and staff management by the time you were out of elementary school.*

Jan: I was eleven, so I was still in elementary school when I had my first three employees, but I did find that children were not very reliable. And you didn't make enough money to really make a difference. That was when I started to realize that these were not my ultimate goals, but they were a means to an end, not the end itself.

I remember I didn't have any concept [about going to college] because no one in my family had been to university, other than my grandmother. She was a school teacher living in Alaska, and she wasn't influencing the application process. But I got a notice, as all seniors did, in the fall that I had to come take this test on a Saturday. I was pretty ticked off about it because it meant I had to be off work for a day.

At that point, I was working in fast food, which meant I had to give up a day's income to take this test. But they said, "If you don't, then you won't get into university," and I knew that I had to go to university.

Jan was always a planner, and her discussion of her career reflects her ability to take a long-range view and to recombine and synthesize her skills:

Jan: That is one of the wonderful things about working in big professional services firms: you work in so many companies; you see the insides of so many things. In time, it became clear to me that Oklahoma wasn't going to be the place I needed to be, longer-term. I had been doing quite a lot of IT-related work, since the partners and senior managers in the firm didn't know much about computers, because computers hadn't been a critical part of their experience over the years.

When clients such as banks, insurance companies, and retailers all began to use computers throughout their businesses, we started needing to audit their key systems. The head of audit went through the university transcripts of all the new hires to see who had IT classes. He noticed I had quite a few. He approached me to help him understand some things about computers, which I did. Eventually, within only a couple of years, I was leading the IT portion of the audit function, and I was actually going to the global headquarters, which was then in Cleveland, Ohio (it's now in London, England) and teaching courses on IT.

In time, they offered me a role to transfer to Cleveland to do research and development of new methodologies, etc. Within the firm, there was a history of people who had spent time in headquarters being promoted to partner. So it seemed to be on my path to partnership, which was still firmly in my head.

I went to the managing partner of our local office and told him that I wanted to go to Cleveland to do this role. He was quite resistant, because he wanted me to stay, make partner in Oklahoma City, and be part of the succession planning there. He is a wonderful leader, but I said to him, "The truth of the matter is, Brian and I are going to leave Oklahoma. The question is whether I do it with the firm or without the firm." He approved the transfer. Then I went to Cleveland, Ohio, where I helped develop methodologies and tools for how to integrate IT into the audits of all of our global clients.

Q. I was just going to ask you to circle back for a second, because I was going to ask you what happened to the parachute boyfriend who became your husband.

Jan: He went to work for Colgate-Palmolive, when we were in Oklahoma, in sales and marketing. I'm very structured, so before we got married, we negotiated a number of things for both of us. Since we both planned to have careers, among the things we negotiated was that we would take every career decision that came along and together decide what was better for both of us. Part of the thing about me declining the CIA and the FBI was that Brian had had a very good job with Colgate-Palmolive which he had just started.

When the opportunity to transfer to Cleveland happened, we both really understood the long-term financial implications to my career development and my chance of making partner, so he changed jobs and went to work for Johnson Wax in Cleveland in a similar sales and marketing role.

Later, when we had the opportunity to advance my career and move abroad, while he didn't have a job opportunity in the U.K., we both thought it seemed a wonderful experience for both of us to be able to live in London for what was going to be eighteen months. While we were in London for over 20 years, he went through a number of iterations in terms of some two major career changes and ultimately ended up in the academic world, which he really loved.

Q. *Okay, so let's circle back to when you moved to Cleveland.*

Jan: While I was in Cleveland, I went to night school and got my MBA. I was finding that my technical studies in accounting—with quite a lot of IT—were great for technology. But as I looked at leadership roles, it would be helpful to have an understanding of a more general management background. My husband went back with me. He had decided he wanted to go back and get an MBA. I figured it was going to absolutely destroy our social life with him doing that all the time. So I thought, *Well, if I ever am going to do it, I should do it now, so we can both have the same commitments.*

We literally took the exact same curriculum, the same classes, same everything. We were in every class together and both graduated, incidentally, with a 4.0 because, I think, we encouraged each other. If one of us was like, "I don't want to study tonight," the other would say, "No, no, no. We have to study." So I think having a study partner was a good thing, which is why we graduated first and second in the class.

Q. *I also love it that you chose to make the same sacrifices at the same time. That seems to me like a great friction-reducer.*

Jan: Not really, as we don't have a great deal of friction in our relationship. We are very different … stylistically, in terms of how we deal with stress and things like that, but we have learned a lot about each other over the years. Some of the things we sat down and organized before we got married, like having some rules on how to argue. We have held to, maybe, seven, eight rules that helped us deal with those stresses. That's been very helpful. And just a lot of respect for each other and support for each other, I think, is quite critical in these things.

When I was talking to world leaders about accounting and tax standards and various things like that, they would say, "So, what are you accountants doing about measuring carbon emissions and greenhouse gases?" So I started working with the team to develop an answer. Simultaneously, when I took the regulatory role that I did not want, I asked for another project to do on the side that was more interesting than regulatory and public policy might have been. So I started looking at where the next big revenue streams would be for the firm. One of them was around audit, compliance, and taxing of climate change and sustainability matters.

Between the two efforts, I was becoming a bit of an expert in the business and reporting aspects of climate change and sustainability. I think in my bio there's a list of some of the organizations that I was involved with, as well.

I began to look at how we were going to set up this new business practice and how it was going to be organized on a global basis. I did a business plan for the NEMA executive board on what we needed to do. I proposed that we hire someone to create it but, in the end, they decided that I would be a good global leader for it because I also understood the business side of it. In particular, I wasn't an environmentalist trying to save the planet, but rather a pragmatist thinking about the business side of it. I always say I'm the Jerry McGuire of climate change, "I will show you the money." But I also know the more we get business behind this, the more likely we are to save the planet.

Q. Great. So what's next?

Jan: I moved into that newly-created role and then started hiring great people so we could set up the global practice, working with audit, tax, consulting, transactions advisory services, as well as every industry group. I traveled the world, creating that practice and building up a global climate change and sustainability practice which had previously not existed. Effectively, this was my third turn within Ernst & Young creating something new. That's fairly unusual in the big firms because, again, they've been around for a hundred years, more than a hundred years, and it's not very common to set up new practices.

Q. No, they don't change that easily, and for you to have been deeply involved and heading up three of them, I would say is quite unusual. It doesn't seem to me that there were a lot of other women around. What were the proportions?

Jan: Well, that's the interesting thing. It's one of the lessons that I learned through this process, that if you have women in leadership, it actually attracts other women.

At the time I was the managing partner of technology and security practice, there were nine business units. The average percentage of women partners was twelve. My practice had thirty percent. What was really noteworthy is that I had no women's programs at all.

Both Susana and Herta's families were forced to leave the Transylvanian area of Romania because of religious persecution.

Susana: I grew up in northern Transylvania, close to the Hungarian and Ukrainian border, still in Romania. I was born right after the World War II, in 1947. That, in itself, places me at an interesting historical juncture because it was the beginning of communism and the end of the concentration camp for both my parents. Both of my parents were Holocaust survivors. They went back to their homeland in Transylvania because they were looking for long-lost relatives, perhaps other people who had survived in the family.

The borders of Romania closed when Romania became communist, and they were stuck together with a lot of other Jewish couples who had just gotten married. I was born a year after they got married and, at that point, although there were other people living in Romania going off to the West, my parents did not leave. So I grew up in a very picturesque village at the foothill of the Cartesian mountains in a very beautiful physical setting, but with a lot of painful, convoluted history.

I went to school in Romania and spoke both Hungarian and Romanian, because Jews spoke both languages and dreamt of leaving; that was always the dream. I had a geography teacher who talked about the smell, the scent of flowers along the Mediterranean, and the oleanders that grew wild. And I dreamt of oleanders growing in the wild and looking at the many, many stars of the Mediterranean Sea; so I dreamt of exploring the world and travelling.

Q. Wonderful. So how did you finally start working towards that dream and how did you end up leaving your country?

Susana: There was a great effort on the part of Israel to free Jews in East European countries. They established a relationship with Romania, in particular. Romania was very interested in money; they were poor in the early '60s. They were also interested in growing their economy, so they established this relationship—very, very complicated—through this intermediary, a British business man who served as middleman. Romania would request either money or—the year that we left, which was 1962, their favorite currency was bull semen. So they had either bull semen or pig or cattle that will be exchanged for the freedom of poor Jews who lived in Romania.

The year that we left—I saw this in a museum of communist atrocities [when] we went back to Romania recently—there were tens of thousands of Jewish families that left. I have just recently found out the currency that was used, so I really like to talk about the fact that my freedom was purchased with a bag of bull semen.

Q. It's a great story.

Susana: Well it's a great story, but … it killed any kind of nostalgia that they might have held for the place where I was born. It kind of squashes any kind of old joy of childhood, because to live with for parents, to live with the thought that they were going to be freed any minute. We have this huge trunk in my parent's bedroom that was called the Israel trunk. That was going to be filled with all the things that they would allow us to leave with.

Eventually, in the spring of 1962, we were allowed to leave. We did, indeed, pack the large trunk with all the stuff that they would let us take, [things] that would be totally useless and meaningless in the West; china and clothes and nothing of value, nothing of great value to the family was taken out, and off we went. In February of 1962 we left Romania. Our first stop was Vienna, where there were Jews from everywhere also escaping communism. After two weeks in Vienna, we went off to Brussels where we needed to renounce our request to land in Brussels, because that was the agreement, I guess, [because] the bull semen came from Belgium.

As described more fully in Chapter 4, Susana's experiences with so many different people and languages served her well in her work as a translator, language teacher, and leader of diversity programs. Herta's story of leaving Romania was different:

Herta: I was born in a German-speaking part of Transylvania in Romania, in the heart of communism. Being German in Romania was simply not an easy thing. Being a Christian in an atheist country was another challenge and then a Seventh Day Adventist Christian on top of that. So it was really being a minority of a minority of a minority.

I grew up very much with the notion that people can take away anything from you, but they cannot take away your attitude and your dignity. That was very much drilled into me growing up. My grandparents and parents had lost everything, pretty much, after the war. The property with the communist takeover was basically expropriated. They were left with limited, limited financial means. I grew up with the sense of: In spite of the circumstances, you can achieve.

I was a very good student, so to me, the intellectual challenges were fascinating and interesting. From the time I was three feet tall, I basically wanted to be a lawyer. I wanted to be a lawyer specifically because I think we are shaped by our history. My mother and grandmother were court-martialed during World War II for no other reason but because they worshipped on Saturday. This was the height of the Holocaust, and this was a criminal offense. The punishment for that type of infraction, even if you did it in the privacy of your home, was many, many years in prison if you were convicted. To make the long story short, my mother and grandmother were, indeed, convicted. I mean, it was an open and shut case. But, through an amazing chain of events, the judge commuted the sentence.

My mother was fourteen years old at that time. So I grew up with this notion that God can do great things, and lawyers can do pretty good things, too. So I thought lawyers were great people and that I would be a lawyer when I grew up. I would actually defend the people who needed defense, and so forth. So that was my desire as a little child.

Q. So you grew up in this German-speaking section of Romania, but you didn't remain there. Where did you go?

Herta: Again, this was an amazing chain of events. You may remember, in the seventies, this really was height of the Cold War. Hardly anybody was able to get out from behind the [Iron] Curtain. The Germans in our neighborhood all had a relative or most of us had relatives in the West. For example, my grandfather lived and died in Austria. I saw him once. He was unable to come back and he was unable to get his family out. So I saw him once in '68.

This was when Russia had become very belligerent and the Soviet Union, at that time, very belligerent. In '68, you had the … Czech uprising and basically, the Soviet tanks just ran across Eastern Europe, brutally extinguishing that uprising. But Ceausescu who, at that time, was the President of Romania, had the audacity to actually stand up to the Russians. So he was really considered kind of a maverick in the west.

The U.S. had its famous foreign policy, you know, "My enemy's enemy is my friend." And because Ceausescu had actually stood up to the Russians, the U.S. in '75 had granted Romania Most-Favored-Nation status. As part of that treaty, Romania had to commit to the United States that the former would allow people to immigrate to the United States who had first-degree relatives in the U.S.

First-degree relatives were basically parents and children; it was a very narrow definition of first-degree relative. Again, in an amazing chain of events, my sister had married an American in '74. In '75, the Most-Favored-Nation status was granted to Romania. Also in '75, my grandfather died in Austria—my father could not even go to his funeral. But as soon as the U.S. granted Romania the favorable status, we applied, my parents and I, for a passport to immigrate to the United States. We applied for the passport, and within nine months we had permission to leave. Then, you know, it took another five or six months to get all the paperwork sorted. But on November first of '76, we landed at JFK.

I was eighteen. I was in twelfth grade. The U.S. was, I mean, the sky was the limit. We had to pay to relinquish our Romanian citizenship. I arrived in the States literally as an alien: no citizenship, no nothing, no money, no nothing. But there was the sense of "the sky is the limit".

I've got a good head on my shoulders. I already spoke pretty good English when I arrived in the States. I was multilingual, so I started right away. I needed only a couple of credits to finish high school. I finished high school, but at the same time, started to take college classes at the community college. I worked my tail off to earn some money so I could pay for my classes. I remember perfecting my English by reading the dictionary. It's a great thing.

What Herta said she learned from this is that dignity and attitude are all-important. This is similar to what Donna learned from her parents, both Holocaust survivors:

Donna: I'm an only child of two Auschwitz concentration camp survivors. That certainly colored my world, because the one thing I was always taught is that everything can be taken from you except your brain. So knowledge and reading and books and learning were very, very important.

The Past Predicts the Future?

We carry our childhood with us, for good or ill. Our earliest messages often shape our later choices. Strong, positive messages create strong, resilient adults; strong negative messages can create lingering doubts and fears. If your messages were limiting—like the one I got from my Uncle Don who, although he barely knew me, insisted I was lazy; or Alice's father, who wanted her to remain subservient to men—it may take a lifetime to move beyond that.

Exercise

- What did you want to be when you were a child?
- Can you identify threads of that choice later in life?
- Does that childhood dream suggest something you might want to go back to now?
- Or skills that you could use for the next great thing you want to bring into your life?

Synthesizing and Recombining

Many of the women I spoke with found interesting ways to recombine their skills. This both informed careers and allowed for some interesting career transitions.

An attitude of enjoyment and exploration supported Natalie's choices, which included co-owning a crafts store, creating new ways of relating to children, adults, and elders in her activities in early childhood education, home schooling, and coaching those involved in elder care. All of these pursuits led to the development of a skill set that helped to shape the creation of Ageless-Sages, a publishing company for books designed for elders as well as an umbrella organization for creating a new outlook in elder care.

Susan S.: Finally, I got into finance. And I enjoyed it. I had enough intellectual gravitas that if an analyst would say, "Well, surely, you can understand that," I would say, "No, I don't. It's not that I'm stupid; it's that you're being unclear. Now if you could explain it, I can translate it."

At the time, I was also writing science fiction novels. In about '85, just when I thought I would go for the Certified Financial Analyst, I sold five books.

In preparing for an academic career, Susan S. had to develop and hone her research skills and become knowledgeable in a wide range of subjects. She had to understand history and literature and she had to be able to write well. Her ability to transfer and recombine those skills allowed her to move successfully into new fields. Not everyone would automatically connect Medieval Studies to science fiction and to finance, yet these connections were clear to Susan S. She discussed how the research skills she developed as a Medieval scholar helped maintain accuracy in her writing and aided her in understanding the financial world:

Susan S.: People in the industry took a while, but they realized I could do Boolean searches like nobody's business. I enjoyed it. I don't just think outside the box; I don't know where the box is. This is something science fiction writers are very good at. And, when you combine it with the Medieval sensibility and put things together, well, it's no wonder that Lewis and Tolkien and Charles Williams were Medieval scholars. Also, my father turned me on to *Star Trek*.

Q. So, you entered the wonderful world of finance and you were writing, both at the same time?

Susan S.: No, I was no longer writing fiction. In 2006, I left my job and my publisher simultaneously. I love the novels I wrote. I wrote historical fantasy. I wrote about five *Star Trek* novels with a collaborator, now deceased. I wrote some hard science fiction and because of, again, the Medievalist in me … one of the things you have to learn is military history.

You have to learn not just military history, but with what and how they fought. So that wasn't considered a dirty word, it was just considered more data. Naturally, I ran into veterans because a lot of the military really likes science fiction—you don't want to know what they think of the various *Star Trek* captains—but they enjoy *Star Trek*. Anyway, they picked up my name; so did some of the Medieval scholars. But they come after you, so you have to get it right. Besides, it's like a tremendous puzzle and game that you can put together.

Susan P. had a variety of interests as a child that seemed to come together to inform her career choices. Although she met some success as an actress, she discovered that she didn't like it and preferred working with people in different ways:

Susan P.: We started a thing called the Actor's Information Project, where we collected information and actors would come, and join, and get the information. Well, the interesting part about this is, why it's a precursor to coaching: people did not know how to use the information; they didn't know what they wanted. So we started developing an introductory workshop, about twelve hours long, on not only goal-setting, but basically, the philosophy that if you're not going to have fun and work with people, it's not worth it. And that your well-being is really important.

We had career consulting. We didn't realize at the time that it was coaching. It went on for quite a long time. Henry House, Madeleine Holman, and [other] people who became famous coaches worked for us.

Henry said, "Well, we could do this for real people [non-actors]."

And Jay said, "No, you don't … no, you can't."

Henry, towards the end [of our business], went out to California, met Thomas Leonard, and hooked up Jay with Thomas Leonard.

We went out of business about '91 because of the economy in New York, and we really did not have enough of a reserve. In the meantime, Jay had started working with Thomas Leonard. After having twelve years of experience—basically doing coaching— he and Thomas, he was able to be at the forefront of coaching. Henry went on to form Coaches Training Institute (CTI). Mad Holman went on, and Cynthia Darst and Loy Darst worked for us. She ended up working at CTI.

It was really quite extraordinary, it was really a precursor … it was nascent coaching. We really didn't care whether someone got an acting job, just as long as they were happy, so it was very holistic. Part of it was from *est* training stuff, but part of it was like, well, "We're all hippie people." We weren't attached to, "Oh, you need to be on Broadway," or "You need to be this." Rather, it was, "Oh, you want to do something in a parking lot! Isn't that great!"

The other thing that was so great about it was that the philosophy was to work together; it was not a competition. You worked with other people. So people worked together and had a great time, rather than having to compete or asking for support. We were brave, but we called for free peer consulting, which was basically coaching.

Jan reached a point in her career where she realized that the next logical step was to combine all of her experiences into a more flexible career:

Jan: I also decided, around that same time, it was time for me to leave Ernst & Young. I wanted to do a board portfolio and to have more choices in whom I worked with and what I worked on. The best way to do that was to "go portfolio," which I've done. It doesn't really matter where I live, as long as I have access to a good airport.

Q. Tell me a little about this concept of portfolio.

Jan: Okay, I've always been a long-term planner, both in my work and personal life. I had my first long-term plan when I was eight, so I was always looking at least a decade out. Sometime in my thirties, after I made partner, I started thinking, *What's going to be next?* Managing partner was, obviously, something I aspired to, but what after that? As I looked at that, I looked at businessmen and women I knew who were ten to fifteen years older than me and looked at the kinds of things they were doing.

In Europe, we call what I have done "going portfolio." Basically, I have not retired, but I no longer work for one organization. I choose the things I work on. Basically, you've got thirty years of business experience working in all different kinds of companies and working in downturns and booms and expanding in different markets and dealing with different personnel issues and all of that. So we bring that to bear on a number of companies, so you choose a board portfolio and you work full-time, but you don't retire.

Ernst & Young is a wonderful place to work, and I had many wonderful experiences. They indulged my creativity, supporting me in creating businesses and things like that; that was great. But the reality is that you end up working, sometimes, with people that you don't want to work with, that you don't enjoy the time with. Sometimes, more often than not, that may be an individual at a client's that is difficult. By difficult, I mean "mean-spirited." Not difficult as in challenging issues to be addressed, because challenging is great, but mean-spirited is not. And you can't walk away from it, because you're a managing partner and there are millions of dollars or pounds or euros of business for your firm. You can't just say, "You know what? I don't like spending time with you, so I'm going to move on."

But when you do a board portfolio—and my portfolio is a bit broader than boards, because I also do executive-in-residence at universities, and I do some writing for magazines, etc., and a lot of public speaking—I only do the things I want to do, that I will find intellectually challenging, and that I feel will be using my talents, whatever they are, to best effect.

Some of the boards I've been asked to be on, when I met the chairman or CEO, I thought, *You know what? He's just a bully and I don't want to work with a bully.* Now I don't say that out loud, but that's what's going on in my head, and I find another reason to tell them that I don't want the board. So the boards I take on are people who are very ambitious for the business, but humble in their approach. And they respect each other and they work toward a common good for the company and the shareholders.

I go through a lot of due diligence with companies before I take them on. I always say that I have just as much stress and I work just as many hours, but it's all joyful stress now.

Q. In my terms, then, this is a form of high-level consultancy.

Jan: You know, I don't like the word consultancy myself because I was a consultant at Ernst &Young and the thing about consulting is, you are hired by somebody. You work to their agenda. If you say something different than what they want to hear, then they will usually fire you. In the roles that I am in, I am my own person.

As a board member, you have a responsibility to support the CEO, but by the same token, the CEO has a responsibility to the board for delivering results. The board, as a collective, hires and fires the CEO. As consultants, that's not the case. So you really get to be authentic in terms of what you do.

Cheryl stayed in related careers, even though she changed jobs and eventually went out on her own. Hers is not a story of reinvention, as she says, but rather of using skills as building blocks that she could reconfigure in different ways to be successful in related fields. She defines her career choices this way:

Cheryl: I've never had any grand plan. I wake up every morning with a million ideas and then I sort through what's doable and what's not. Then, the ones that stick around for a while and then keep coming back to me—and I find that happens a lot—I'll try and pursue those.

Q. So what led to the Three Tomatoes?

Cheryl: Well, when I left the ad agency business, I started this marketing consulting firm. I had this idea in my head because I knew all the bright, smart, wonderful women in New York City who were over the age of forty-five, some of them well over the age of forty-five, who not only were very accomplished in their careers, but in their lives. They are people who sit on boards, they're involved in philanthropy, but they still love to have fun, they still like to go out and have a good time, feel great, and enjoy themselves.

Looking around, I felt that to marketers, in particular in New York City, we had become the invisible women. We were being completely ignored and everything was being focused on what I call the "smart twenty-something size zeros." They were missing a huge market! We actually had money to spend and disposable incomes but really, no one was talking to us about where to go, where to shop, what to do. And I thought, *That's just silly.*

I had these great friends who were having these great conversations and I thought, *Well, I'll just start an e-newsletter*—because e-newsletters were starting to get popular around that time—*and it's just going to be about the kinds of conversations I'm having with my girlfriends.*

I sent the first newsletter out to sixty friends. This was a little over five years ago, and it just took on a life of its own, really virally, through word of mouth. It has grown to 12,000 subscribers and we now have this robust website and fantastic, amazing contributors. Many of them come to us and say, "We'd really like to be part of this. We love what you're doing."

It has been the most extraordinary experience for the last year-and-a half. My husband actually said to me at some point—you know, I was just doing this and watching it grow and seeing what was happening—"You really have to get more serious about this and treat it like a client."

That is what I have been doing for the last year-and-a-half. That is where ninety-eight percent of my efforts are going … and really trying to grow it as a business and see where we can take it. It has been just an amazing adventure. It's really the most amazing thing I've experienced, career-wise, business-wise.

Q. That's wonderful. I just love it. I look forward to it, always delighted by something. It seems to me that what the Three Tomatoes has done is really captured the essence of a certain kind of woman in ways that other sites haven't quite.

Cheryl: Yeah. We're celebrating who we are … we're just sharing. We're not about empowering you. At this stage of our lives, these are women about whom I like to say, "Have so much power they could light up Manhattan." We don't need to be telling you what to do with your lives. We're really sharing things we enjoy doing. As I said, it's the conversations that you and I are having and we're having with our other friends, so I think there's an authenticity to it that you don't feel with some other media properties, whether they're websites or magazine that are trying to talk to this particular group of women. I think that was what struck a chord. As I said, it has been amazing. I've met some of the most extraordinary people through the *Three Tomatoes*, and every day brings something new.

Q. So what do you see as the future for the Tomatoes and for you?

Cheryl: What I'm really trying to do now is to see where we can grow it as a business entity. We really want to grow that subscriber base. We're bringing in marketers and advertisers now who are now realizing the value of reaching this really-hard-to-reach demographic. You know, it's not really a demographic, I shouldn't say that, because not all women over forty-five are lumped into one group. But certainly, the way I like to describe this audience is, smart and savvy women, accomplished women, who also have substance and they're multi-dimensional with a lot of interests. So we're definitely focusing on that, growing it.

It would be great one day for someone to come along and say, "We want to buy you," which would be the ultimate dream. But just working it through and actually saying, "Yeah, we're making money on this, we can grow it, hire people, bring in more partners."

It has just been a great experience. It has just been fun. Of course, I am working harder now than I ever have in my entire life because it really is a 24/7 kind of a deal. But as I said, the opportunities and the incredible people that I have met.

Jeannette moved through a series of positions that allowed her to use her writing and communication skills in different, but related ways:

Jeannette: This is, again, "If you see a fork in the road, you take it." I interviewed for two jobs: a house editor at BBDO and, at the time—this is way back when very few women were reporting on business—I went to McGraw-Hill. The head of human resources there, a man who was way ahead of his time, said, "I would love to get you as a writer for *Business Week*. It will be tough, because at this time Chris Hawkins says they don't like to hire women, but you have such a great background and portfolio."

In the meantime, he sent me to a few trade publications there. I was waiting and then I was called by BBDO. I was having these concurrent interviews and I said, "Whichever job comes first is the one I'm taking." The BBDO job came through, so that was the fork in the road that I took. It led me to a career in public relations, I mean, as simple as that. I think the really interesting point here is that I didn't start as a professional; I started out as a secretary. In fact, I wanted to start as a stenographer.

Betsy was looking for a sense of connection early in her career, and eventually used those connection-building skills to grow The Transition Network:

Betsy: So in some sense, the Financial Women's Association was a great way to connect with women. Many of them were single. I mean, I got to a point also where I thought I probably wouldn't get married, and that was okay. I certainly had a great life. But the right person came along, and it's incredibly wisdom-enhancing to be married.

Anyway, going back to my parallel life: after I finished as president of the Financial Women's Association and had a little more free time, I got very involved with the women's networking group at Chase. In fact, I was working in Jersey City at the time, so I helped to start the Jersey City or the New Jersey chapter of that internal women's networking organization.

I felt it was absolutely the right thing to do and it was also a way to, again, connect with women across the organization, to connect with a variety of women in my location in Jersey City, and [do] something I believe very much in. So in hindsight, those activities were really leading to my future career. I didn't necessarily think of it that way, but they were just life-enhancing activities that I wanted to invest time in.

Fast-forward to 2005: I was finishing up a project at Chase—it was almost a two-year project—but one that was defined as something that would come to an end. We were in the midst of our latest merger with Bank One, so I was interviewing for my next job within J.P. Morgan Chase.

My two alternatives were to find my next job within the firm or take a one year severance package. My decision date was April 15. On about March 31, I woke up in the middle of the night and said, *It's time for a change. Get out of there, take the severance package.* P.S.: I was forty-nine and three-quarters; I was just about to turn fifty. I said, *If you're going to start your new career, don't wait. Get out there and start it now.*

Q. And that's an interesting sort of pinnacle age for so many women.

Betsy: Yes. I mean, I felt great about turning fifty. I had no problem with that, turning fifty, but I just felt life is finite My work with the women's networking and the Financial Women's Association had really led me to the conclusion that in the next phase of my working life, I wanted to work in a permission-driven organization. I was looking for a full-time job. I have always worked long hours and I knew that I would work long hours in the new job, but I wanted something where the mission was more and [the organization] was really making a difference in the world.

Q. It's interesting though that—and this is true for both men and women—that at midlife, we tend to shift from achievement to looking for meaning in what we're doing. It sounds like that's exactly what happened for you as well. So, ready for your next job…

Betsy: I was in my countdown and a couple of things happened. I had obvious job prospects, although I had learned that The Transition Network—the organization of which I'm now executive director—was looking to hire its first executive director. I found out about that job through the executive director of the Financial Women's Association. So, through a networking contact, she knew I was looking to leave, and she knew I was interested in an organization working with women or girls. I had effectively planted a seed in the minds of people and that seed started to sprout: that was one thing I had heard of.

I sent in a resume with a cover letter. Hadn't heard anything and so, as I was leaving, I sent a note to the usual 150 people that you worked with, saying I was going to be looking for a job in the non-profit sector. One of the people I wrote to said, "Congratulations, I'm excited for you and by the way, I'm on the board of a non-profit. They're looking to hire someone. I think you would be terrific, so please send your resume to so and so."

One of my takeaways with that is, Get out there and tell everyone what you're looking for, be as specific as possible, and good things will happen. I ended up getting an interview with The Transition Network because I identified two networking contacts so well that the founders, when they first saw my resume, did not click. Somebody called them and said, "You have to absolutely interview Betsy." Obviously, she is very persuasive because I was the last person interviewed, and I ended up getting the job.

Q. So what do you see next in your life?

Betsy: This is a timely question, Susan. Actually, I have just announced that I will be leaving The Transition Network in July. My husband and I are making an extended cross-country trip. This has been his dream since he was a boy. It was going to be in a Volkswagen camper, although we've decided no, it won't be in a Volkswagen camper. So I am going to go off on an epic adventure.

The Transition Network will find its second executive director and certainly, when I'm back, I am excited about finding my next encore career. I don't know what it will be, so that's scary. I haven't done a resume in eight years. On the other hand, if I don't know if I can figure out how to make a transition, shame on me, because I've been talking to people about this for years. I think change is healthy and I am, of course, absolutely committed to making sure that the next executive director is successful and has a great starting point.

Among other things in my life, my husband and I have lived in the same Upper West Side apartment … I have lived there for twenty years. We moved in after we got married. I began to feel—this is probably five years ago—that it was time to move.

I absolutely love my work; I love the people I work with. I hope that in my next job, I will find as much satisfaction. I'm sure I will, but I just felt it was time to repack myself. In fact, moving to my new apartment, also in the Upper West Side, was a bit traumatic. [Laughter]

I saw in William Bridges' [book], that here's change and there's transition. I thought it was just going to be change and it turned out to be [a transition]—I really went through a very tough period, which was totally unexpected. It was much harder for me than changing jobs.

Q. Yeah, it is a transition and it's not a change.

Betsy: And yet, it has worked out wonderfully. It has been life-enhancing and so, I think part of my philosophy is, "In order to grow, sometimes you need to make a change. Get out there, and take a risk."

Q. You do, and congratulations on being ready to do it. What have you decided to travel in?

Betsy: We're going to be in a sedan, so just pretty plain vanilla.

Q. I know a few people who are doing the Winnebago route, so I had to ask.

Betsy: We thought about that, but it's so much more expensive and also, when my husband had this childhood dream, he was eight or nine. At that time, he was probably five feet tall and now he's 6'4", so by the time you get the Winnebago where he could stand up in the shower, you're really talking big bucks. Three months of not being able to stand up in the shower is just not going to enhance the experience of the Grand Tetons or the ...

Q. No, probably won't. You may want to leave this open-ended too.

Betsy: Well, that's true. That's true, so it's an adventure, it's a break, it's a risk, it's an opportunity, and it's exciting.

Q. It's tremendously exciting. Very excited for you. There are so many wonderful things to see and, at this point, I'm assuming that The Transition Network is going to be a little more useful in this, because you probably know people practically every place, just in case you want to make contacts along the way.

Betsy: I do. Yes, exactly so. That's another wonderful part of the organization, is that we connect people in a dozen locations in the country, and more to come. A number of our members who have moved have been able to find a new community in a new city because of The Transition Network, but I'm coming back to New York.

Nancy E. started as a social worker, but eventually realized that she would need to find less traditional ways to use her skills to create a life that satisfied her:

Nancy E.: I worked at Cornell. That was a real growth period for me, because so much was being developed in the area of child abuse at the time. I got to help create the curricula, work with some really preeminent people in the field, worked with academics who didn't know how to train, so I would often work with the curriculum. I got to go to England and do training with people who did the sexual abuse interviewing, people who had done a lot of the research on it, and I was paired to go with them on these various training assignments across New York State and then over in England. It was good, but it involved a lot of travel.

I decided I wanted to start my own business—that was in 1983. I started my own business, People Potential. So I think, for Cornell, I only went there four days a week. I had my business in the background, and would pick up a day of training here and there. I wound up leaving Cornell, but then they hired me as a consultant. So I had a long relationship with them, in terms of a work partnership.

Q. So what else was going on in your life? Were you doing other things outside of work or were you just working?

Nancy E.: I was married for a few years. That didn't work out. When I was single again, that's when I was doing a lot of this traveling. That was really interesting. But I think a lot of the social activism in the seventies had really quieted down. I didn't stay in an activist stance. I needed to earn an income, pay my rent. I think things like going to plays and a little bit of travel ... I always went back to Mexico. I loved going to Paris; that was a favorite spot. And then England, did a lot of that for work.

Q. So basically, your job was, to some degree, social activism, but you were doing the young single New Yorker thing.

Nancy E.: Yeah, but it was like doing training. The thing about it, Susan, which is interesting—this is the thing that I think is very complicated about social work—is that, eventually, nobody's happy about how these services are done. A lot of it is very judgmental, and you have all these eligibility requirements, and the whole thing about fraud, and all those kind of things. So you become an agent of the government, for people to fill out applications, and you have got to verify things and then you have to interview them, and you have to determine whether they are lying or not.

It's an interesting dilemma because, without noticing it, you wind up being complicit with the system. It was the best we knew how to do, so I can't criticize it that much, but it was hard for me to do some of the direct practice because it felt terrible to do this stuff to people. They're in need, and you're, "I'm sorry, but you need to prove this and you need to prove that." And then as a trainer, you're training people how to do these interviews. I mean, mostly, my work was more about determining if a child was safe or had been abused, so it wasn't that bad.

Q. No [it wasn't that bad]. I became an expert at the other part of it myself, so I know what you are talking about, because we were trying to get students four-year degrees and the Department of Social Services did not want to approve Bachelor's degrees.

Nancy E.: Right. Right. One of the things I notice about myself is that I used to question myself, "Why don't I like to take a job and stay in it?" And I realized for myself that my role in life was not going to be to enter the mainstream of an organization. The place that I liked to be was a bit on the rim. Having a foot in understanding those environments—I really liked the public-sector environment and not-for-profit, that's really the area I stayed in—and then having one foot out so I could have the freedom to look at new things and then bring it into my work with training and things. Always looking for some innovation, something interesting, what were some of the new ways of looking at things, but staying on the rim, and not joining in.

I mean, I had two times when I took jobs, and they were very short. I was training director for the Department of Juvenile Justice in New York City. I met one of the deputy commissioners at a conference and really liked her. This was Ellen Schall, who became Dean of the Wagner School. I was so taken with her and her leadership that I felt I could learn a lot, so I went in and did that. But then, that's when I got married, and we lived in New Jersey. At that time, they were enforcing the residency for New York City employees, so I had to resign. I mean, I probably would have stayed longer there because they were doing phenomenal organizational development work. To be part of that was just wonderful. Another time, I became the director of training at the Federation of Protestant Welfare Agencies. I did that for a little over a year.

It was the last time that I got inside, and that's when I really realized that wasn't my work. I haven't tried that again; it's been a long time since then. Then, because I got to know people in the city, I ran into Richard Gitlin somewhere. They were doing those interviews for trainers with the city and then Susan Blau, who had been with Cornell and did some of the child abuse training years ago; she was the training person at Department of Citywide Administration Services (DCAS).

I found it fascinating to work with city agencies. I love New York City government; I think it's fascinating, and to learn about how each of the agencies [works] in a city as big as New York. And some of the projects that you and I worked on together—some of them were quite challenging—but I still like most of my work at DCAS, and find it really, really interesting. I am in the middle of some stuff with the fire department. So it's all just fascinating to me.

Q. Tell me more about why this is fascinating.

Nancy E.: Well, I think you have people responding to Bloomberg's initiatives or whatever and then you have certain commissioners coming in. Definitely from a change perspective, and to see some of the innovation; but also, where the city has started to pay attention to leadership training.

We were on the cusp of this real push toward people learning how to lead, how to run a project, how to be efficient. I mean, there was a time [when] people had no training in any of these things, so you had the corporate business people almost mocking government. Meanwhile, that was not fair, because government had not yet woven in training.

So some of that was cutting-edge. Being involved in some projects—one of them involved a court order—so the notion of trying to help clean something up or right a wrong that was going on, that's very appealing. And just how the city functions—I mean, how many cities are there in the world that are as big as New York? It's a remarkable place.

Q. Part of the thrill for me, was—I have to admit—sort of sneaking things in that we ... training professionals ... knew was good for them, but the agencies didn't necessarily want to include in a program.

Nancy E.: Right. Yup, that's true. Then, another turning point for me was reading Meg Wheatley's books, all her books, *Leadership and the New Science.* One that just put it so simply was *Turning to One Another.* Meg Wheatley has done a lot of work with Fortune 500 companies, and she had been a big high-falootin' consultant, and worked with the Marines and all that. Basically, what it all boiled down to, was how important it was for us to have the relationships, be in a conversation, and learn to listen to each other.

That is what led to my journey, where—for the first time in my whole career—I paid for a training program for myself. I went to the West Coast and took this Art of Hosting training, and that was in 2005. Now it's been going like crazy world-wide; it's being used in all kinds of situations. We are doing training now up at Riverside Church, working with people outside their silos. For the last one we just did, in February, we had a whole group of people who work in the field of disabilities. They were at this precipice in their work where they felt they had been inside their own silo and only spoke to people when someone had a family member, or they were [themselves] disabled. It was a fascinating thing because they felt refreshed by just being a part, and welcomed. I mean, it's not even like any of us even noticed anything, but it's so incredible what can happen. You bring up World Cafe, but just to have people who can talk across their differences and outside their silos, whether it's a department, or a community, or an organization or something, it's quite remarkable.

Years before she became a social worker, Isora combined her interests in adult learning and organizational development with her personal experience as an immigrant to the United States to find creative ways to work with a population in need. Her skills in helping families affected by a fire in a Bronx social club gained her international recognition:

Isora: After Teacher's College, I was still with the Department of Mental Health. I remember that we celebrated my graduation when I was an Assistant Director of the Office of Program Review and Evaluation. Later on, I became an assistant commissioner for the Bronx. While I was an assistant commissioner for the Bronx, I became the principal investigator of the Happy Land fire, the second-worst arson fire in the United States.

Q. Talk more about that.

Isora: I remember they decided that, since I was the assistant commissioner for the Bronx, I had to help do the family coordination for the mental health services for the victims. The way they did it, in the beginning, was like making a list of the victims, the relatives of the people who died in the fire. Then they wanted to match their names and addresses with the mental health programs in their neighborhoods. But because of this stigma that we still have regarding mental health, that didn't work out.

So I said, "Well, let me do it my way." I went to the Bronx and I went to a church that was almost across the street from the social club where the fire happened. I remember it was Santo Tomas de Aquino church. When I spoke to the priest and told him who I was and what I wanted to do, he said, "Oh, you want me to help you look for the victims? They're right here in my basement. So, I'm glad you're here." So we did look for people who were already known and trusted by the community or who were community leaders, and they helped us provide services for these people.

Number one, we rented [privacy] screening and the initial evaluations took place in the church, because I found out that you need to identify natural settings if you want to provide services to this population. Most of them were black from Honduras, called Garifunas. We would also do some psychological screening to identify the impact of the stresses that were caused by the fire.

It was a great project because I also had to train the workers who were providing services. At the end it paid off, but I was totally stressed out. At that point, my parents were both sick, suffering from cancer. So I was taking care of the victims; I was taking care of my parents. After my parents died and the study was completed, I decided to resign. I spent a whole year doing consulting on a part-time basis. That's the year I went to China.

Her personal background also helped her to work with a business partner to develop a unique diversity model that she used in training programs.

Isora: I learned how to use music as an engagement tool with people trying to cope with stressful situations. After that, well, I am still involved with the Institute. For six years, I've been working with seniors. We provide mental health services, site education, and presentations to people sixty and over. It happens in churches, in their homes, in senior housing programs, senior centers. It's very rewarding.

Q. Yeah. Okay. I want to come back to that. But you also did some diversity consulting along the way.

Isora: Yes, you see, that's the thing. I've done so many things that I really don't remember. Yes, and I remember I came up with this … reflective diversity learning concept … saying it is not only the responsibility of the one who is the victim, the one who is discriminated [against], but it is also … the responsibility of the victim to tell the other person, "Hey, you're discriminating against me. Let's find out why. Where does it come from?" Race relations problems exist also within the family in Cuba.

Q. So even within your family, there was a certain amount of...

Isora: Oh, yes, even within the family, so I'm used to that. I was raised in an all-white neighborhood in Cuba, so they called me all kinds of things. I was a victim of bullying when I was a child. The only thing, I guess, in those times [was] we reacted differently. I would have never thought of committing suicide. It made me stronger.

It was interesting how I learned about diversity. When I went to school in Miami, I went to Robert E. Lee High School, which was a mostly-white school. I remember my parents' friends were very concerned. All the Cuban people there didn't know what was going to happen. I have to say, it was a wonderful experience; I ended up being the teacher's pet and I was on the honor roll two months after I was in school. I had a lot of friends and it was a nice experience, so you never know.

Scanning the Environment – Looking for What Might Be Next

Several of The Fifty, including Donna, Jan, Susan M., and Corbette were always looking for different ways to use their skills. Corbette, while remaining deeply involved in whatever she was doing, was always scanning the environment to see what might be next:

Q. You have always had, it strikes me, the ability to maintain multiple focus. It sounds like you focused on your current position, doing the absolute best that could be done in that position, and growing in that position. There also was a piece of you with an eye to "What's next" and "What do I want from myself?" That's less common that you might think, so I'm a little curious about that.

Corbette: Actually, I'm glad you raised that because I do think and advise other people who are trying to figure out how to make real transitions. For example, when my old company, when they announced I was retiring and taking on my dream job of teaching in college, people came out of the woodwork saying, "Oh my God, that's my dream too! I've always wanted to teach college. How did you do it? How did you do it?"

One of the key things I said was, "You can't start that process when you're ready to do it. You have to lay the groundwork all along the way." For me it was not intentional, it was more my passion for information and networking. I've always approached networking from the standpoint of it's fun and invigorating, rather than, *What can I get out of it?* So I spend more of my time trying to do three-way networking and connecting other people.

The result of that is the door constantly opening and, I think for me, it's a matter of choosing which of those doors you are going to walk through. My challenge is constantly not saying "Yes" too, too much. I am a firm believer in avoiding over-committing, but I still do say "Yes" too much, as I don't have the quality of life that I might like.

But I think it's intellectual curiosity that has opened the doors that have led to other doors. I agreed to a meeting last week for a business magazine. They want to make their first issue about innovation and diversity. It was seven thirty in the morning, downtown, way back at the Vanderbilt campus.

I live in the suburbs, it's the first day I don't have to be downtown because classes had just ended, and I'm like, *Oh I agreed. I have to go downtown. It's seven in the morning on the first day when I can just stay home and relax.*

But I did it and my husband was like, "What are you doing?"

It was the most amazing meeting. I met the most amazing people. There were almost no people in the room other than the publisher that I knew, but there was this amazing energy and conversation with really interesting people—that's what happens, right?

Synthesizing Outside Experience

A few of The Fifty were able to synthesize experiences outside of their own knowledge base. They could see connections even when they were not grounded in that field. Susan M. used her ability to scan and synthesize in her professional life.

Susan M.: For me, it was more a matter of synthesizing. I was always able to recombine my own skills and spent most of my career helping others figure out how to recombine theirs. One of the things I learned early on, when I was doing the co-op work, is that I am very good at helping people be better at things I do not understand in the least.

I guess what I knew early on was how to help people think about learning and think about what they were learning. That's a skill that I was able to use straight through my career. My thing was, "What's the best way to learn this? What's going to help people really get this?"

They started calling me "Doc" because I was such a good script doctor and I was a script doctor of training curricula. You could show me a curriculum and I could tell you exactly what was going to work, what wasn't going to work, and figure out how to fix it. We would do run-throughs of the program and I would help people find better ways to present the material. So that was the kind of thing I did; I was really facilitating learning.

Deb L. also worked with people whose work she didn't initially understand. She learned about leadership and about the medical field in the moment as she set up a call center. She discusses learning from her mistakes:

Deb L.: The call center was being built, so these were temporary lodgings. I was the first person there, so I had to hire my own staff, and it ended up being forty-five people; mostly background check people, interviewers, and people with some human resources, one techie person who could, kind of, interview the tech people.

We got that together in a couple of weeks, had our job fair, and thirty-five hundred people showed up—we had expected three hundred. So it was like jumping in with both feet. I've never worked harder, ever, than in that job. That was a six-month stint. We processed seventeen thousand people, staffed the call center, and got it ready for the grand opening.

I said to my husband, "I can do this. I can do my own."

He said "You have to have a client."

So I put my resume out, again, and got hired within a week for a medical services call center in Buffalo Grove.

It was medical and I didn't know about medical terminology—lots of acronyms in the medical world—COPD, CHF, CAD. And it was telephonic management of people … the health manager for people who had chronic illnesses … it was nurses on the phone.

They hired me to build a centralized call center in their corporate office in the Chicago area. They had twenty-three little satellites, and they needed to merge them down. So I did that. I was there for two-and-a-half years and was really successful. I changed the culture completely because we didn't know how to sell and they didn't know they were selling.

Q. I'm watching this thread of how you used different things you learned as you moved on to the next thing.

Deb L.: Yes, it all just kept building and building. It was interesting because these were nurses who really cared about who they were talking to, but they couldn't get anyone to trust them and to say, "Yes, I'll talk to you."

So the first time they would reach out to say, "I'm calling because …" they'd say stupid things like, "Well … you have heart failure and I'm going to help you."

People would say "Well, first of all, no one told me I have heart failure," or, "I was just told I have a touch of sugar. I don't have diabetes," those kinds of things and, "Who are you to call me?" because they didn't know how to build rapport.

They didn't know they were selling, because if I call you—even if you don't pay money, you are paying time and trust—I need to convince you that I'm there for you.

So we had to rip everything apart and start all over. Nurses are not known to be real accepting of change, so I had to sell them on why they would feel better if they got less "No's" on the phone and how, by getting people to say "Yes" they were really helping them. You weren't forcing them to do something they didn't want to do, you were helping them. It doesn't matter [what] the words [are]; it's more about how you say them, and when you say them, and all of that.

We transformed that whole company, and they were paid every time someone said "Yes." They got paid by Humana or United Health Plan—paid them for every person who participated. So the company went from enrolling, like, nine percent when I started there to seventy-nine percent when I left.

The revenues went through the roof. It didn't make a difference—I got one promotion in two-and-a-half years. Now, you see, I'm naive at this point. I think you are supposed to get promoted every three months because that had been my experience. At Sears, I got promoted a lot and at that other call center I got promoted. I thought, *They're not promoting me! What's wrong with them? Don't they see how good this is working? How much money I'm making them?*

But I didn't know how to promote myself. I didn't know how to sell myself and my talents. That's a thing that women, I've learned, do not do well when they go to negotiate a contract; they don't ask for it.

I didn't know how to translate because people are busy doing their own jobs. They didn't know how to say, "Look. I just made you a hundred million dollars in revenue you didn't expect, and your company is a hundred million. So our department doubled your revenue in a year. So don't tell me …" I mean, seriously.

When Deb L. decided it was time to move on, she transferred everything she had learned into creating WhiskerDocs, a call center for pet owners:

Deb L.: I've started another company and my son is in it, which makes my heart happy. I am at the phase of my life where if it does not make my heart happy, I don't have time for it. So, it makes my heart happy to get to mentor him and watch him grow. He has worked in our call center every year since he was fifteen. He was really good, and he loved it. He was a loyal, wonderful employee, and he was stellar on the phones. He can sell anything. It's because he's heart-centered, and people love him. So, I'm like, "Why not have him go and sell whatever we're doing next?" So, we're doing that.

Q. What gave you the idea that this was a service that there was a space for, that there was a market for?

Deb L.: Well, you know, we're animal-crazy people. We have had ridiculous numbers of animals in our house. I've put a limit on that now, I just can't do it! We can't have seven cats running around. So, we're down to two cats right now, but when I was growing up, we had cats, dogs, and birds all at the same time.

Our previous company was a twenty-four-hour-a-day nurse line … for helping patients understand what to do. Not diagnosis, but decision support. It was not, "We know that your baby has this." We just [said],"Presenting these symptoms, here's what you need to do."

We did some really cutting-edge things, in that we were the first call center in the world to put nurses on secure live chat, where people could be looking up something on WebMD and go, "Oh, shit! It sounds like I'm dying. I'd better go talk to somebody!" That's what the other company primarily did as our main service.

So Rob kept saying, "I feel like that about our animals. I feel so stupid … I don't know what to do." We were running up to the pet emergency room and it costs three thousand dollars. They do MRIs and all sorts of shit, and he said, "Why don't we do that for animals?"

I said, " I love that idea! I don't think anyone has done it, but we have no time for it now."

So, of course, as the universe would have it, people showed up immediately that were in the pet industry, and I ended up on the phone with a guy who had been a CEO. He had had a company that sold his pet food line to PetSmart and he's a serial entre-preneurial thinker. I got on the phone with him and he said, "Are you kidding? This is brilliant and here's why … " He explained the marketplace, he explained the needs that were upcoming in the marketplace—and there's a lot coming. We had also done some research about the size of the market. I mean, there are two hundred million pet-owning households just in the United States. In the U.K. and Japan and France, they're all as nuts about their animals as we are, if not more.

It's a bit scarier, but it's more fun because we actually get to define for our clients how it should work. It's undefined.

And because we did the same thing for people, on the back-end side of it, the opera-tional side, we do know exactly how to put out a really comprehensive, good product that people really love using. They can text, they can chat, they can pick up the phone, they can send pictures—we have all this beautiful technology. But we understand the reason why they would call—because they're scared—and how they need to be handled when they call because they matter; and how we need to listen; and how we need to follow up with them and make them feel good about the fact that they called. Because it is a sale.

All those things come together, and you take something like this, and everyone says to me, "I can't believe it's never been done before!" And I say, "I know. That's what makes it so amazing. No one has done it! Nowhere [else] in the world is there a 24/7 veterinary call line."

Q. I know! I love it.

Deb L.: It's like "Whoa!" Of course, we could end up being insane, but the cool part is my life doesn't have that kind of pattern to it because it's fluid. So you just shift, right? You just say, "Well ... I guess it's not going to look like this because nobody likes that idea; but over here there's another approach, and let's do that." So you just kind of shift until you find the sweet spot: this is what the customer wants, and this is what we want to give them.

Melinda seems to combine scanning, synthesizing, and making connections to create new opportunities:

Melinda: It was basically marketing messaging and creating visuals to the limited extent I could, as a person without an artistic background, using the tools that I had. I did really well. I had a box full of excellence awards. There are a ton of people I worked with who benefitted from my work and I benefitted by knowing them. It just created this whole wonderful—I'm not sure what to call it—but just this whole bucket full of goodness doing that work.

I also got the experience of growing a business, of doing the research to try to find out where to take it, how to grow it, and how to get the money and resources to take it to the next level, which I did. I had to buy a couple of new systems as time went on because I outgrew what I had. I worked with outside service vendors and twenty years later, we both evolved and we've come back to getting together again, which is kind of interesting. But that was a really good experience. I was there through, like '87 or so, when I finally said, "This is crazy." I left because ... I had nowhere to go. I was just there as a graphics person and wanted to do something else.

Q. "Crazy" as in "limiting" and you needed to be doing more?

Melinda: Yeah, you know, the people see you as doing one particular thing and it's kind of hard to break the mold. After that, I got a job I really liked working with computer graphics—I liked working with technology a lot. I was very independent and capable of determining what I needed, getting what I needed, and making it happen. And I was very, I wouldn't say ambitious, but very achievement-oriented.

So I was looking for a place where I could take all the things I liked to do and make some money and learn something else. I ended up at a company called The Slide Center in Boston, which was a small independent business that was doing presentations for corporations. They did some other graphic services as well. I was a sales rep and, as it turned out, I really sucked as a sales rep. I did not do a great job there, but I made some good connections and it was kind of fun working in Boston.

Ironically—this has been a touchstone through everything—one of the guys, the guy that actually owns that business turns out to be somebody I reconnected with a couple years ago. I reached out to him and I said, "Hey, didn't I work with you at The Slide Center?" It turns out he's doing really advanced web development stuff. He does a lot of work at MIT and Harvard, and he's a very well respected and accomplished guy. I'm always reconnecting with people and connecting with people. That's been a kind of a touchstone of what I do. Not trying to be the glue that gets people together, but really flourishing in an environment where people are connecting.

Lynda also commented on scanning, recombining and synthesizing in her personal and professional life:

Q. So it seems like you have always done a number of things at once and you are continuing that same path?

Lynda: Yes. In fact, I need that kind of stimulation, having several things going on at once. I think I've been successful in doing a lot of juggling and managing chaos in my work. At the Foundation for Community Vitality, where I was for ten years, I had an opportunity to work with an organization—Plexus Institute.

Plexus is a group of scientists. They study chaos theory and complexity and do a lot of work in healthcare. But anyway, at the Foundation for Community Vitality, I was able to put together what we called a Leaders Learning Network. We had two facilitators that came from Plexus, two board members. We invited the executive directors or leaders of the non-profit organizations in Montana and Wyoming and Argentina (that the Foundation supported) and we spent about two days just talking about Complexity Theory and leadership skills and things like that. So, I've used a lot of that type of thinking in my personal and professional work.

I'll add something, Susan, that in my work as an administrator, I was always thinking in the back of my head: *I probably should have gotten an MBA instead of an MFA, Master of Fine Arts.* Several years ago, I was reading something about leadership and the world today—the changing world that we live in. There was a comment that the MFA is the MBA of the 21st century. I feel that an MFA certainly provides the individual with those skills you need—the ability to take risks, to not see any particular work experience or product as precious, that you're always re-inventing, re-designing and going through a whole ecosystem of destroying and re-imagining. So I think the fundamental work and training that I've had as an artist has really helped me in my professional work.

Q. Yes. I can see a lot in terms of identifying patterns; that really comes with creativity, you know? Seeing relationships differently, which an artist would do and somebody else might not do. That really makes for a marvelous addition to management.

Lynda: Sometimes I say that it's "network weaving" and that is one of the aspects of the work I have done and am still doing—bringing people together and creating opportunities for collaboration and exploration and opportunities for people to be part of that creative process.

I also used those skills in my legislature experience. At one point, I had a colleague across the aisle. We were always at odds on our positions on various pieces of legislation. One day, he just looked at me and he said, "Senator Moss, we just don't know where you've come from and what kinds of experiences you're bringing here. It's very different than what we have ever had before." I was, really, one of the first artists that was ever an elected official. So it was great to bring that perspective to the policy-making process, too.

Robyn commented on assessing and reassessing your life:

Q. *Anything that you can think of that we didn't cover, that you want to share about your career path, making these transitions, adding new things, new twists on things past fifty, that kind of thing?*

Robyn: Having new twists past fifty? I just got this image of picking flowers because I feel like that's what it is. Once you are past fifty, you turn around and say, "Okay, what flowers did I grow along the way and forget to pick up?" I feel that when you do that, then you have this amazing bouquet. There are a lot of times we fail to notice that we have planted these beautiful flowers along the way, and we trample on them.

We are gathering this bouquet and they are all different colors and that is what I feel like right now in my life; it's like this bouquet of all different-colored flowers and different shapes. Now, I'm just making this bouquet and just want to share it and be happy about it and be able to just give it away and display it. I think that we can all do that. I love helping people to do that, too. It's one of my goals to make people see what they've dropped along the way.

Herta is one of several women who has made a career transition and is scanning the environment to see what might be next:

Q. *What's next for you? What's next for Ariya?*

Herta: Oh, great question. For Ariya, I have a very clear vision and I'm incredibly grateful that we did not give up; that I did not give up. We have a number of the significant projects that I talked about in the works, but we don't have anything that's finished at this point. So I really looked at the next, and you can hold me to this, because probably by the time you publish the book, there will be an epilogue to this.

The plan right now is to move to Nairobi, because I feel I need to be closer to the influencers and to the project that we are working on. That will be the next step, and my husband and I are basically committing the next five to ten years to really building this business. I see Ariya becoming a major, major developer of clean and renewable energy projects in Africa. In addition to that, a significant financier of these projects, because on the back of these clean energy projects, I plan to raise a large infrastructure fund. So that is where I see the future and it is a perfect alignment of my business interest and my philanthropic business. I can say that, for the first time in my life that those interests are aligned.

I feel very strongly my philanthropic work, that is very, very important and becoming increasingly important, because my definition of sustainability is basically that the world is sustainable when everybody sits on the stool and the three legs are free: education, at least at the tertiary level; affordable health care, and this may vary from place to place but it has to be some affordable health care; and thirdly, an opportunity to make a living.

I don't think we owe people a living, but we owe people an opportunity to make a living. I think that's a fundamental difference. Obviously, civil society needs to support people who cannot take care of themselves, but civil society may have doubled the responsibility to support people who can really take care of themselves and just choose not to; and so, the emphasis on an opportunity to make a living.

On the philanthropic side, I think there continues to be a need in the educational space, whether that is philanthropic or the government; there continues to be a need, particularly in places like Africa, for aid when it comes to healthcare. But the private sector has to drive the opportunity to make a living. I still believe that the best charity is a job. The best way to support somebody is actually to give them employment opportunities. And the private sector has to drive that.

We raised the money for a school in Uganda, for example. The proceeds from my book largely go to charitable purposes. We've just raised the forty-five thousand dollars to build a school for seven hundred students in Uganda. We continue to invest in education in arts, like the film that we produced, etc. So that's what I'm doing on the charitable and on the philanthropic side and leadership.

There is a significant leadership element on the philanthropic side. On the business side, the work that I am doing through Ariya is so nicely aligned, and I am incredibly grateful for that. And just to keep my fingers in the large corporate world, I just came off a board of a smaller publicly-listed company.

I'm interviewing right now for a couple of other boards, so I will, if things go as planned, go on a corporate board as a non-executive director or chairman, to keep my hand in the game. But my top priority is really to continue to build and grow Ariya. That's about as far as I can see, and that's probably almost too far at this point.

Strategic planning experts speak about the importance of scanning the environment and assessing information. The Fifty had that ability. As they absorbed information, they were able to fit it into a larger picture of the world and relate it back to their own lives. There are lists of predictions from famous people who weren't always good at scanning.

Possibly one of the most famous incorrect environmental scans:

"There is no reason anyone would want a computer in their home."

-Ken Olson, president, chairman and founder of Digital Equipment Corporation.

Here are a couple more examples of shortsightedness:

"A cookie store is a bad idea. Besides, the market research reports say America likes crispy cookies, not soft and chewy cookies like you make."

-Response to Debbi Fields' idea of starting Mrs. Fields' Cookies.

"We don't like their sound, and guitar music is on the way out."

-Decca Recording Company, rejecting the Beatles, 1962.

Contrast these with Herta's ability to foresee the need for funding sustainable projects in Africa or Deb L.'s and Audrey's understanding of people's attachment to their pets and what supportive services they might need.

Elements of Scanning and Synthesis

Scanning the environment involves careful, on-going observation of the world around you. It means keeping current on world and community events, your family and friends, your community, and yourself.

Synthesizing and recombining are similar, but not exactly the same. Synthesizing is putting different, perhaps seemingly unconnected things together. Recombining involves taking things that are already familiar to you—generally, skills and experiences—to create something new.

Phoebe and Susan M., among others, recombined skills from their childhood roles as would-be Western heroes into organizational leadership roles. Deb L.'s love of school led her to continuously scan her environment. Later, she honed this ability during her travels and finally found that this ability to see the big picture and intuit what people need underscored her success in running call centers.

For Susana, recombining elements, including her linguistic skills, enabled her to build a successful career with the CIA. Susan S. understood that the skills she had acquired as a Medieval scholar could be used both in writing science fiction and in developing materials for a financial institution.

How You Can Develop Recombining Skills

The exercise below will get you started learning how to do an environmental scan and how to synthesize. Use the tips below to expand your abilities.

- Keep a running list of things you would like to explore—skills you want to master, topics you'd like to know more about, places you'd like to visit. Draw lines to connect items you see as similar.
- As you explore items on your list, make another list. This one will contain ideas that came to you in each exploration.

- Create a list of the skills and abilities you most enjoy learning. Make a separate list of as many ways as possible these skills could be combined into different work possibilities (paid or volunteer).
- As you look around your household or neighborhood, imagine what you would like to change or improve by reusing what is already available to you.

Exercise

Practice expanding your own ability to scan and synthesize.

1. Pick up any simple household item. List as many unusual uses for that item as you can.
2. Next, create a quick-and-dirty demographic profile of your neighborhood: Who lives there? Ages? Families or singles? Children? Guess at occupations and income levels.
3. Make a short list of services nearby.
4. Add to the mix two articles from the newspaper or a magazine or items from the news.

That's an environmental scan. Now, synthesize. Look at all the information you've collected. Devise two products or services that, based on the information you've collected, would be successful in your area.

Chapter 8

Taming the Cowardly Lion – The Ability to Keep Fear In Perspective

Keeping fear in perspective is most simply accomplished in two phases. The first phase involves evaluating situations and assessing risk factors in both the physical and emotional worlds. The second phase involves planning actions that address fears and allow for either forward motion or a clear decision to stop, when that is the realistic option.

For example, speaking in public or getting on an airplane are fears that can be overcome with evaluating and planning action steps, but when faced with a bear in the wild, a quick retreat is the best option.

The hesitation and fear that keeps women in dead-end jobs or stuck in boring lives is the same force that can stop us from critically examining our lives and making necessary changes.

I've discovered in my coaching practice that what appears to be procrastination or avoidance is often unacknowledged fear—sometimes so deeply rooted that it may take deep work to reach the level of recognizing and admitting fear. You may see this in friends who refuse to consult with a doctor, even though it is clear they have medical issues. They rationalize their behavior by saying, "He will just find something," as if avoidance will make the issue disappear.

This type of fear-based block or denial keeps many women in unsatisfying and unproductive lives. It takes a certain amount of courage to even acknowledge fear and then to evaluate that fear. While it may be natural to be fearful when facing something new, The Fifty figured out how to face and evaluate fear, keep that fear in perspective and then move forward.

Herta said it best:

Herta: You learn how to fear the things that are worth fearing as opposed to things that are not worthy of fearing; and that trying something new shouldn't be something to fear.

Agenia recounted a discussion she had with a young woman who was acting as if it was fine to get passed over:

Agenia: No one sets your expectations for you but you. No one [else] sets them. No one determines them, no one says, "Yes. No." No one makes that decision for you but you. And as soon as you own that decision, you'll be okay. There is nothing—I mean nothing—to stand in [my] way, except me.

I had an interesting conversation with a young woman. A few weeks ago, I was asked to speak at a lunch program with a group of about 125 employees of the state of Tennessee. I wrapped up my program, answered some questions, and was leaving the building when this one young woman walked up to me and started a conversation.

Her story was along the lines of, "Well, you know, I really am okay with the fact that I didn't get the job promotion that I thought I would be getting. I'm okay with that. But they put someone else in and they are telling me if I do this and that, then maybe the next time I'll be ready. I'm okay with that."

Finally, I just stopped her and said, "Stop saying you're okay with it, because you're not. You're not okay with it."

I think the minute we can be honest with ourselves and say we're just not okay, then maybe we will wake up and realize that if they're not going to give it to me now, they may not give it to me later either, so maybe I'm just in the wrong place. But stop telling yourself it's okay.

I think that is one thing we as women—and maybe this is a Southern trait—we're conditioned to believe it's okay. "Your time will come," you know, being patient is okay. No, some days, it's not okay and there's nothing wrong with admitting that, saying that, and more importantly, taking action on that.

But it was just disheartening standing there, listening to her constantly say, "But it's okay." The whole time I'm hearing her talk I'm thinking, *It is not okay*. I'm standing there looking at her and again, I'm on my way out of the door, I've got my keys in my hand, and I'm listening patiently and intently.

More interesting was the look on her face when I just said, "Stop convincing yourself it's okay. It's not."

And she just looked at me.

I said, "You said three times, 'It's okay.' It is not. It's not and you know it's not."

And she admitted it was not.

I'm like, "Okay, now you have something to work with."

Q. Well, I'll tell you, I would like to see that habit just wiped off the face of the planet.

Agenia: I would too. I would too. It's quite interesting, because there are so many women I get a chance to meet. I just met with one earlier this week who shared with me about … listening to the voice in our heads that tells us what we are not worthy of—and we begin to believe it.

I thought to myself, *Isn't that interesting?* because I never had that voice in my head about what I'm not worthy of. I've always had the voice in my head, *Do I have enough time to make happen what I want to happen?* but that's really about it. I think I got rid of that voice a long time ago. I think that's the voice we get in our head in our teen years.

Cheryl and Victoria also both discussed taking risks:

Cheryl: I very much consider myself an entrepreneur. Entrepreneurs are kind of fearless; you don't know what you don't know, which is probably a good thing. Because when I look back, had I known then what I know now, I probably never would have done it.

I didn't know anything about the ad agency business, but that didn't stop me from jumping in. It was a great, amazing learning experience. I mean, obviously, I learned a lot and it was terrific.

Victoria talks about the fear writers and entrepreneurs face around both turning down projects and getting older. Many women, regardless of their actual resources, seem to entertain "bag lady" fantasies, always afraid that each opportunity will be their last. This fear can easily block the ability to exercise good judgment in making choices.

Q. I think there is a lot in what you have shared for women who are operating out of fear and think that they have to say "Yes".

Victoria: Absolutely. And that fear, of course, is like turning down a date. When somebody calls and asks for a date and you're busy, you're afraid to say, "I'm sorry, I'm busy" because you're afraid he'll never call back and ask again. It transfers over so much into our lives and especially, I think, for women. Men probably have the same insecurities, but they don't discuss it as openly. But with women, we are programmed not to let people down, not to say "No," not to disappoint people. You're being the good girl. And you get to a certain age where you say, "You know what, this doesn't work for me." I'm not infinite. I have a finite time on this universe. I'm 68—I may not live to be 69—who knows?

It was my first experience with really serious work with personal essay and also serious work as an editor, because it was my job to edit. The first essay that came in was by Jane Smiley.

I called my agent and said, "How do I edit a Pulitzer author? I mean, come on."

She said, "You just do your best, you can do it."

I made myself physically ill for a few days and then I sat down and edited the first essays that came in. When I sent Jane the essay with my editing notes on it, she got back to me and said, "Oh, good eye. I like that. Go ahead and put that sentence there and yes, that's a good thing."

I said, "I see where you're confused. Okay, that's fixed."

She said, "No, no, no. That word stays just the way it is. That's what I intended it to be."

I learned then that writers want their very, very best work out there, and if you have an editor who suggests something that does improve what you've got, a good writer would say, "Absolutely, let's do it." And that's when I learned to enjoy my work being edited. I mean, I have a wonderful editor, a freelance editor that I use. I never let my introductions or my essays for any of my anthologies go to the publisher until my editor looks at my work and gets back to me and we edit it together.

Agenia also speaks about not being afraid to try new things:

Agenia: Jim Hart was the general manager of the television station and Jim Swinehart was the news director. I guess they thought it was important enough to them that I get my MBA. Roger Jenkins was at the University of Tennessee-Knoxville College of

Business and the head of the department at that time. He encouraged me … and off I went to get my MBA.

It was wonderful. I enjoyed every minute of being in the MBA program and understanding more of the nuances of business and business operations and all the important factors. While I was in my first semester in the MBA program, they made it clear we needed to get a business-related summer internship. I worked really hard, ended up with an internship at Pepsi, and spent my summer in New York working for PepsiCola. That was just phenomenal. They offered me a full-time job, and I worked for them throughout my second year of the MBA program.

I secured an offer from American Express and was torn between which to take when Charles proposed marriage. Then he explained that he had no interest in being in the Northeast, and he had accepted an offer from the Saturn Corporation right here at Springhill, Tennessee. So, that's how I ended up in Nashville.

Rita faced danger and risk in her personal and professional life. First, she extracted herself from an abusive marriage:

Rita: I got pregnant when I was eighteen and married the father. I had my second child while I was with him. He was extremely violent, and I was able to leave him because of LBJ (Lyndon Baines Johnson) and the creation of Medicaid and food stamps, and the AFDC program. I knew I could leave that situation and take care of my children, and that's what I needed to know. So I was able to leave.

Q. And then you moved to New York where you went to Columbia?

Rita: When I was accepted by Columbia Journalism School, I moved me and the kids to New York. We lived in student housing — married student housing, even though I wasn't married.

Q. But you had kids, so that counted. So what was that like, moving to New York?

Rita: Well, it was very scary, and it was very exciting. I had no idea—'cause I had never visited Columbia—so I had no idea what it was like.

Rita's earliest experiences as a journalist working on her college paper showed her the power of the press:

Rita: I was handed this story to do about an African-American woman in Ohio State University Law School who lost custody of her child, her son, during a divorce. Not to her ex, but to her father. The judge had made this very idiosyncratic, off-hand decision with the explanation that since she was going to law school, she wouldn't have time to be a mother. And since the dad wasn't around, he would give the child to somebody else to raise. Part of the evidence against her was that she took flying lessons on the weekend. I was so outraged that this happened. This was crazy.

I met the mother and the child, and then I called her lawyer, who was a professor of law at Ohio State. He explained to me, so eloquently, why this was outrageous and it violated the law. I thought, *This is so cool. I can interview these smart people, write down what they say, and tell other people. This is great!* And he expressed it much better than I would. That's sort of the essence of journalism, anyway.

Rita's focus on women and her politicization began when she was an undergraduate and carried through to her studies at the Columbia School of Journalism.

Q. *Were you politicized before this interview, or did that politicize you?*

Rita: I think my politicization was being part of an organization called the Single Mothers Support Group. Early on in my college career, there was a small group of women, all of whom were going to Ohio State, all of whom had little kids, and all of whom were very much in need of mutual support. We bonded together and then we became part of the umbrella organization of campus women's organizations. So I began to learn about women's rights, but in the context of being part of this close-knit group who had committed to helping each other.

Q. *So, you were in journalism school. What was that like for you—that experience?*

Rita: Well, you know I was an outlier, right? I was politicized. I was on welfare. I did have children, I wasn't married, and I was older than most of the students — all the students. So it was pretty lonely. I loved the work, but nobody saw me as a rising star, which is something that happens in journalism school and, I suppose, all schools. I got pretty good grades. I was an honor student. But nobody took me aside and said, "Things are looking good for you, kid!" In fact, I can remember the head of the department, when I told him I had been accepted by Columbia Journalism School. He almost fell down, he was so surprised. So yeah, it was a surprise to everybody, in part because I was so politicized.

Q. *But Columbia was pretty political at that point. I don't know about the journalism school.*

Rita: Yeah, but not compared to Ohio State. But still, I was an outlier. I was part of their recruitment; a deliberate recruitment of people who were not from the Ivy League. But the majority of the students were from the Ivy League. I had never met anybody from the Ivy League before, and I certainly didn't share their assumptions.

I can remember a women's group formed within our program, and we all went around the room and then one said, "Oh, my mother did this and that," and another said, "My mother did this and that." I felt so intimidated, but we were coming to a Puerto Rican in the circle, so I'm like, *Oh, I'm going to be able to bond with her*, but no—both her parents were pediatricians. Then they got to me and I said, "My mother was a housewife. She had six kids," and they're like, "Oh, how nice for you."

Her unique perspective carried over to covering difficult and controversial stories:

Rita: I finally, with the help of Columbia and my classmates, was able to get an interview with the *Record* (Bergen County), which was the premier starting-job newspaper that you got when you came out of Columbia. I had written to them before, but they had ignored me. But now I knew somebody who actually worked there. So they invited me in for an interview, and the man said, "Well, we're not going to be able to hire you, but there is somebody who might, and that's the *Patterson News*. They have a new editor, and I think you should give him a call." So I did. His name was David Bergen, and I gave him a call.

He was very impressed with the Columbia degree and hired me right away. That was such a relief. I can remember the feeling of seeing a desk, and like, *Oh my God! They've given me a desk, a phone and a typewriter! This is wonderful*! So I went to work at *Patterson News*, but—I don't know the words—but I was really so hungry for the story. And, on the other hand, because I had been on welfare and in and out of marriage, I understood a lot of what was going on in *Patterson*, which is an extremely poor town, and what was going on institutionally that made things worse for many of the residents.

So I quickly began to win reporting awards. I don't know if you saw the Public Broadcasting System (PBS) special recently about the girlfriend of a deputy sheriff being found dead … with the deputy sheriff's pistol in her left hand (she was right-handed.) There was a big story in the *New York Times* Magazine and a documentary on PBS, and I'm like, *Oh, I so did that story*! I did that story in *Patterson*, and it was the chief of detectives whose wife was found dead on the kitchen floor with his service revolver in her left hand. And she was right-handed. He ended up being prosecuted for murder, in part because of the stories we did; he hung himself the night before he was to be arraigned. This was a big-impact story about officers of the law who killed their loved ones with their own service revolvers. It's all very tragic.

Q. And, I imagine, covered up as often as possible.

Rita: That's mainly what this story in the magazine and on PBS was about—the cover-up. I mean, it was assumed they were going to cover-up. When they did this story in *Patterson* about the chief of detectives, immediately the ruling by the local coroner was suicide. What made a difference, in this case, was she had filed for divorce. In the divorce papers, which were public, (in New Jersey) she had described an enormous amount of abuse. I still remember excerpts from those court documents vividly.

So we, with the woman's attorney helping us, got the documents from the court system. We were able to run that story verbatim from the dead woman's own words of what she went through. And that caused a ruckus. Then the attorney filed civil murder charges against the chief of detectives. And then there was another autopsy, and another autopsy. It went on, but finally, he was indicted.

Q. That's amazing. I mean, when I think back to the time, it was, as often as not, clearly "the woman's fault." And for you to be able to write a story like that is so amazing.

Rita: I had fun there. It was very rich in stories.

Rita's desire to get at the truth and her family responsibilities affected her ability to get a job, but didn't deter her:

Rita: I was only there two years. That story was generated because people called the newsroom and told us that they were suspicious about her death. There was the case of a vice principal—who was also on the city council and also on the county services commission. Therefore, he had control: if people didn't get their food stamps or didn't get their checks, or whatever, he could fix it. He was molesting the girls in the school. And people called us. That was a tough story to do, but we did it.

Q. Sure. Wow. So where did you go from Patterson?

Rita: I went to the *Stamford Advocate* as a night copy desk editor because no one would hire me as a reporter. I was too much trouble, I think. But also, the same barriers—I couldn't work nights. If you're on a night copy desk, you get there very late, like ten p.m. and you get off at six a.m. So I'd tuck the kids in at a coworker's house, and they slept there. I would wake up in the morning and pick them up, and we would take the train back into New York City. They would go to school and I would sleep during the day. That was a tough year.

Q. So you have a real consistent social justice theme to your writing.

Rita: Yeah, I think so, and part of it is I would go back to the lies they tell about welfare mothers. It's like, "Wait a minute! This is not true!"

You know, it was not just about me, but all the women on welfare, and this is punitive, right? They have so many stereotypes and they make laws based on those stereotypes and that hurts lots of families. I can remember going to a party at a National Organization for Women member's home after a lobby day for better welfare payments. Her home was in the suburbs, and a state representative was there.

He came up to me and said, "Well, I can tell you what they can do to prevent having babies."

I ask, "What?"

He said, "They just put an aspirin between their knees. Put an aspirin between their knees." He thought that was hilarious. I did not. I think somebody, some current member of Congress said that publicly, recently.

Then it became part of welfare law, in TANF (Temporary Assistance for Needy Families) legislation, that welfare recipients could only go to school for one year. When Bill Clinton and Newt Gingrich got together to "end welfare as we know it," I was unprepared for how severe it would be.

Originally when they were talking about it, I'm like, *Oh, he's not going to do that, because it would hurt too many women and children*. But then, the news about the proposed legislation was all about blacks and often men. There was one story in the *New York Times* magazine about Mary Ann Amour who lived in Cabrini Green, was African American, and had four children. The last two—twins—were conceived when she was high on cocaine. They had a picture of her on the cover, and I'm like, This is so racist! This is such lazy journalism. And it was all beautifully written, right? And so it reinforced every stereotype: she was overweight, etc.

I can't go back to covering the law. I have to figure out a way to use journalism to advance women's rights, because this is just outrageous. (That was in '96, and I was on my fellowship at that time.) This was a result of the media's failure to tell the truth about what that legislation really meant … the interpretation that it meant they should go out and get jobs. Excuse me, right?

Q. Right.

Rita: They have a job—to raise a family by themselves. Anyway, I said, "Well, I've got to figure out how to do this." It took me several years, but then I got an opportunity with the National Organization of Women (NOW) with their Defense and Education Fund. [speaking about the creation of *eWomen's News*] They wanted someone to create an online news service covering women's issues. I'm like, "That would be me." Right? They had a search committee, but I'm like, "Yeah, that would be my job." They quickly agreed and I got this job that, with NOW Legal Defense, would allow me to do a startup, basically. I had a blank computer screen and no idea, actually, how to do this although I'd been online since the seventies.

I set out to interview people who would design the website. I had no idea what the difference was, what design meant. I was quickly educated that there's the design, i.e. the looks of it … and then the design of making it work. The two work together, but they're two very different jobs.

So I hired the only company whose presentation worked during the interview. Everybody else's froze, or whatever. That's how I selected them. So we launched in June of 2000 and we have published every day.

We published a very short message on September 11th, 2001. But September 11th, 2001 took a real toll on NOW's legal defense. They had a budget crisis because they didn't have their gala in the fall, where they [usually] raise a lot of money. The year-end donations were off as well because people were sending their money to the Red Cross for the 9/11 survivors. So they told me we were going to shut down; lay everyone off.

I'm like, "Can't do that." So without knowing how, I spun us off and we've been independent since, which is where we should have been. I mean, people are suspicious of us if we are part of an advocacy organization, so we have been independent since January 1, 2002.

Cheryl and Phyllis C. talk about jumping in without thinking:

Cheryl: Seeing something you started from basically nothing, to see it grow and thrive and become something that actually had value, it was terrific. Then, when I moved into the world of big ad agencies, it was great because I got to work with some really world-class clients and some terrific, smart, sharp, bright people. The ad agency business is terrific and wonderful and I still have great friends that I've known all these years through being in that business.

Phyllis C.: I was addressing a regional group, one of the districts for Rotary. I had been asked to get up and speak in front of about 300 people, and I was petrified of public speaking. When I got up to the podium and they turned on the microphone, I started to speak. I was shaking so hard that the podium started shaking, and I was stuttering and crying. And I gave my speech.

When I was getting my bachelor's degree, one of the courses had to do with speaking. I went to the faculty advisor and said, "I need to drop out because I can't speak in front of the group. I will not be able to do it. I will fail."

He said, "Well, you know, let's give it a go. Do you think you have the courage to do this?"

I thought about it and said, "Well, yes. You're asking me if I have the courage to fail, and yes, I think I have the courage to fail."

I went up and gave my speech and passed. I didn't think they would be hiring me at Toastmasters anytime soon, but I did fine. I have gone on to speak; I do get asked to speak two or three times a year at various events, but it takes everything I have. I agonize over it two to three weeks before the event. I'm a nervous wreck, but I now accept those engagements because I'm not going to let it master me.

Q. You see, I think that's a big part of what the difference is between the women I'm interviewing, like you, and the women who just say, "It's hopeless. It's over. There's nothing I can do. I'm stopping." It's that courage.

Phyllis C.: Do you have the courage to fail?

Q. Do you have the courage to fail? I think that's gorgeous. Oh, am I going to enjoy using that line.

Similarly, Nancy C. attributed her success to fearlessness:

Q. How did you manage to move from almost a clerical position, reporting scores? How did you transition out of doing that into an actual [reporters] beat again?

Nancy C.: The fire in my belly. It was phenomenal. Looking back on it, I just marvel at my own initiative, because sometimes I forget. You know, how you're so into your own story that sometimes you forget what you've done? They had every week—and this is a broadsheet newspaper, very well respected, very well done, mid-sized—every week they had a community section.

Now, keeping in mind that community to them did not mean high school and college sports. That was a whole separate thing and they had many pages of that. But they had a community section which was just, you know, little Joey Junior's karate and little eight-year-old soccer stuff. This community section was called "Sports Scene" which was, maybe, half a page, maybe a third of a page.

Deb L. was another woman who just jumped in. This allowed her to become a public speaker, and that led to deciding that she could run a call center:

Deb L.: At that time, I remember we had met a fellow who was doing a lot of public speaking, and I thought, *Oooh! I've always been terrified of getting up in front of a group. I really want to learn how to do public speaking,* so I asked him if he would teach me.

He said, "Sure. Next talk I'm doing, I'd like you to just introduce me." I said, "Sure. That sounds great!"

We're at a talk with maybe, fifty people. So the next talk, I walked in and there are a thousand people in the room. And I have no preparation! You know how hard it can be? I stood up on the stage, and there were these people. And they got quiet!

They stopped talking. I went to talk, and no noise came out of my throat. It actually closed. It closed! And I could hardly breathe. No matter how hard I tried, no noise came out. So I stood up there for … it felt like forever, but I'm sure it was maybe a minute, trying to make noise come out. I finally had to set the microphone down and leave the stage because it just wasn't going to happen.

So, of course I was mortified, and I went way to the back of the room and just sat there going, *Oh my God, I can't believe this. Oh my God.* I had no idea what people thought, but he said, "Don't worry. We'll do it again."

So, the next week, I got up and introduced him and words came out. They weren't the best, but it wasn't bad. And he had me do it again, and the next time everything came out okay. I got to do it again, and the fourth time it was actually quite good. And he said, "Next time, I'd like you to give a talk."

He was a wonderful mentor. I will be forever grateful.

Five or six times I gave a little piece of his training. (He was doing training on sales.) Afterward, he said, "You know, you would make a phenomenal call center director. Why don't you come work for me?" He was the president at a call center.

I said, "Okay. I'm in." Then I had to go home to find out what a call center was!

I just knew I needed something different. I knew that he was all about sales and marketing, and I was intrigued by that. So, I bought a briefcase and a couple of suits. I showed up to be the call center director!

Tish had to deal with fear on a very different level. She was facing the very real possibility that she might die soon:

Tish: I had been pretty active. You know, I had played tennis and was playing tennis, even when I was pregnant with my son. So it was very, very hard. By the end, I really couldn't participate in any meaningful way in my children's lives. It got to the point where, for over a year, the only thing I could really do was sit on my couch. If I went up the stairs, I would have to crawl up the stairs. So there wasn't very much that I could do to be a part of my kids' lives. That was probably one of the saddest aspects of that.

Q. How did you manage to keep your spirits up through all of this? I mean, it sounds like you fought really hard.

Tish: Yes, I did. I fought really hard because of my kids. There was a reason that I tried for … I tried as hard as I could, and for as long as I could, to keep life normal for them. It was a balance—how much do you tell them and when? We made every effort, to the point where we would go on skiing weekends. We would pack up my concentrator, which provided the oxygen I needed at night, throw that in the van, and away we would go. I'd sit in the ski lodge all day, but my family would ski. It meant a lot to me that they were able to continue to do that.

Q. And that you were able to maintain as much quality of life …

Tish: Exactly, a family life. The other difficult piece was navigating the whole question of lung transplantation. Where that should be done was tricky. At the time, the criterion for actually getting a lung transplant was how much time you had spent on a waiting list. So you could be very, very sick, but if you didn't have as much time [on the list] as someone else who wasn't as sick, well, guess what? They were going to be given the donated organ first. When my doctor first said, "Look, your only answer is to one day, have a lung transplant, and it is very risky."

I thought to myself, *I will crawl on the streets before I ever go for that. It is just too risky.* You're not thinking it would ever get that bad, that you would need to do that. But then you get to a point where you realize it's riskier for you not to have the transplant. Without it, you're definitely dying.

And kind of the same way, it was, little by little, you realize that you have to accept this help, and also that your friends need to be able to help you—and that you were actually doing something for them, because they and your family members were standing by helpless. For them to be able to drive you to your pulmonary rehab sessions that you needed to go to, was something they could do and they could feel better about themselves. In a way, you were kind of helping them.

She also spoke of the tremendous shift and new set of fears that occurred after her transplant:

Tish: There was also a kind of mental switch, because as long as you were waiting for a transplant, you were always waiting for something. In your mind, everything would be fine once you got it. Now it was … now you have it. If something goes wrong, you will have to deal with it. So it was a mental switch.

For example, rejection is something that's, well, the enemy of all transplants. So the reality of, "Okay, if I do [have a transplant] and if it rejects right away, I'm really in trouble." So it was kind of a different shift. But I was very blessed. I did have a couple of challenges, but I was well enough to come home after about three months and slowly start to build my life again.

Let me tell you, it was so great to wash dishes again. It's going to sound so corny, but the first time I went to Costco and was standing in line, I had tears in my eyes. This is great, you know. Just that semblance of everyday life that had been so closed off. It was great. I certainly loved every second being with my children again. And I really took every moment I could to revel in that.

Tish tells part of her post-transplant experience in Chapter 5, focusing on the change in mindset. Here, she addresses dealing with the fear:

Tish: Here's the reality: I'm going to take all these medications every day; I'm going to go four times a year and I'm going to be petrified every time I'm there because you get the results right then, and they can tell if some rejection is creeping in. But I'm going to deal with it. I'm going to be strong enough to deal with it and I'm going to try to have a normal life.

The way life is, your child could be exposed to something and could bring it home. So I made my peace with it—that I'm going to live my life and deal with the consequences of that. The medications are really toxic. So you accept all that.

But what do I do? Do I just live every day? Or, thinking about going back to work—should I do that? Is that the right decision? So there was a lot of kind of coming to terms with how do you go on with your life once you've been through something like this.

Like many women, both Betsy and Sharon took risks in their careers and saw the relationship between risk and reward:

Betsy: I think that some of the important things are finding ways to get comfortable with taking risks. That will give you many opportunities to see what you like and what you don't like. Second is, certainly, don't think so much about failure. I mean, my own feeling is, as long as I learn something from an experience, it's not a failure. So try things; see if they work. If they don't work, figure out why they didn't work and dwell on those lessons. I think the more open people can be to new experiences, to putting themselves in different situations, the better.

Sharon just dove into a whole new career, saying "Yes" to everything. Her concerns about lack of knowledge were offset by her excellent skills with people.

Q. Let me just stop you for a second. This is so cool. I have to stop you for just a second to ask, "What do you think it is about you that you just chugged along and said, 'Okay, I'm going to say yes to everything and I'm going to make it up as I go along.' How did that happen?"

Sharon: Because I knew that I wasn't afraid to talk to people. And there had to be answers; there had to be people who knew what I didn't know. Phyllis is a funny one, because Phyllis has been my friend forever. At one point, I called her. I said, "Phyllis, I'm making money. I'm doing these things, but you know what? I don't know anything."

She said, "Oh, Sharon, yes you do." She said George Goldman had told her that it isn't what you know; it's how you get other people who do know things to do things. And she said, "So, yes, you do know."

That was like freedom, because I started to feel really horrible like, well, I'm not an engineer and I'm not this, and I don't know that. I don't have this education.

But one thing led to another, and I got a job. I walked into another plant. I had a door problem and I needed a different kind of contractor, a cold storage contractor. I called this guy—this is an important part—I called this guy, Rich Schellenberg. He had a company called Unified Building Systems. I asked him if he could fix this horizontal slide that is used in food plants as cooler door, big industrial doors. He said that he could.

I said, "Well, you would be working for me, not for the company. And you would have to come in under my name."

"Well, I don't do that. I won't do that. No, I can't do that."

Now, one thing led to the other and he finally did it. Well, I wound up on another job where he was also on it,; but he was doing a big freezer there. I saw him and I thought, *Oh, my gosh.* So I called him and asked him if he would do my work, and again, "No, no, no. I don't do that." Well, today, we are building a $10 million plant. He is still working with me.

We're doing Peter Pan in Chicago. We actually lost a $20 million job because he couldn't get a bond fast enough for that amount. He didn't have the right contacts until about a day late. The New York office—not the people here; they didn't know us whatsoever—said, no, they had to go on because they had to have [the bond] that day. And we lost a $20 million contract. So we went from a door with probably a $500 ticket on it, to today. So it's been quite a journey he and I have had.

Susan P. took risks that ultimately ended her career within the prison system. She felt she had no choice. Every part of her needed to fight to correct the system within which she worked:

Q. So did you choose not to fight the firing?

Susan P.: Oh, no. For a couple of reasons, no. It was time for me to leave. It was just not healthy for me. Everybody knew it wasn't healthy for me 'cause I couldn't stop. I wasn't winning. There was no way—I couldn't win and I couldn't change. Other people could let it fall off their backs; that was not a possibility for me.

Q. No.

Susan P.: It just wasn't possible. I mean, I tried. It was what it was: oil and water. I could not stop e-mailing people. I thought, *Do you know about this stuff?* It's a military format you know, and there's a chain of command, and that's antithetical to anything I had experienced in my life. It's not any way I can operate.

It was interesting, in terms of my karma; I really wasn't able to leave. I knew I needed to, but it wasn't going to happen until I was fired and until my cancer acted up. And that's what happened. It was absolutely the way it was supposed to be. It was not going to end any other way. So, it was a blessing.

The problem with that was, being fired, I wasn't able to get unemployment. I could fight it, but I really didn't want to fight it because it was going to be emotionally hard for me to fight it.

Nancy E. had her first experience with activism, violence, and fear when she was an undergraduate at Kent State. This planted seeds for her current focus:

Nancy E.: I had a final or a mid-term the next morning at 7:45 a.m. . All this had been going on all weekend and the campus was still occupied, so I walked to my class. The professor said, "If you want to take the test, you can, but if you want to leave, you can." You know, just sort of acknowledging how uncomfortable everything was.

There was already a protest forming, so I went and joined in with that group. Then helicopters came in and started to drop pepper gas—that stuff really stings your eyes. So people were running from that. You have to close your eyes or get water into your eyes because it's like getting a bad kind of soap in your eyes. We were running; I was running—actually, it was not far from my dorm—and then I heard what I learned were shots.

I was standing next to a guy who was a Vietnam veteran, and he said, "That's a … [he identified the weapon]," and said, "Get into a building." So he seemed to know more about what was going on. Then we walked out and right near there were students who had been shot. My dorm was right near the parking lot where some of those famous pictures were taken. And then they declared martial law.

Again, there were no cell phones. We were told to get onto a bus; they were renting buses. You could pack up a small bag. If you didn't have a car, which I didn't, you had to get on a bus. The [buses] were being sent to the major cities around Ohio. And you had to try to call your parents to come pick you up.

My father, coincidentally, was coming to have dinner with me that night because he had a business trip at Cleveland. So he's in a car, driving up to Kent, and hears what happened on the radio. So he continues on, and by then, I had to get on a bus, but I left him a note. I eventually got home. I had to calm my mother down; she was crying like crazy. Then my father called and said that driving into the town, he felt physically sick because there were more troops and ammunition in Kent than in an occupied town in Germany when he was there in World War II. So it was pretty dramatic at the time, as you know.

From there, I was fired up, and got … it's so hard to remember what it's like not to have cell phones, but I imagine we all used to call each other up on land lines. But I got involved in the legal defense fund. I did some speaking; I wrote a letter to the editor. Then I started to get hate mail, although the letter was very benign as far as I was concerned. In the town we lived in, I actually asked to speak to the editor of the paper because they used to change people's letters to the editor, and I didn't want my letter changed without my permission. So I actually went and sat with him, and he went over it, and we agreed on a few changes. When the letter was published, it was pretty much that.

Really, to me, there was no reason to be shooting at students, no matter what. There was never any evidence that rocks were thrown, but even if they had been, you don't use bullets against that.

I started to get some hate mail sent to our house, because you also had to put your street address on your letter to the editor, so then everybody knew where I lived. My father knew somebody from his business that had a restaurant on the Jersey Shore. So he drove me to New Jersey, and I wound up getting a room in a boarding house, and I was a waitress for the summer. I met some wonderful people, but was also close to friends that I had had in high school. Having only been in Ohio for a year, I still had a lot of good friends in New Jersey.

I went back and got my stuff, and then when we went back in September, it was like an armed camp. Not so much the tanks, but every class had a sheriff or a state trooper or somebody in it.

That was a turning point, and I decided okay, I need to work on social justice issues. I wound up entering into the social work curriculum they had at the time. There was a sociology professor who had this experimental program called the Akron Neighborhood Faculty program, and you could register for sixteen credit hours. It was a small group of people, and you were taught by an ex-con … a prostitute—street people were our professors. So instead of reading about them in books, they actually were our professors, in addition to having traditional professors holding seminars. But it was very intensive. We had all-day sessions. We did things like a protest around social issues in Akron. It was quite informative. We even, one night, were taken by a van, with hoods over our heads to meet with the Black Panthers in Cleveland.

That was quite phenomenal, because I got exposed to some remarkable, really local activists. I don't know if any of them were ever on the national scene or anything, but it was really quite phenomenal. Then, it was really all the military on the campus.

I stayed one more semester because they had another program, an exchange program with Mexico. I wound up going to Universidad de las Américas for a semester and that was wonderful. So here I was, officially a French major, going to Mexico. That was a little weird. But, you know, I actually learned Spanish a lot easier because of having French. I could really only acquire [French] by reading it. It's very difficult for me to speak it and Spanish was a lot easier. I traveled around Mexico. That was wonderful; it was a great semester.

After that, I left school. I just couldn't deal with it. My parents were supportive. I went and got a job, stayed out for a couple of semesters, and then went back. I knew I needed to finish. I went back, and I wound up taking twenty-six credits, every semester, and I wound up graduating on time, so I could get out.

Herta discusses stepping up to make a career change, despite being comfortable where she was:

Herta: I was the corporate lawyer doing mergers and acquisitions and international tax in the '80s. This was the height of the corporate raiders, etc. I felt being in law was good and being in an advisory and transactional capacity was good, but I felt I was quite commercial and I was comfortable making commercial decisions. So in 1989, I moved from law into banking.

I went to Citibank, initially as Senior Tax Counsel for Europe and then moved from New York to London in 1990 because I really needed to be in London. That was the time when Citibank was going down the drain and the share price was at $80. It was just a very, very difficult time, and I was supposed to basically bring the $400 million tax liability under control and see what could be done because we were in an awful tax bracket. So I basically said, "I need to be in London to do that. This is a matter of trust and I need to be close to the country heads, etc."

There was a sense I had—I was with Citibank for almost ten years—there was a sense of camaraderie. The sense of "even if we're going through difficult times, we can make it." I had this wonderful boss, initially.

Even though it was such a large organization, Citibank created an entrepreneurial environment where you could run your business in an entrepreneurial way. I saw it changing in front of my eyes because a lot of the people who were very skilled and very high-caliber professionals with tremendous integrity were either retiring or leaving. Then the merger with Travelers destroyed Citi, in my view. It really destroyed that entrepreneurial culture.

Q. So you were with them; you were in London.

Herta: I was with Citibank in London and had a great run. The things I learned and was able to do and the community I was a part of … I have very, very good memories of that time, the deals that we made and so forth.

I wanted to move from risk management tax counsel because at that point, I was Senior Tax Counsel for Europe and Global Market, so it was a huge job. But I actually wanted to go into a business [unit]. As part of that, I just put my hand above the parapet, because I felt if I was going to make a transition from middle office to front office, doing it within Citibank would probably be the easiest because I was a known quantity. And sure enough, I spoke to the head of Global Derivatives. He basically asked me to run the Financial Engineering Group, which was the group that needed some structure and some leadership and so forth.

So I did that and felt that I liked to run businesses. I was comfortable with this, even though the environments were not always conducive. The idea of being responsible for my profit and loss and so forth. I felt the love, but then decided to leave Citi because of what was happening internally. I felt it was no longer the firm I had signed up for, if you will.

I very briefly went to Rabobank. I always find that you learn so much more from the things that don't go well than you learn from the things that do go well, human nature being what it is, you know. The things that don't go well somehow shout louder. And at Rabo, it became very clear: Here's an excellent stipulated bank but they have absolutely no aptitude for an investment banking operation, which is what they were trying to build. So, I basically had time to go to J.P. Morgan here in London to build the structure tax business. I was with Morgan for a year. In the meantime, I had also met Sandy Warner and I had deeper insights about how things get done at Morgan.

We had built a strong pipeline and couldn't execute anything. It was during this time that a headhunter friend of mine approached me. AIG basically made me an offer I couldn't refuse. I really felt it was only a matter of time before J.P. Morgan would be taken over by somebody. I accepted the offer from AIG Financial Products on Tuesday night. Wednesday morning, I walked into Morgan and it [the news] was everywhere that Chase had just bought Morgan.

My exits have been absolutely uncanny. If I look back over my career, it's almost spooky. Because with J.P. Morgan, where we had built this very strong pipeline and because I had the niche in the market, I basically felt there was a really strong niche in the market for corporate structured finance, not just between banks but between banks and/or financial institutions and corporations, sophisticated corporations as well.

I really saw this niche and when I arrived at AIG. I said, "I see this niche in the market. I really think we can build something."

And to Joe's credit, he basically said, "Go for it."

Literally, within a little over three months of being at AIG, we closed the first $750 million deal with a major multinational. We took a business from zero revenue, [with] a very good platform but zero revenue, to $50 million in net revenues in less than two years. I'm very proud of that because the relationship that I had, that I was able to bring into the firm and to actually get this multi-billion dollar deal done was remarkable.

The great thing about AIG, at that time, was it could look the counter-party in the eye and say, "You don't have execution rate with me." And that was very unusual in the financial firm, as it is in the industry. That was one of the reasons why we were able to get things done. That was really textbook. So this was really the second part of my career. If you look at my professional life, in the first part of my career I'm a lawyer. In the second part of my career, I'm a banker, and I stayed with AIG until 2005.

I left for two reasons. One, because I really felt I had achieved what I wanted to achieve. And second, because I genuinely didn't like the direction in which the firm was going. At the time, people thought I was nuts because, quite frankly, since we were comparable only to Goldman Sachs in terms of fire power, in terms of capital income, etc., and people just didn't leave AIG. It was one of those things—I felt it was the right time to go, and that really concluded the second substantial phase of my career.

At that time, I was still quite young and I thought, *Well, you know, I can never have a fabulous portfolio,* so I started to go to a couple of boards. They were actually very significant, because at that point, I had been one of the very few female managing directors in the city. I had done things that a lot of people only dream of. So it was really successful in financial terms and so forth.

But there was something niggling at me and it was basically, "Okay what can I do that's significant? And how do I really make a difference?" I mean, my husband and I had always been charitable in terms of making donations and whatever, but it was never hands-on because I had no time for anything.

After many years of avoiding a major part of her talents, and an integral part of who she is, out of a deep-seated fear of what others might think, Deb Roth came to grips with being who she was meant to be:

Deb R.: I have been calling myself a G.P., a general practitioner, you know, like a doctor. And I do not feel—I know you're in this boat too—I do not feel like you can compartmentalize your life. As a coach, I do not want to do that. I do not want to encourage people to compartmentalize their home life from their work life from their relationships from their friends, from whatever. Because business has been down the last couple of years— I was really starting to doubt. It's like, God, should I? Maybe I should ... maybe the universe is telling me I should be doing something else.

When I started coaching with Donna over the summer it was like, *No, I am doing what I love to do. This is what I'm supposed to be doing.* I've just got to think about how I put myself out there in different ways to audiences that I may not have focused on as much, like corporate women, but not doing corporate coaching.

The other big thing has just been — you may not believe this — but I feel sometimes that I've homogenized myself a little bit when I present myself to groups. I don't talk about my tarot or astrology. I tend to talk about women's circles, but I don't use "woo-woo" language. I've just decided that, you know, I've just decided that I'm going to start saying things like astrology and tarot and goddess circles and that kind of thing because that is what makes me different.

Something I was so aware of when I first started doing this stuff years ago was how all the Libra in my chart is so concerned with pleasing people and not making anybody uncomfortable. When I first started studying all of this stuff and people would ask me what I did, I'd roll my eyes and I'd call it "the weird stuff."

I'd be very self-effacing about it and at some point—and I remember it so clearly— Chris was probably like ten, so it was right around the time I had started working on my master's program—being at a season-end soccer potluck with all the parents and the kids. The little boys were playing video games in the other room. Peter and I were with the parents eating while standing up, and talking.

When I started to talk about what I did, I could palpably see, like, a third of the people's eyes kind of glaze over, who didn't know or care about what I was talking about. I found myself talking about what I was studying; what I was starting to do in a very matter-of-fact way. Not apologetic. Not self-effacing. Just—this is what I do. So, I noticed that a third had that response; then another third were kind of curious, you know, politely curious—and wanted to know more. Then the last third were like, "Oh, wow! My sister just gave me a tarot deck." Or, "Oh, I just went to my first new moon circle." People who were, like, actively, "Isn't that cool?"

What was a revelation for me is that, rather than feel like I had to explain myself or jump through hoops to get the first glazed-over group to like me, it was like, okay, that's cool. It's not for them and that's okay, without judgment. I feel like I have been in a second octave of that lately … remembering to go back to my passion, to not be apologetic about it. You would have really heard it in our spirit calls, particularly since, like, a year between last summer and this summer, just feeling very vulnerable and lost and tentative and invisible … just weepy.

Yes. I can look at my chart and I can read off all the things that have been going on with me, particularly for the last year and a half. But whatever it was, even if I didn't know about it, I was really clear about how I was feeling. And it's starting to shift. It's coming back into owning the stuff that I love. I know, definitely, one of my big lessons this lifetime is not to run myself by what I think other people want to hear or worry about if they're going to take me seriously. You know, that's that is always been like this big … "I'm smart and I'm articulate." And *Oh, God. People are going to think I'm some flaky broad … if they really know who I am.*

Q. Well, instead, you bring this together in bigger ways … in the way that you support conferences as well, which is something else that you've been doing for the past year.

Deb R.: Well, it's funny. It's so true, Susan. One of the things I've always loved to do is organize social "people" things. I was, literally, a social chairman in college, social chairman of my class. But it's also about service, which I realize more and more is such a big piece of who I am. And so the organizing, the service, and all that stuff that goes into the conference support you're talking about. It's certainly one of the key things in the work I do about V-Day [the Vagina Monologues' event] which is huge, which is very wonderfully consuming. That brings together so many things that I love to do and that I'm good at. I'm a good mediator, moderator, and motivator; I get people working together, you know? And all that stuff comes in from the conference stuff—I mean, I'm not running that conference, but just to be able to support it happening the way I've been doing is just … lovely.

Q. You're an emotional touchstone for that conference. And you know how to shift—and you've done it more than once—how to shift the tone, whether it's one-on-one, as you did for me, or for the entire group, as you did when we reached that interesting point on the last day.

Deb R.: Yeah.

Q. So, that's another skill.

Deb R.: I'm bringing that more into how I present myself in all those different networking groups; in Adrien's Network and this NAWBO thing yesterday. Any time I get a chance to get up and talk about what I do, I've just been allowing myself to be much more … playful.

I'm also an astrologer and I do these really magical new moon circles for women. Instead of just saying, "Oh, I do these women's circles, these women's groups," now I say, "I do new moon circles." But you know what gets me about it, Susan, is like, shit, how many times do I have to remind myself? Yeah, I know this is my life's work to just be comfortable in my skin with all the funky stuff I do, but God, you would think I would have learned it all by now already.

Q. It's not funky stuff. You're not allowed to say that.

Deb R.: I know. But it is. I'm allowed to say it if I embrace it as being okay. It's not mainstream.

Sometimes, we make changes in a moment of courage—or maybe impulse—without a plan for what will happen next.

Susan M.: I've leapt before I looked more than once. Twice, I quit jobs with no idea what I would do next and no fear as to the outcome. I was confident that something better would turn up. The first time, when I stopped teaching pre-school, I was fortunate to win enough money on the $20,000 Pyramid game show to finance my expenses while I finished graduate school. The second time, I felt that my job was affecting my health.

All right, I was fifty, so this would have been 1995. I had discovered there was this thing called coaching, and I knew that was what I wanted to do. There was a coaching school called CoachVille where everything was on the phone and it was free. So I signed up for CoachVille and it was a wonderful thing. I had found my people and I had come home and I loved it, because I'd been doing this kind of thing my whole career, I just didn't know that it had a name.

So, I turned fifty and I quit. I quit my job and never looked back. I said, once again, "Okay, I'm going to set myself up as a consultant. But at least this time, I know what I want to be consulting on." So I was going to be a coach and consultant and I was going to do organizational development work because I had a good foundation in that. And I could do stress management and I could do emotional intelligence and I could do anger management and trainer development and I could continue my coach training and start coaching individuals.

I had a business partner and we did some work together over the next couple of years. Also, she found me a part-time job with a friend of hers who ran the Institute for the Puerto Rican-Hispanic Elderly, so I worked there a couple of days a week, trying to be her executive coach and trying to get her organized. I've never had such a resistant client, and that's where I learned about solopreneurs. Solopreneurs cannot necessarily make the transition to becoming the boss of their business: she was one of those.

I got involved in an action learning project out in New Jersey with Roche Pharmaceuticals. That was a delightful experience because I was training the facilitators to work with small groups, small learning groups. At one point, they needed an extra facilitator, so I was facilitating a group of my own. I did that for about a year-and-a-half. That was wonderful, because this was really group coaching. I would go out there and, over the month, I would see these people change; there would be physical changes in these people. They would be looking better and standing taller and more self-confident. So it drew on the work I had been doing at Medgar Evers around self-esteem. I said, "Aha, now I see how this works."

After a while, I felt like I was so dragged into working at the Institute that I wasn't really focusing on building my own practice, so I decided I was going to quit that job. My timing was impeccable; it was September 2001. My last day of work actually was 9/11, and, like everybody else in the city, I was just devastated. I went home. I didn't know what to do. My heart wasn't really in marketing at that point and nobody was really looking to buy anything at that point either. I had started to do some teaching at CoachVille; I was what they call a Community Coach, where there was a particular subject matter and you taught classes and did some curriculum development with them as well.

After a while, I had to do something, so I ended up taking a job at Good Shepherd as their Training Director. They had spent something like a year-and-a-half looking for the right person to fill this job. It took them nine months to realize they didn't need anybody in that job at all. So that was the only time in my life I was ever actually fired from a job. I was just devastated, still not back together from post-9/11 and didn't knew what I was going to do at all.

But I had to do something, so I went to my old friends who were working for what had been the Department of Personnel and what became Citywide Training. I said, "I need a job. What am I going to do?" The guy who was the Head of Bureaus was somebody I had hired as an intern, and the guy who was in charge of the training program had been a colleague of mine for many years when I was still working there.

As it happened, shortly after we had this conversation, they put out a request for proposals looking for consultants to come in and do training. I jumped on it, got hired as a consultant, and started working for them doing curriculum development, doing training. The city-wide Department of Environmental Protection was under severe sanctions for the mistakes they had made, so a colleague and I developed training for them. We trained every manager and every supervisor in the entire agency. We ended up with a whole team of people teaching the courses because it got to be too much for us. I developed trainer development courses again, and I developed a managerial certificate program.

All this time, I kept on saying, "Michael, we need coaching; the city needs coaching." So three years ago, I was actually just doing one thing—trying to build my coaching practice and doing this consulting work.

The Commissioner of the Human Resources Administration read an article in the *Wall Street Journal* about coaching and said, "We need some of this. We need this at HRA."

It was funny because the Commissioner said, as part of selling the program to him, "What's this like?"

I said, "Well, is it okay to coach you?"

He said, "Sure." So I ended up in this meeting for the whole team, coaching the Commissioner.

Q. Did that sell him on it?

Susan M.: It did. He liked it, he did it. He saw that it can be very practical. We are now in our sixth cohort of senior-level managers within HRA. It's been great fun. I mean, they're wonderful people. This year, we allowed some people to come back for a second round because they said, "We've grown, we've changed; now we need the next step." It's been really successful; it's been really rewarding; it's been a lot of fun.

Elements of Keeping Fear in Perspective

Identifying fears, moving from that state of free-floating anxiety to dealing with something tangible is the first element. This is followed by deciding if the fear is fact-based (it is probably a good idea to remain afraid of exiting a plane midair without a parachute—the results are well documented) or psychological (fear of public speaking, fear of success). The second element is devising a plan to keep the identified fear in perspective. This could include fact-based and psychological fears, such as an individual with a life-threatening disease.

Victoria describes facing her fear of editing the work of well-known writers. Her agent told her to just do the best she could, and she was praised by the contributors to her anthology. Rita took great risks in reporting the difficult stories. Deb L. found a mentor to help her work through her fear of public speaking. Sharon was never afraid to ask questions.

Exercise

Developing Perspective on Fear

- Sit very still with your fear. Let it wash over you as you feel into it. Identify any related feelings.
- Rate your fear on a scale of one to ten. Rate your desire to change your perspective on the same scale.
- Decide whether you are dealing with a primarily fact-based or psychological fear.

If fact-based, gather and evaluate information about your fear. Use this information to develop a realistic perspective: what are the odds that your fear will become a reality?

If psychological, trace the fear back to find the roots. Do those same circumstances still exist? Is there a hidden benefit for you in holding on to the fear?

If you let it, fear will overwhelm you and prevent you from doing anything. Many famous actors are notoriously shy. They push their fears aside in order to appear on stage. Writers fear going dry. Fear of flying stops some from ever getting on a plane and becomes just another thing to deal with for others.

There is an element of risk in every change we want to make in life. Which risks are you willing to take?

Chapter 9

Lagniappe – Legacy, Creating Meaning, Having Fun and Other Important Life Lessons

LEGACY is generally defined as money or property left to someone. In a broader sense, though, it is an integral part of second adulthood. It is part of making meaning. The definition of legacy used in this chapter is what an individual contributes—ideas, teachings, a favorite recipe, work for an organization. Jung says that the second part of our life is about building meaning rather than building achievement. Having fun—enjoying life—needs no definition.

When I was trying to sum up this book, to find a single idea that best represented what life could be like beyond fifty, I went back to the interviews for inspiration. I think that Robyn's comment in Chapter 7 summed up my thinking beautifully and is worth repeating:

Robyn: Having new twists past fifty? I just got this image of picking flowers because I feel like that's what it is. Once you're past fifty, you turn around and say, "OK, what flowers did I grow along the way and forgot to pick up?" I feel that when you do that, then you have this amazing bouquet. And there are a lot of times, what we fail to do is to notice that we've planted these beautiful flowers along the way and we trample on them. We're gathering this bouquet and they're all different colors.

Although I've tried to create categories that made sense, as I read and reread the stories, there were always pieces that excited me that didn't fit into any of the categories. Three themes seemed especially important. Especially for the oldest women in the group (seventy plus years), there was a sense of creating a legacy. They wanted to have made a difference. This tied into another thread about doing meaningful work. For some of The Fifty, that sense of creating meaning came from their primary careers. For others, like Sally, it came from volunteer work. Finally, whether they mentioned it directly or indirectly, these were women who wanted a full life, and they wanted to have fun.

For Barbara, fun comes through her regular job and through her love of softball. Both her current job and her involvement with a national sorority add meaning and opportunities to give back.

About an Early Job and Fun:

Barbara: It was the start of what became E! Entertainment News, but at the time it was just called HBO Entertainment News. The major players—who then went to California and started E News—were there, and I was the production assistant for it. It was really fun. I got to go to all these premiers and openings, and things like that. Every week, we had different celebrities come in for the entertainment news, and it was a lot of fun, and I really enjoyed what I did. It wasn't altruistic in any way, but I just loved all of the stuff.

Through that job, I got to go to Wimbledon, which was one of my favorite things! And I got my friend, Sally, to be production assistant there! That was a lot of fun.

Her volunteer work:

Barbara: I did get into a sorority, which was another thing with my Dad, like, "Try this," and I'm really glad that I did, because it's been a huge part of my life. It's like a grounding thing with other people, mostly in New York, to come here. Even though I don't know or go to school with the people, I felt we had a common thread. So through that, I've been involved in a lot of volunteer projects. Alpha Omicron Pi is the name of it.

Q. What kinds of projects?

Barbara: Currently, we're working with a chapter at Barnard College, Columbia University. In the early thirties, I think, was when all the sororities and fraternities were not wanted at Columbia anymore. So anyway, we got ours back, and it has been very hard for all of us; rewarding, but hard, because it's like having eighty teenage girls that you're taking care of. But an interesting experience! And then, of course … you learn so much about yourself, too.

And her current job:

Barbara: I did things, specifically with the employees, and got them engaged. I have been doing that, pretty much, for the last seven, eight years.

Q. I'm wondering also … you went from all these really glamorous careers to public service. I'm wondering if you could just speak a little bit about what you found rewarding about public service.

Barbara: I'm so glad you saw some of that, because I have absolutely loved how much the staff appreciates what any of us do, when we're able to do something for them that touches them in some way. People stop me on the elevator and say, "Thank you! No one else ever paid attention." Or, "No one did …" And a lot of times, especially in the entertainment world, you could practically swim in with the videotape, and people would go, "Next!" The appreciation was so much more meaningful here from people that—you give them a glass of water when they've trudged a couple of blocks to an event. Meanwhile, at some corporate situation, they can have … lobster! That really summarizes it for me. I've said that to so many of my friends who are still in the corporate world, what a difference it is, what a refreshing difference. And the importance of being involved in a group of some kind. For her, enjoying softball in the park:

Q. I want to ask about a broader picture. What else is going on in your life? Are you still volunteering? You talked a little bit about that. Are there some other things that get you energized outside of work?

Barbara: Sports? I'm involved with playing softball, and I probably am the oldest woman playing softball in Central Park on the weekends … catching for two hours, which is not easy for men in their twenties and thirties. [laughter] Here I am, I'm almost sixty and I'm playing softball. I actually really, really enjoy that a lot.

Sports were such a big part of my life, unfortunately, during that time before Title IX. I feel like that would have been a different direction in my life, because there really weren't the opportunities.

There were times that I would go up to somebody and say, "Can't I be on the team?" And they would go, "No, we don't have girls on the team."

That kind of stuff. And there just wasn't the money that there is now, for sports in college and high school and everything. I think, actually, that being involved in sports and something like—it doesn't have to be a sorority—but something like that grounds you, helps, and supports you is just a wonderful thing to have. I almost cut it out of my life, thinking, Oh, no, I don't want to be a part of that.

As a teenager, I thought, *What? I don't want to be around a bunch of women in a house!* Or, you know, even being involved with teams. I just think those kinds of things really help you in so many ways. Especially now, with people that are completely involved with their computers and their phones, and they don't get out and get involved with those kind of programs.

Sally found opportunities to give back throughout her career and developed a deepening interest in service that grew out of her travels. She took advantage of travel discounts offered to airline personnel to travel widely:

Sally: When I first started flying, I would take my days off and take a pass and go to Bermuda or Miami, around the United States. Then, after I got to New York, I met this girl who became a friend of mine, and we decided we were going to see the world. The other airlines offered us discount travel, so for about ten years, every chance that I got I would take a pass and go to a different part of the United States and the world. I got to meet loads of people, and I actually got around the world several times, just visiting other countries, and meeting people, and having a great time.

I still had the desire to travel. So in 1980, after many years of wanting to go to China, I was able to get a visa when they first opened up the country for people to tour throughout their country. We spent three weeks, and it was just so incredible seeing how the Chinese people lived. We did not know any of this because none of the way they lived, really, [was] in our newspapers or on our news. So it was quite an experience, as I was one of the first people to be able to get a visa into China.

Q. Right. That's amazing.

Sally: I came back from China, and then a friend of mine decided we should learn how to sail. So she and I went to the offshore sailing school in City Island. We wanted to do a trip to Turkey we had heard of. Each year, they took three boats, and whoever [had] learned to sail and had the desire to go to these different places. Our first trip was three weeks on the coast of Turkey. Instead of doing much crewing on my boat, I bought a

Turkish cookbook, and I ended up doing most of the cooking on the boat, trying a lot of the Turkish recipes. It was really a great three weeks, as I had really never been on the Mediterranean, or the Adriatic Sea. I had never been on that coastline, in those waters.

I actually fulfilled the dream trip I had had for many, many years, and visited Tibet. We were able to fly into Lhasa from Nepal and then we spent five days in a bus, winding down through the Himalayas. It was absolutely the most beautiful, breathtaking trip I had ever had. We stayed in very poor hotels, which were not really hotels, on the side of the mountains, for these five days. It was just incredible. Also, I met quite a few people because there were twenty-six of us on the bus. I think one of the most exciting parts of the bus ride—we would look out to the right, and our tires on the bus would be right at the edge of these cliffs, and the drops might have been five or eight thousand feet down. So many times, when we went around a corner, we would have to get out of the bus and walk, or we would not have made it.

At one time, one of my friends and I, we were taking pictures, and they were yelling at us to hurry up and run, and we didn't know what they were talking about. So the girl who was head of our tour group came back and grabbed me by the arm and said, "Run!" And I said, "What's wrong?" She said, "Look back." There was a mudslide coming down at that corner. So she saved both of our lives. After that, I listened to what she had to say and did what I was supposed to do.

I also got my pictures. One of the pictures that she made me take was a Land Rover that, a few days before, had gone over the cliff. It looked like a little fly, it was so far down the cliff, but I have that picture!

Phoebe also enjoys traveling. She sees it as a good way to create quality family time and to enrich the lives of her children:

Phoebe: One of the things I have not talked about is how much I've travelled. When I was in the corporate finance job, I spent time negotiating in Venezuela and in Indonesia. I spent good amount of time in Indonesia, in particular, and learned, sort of, that culture and how it operates. Those are experiences you can't really take away from people. They can never take away education and you can't take away some of those deeply rich cultural experiences, like having them describe the welfare system in Indonesia, for example, and how that really works.

We, as a family, have done international trips each year. As a family, we have been to Africa; we have been to China to see the total eclipse of the sun—something you should do in life—that's a spiritual experience; we have been to Scandinavia; we've been to London; we've been to quite a few places in Europe. Last year, we went to the Olympics. So we have tried to expose our children to many different cultures—I've been to Japan with Kate, I have been to Mexico—so we tried to expose them to cultures and different ways [that] Homo sapiens live on this earth. That is a pretty important thing for us to inculcate in them, I think. We have done that; that's good. We've had the resources to be able to do that, and so we have done that, and that's richly positive. I've worked really hard, just in terms of parenting, to make sure my children know how to interact with adults, how to entertain, how to be engaging, and so they're both that. They're just very, very comfortable in the international, global world.

Having fun at work was important to The Fifty. Some women spoke about this in terms of not being bored (Chapter 7). The following women seemed to speak more about a conscious effort to enjoy what they do:

Natalie: So at that point, I was still determining what it was that I wanted to do. I have always done something; I have always gotten involved in what my husband used to call "one hare-brained scheme after another." As it turns out, they were not so much hare-brained schemes, but again, that interest in wanting to have fun and that interest in people drove me. That's what always drove me, and I always allowed that to drive me. So I took a job here and there doing a variety of things. Seriously, I mean it when I say variety of things: I was mowing lawns for the summer; I was a janitor at a church for a while. I mean, I just did whatever I could, because shortly after I moved to Vermont, I was pregnant with my first child.

For Marla, enjoyment was a constant theme. If she wasn't having fun anymore, she moved on:

Marla: I enjoyed it. It was fun working for a big organization like that. I enjoyed the marketing end of it. I enjoyed figuring out what people wanted and selling it to them. So that was a lot of fun. I decided, at that point, that I wanted to stay at CitiBank, but I wanted to experience different opportunities. When you work for a big company like that, a huge benefit is that you take a position, you train in it, you work, you excel, and then you are encouraged to move on. So I was at CitiBank for quite a number of years, and I was able to take on quite a number of different positions. And that was definitely encouraged.

Q. Okay. And what were some of your favorites among those?

Marla: Well, one position that I really liked a lot was called the Area Marketing Manager. The way CitiBank set up their branching system at the time was there was an Area Director. The area director I worked for managed the biggest Midtown CitiBank branches. I was brought on to do marketing support. The Central Marketing Department was pumping out a whole lot of new materials. They were creating new products and it was my responsibility to make sure that the branches understood the features and benefits of the products and were able to market them appropriately.

That was fun for me, because it was a really good transition into the marketing world. It was working and leveraging my people-management skills because I had to work with a lot of different store sales managers. I had to teach them a lot about how to market and sell CitiBank products. It also enabled me to interface with the Central

Marketing Department. I did that position for a while and then was promoted into an Assistant Manager position at the Central Marketing Department in CitiBank.

That was great—I really felt like I was at the core of things. I worked in the New Product Development Department and our job was to figure out how to create new products and services for CitiBank. At the time, it was fun because they were experimental; there was a lot of flexibility. CitiBank was on the forefront of financial service products. It was something I really enjoyed.

That was the heyday of American Express. It was very entrepreneurial, very aggressive, very creative; a real focus on marketing and the customer. I enjoyed every second of it. It was just such a wonderful experience for me. I was there for quite a while … just about twelve years.

Let me take a step back. When I first started at American Express, I would say a year or two into that [job] was when I had my first child. It was a very heady time for me. I was young, married, just about finished with my MBA, had my first baby. It was really an awesome time for me and somehow, I managed to do it. I wonder … I think back to those days and I think, How did I make it all work? But somehow, I did.

Q. *Women, in general, seem to somehow expand their available time beyond all imagination to make things like marriage and family and work and school all happen at the same time.*

Marla: Right. And I made it happen because I loved what I was doing. I loved working at American Express. I was there for twelve years. I had a lot of amazing positions there. I was there during a time of very rapid growth of the company. The management team was tremendous. I learned so much. It was just such a great place to learn and grow. After a couple years, I had my second child and, again, just managed to make it all work because I really loved what I was doing. I had a lot of passion for it.

I really believed in the company; I really believed that they were trying to create the best possible products and services for their customers, and I felt good about that. It was a truly wonderful experience, the kind of place where you got into a job—there was a lot of pressure—but you were given a lot of tools and resources to help you grow and develop. I really adored it. It was a lot of fun.

I was able to leverage a lot of different channels: direct mail, email, and in-store marketing to market the Readers Advantage Program. I did market research. It was fun because we worked with the buying group within Barnes & Noble and we were able to support some of the very key book launches; for example, one of the Harry Potter book launches. That became a very integrated marketing program. We did some promotions—it was a very multi-channel approach to launching a book—and that was fun because it leveraged all the creativity, a lot of creative tools.

I took a position with a company called WebMD. WebMD was a very cool company, a very interesting company. It's still in existence today, but when I started with WebMD, it had just formed. Again, it was the era of the dot-com boom and there was lots of money. They were doing very cool things and it was just fun to be part of their marketing team. I was there for about a year.

But what happened was there was a very distinct change in management. I think the company had spent a lot of money and it was time for a second group, a second management team, to take over and try to steer the company to a more profitable position. When that happened, a lot of my responsibilities changed, and it just wasn't a whole lot of fun for me anymore. So I decided to leave the company.

You know, when I'm doing something I love, I feel very creative and entrepreneurial, and that's great. There's a freedom to create and grow. What I found most challenging in the positions that I've had over the years is when company politics get in the way and sometimes, [there are] very strange corporate policies. And that's not what I'm about; that's not what I want.

Q. The two things that I'm hearing: one is that when the job starts restricting you in some ways, then it's time to move on; and the other is, if you're not having any fun, you don't want to do it. If you're having fun, you're just full speed ahead.

Marla: Right, because to me, the creative process requires a lot of energy and passion and freedom. You know, I certainly understand corporate requirements and financial requirements—that really wasn't the issue. The whole point is to create products and services that meet the needs of customer but ultimately are profitable for the company. There's no issue there. But when I was in a situation where there was some conflict, in terms of decisions and inconsistencies, I realized I was feeling very suffocated. I was feeling very constrained. It was time for me to move on. I was fortunate; I was able to do that.

Charlotte also speaks of being able to pick and choose. At a certain point in her career, feeling that she was adding value and her relationships with her clients were much stronger motivations than earning potential:

Charlotte: Two years ago, we attended a class called the Supernova, which developed out of Wharton, I believe, about doing business. You know, over the years, you can acquire quite a lot of clients that maybe don't get the full services, they don't want them. The top clients are not the ones that have the most money, necessarily. They're the ones I truly enjoy working with, the ones that appreciate what I do, and go with what I do, and don't argue with what I do. I let go of some clients to give me more time to actually give the ones that I do enjoy the most more service. And to take advantage of what we can offer them.

Q. Good for you.

Charlotte: This is something we talked about at the women's conference last Tuesday: The fact that I have one client, and I really like him, but I called him and told him that

I enjoyed so much working with him, but I did not enjoy his wife. I could no longer feel like I could do a good job.

She goes to an investment club, and she calls out of the blue, and she's got to have you right that minute, show how important she is by quizzing you and telling you, "Now, what do you think about this? Tell me what you think about that? Give me the reasons to buy this. Give me the reasons."

She wanted to have lunch on a regular basis, and usually she was thirty to forty-five minutes late, and she didn't take me as a professional. She tried to treat our relationship as something to educate her or be about her.

I have one client who has a limited amount of money. She hadn't worked with me until, probably, ten years ago and already had had some bad experiences. I don't make any money working with her. I don't charge her to do certain things because she doesn't have it, and she can't take any risks. I put her into safe investments like certificates of deposit. She doesn't get a lot of growth, she doesn't get a lot of anything else, but she can't afford to lose principal.

And I have had more referrals coming from this woman because she'll go to the doctor's office and she'll say, "You will not believe what Charlotte has done for me!" So, here you've got a client that doesn't have much money, is not a big contributing factor to your income, yet I enjoy her, I check on her, I talk to her daughter who is in Seattle. You know, things like this ... it gives me pleasure. It's about working with people you enjoy. I say now I'm a wealth manager and I'm a risk manager.

Almost all of the women I spoke with are involved in some sort of mentoring or other volunteer work. Phoebe speaks about giving back:

Phoebe: One of the things that I would say for me is, sometimes, I've done things because people like what are you doing about it or people have made me think, What am I doing? You know what I mean? Like, What am I doing to help women, and What am I doing to help? With age comes more courage to talk openly and more freedom to talk openly.

Q. Yeah, and I think a shift to having deeper meaning in the larger world.

Phoebe: My ninety-year-old mother asks, "What is my purpose ... what am I doing to help someone with my purpose on earth at the moment?" That's what she's asking at ninety-one.

Q. And these kinds of things are wonderful. I love your mother's philosophy ... I think we're seeing more of that. Maybe there's still hope for the world.

Phoebe: Yeah, yeah. You can't have children and not have hope for the world. They're wonderful, wonderful; at least some of them are truly wonderful. I'm unusual, I think, in [that] I'm among the first wave of women.

I had children, but very late in life, which is very typical of that group of women ... if we had children at all. I have many friends with no children; many, many friends with no children. That's a characteristic of our particular era. And I have international experience, which I consider a wonderful gift in terms of my world view.

For Connie, her involvement in a professional group, The Committee of 200, took her from an interest in women's issues to what has become a full-time post-retirement volunteer project:

Q. So you retired, and ...

Connie: People gave me excellent advice, which I now give everyone who asks my thoughts on retirement; advice which I, unfortunately, didn't follow.

So now I tell people, "Please follow this advice. Don't be like me. Don't sign up for things. You'll get calls on lots of different things, but don't do anything, commit to anything for about six months, because you need some time to decompress and to really figure out where your passion lies."

So, I had about two years of what I'd call "transitional" activity. It was at that time I assumed the chairmanship of The Committee of 200. I had been on the board for a while.

Q. Tell me a little bit about The Committee of 200.

Connie: Well, The Committee of 200 is the organization of leading women business leaders, both entrepreneurs and corporate women, line women. It's been a great organization. I joined, probably, twenty plus years ago. It's really been a source of friendships, because everyone who's eligible to join The Committee of 200—it's an invitational organization—has really walked many of the same paths that the other members have.

They get that you're spread very thin, managing a business, running a career, plus a family, plus the other things you do. They also understand that, you know, in that kind of juggling, what goes first are your own activities and friendships. So there's an almost instant bond of friendship with this group. I found that to be the case.

It's a phenomenal group. One of the older members initially told me, "You know, we check our guns at the door here." And that's always been the case. It's just a very unique organization. Anyway, I'd been on the board and they asked if I would chair the board for two years. So I did that. At that time—I also started doing some angel investing with a group of women—some Committee of 200 members and some others in Boston. And our creed was: Women-Led Businesses, Women Entrepreneurs.

These were very early-stage businesses. So I did that and had a portfolio of early-stage companies. We did a lot of mentoring of the women in addition to providing some angel capital. Out of that grew an activity where a couple of us co-authored a book on entrepreneurship, specifically targeted at women. It was really kind of a give-back. We got asked so many of same basic questions by the different women who would come and see us that we just felt that it would be great to offer a primer on some of the basic aspects of entrepreneurship.

So all of that took place in the first two years, along with an invitation that came through a Committee of 200 member to join a bipartisan State Department

Commission on Afghan Women, which was formed in early 2002. I retired at the end of 2001 and I was in New York for 9/11, which was, sort of, the final sign that I wanted to be back in Chicago.

This Commission was being formed by the State Department to help women have a seat at the table in new Afghanistan. They needed a business representative, so someone put my name in. That was really my entré into Afghanistan, something completely unanticipated, which also started me down the road on what's become a personal journey in founding ARZU, the social business I have founded to employ women in Afghanistan.

I have been at that now, for almost ten years. If you'd asked me ten years ago, would I be deeply involved in thinking about issues, thinking about solutions to this intractable problem of global poverty alleviation, I would have said, "I don't think so." And yet, here I am. I have to say, it has been truly some of the most interesting work I have ever done.

Q. Tell me a little bit more about actually getting interested in these women as a group, and figuring out that you could do something that would help them.

Connie: Well, "women's rights" has always been my own personal soapbox. Throughout my life and my career, I've always been into women's issues and followed them to the extent … supported different initiatives.

Early on, Goldman was under Bob Ruben, a leader, an innovator in this whole idea of a diverse workforce. That wasn't really a term that was being used in corporate America then. He was thinking not just about gender diversity and racial diversity—which is what we think about here in the United States—but also about cultural diversity as the firm became more and more global.

For about five years, I led the efforts to institute and think about this issue of managing a diverse workforce, instituting many of the family-friendly policies that are just part and parcel of the firm's culture today. Again, all of that was in line with my own passion about women's rights, particularly about women's economic empowerment. That's what I've always been specifically interested in. That is why that followed me or sort of led me into the angel investing arena; helping women entrepreneurs, because women still get a very disproportionately low percentage of venture funding. Again, it's a continuing theme, or thread, as we say in ARZU. We use a lot of thread and yarn analogies, weaving analogies.

I had been following Taliban abuses of women, just generally in the newspapers. It was really brought forth in the feminist majority, I'd say, in the late '90s. So when I had the opportunity to visit Afghanistan —I did not know what my role would be on this committee—but thinking about having some exposure to this, I was very fascinated.

When I went on my first trip there in January of 2003, this wave was the first women's delegation allowed to overnight in the country. So this was a really—what's the right word—it looked like Berlin after World War II. It was not only half a world away, but it was like stepping back in time two thousand years. Women were clearly at the very bottom of that pyramid, if not in the cellar of that pyramid, under the Taliban. It really stoked both my passion and interests.

Going back to that advice, I forgot to say what the advice was that I had ignored. It was, "Don't sign up for anything for the first six months or so," because you get calls to do random kinds of things. You look at your calendar and think, *Gosh, I've been so scheduled for breakfast and lunch and dinner that sure, I could participate on this committee or participate in a fund-raiser four months from now.*

But what happened was I looked up six months forward, and every single week I was committed to do something that I hadn't necessarily thought through in a cohesive way. Then it took another year to gracefully unwind out of those commitments. So over time, I thought very much about my portfolio of time and how I balance that portfolio between business activities, philanthropic activities, and family, friends, and me activities.

So that's the advice I give to people: "Don't commit like I did in the early days. Wait, and sort of decompress, and let things sort of unwind." So, they all ended up in the right place. It's just ... there was that interim period where I didn't listen to good advice.

Anyway, that's how I got to Afghanistan and why I was particularly intrigued about this idea of figuring out how to employ women in Afghanistan ... the nascent days of social entrepreneurship. I had no direct experience with Afghanistan, with international development, traditional practices, or with rugs—certainly not. I now know quite a lot about all three, which has been this learning curve. I have been able to develop, through that, strong opinions about why international development practices are so off the mark and why, as a country, we waste billions of dollars when there is such need in the world. I knew nothing about this industry. I knew nothing about the international development sort of approach, standard operating procedures.

The "What's next?" is, I do think I would like to write a book or in some way share the operating principals that I've learned as it relates to social entrepreneurship and its impact on grassroots economic activity.

Q. Oh, yes. I mean this whole business of thinking, coming to the notion that this was a business that you could make viable for these women in the first place, I think is pretty amazing.

Connie: I am still amazed at how far we've come given where we started, which was a junky product. Weaving has always been a traditional activity. In fact, it's just about the only culturally-accepted activity that women in rural areas in Afghanistan can do because it's home-based work. But you know, given that I was entering the picture twenty-three years into a non-stop war, and you think about what that does to the economy of a country—it just literally blows it to smithereens. So, the supply chains were disrupted, and the weavers were displaced in refugee camps. The product had increasingly developed a junky reputation on the international market.

I didn't know all of that 'til I had already jumped into the pool. It's one of those things where the old "ignorance is bliss" is probably true, because if I'd actually understood exactly what I was getting myself into, I don't know that I would have taken the punch. But once I was in, I had to start doggy paddling to keep my head above water. It took about five years to establish our footprint.

As soon as we got the lay of the land, we went straight out to the rural areas, away from the central government corruption—as far as we could get—at a time when there weren't a lot of organizations working out in the middle of nowhere. That allowed us to do a couple of things. One is, we worked … we built our footprint with the Hazara tribe in the Bamyan province; that's where those giant Buddhas were blown up.

The Hazara, if you remember from *The Kite Runner*, was the servant family. There are about forty tribes in Afghanistan. The Hazara tribe, because they are the minority Shiites, have been historically the dog that everyone wanted to kick, so it's one of the poorest regions. Ironically, we have found the people there incredibly receptive—in the context of a conservative Muslim country—to new ideas. They are clearly willing to learn, to do whatever it takes to improve the lives of their communities and their families because they have been so disadvantaged for so long.

That came out of what I'd call "on the job training." That has been a powerful instructor in this whole process. We just made it up as we went along. I had no idea how to do this. I did it from the standpoint of, "What would I do if this were a business? That's how I think of it, although we are structured legally as a 501(c)(3) non-profit in the United States and a registered local Afghan NGO [non-government organization].

I've thought about this model since Day One: to be sustainable, you have to be profitable. The whole model that we're trying to prove out is: If you can bring to the market products with purpose—and here we're on the front edge of a wave because, since the recession in 2008, I think consumers are increasingly conscious of how they're spending their money—if you can bring products with purpose that are competitive, both from quality design and pricing perspectives and then it has the back story of, if you buy this product, you are directly transforming the lives of a woman and her family, people go, "Wow, why wouldn't I buy that?" vs. buying a rug. And the rug industry, after trafficking, is notoriously exploitive of women and children.

Q. And not to mention, these are some of the most gorgeous rugs I've ever seen in my life.

Connie: Well, thank you. That's again, that slow, patient build; starting from junk, slowly building this up over a five-year period. We, five years into it, in 2009, got the market validation that we had arrived because we won Best Rug of 2009 by *Interior Design* magazine. We beat out some very high-end, well-known names. So that was enormously validating for us.

What I spent the [next] four years doing then, is building up to the product that we know meets the standards. We have the scale now. If we can build our distribution channels and sell through the volume of product that we have the capability of producing now, then we'll be profitable. And that's the last piece of the puzzle.

Again, I've been working on this for four years and I feel like we are at a tipping point, because we have been slowly and organically building a brand, again, as a small non-profit organization.

One of the challenges we had is, how do you build a brand and compete with commercial entities when you have no marketing, public relations, or advertising budget? It's an interesting question. We've used social media extensively. We use word-of-mouth … literally, one buyer to the next. People who have purchased ARZU rugs and are aware of them have a high degree of customer satisfaction. The issue for us is getting the brand better known, you know, on a shoestring.

So, it's a challenge, without question. But this is the last piece of the puzzle. When we tip into profitability, then we will have a model that has been built in, I would argue, the hardest place in the world to build a business.

There are a lot of places that are difficult around the world. There are a lot of places that have conflict. But when you look at Afghanistan—which Thomson Reuters Foundation deemed the worst place in the world to be a woman in 2011—that was the same year we won two awards. We won a gold medal Edison Award, which is a big corporate award; we won in the Lifestyle and Social Impact category. That was the year iPad won in its consumer electronics category. We also won the ASID, the American Society for Interior Design's inaugural award for the company.

Again, we are a social business, but a non-profit company changing the environment of humanity by design. So that's all happening and it's all happening at the same time.

We are getting significant positive press just since we launched in the early February timeframe. Part of it was to demonstrate, to elevate, our brand by demonstrating that we really are on the luxury high-end of the market. Much like in retailing, in home décor, and most consumer products, you've got the luxury end of the market and you've got Wal-Mart and there's really not much left in the middle anymore. So we are on the luxury end, but when people see the quality of what we do, they look at it and they say, "Well, this is no more expensive, in fact, this is more reasonable than if I just go to my local rug store and buy a rug," a rug that you really do not know how it was made, but you would be appalled if you did or, you can buy an ARZU rug.

We are just thrilled that we have the opportunity to associate ARZU with these renowned Hall of Fame winners. Again, it's great for our brand and it also is being marketed by order only, as a numbered limited edition collection. So it has the other benefit of giving us an influx of cash, which is very important, because we are still trying to become profitable. So it helps us on many fronts, but those would be the two key ones.

Q. Yeah. Wow. It's just incredible stuff. So you were starting to talk a little bit about what's next, and you mentioned a book.

Connie: Yes. And I really feel that the way. ARZU is basically a prototype; we're a learning laboratory. Again, it's been so long and I was so unrealistic about what I thought I was doing, I honestly can't remember what I was doing. Oh, they make rugs. People buy rugs. Maybe I could just make a few introductions and it will take care of itself. But it doesn't work that way. So what we really have morphed into, because what we've also learned is, I believe, is that a job comes first.

Others believe education comes first. Well, you get the Arab Spring. You didn't have tens of thousands of people pouring into the streets in Cairo because they were demanding an education; they had an education. There was a 35 percent official unemployment rate, and so the real rate was fifty percent, sixty percent? Who knows? And these were young people who had no chance of getting a job. So I argue that a job comes first. But, in order to really afford people an opportunity, you have to pair it with education.

So we developed simultaneously during this first five years. What we learned is that you have to create this ecosystem of social programs which help provide and meet basic needs. We're talking Maslow's basic needs: food, air, water, heat, clothing, because there are still some three hundred families in our immediate vicinity. They're living in caves—think Colorado—these are mountains with lots of snow in the winter. So we started looking at affordable, low-cost housing that could be made with local materials—dirt. There's a form of adobe called Super-Adobe.

We realized that we had to look at how we get people access to clean water, because if they're too sick, they can't work; or if the kids are too sick, they can't go to school. We require that the women attend our literacy classes. We require that the families enroll girls and boys in school. And our third requirement is that the families release pregnant women to our ARZU-chaperoned car and driver to be physically taken to and from pre- and post-natal care, and babies for immunizations. We call that our maternal health program. Now, maternal health is the country's, is the government's, single biggest health priority, because Afghanistan has either the last or second to last highest maternal death rate in the world. The average Afghan woman has an average of eight pregnancies, each one a life-threatening event. In the rural areas, ninety-five percent of the women will never have any trained [child-delivery] system. They'll deliver at home in their mother-in-law's house. So, even if there is a clinic or hospital, the mother-in-law with whom you live, is like, "I delivered my ten children at home. Good enough for me, good enough for you." So even if women are hemorrhaging, they don't get taken to these services, even if these services are available.

What we do on the social program side, we really look and try to fill gaps. What we observed is that there is a regional hospital; there are some clinics. But if the women can't go, they might as well be sitting on the moon. So they're still at risk of dying. By making this relief a requirement, in effect, what we're doing is, we're providing logistics.

That's what we're doing, and providing a four-wheel drive vehicle, a driver, and a female chaperone known to the community. We track everything. Since we've been doing this, since 2006, we've not lost a single mother or baby in childbirth, in the country with these kinds of statistics.

We're in the middle of nowhere with limited resources available to women. But I think the point of all of that is, what we've learned along the way: job first. But then you have to wrap it in this ecosystem where you can, at least, minimally address these basic needs, because until people can put food on their table, drink decent water, have reasonably decent health, they can't start to think about the second-order needs. One of those needs is security, which in Afghanistan, I translate, and other places, into peace. So, for desperate people—it's hard to talk about civil society until they actually can feed their kids.

It's like that guy on Ed Sullivan who was spinning the plates—you know? There are like seven of them; you've got to get all going at the same time in order to make the whole package work. You know, you get the first three going and suddenly, you've got to go back and re-spin the first one. So it's an iterative process. Some of them wobble a little bit, but that's what it takes. You can't just immunize babies. You can't just educate primary school kids. You just can't do some of it. You have to do all of it.

Q. Sure. Sure. Wow. So this is just amazing. Anything else in the "what's next" category that we haven't already talked about?

Connie: Well, the "what's next:" I'm very-laser focused on completing this last piece of the puzzle because, in my mind, until we are profitable this model is not proven. When we are profitable, it will stick. The way we'll scale—because I get this question about, "Well, you're only working with thousands of people. What about tens of thousands of people, millions of people?"

Before the crash, I started looking at the idea and thinking about the idea of creating sort of an umbrella network of high-end, women-artisan craftsmanship, because I've looked at weaving co-ops in Peru. There are fabulous textiles in India. Ethiopia—they weave hand-spun cotton-which is fabulous. So there are a lot of intrinsic, women-made, high-end skills that are number one, being lost because everything's made in China, right? But I think, at the same time, in the luxury end of the market, there is this new and increasing trend for product with purpose and authenticity.

What I've learned directly through my work with rugs in Afghanistan is that all of these women's co-ops have the same issues: they need design input. You've got to start with what is appealing in the developed markets and relate that with what you produce. There are hundreds of Afghanistan patterns and hundreds of color combinations. So it takes a woman the same amount of labor to weave what you would look at and say, "That's ugliest thing I've ever seen in my life" vs. "This is spectacularly beautiful and I'd love to have it in my home."

How is a woman in the middle of nowhere supposed to have any sense of what the Western eye values?

So, it's this design reconnaissance ... that's Step 1 in product development. Step 2, which is the absolute critical issue that all of these co-ops share, is how do you get distribution channels for your product into a mass market? How do you build your brand and reach that?

We can identify, again, many, many appropriate, interesting co-op groups. Too often these skills are now being put into work what I call, making the tribal tchotchke (worthless bauble), right? A beaded change purse. The little silk scarf. Those are blankets, not export products. Those are souvenirs that people buy, but they don't kick off enough cash systematically to actually create a real business, a profitable business. So, back to scale. After the recession hit—and ours is still, four years later—we were growing at a great clip. Things flattened and we're still working to achieve profitability ourselves.

The way I think about scale is not about ARZU expanding, but rather ARZU sharing what we have learned from a protocol perspective and scaling through others. Replicating how we've we what we do, albeit based on the constraints we work in—no infrastructure, no electricity and very little water.

We work in very water-constrained areas, which eliminates the possibility for agriculture which, at least in South America and Africa, you have in many places. Working in a conflict zone, working in areas that now have cell phone service but still have very limited Internet. When we first started, there was virtually no Internet. We were working within a culture that is incredibly complex and layered from the perspective of cultural mores. You've got religious mores. Tribal mores. Local customs. Gender-segregated society. I mean, there's just one layer upon the other that makes it difficult to create a business in Afghanistan.

So my thinking is, if we can do this there, it is transportable anywhere, because I just don't think there's any place that has all of these factors and constraints. It would be my honor to share what we have learned with others. So ours is definitely small. It's prototypical. It will always be that way because we will be experimental. But we also will be profitable.

Q. *That's great.*

Connie: When we are, then I can be chairman of the board and I will have a sustainable organization that someone else can run every day, since I work *pro bono* ... and I do this seven days a week!

Agenia also spoke about giving back and about mentoring other women:

Agenia: You know, I was one of three children born in Mobile, Alabama to parents that did not have a college education and didn't know what a career was: they had jobs. I think that—if nothing else, what I feel has been really poignant in my life and poignant for me to experience—is while that may have been the circumstance you started with, it is not the circumstance you have to end with. I'm glad to know that that really is possible, that you really don't have to end up where you started if you don't want to. In my case, I did not want to end up still living on Bragdon Avenue, off of Mobile Street in Mobile, Alabama.

I think that from being exposed to these godparents and reading about the world that existed outside the boundaries of our zip code, life became very exciting and very interesting for me. I treat everything like it is not a barrier; it is not a hurdle. It's just something else that may be in the way that you have to figure out how to get around, not just professionally, either.

Agenia: I think I shared with you earlier something about me and swimming. So, I've done a couple of sprint triathlons, and I really like them. They are short swims, short bikes, and short runs. I've done a bunch of half-marathons. I like the challenge of pushing myself far enough to do just that. Growing up in Mobile, Alabama, that was not a part of the expectations that were set for a young black girl that lived in Toulminville, which was the black neighborhood. That just wasn't the expectation. I'm glad to know: no one sets your expectations for you but you.

Q. That's a huge thing, and some young women just never have the opportunity to learn that, you know. I mean … you did something to attract all these people into your life, mind you. But you were also truly blessed to have the people show up in your life that showed up.

Agenia: Oh boy, do I have … such a great list. My list is so fascinating and sometimes I look at it with a big smile on my face. I was here in Nashville recently, and someone tapped me on my shoulder. I turned around and it was Rick Johnson. I met Rick when I was a waitress, waiting tables.

The restaurant was the flagship Ruby Tuesday restaurant, started and founded by Sandy Beall, and it was located right there on the University of Tennessee campus. They were known for having the most amazing hamburgers and French fries. They charged a premium for them, and they had other food items on the menu too.

Rick and his wife would come in and have brunch at Ruby Tuesday on Sundays. What I didn't know was that he was the CEO for his own public relations agency, and they did the communications for Ruby Tuesday. I waited on him and his wife numerous times. I'm in there, doing my regular Sunday work over brunch, because it was my favorite strip to get assigned to.

One day he gave me his business card and he said, "Knoxville is going to get the 1982 World's Fair, and I'm going to have to hire some extra people while the work on hand is going on. Would you be interested in coming and working for me for all the accounts I have for the 1982 World's Fair?"

I remember saying, *What, now? Who are you, other than this man I've waited on every Sunday?*

So, I took his business card, called him back, had an interview, and worked for Rick Johnson. I had a magnificent, magnificent nearly-two years working with him, with all these fabulous accounts that he had.

And, there he is, here in Nashville, too many years later tapping me on the shoulder and saying, "Agenia?"

I said, "Rick!"

He was a great mentor, a wonderful coach, and a fabulous, amazing leader. He and I have since sat down and had dinner and just enjoyed reminiscing. He will go down in my mind as one of those amazing people that I met along the way.

When I was thinking about people I met along the way, I liked the fact that they have been men and women and racially and ethnically from all walks of life.

Q. *You know, I think it's an interesting point, because a lot of women I've met over the years, as I've run mentoring programs for organizations, don't necessarily think broadly about the mentors that they chose for themselves. Sometimes they don't think about, you know, what you could learn from a man; what you could learn from someone who's ethnically different from yourself, and just that reaching out. Once we got past that barrier, people had some incredible relationships.*

Agenia: I'll be honest. I also see that there is this formalized idea of what mentors are. I think the most important mentors we have in our lives are the friends we choose to surround ourselves with, too. You know, there's an old saying, "You are who you associate with." I had an aunt who told me that years ago. She said, "I can tell a lot about you just by your friends." I think that is so very true.

So in my life today, some of my best mentors are some of the women I've surrounded myself with as my friends. I have a long, long friendship with one woman, her name is Deborah Roberts. Deborah and I met almost thirty years ago, but the reason she's still a friend and still a mentor is I like and love her positive spirit and even better, I like how she's willing to pass that on and motivate and encourage me through all parts of my life.

I mean, we've gone through the marriage thing, and the having kids thing, and being working moms thing, and trying to stay physically fit thing, and all of that. It's just so helpful for someone to send you a text message that says, "Don't forget to drink lots of water today," or "Don't worry, today may seem challenging, but tomorrow it won't be." It's just wonderful to have that kind of day in and day out mentoring that comes from a friendship.

I've gone to a place where I truly have divested myself of toxic friendships. They're just not good, because your friends are your mentors and those that are toxic are not good for you, personally or professionally.

Q. I look at, you know—talk about friendship circles—I look at the group of women that Jan suggested to me.

Agenia: These are women I see as friends. I am so excited they are part of my life. I see them as friends, but a friend who can mentor at the same time. It's just wonderful to have people like that you can extend a hand out to and they're willing to turn around and then grab it and take you with them.

Sharon also spoke about the importance of friendships, maintaining a sense of purpose, and honoring relationships:

Sharon: I look for some of the things that, to me in my life, stand out. One is not losing sight of what you really want the most. Not saying "No" to yourself, "I can't have it because." Instead, looking for, "I can have it, because ..." or "I will do this or I will do that," you know? So I guess that is more of where my thinking has always been.

Q. I'd like to say it's easy to see why you and Phyllis are such good friends.

Sharon: Well, you know what? That's another thing I wouldn't mind having in the book, that is, I have my one friend who was my first customer. She is the only plant manager I have ever met—and we are friends to this day. And other women I met when I was in Dundee are friends to this day. The power of, the joy of friendship has been a lot in my life.

Q. You're speaking directly from your heart, and I think that's what other women are going to want to hear.

Many of The Fifty spoke about giving back and being of service as an integral part of their lives. For most, this was in addition to work. For Susana, helping others has always been central to her career. She drew on her own multi-lingual background early in her career to teach English as a second language and is now refocusing to develop a spirit-centered practice:

Susana: I thought teaching English to people who came here to seek a homeland was just a brilliant, wonderful thing. I've always been an idealist, so the beauty of being able to give back stuck with me. Then in the early '70s, I got married and we moved to Washington. By then, I had a baby and I fell into English as a second language rather than French and Spanish. That felt so wonderful to be able to give back to the immigrants what I had gotten before.

In the early '70s, Washington had a huge population of Vietnamese people who were boat people, essentially, and landed in Washington. So my students, adults in Prince George's County and in suburban Washington, were Vietnamese. There was an influx of Koreans and there was always a huge Hispanic population, so I had the joy of being able to teach English to foreign adults trying to integrate themselves into American society. I am still in touch with some of those people.

There was a group of Laotians who then wound up in Oregon, because somehow, people from Laos did not like Washington, so there is a large ethnic population of people from Laos in Oregon.

It was like pioneer days, like I was witnessing again and experiencing and living with again, a migration of humanity. A different kind of migration, different circumstances, but still seeking a land where they could live and where they could establish themselves. There were some wonderful stories of people who did make it, and there were horror stories about people who had to give up their prior identity and become something that they had looked down on in their country, and families who committed suicide together. Just that—a whole kaleidoscope of humanity that I loved so much all those years, which set my idealism and made it meaningful for me to be a human being; a human being that experienced transition and who was helping people through transition.

I can be an entrepreneur and I can run a business with the help of very, very loving partners, but I'm ready for something different. I love your question on the fact that I was always leading with my heart. I want to go full-time into leading with my heart. I'm not interested in being smart anymore; it's not enough.

Q. *That's so wonderful.*

Susana: I enrolled in a spiritual direction program last summer, and this program is dedicated to working with people who are searching to speak the language of their souls. It is no longer the guise of being smart or being intelligent or being articulate, but being in touch with their soul and, therefore, with the faith part of us.

I really, frankly, had not paid a lot of attention. I did not have an articulated theology. I knew what I believed in, always, but what I'm learning in this program is to articulate how I believe and why I believe and how I translate it into words or into a language that understands other people's desire to do the same thing.

Q. *Oh, this is so lovely.*

Susana: My learning edge, right now, is to help myself and help other people communicate what's in their hearts without the disguise of their brains—in fact, moving away from their brains.

Q. *Oh, I so love this.*

Susana: Thank you. I don't know where this is going to take me, moving me away from our business. I am cutting back on that and I still have another year-and-a-half to go with my program. It's a new community, it's a new language, it's a new beginning. I'm not so good at it; it's a language I don't speak so well. But I'm pretty good at learning new languages, so I'm looking forward to seeing what happens next.

I am not sure I want to practice as a spiritual director; it's a very specific kind of discipline. Again, it's a very different discipline than my discipline. What's confusing is that on the outside, it looks a little bit like coaching, but it is totally differently motivated and differently internalized than coaching. So that's who I am.

Phoebe and Marla speak of the need for balance:

Phoebe: I have always been interested in non-profit work and have always supplemented my life with those activities. So I was really pleased to be on the board of trustees at Smith College for ten years. I'm now on the board of trustees at the University of Louisville. I'm in my fourth year there, appointed by the governor, and I serve also with the American Printing House of the Blind, which is a federal agency that produces books for those who are blind and visually impaired in America. A very interesting group of companies, and I do one more. I sit on a foundation of about a hundred million in assets where we give away one large grant each year.

Marla: I have not talked a lot about my non-profit work, but I try to do as much as I can. I have done everything from Boys and Girls Clubs to the board of trustees where my children have gone to school, etc. I don't think that's terribly important for the scope of your work, except that it adds richness to life. I think that's important.

I don't want to denigrate the work I've done parenting, which is important and very satisfying to me. I sort of struck a bargain in my career, I said look, I'll work really hard from Monday morning to Friday evening and I'll travel as much as I have to and I'll work as much as I have to but I'd like two days per week for my family with the exception of maybe some Sunday nights. I really kept that bargain, and so that meant I was able to spend time, especially with my daughters as they were growing up.

So I was there [at Barnes & Noble] for a bit. And what happened was, there was a reorganization. The margins in the book business are razor-thin. I think Barnes & Noble was starting to feel some competitive pressure from Amazon. At that point, they decided to merge the brick-and-mortar marketing group with the online dot-com business. So, essentially, huge chunks of the department were eliminated.

At that point, there was really no reason for me to stay at the company. It wasn't going to be fun for me anymore. It was a purely financially-driven decision, and I totally understood that. But it was, essentially, a blessing in disguise, because it gave me the opportunity to take a step back and to figure out, "What do I want to do now?"

I've had some amazing corporate experiences. I've learned a lot. I'm very proud of my accomplishments in every single job. I really feel that I added quite a bit of value to every company that I worked for. But I was at a point in my career where I was able to take a step back and just try to figure out what to do next.

It was a good time for me to take a pause. My kids were at an age where I wanted to spend a little more time with them. I didn't want to stop working because that wasn't really the issue. The issue was … balance is tricky. There really is such a thing called "balance." To me, it's trying to make things work at every stage in your life. At some stages, you can devote more time to your career. At some stages, you need to pull back a little bit so that everything is working in harmony with your family. My kids and my husband were very important to me, so I opted not to look for another big corporate position.

Q. *Can I ask you about how old you were when this was happening?*

Marla: I was in my early 40s. In retrospect, it's … the time when a lot of women are in my position, where we've done the corporate thing, we've learned a lot, we've had fun along the way, but our kids are at a certain age where it's getting more and more difficult to hang everything together. I know I'm not alone; I had friends in similar situations.

I was very fortunate I was able to take a step back and give myself a little bit of time to figure out what I wanted to do. At that point, it was really about looking at all the things I liked about my career and all the things I didn't like so much about my career. I realized what I really did like was this whole segmented marketing—working with particular customers' segments and figuring out what products and services should be developed or marketed to meet their needs.

You know, timing is everything. My daughter was a teenager at the time. I realized that I was really interested in teenagers because I had one in my household and my son was growing up as well. So I started doing an investigation of what is out there to meet their needs? My daughter is a typical teenager; there was, at the time, lots of teenage magazines coming in the door and lots of TV shows and whatnot. I realized there was something missing. I realized that there wasn't a whole lot of focus and attention on the more serious aspects of life for teens, which is the whole concept of, "What do I want to be when I grow up? How can I be the best I can be?"

This is the time when Oprah was pretty big and I realized that she's really great at doing this whole self-actualization thing for women. But girls have lots of questions as well. So this started me down the road of thinking about, Well, maybe there's something I can do to help support the growth and development of teenage girls. That's when all the threads came together, which was kind of cool. I looked at different options: do I publish a magazine or do I create products? What do I do?

It really came to down to figuring that the best thing to do was to leverage the Internet, which was booming, and figure out something that would be appropriate and would meet the needs of at least, a core population of teenage girls in the U.S. That's how I started the development of Heart of Gold.

What Heart of Gold is; it's a website community and an experience for teenage girls. But mostly it's a place where teen entrepreneurs and teen social activists can connect and grow, learn valuable entrepreneurial skills, good citizenship skills. It's really a place where teens can find a lot of tools and connections in a community to help launch a business or take a stand and make a difference. It's a place where they can learn tips and tools to help care for themselves and their future. That's what Heart of Gold is about.

In looking at different ways to think about teenage girls, I realized what really intrigued me was those girls who were making a difference by starting or working in non-profits and those who actually were able to successfully merge the two and be social entrepreneurs. What blew me away was there were a lot of these girls out there. I found that to be very astonishing. I realized that this is a group of girls who—they're bright, energetic, hopeful, definitely normal kids—have lots of the same issues, worries, concerns and fears that most teenage girls have. But somehow, they have this "extra secret sauce," extra desire to grow something and to develop something and make it special.

I realized, Aha! These are the girls that I want to focus on. I want to help these girls. These girls were important to me because I think they are the future. I think the timing has been great, because we've gone through such an economic downturn and … not only are girls doing this for their own self-development, but a lot of girls are starting businesses to help their families. So all the pieces started to come together.

What I did was, in thinking about what I wanted Heart of Gold to be, I leveraged all the skills and tools I learned in all of my marketing positions. I did as much market research as I possibly could. You know, digging and digging to try to find a lot of data on teenage girls: their wants, their needs, their interests.

I did a very deliberate research project—reading a ton of books and spending hours and hours on the Internet, because I wanted to have a good handle and good understanding on the needs and desires of these girls. So I did a lot of work on this; did in-depth market analysis, figured out what the market opportunity was, what the potential was. Then I realized, OK, I'm sort of getting a handle on where I want to take this business.

Here's what I love about it—this is my business, and I can make it whatever I want it to be. That is so much fun for me, because I can leverage the learning about needs, wants, and desires of these girls. But I really can dig deep within myself and be very creative, and be very free with how I build and structure this business. It has been an absolute joy. The process has been phenomenal.

It has taken several years. I've grown it and it's developed through a bunch of iterations until I felt that we were actually on the right track. I would say that, for a couple of years that I did an in-market beta test. I created the website, but played around with its features and benefits and the website then evolved into other things.

Q. It seems to me that I remember you saying that you deliberately did not want to create a non-profit.

Marla: What I wanted to do was … I wanted to create a business that was for profit. At that point, that's really what I wanted to do. Heart of Gold will, at some point, have a non-profit component, but that's not really where I wanted to focus my efforts at this point. I wanted to create a business that met the needs of its girls, but also that could be self-sustaining.

Q. *I felt like there was sort of a philosophical stance as well.*

Marla: Yes, there was, because there are non-profits out there supporting girls. But they tend to be focused on a single issue for girls. I was trying to look at girls a little bit more holistically. I wanted to create something that met their needs, both in terms of developing a business or a non-profit, if that's what they wanted to do. But there is also a lot of life cycle content on the website. So I wanted to make it something that really focused on this girl in a bigger way: this girl may develop a business, but she's also preparing for college; she's also worried about her health and well-being; she's worried about relationships; she's a typical teenage girl with a special interest.

Rather than focus on one aspect of who she is—which a lot of the non-profits tend to do—I wanted to focus on the girl a little more holistically. That's really the philosophy of Heart of Gold.

Q. *And there also seem to be a certain, to me, amount of modeling here. In being a woman who has created a business, making it a for-profit rather than a non-profit, There's something in there for the girls to come to you to learn.*

Marla: Exactly. And that's very accurate, because what we do is for those girls who want to develop a business or non-profit. We want to show them how they can maximize that business or non-profit to make it profitable, to bring it to life, to make it as big as they want to make it. It's interesting: my background is for-profit businesses, and that's been my learning and development, which is, you create something you love. You create something that you believe your customers will love and it becomes very profitable. That has really been my orientation.

What started out as an outgrowth of a crafts project for Marcia, as described in Chapter 5, grew exponentially and has now become part of her legacy:

Marcia: So that has really become our mission: to improve the overall environment in the schools by purposefully thanking teachers and by positively impacting students with tools they can use to make others' lives better.

We define kindness as "actively extending good to others," because we don't think it's something you just hear about; it's a thing you have to do. You have to make a conscious decision to be kind, to say a kind word or to do something, and that's a learned behavior. So we help classrooms have ways that students can practice how to be kind to others.

It's been a wonderful journey. We are now getting ready, next month, to deliver about 30,000-35,000 posters into classrooms that have the Be Kind Pledge, which we are asking kids to sign. We hope to have one million kids sign the Be Kind Pledge, [committing] that they will work to make the school a more positive place. If we can have a million kids sign this pledge by sixty days from now, I'll feel really happy, because it's a million more than if we wouldn't have done it.

We are nationwide. Not meaning every place in the nation, although we could be. We're letting it evolve as it will, but we've been in Los Angeles—in Watts and East L.A. We've been in the Midwest and in the Kansas City and Missouri and Oklahoma City schools that are so difficult. Kansas City schools actually lost their Federal accreditation. It's an education system that teachers are trying so hard, but they don't have any fringe benefits. We provide those fringe benefits.

We've been in Harlem. We've been in the Bronx. We've been in Brooklyn. We've been, of course, in Phoenix. We've been across the country and we'll expand even more as we go forward.

We've continued our relationship with Teach for America because they were the ones who told us in the first place, "Be loyal to all teachers." Our program is offered free of charge in the markets. We're into any school that has a Teach for America teacher. So we try to help Teach for America in those schools where they place their teachers. We don't get any side benefit from that whatsoever, but it's the right thing to do because it was Teach for America who got us started on this journey.

We try to apply those same values about treating people right to how we operate. We have a wonderful group of volunteers and a teeny, teeny tiny staff that does great big things, and I'm working harder than I ever have in my life.

Q. You've come full circle, in a way. You're back to teaching for even less money than you started at. I just love it.

Marcia: Oh, Susan, that's a wonderful way to look at it. I'm going to copy your line.

Q. Feel free. I love it that something that was so ingrained in you from childhood and then your father's wonderful advice has turned into this incredible organization.

Marcia: Well, it's something I could not have planned. It goes back to not being manipulative or shrewd or anything else. But if you live your life right, and work hard, and listen, I think it's just been a blessing. By the way, the school bus is still parked right behind our garage. It's the cutest little thing in the world and we get it out three or four times a week and drive around. My husband loves to take the little Be Kind school bus and drive through Starbucks and pay for the person behind him and all that kind of stuff. So there we go. I mean how many people get to have their own bus (which we have to buy a registration for and everything)? [laughter]

We did this party that went on for ten years and became this major event; I established a board and I tried to give a board experience to women in life who may have never had one before, which was very fun. So we chose women from every decade of life to be on our board, because kindness doesn't have age barriers. Certainly, there are no ethnicity barriers; there are not even gender barriers of course, but we only had this party for women.

So our board was really instrumental in putting together what happened for the teachers. They were the ones who developed the Be Kind Pledge. I was sitting at a table and saying, "What do we want kids to know?" The youngest one was eight years old. The oldest active one was eighty-seven. But that has been an incredible experience to watch women at our age of life be able to help women in their twenties and thirties participate in something for the community and participate selflessly in an organization has been fabulous. The teams in the junior high and the eight-year-old, who is now ten; that was one of the most wonderful experiences in life, to see them sitting and working on committees side by side.

I don't know if it's true or not, but I'm going to say it anyway—we probably were the only board in America that had every decade of life covered. They [the board members] are still so involved. These are my volunteers. The young ones have their schools involved. The older ones are out volunteering in the community. It's just been wonderful. So that's the other thing I think is important—wherever we are in life, we can mentor and help other women along the way.

My daughter, who is thirty-eight, has been on the board. To be able to sit in a meeting environment with my daughter and watch her take on some leadership role in this last event that we had has really been fabulous, because that's the sort of thing that she never got from her mom. She never saw that sort of thing happen when she was growing up, because I was always working. Now she can see both sides of it; that you can work really hard, and when you work really hard, it really affords you the opportunity to do other things. I feel very, very blessed that that's happened.

It's been very fun. Some of my very best friends now are twenty-two years old. I like to hang out with one of the girls who is twenty-two and is on the board. I like to hang out with the hip-hop dancers that came and volunteered. So life is wonderful.

Q. Well, it sounds like you're having the best time and what do you see in the future?

Marcia: I see, in the future, turning this whole effort into someone else's hands that will grow it and help it really flourish. I know when to close the door and know when to give things away, so I look forward to giving things away. I was a U.S. Delegate to the World Kindness Movement Conference this year in London, and I've just gone on to the International Council of the World Kindness Movement. I think there may be some things that we can help schools and teachers in other countries benefit from. So I'll be involved in that. I don't know where that will lead, but I'll be real involved in finding what the common denominators are, not what the differences are.

I hope that my role will change into that, being more of an initiator of actions: we plant a seed and then let other organizations or other countries run with it and see what is best for them. It's about giving things away. It's kind of like kindness—actively extending good to others.

I hope when I have an obituary, the first thing is not my title and what I did in my career. I will be very happy if my work life is buried in paragraphs three or four, and that the remembrance and the legacy will not be in what I did, but maybe who I tried to be and what lives might have been affected positively. That would be the thing that I would hope would be next.

Corbette has been able to give back through mentoring and through advising her students:

Corbette: I have been absolutely blessed by people who have taken a very strong interest in my career and helped to nurture that career. Of interest: I never worked for women until I came to Vanderbilt.

Q. Now, one thing that sort of jumps out at me that I didn't ask is, Who did you mentor and did you sort of reach out to women when you were in that life?"

Corbette: I am very, very focused on mentoring, so before I was in the diversity role, one of the things I had started was a group of thirteen women. We human resources to support me. I couldn't get any help from them. It was very, very frustrating in terms of formalizing a program. To this day, I think it's absolutely absurd.

One of things I did when I was the head of diversity is, a woman in HR at the lower level, who also had set up our African-American employee network, approached me because she couldn't get the company to invest in a mentoring strategy. She had identified this amazing software tool, much like Match.com, but for mentors. So I gave them the diversity budget and we launched it as a diversity strategy, because they couldn't get the company to do it.

I had been recruited by Deloitte as a mentor; I can't remember now what year. They had a brilliant mentoring strategy—they would recruit executive women in the community to lead a mentoring circle for their young women. So they accomplished two things: one was they acquired mentors for their women and had enough in their office, and two, it's really hard to get a partner unless you have that rainmaking status. They help the young women build relationships with very successful women in the community.

I actually did that for Deloitte for five years. I was the longest lasting mentor and I was the most successful. So they would have other people come and join our group to see what we were doing and why it was working so well. I'm still in touch with several other women from the very first group I mentored, and some don't live here anymore.

I'm in this male-dominated industry and I would have men approach me, asking me to mentor women for them. I would have fathers approach me about meeting with their daughters, and I would have men who were managers approach me about mentoring a bright young man in their group who they wanted to ensure were retained.

So I have always done that. Even at school I have to mentor, I mean, advise a lot of students, but I volunteered to advise freshmen. I also have students who approach me who are not my advisees just coming in for advice all the time, looking for that real world perspective. At Nissan, I sit on the executive diversity council and I do a lot of things for their women in different locations. I would be hard-pressed to actually count how many people I am currently advising or mentoring but it is seventy-five or eighty.

Q. *Wow, it's a lot.*

Corbette: It's a lot, but you know what? I love it. I do. That's why I like teaching. I like the opportunity to give back and help somebody else be really all that they can become.

Q. *It's so energizing and as a bonus, somebody wants to pay you for it.*

Corbette: Right. There you go, there you go. Perfect, right?

In a similar vein, Cheryl speaks of meeting many women in different roles as the Three Tomatoes grew. Through these connections, she found a volunteer activity that aroused her passion:

Cheryl: One of the things a friend of mine said to me, many years ago, was that when you live in the circus, you only meet the circus people. That's your life. For many years, my circus was the advertising agency business.

Lynda stressed the importance of a personal support network:

Q. *Friendships, also, is another theme that I'm hearing here. It sounds like you have a pretty large circle.*

Lynda: In some ways, that's what has brought me to my work with Ann Clancy. I was transitioning out of my job at the Foundation. Knowing my work in the legislature was concluding, and still, even with nine years behind me of this sadness and exploring new pathways, I just thought it would be helpful to work with Ann. I was able to allocate some funds from my work at the Foundation to coach with Ann for a year.

My conversations with Ann are certainly about my professional life and sort of exploring these new paths and being aware of my skills and interests, but also talking a lot about this process that I've gone through—intuition and being aware of the ability to sort of communicate with people on a very personal and deep level.

Carole has been able to integrate several strands that ran through her life to create her current situation:

Carole: First, the background. My grandmother—who was a maid and a cook—cooked for Jennie Tourel, who was a very well-known opera singer of the day. We always picked her up on Friday nights, because she was a live-in. My mother used to take us to pick her up and bring her home on Friday evenings when we were very little. I remember going there. She lived a block from Central Park South, right across the street from Carnegie Hall on 58th Street.

Ms. Tourel had this huge apartment with two entrances, a regular entrance and a maid's entrance. My grandmother lived in the maid's quarters behind the kitchen.

So we went in the maid's entrance. We got so much good stuff from this woman and she taught us things as well. She would make me go to the piano and demonstrate my lessons to her, because I was taking piano. She would let me go into her den and read. She was the first person to give me a grown-up book. I fell in love with *Anna Karenina* in her study. I also fell in love with the picture across from the chaise where I would read it, which was a picture of Leonard Bernstein. They were very close friends. I remember very clearly going to Carnegie Hall for concerts, for dress rehearsals we would get tickets for, falling in love with Leonard Bernstein, and thinking, *This is good.*

So I have a very vivid imagination and memory of Manhattan, of Carnegie Hall, of going home together. As a treat, my mother and my grandmother would take me and my brothers to Horn & Hardart's on 57th Street, around the corner, and give us coins to put in the glass doors and get pie. I grew up wanting to move to an apartment—because I lived in a house that was too far from the city—and it had to be in Manhattan.

My grandfather came from a little island called Grenada, which is in what was called the British West Indies. But they came from a part of the island where they never gave up the patois of the long-departed French colonialists. My grandfather grew up speaking English and patois. He married a woman named Isabella from Cuba. I don't know to this day how they met. So my grandfather learned Spanish because of his wife. So when I was very little, he had a little desk in a little library inside what was really my brother's bedroom. But he had a desk with all his books and he used to give me books, too. My grandfather actually was the first person to teach me how to say my name and count from one to ten in French and Spanish when I was five.

Q. You got an early start on being multi-lingual there.

Carole: I thought that was wonderful. I thought, *Isn't it cool? I can say who I am in a couple of different ways.* The funny thing was, we didn't speak anything but English in the house. My father told my grandmother and grandfather he really didn't want us to experience anything but English. So, if they had to speak patois, they were supposed to do it elsewhere, which really worked most of the time, except when my grand-aunt Ivy came from Grenada. She and my grandmother would go on the porch and speak nothing *but* patois and drink lemon tea. Then we heard them speaking patois.

That must have been a really vivid memory, because there's a family story that when I started school, Catholic school, at the age of five, the nuns sent a note home to my mother saying, "Could you please stop speaking French at home? "It's ruining Carole's English vowels."

My mother laughed and said, "What is she talking about? French? We don't speak French." Meanwhile, my grandfather was sneaking me French lessons and my grandmother was being spied on [speaking] in patois.

I had a boyfriend who was very much a philosopher-activist. We used to read each other *Letters from a Birmingham Jail* by Martin Luther King, Junior. Then he became a philosophy major and we used to talk about Eric Fromm, Jean-Paul Sartre's "being and nothingness," and Teilhard de Chardin. I don't know; I was a really strange kid. But in high school, I started to write more. Basically, that was something I realized I could do. The other thing I did in high school was I did every manner of speech club you could think of. I did declamation, or dramatic speech. I was in debate. And I did extemporaneous speech, which I actually loved the most. That was the first time I really became a speaker, in high school. So writing and speaking became my kind of badge of honor and my claim to fame in high school.

I went to a girls' school, but I met people who were debaters from other schools, from boys' schools. That's where I met the guy who became my boyfriend in high school. He was the first person who took me to Washington Square Park and introduced me to the idea of New York University (NYU).

My father actually took me, when I was a very little girl, to the Waverly Dispensary in the West Village. I remember getting off the train and being in this interesting place with my father. But I never had gone to Washington Square Park. And when we started dating, he was totally into the beatnik generation and folk music and Bob Dylan. We totally got into the Joan Baez/Bob Dylan thing and folk music. He took me down to Washington Square Park and we walked around. That was my introduction to NYU and Washington Square. And I thought, *I've got to apply here.* So I applied. I was going to be a political scientist or a diplomat.

When I got there, I met Phyllis and we wound up working for the Republican Party, stuffing envelopes for the state Republican Party and eventually, for the re-election of Nelson Rockefeller in 1965. At that time, we actually started getting invited to Young Republican things. The first of which, I think in '65, was one of the victory parties for John V. Lindsay. We became completely involved in working for the Republican re-election of Nelson Rockefeller, Jacob Javits, and Lefkowitz. That was the ticket. We had a great time. We were a bunch of these kid volunteers that stuffed things and made signs and went to rallies.

While I was there, one of the people we met—first of all, this was the dying days of the liberal wing of the Republican Party—I met Jackie Robinson. Jackie Robinson adopted me and Phyllis because we were the only two black girls there and his job was to take care of us. He was a lovely man. A lot of people don't realize that Jackie Robinson was a Republican, but he was.

At some point, they needed somebody who spoke Spanish because the governor was going to go up to Spanish Harlem and they wanted to have someone on the sound truck announce the fact that he was going up there. And I volunteered. So they put me on the sound truck any time they were going to Spanish Harlem, or anyplace else where I needed to speak Spanish. So I was on the sound truck for the governor's re-election campaign. And I also joined the Speakers Bureau. So that was kind of cool.

A couple of years later, we were still involved in Republican politics, so they invited us, both of us, to the Republican Convention of 1968. I always say to people I went to the wrong convention in 1968. We were in Miami, not Chicago. So we did that political stuff and the social stuff that went along with it. So I guess I'm saying there's a line through my young life of politics. That may have had something to do with why I decided to major in political science. But really, at the end of the day, I realized that I didn't want to teach political science. And politics has little, if anything, to do with actual political science. So eventually, when I came back to NYU, I was already in journalism.

I wound up at the International Students Association. They did the international festival every year at NYU. NYU New York University had the largest foreign student population of any private college in the United States and we made use of it. We cooperated with International House, which is still there up on 125th and Riverside. We just did all these activities. The festival was in the spring every year and it was a big deal. I met a lot of people that I still know to this day. Basically hung out with my girlfriends [who] I went to high school with; one of them was Ukrainian and spoke Russian and Ukrainian. She introduced me to another girl who was Russian. And then, of course, my Cuban friends. Then I was taking Brazilian Portuguese and I started getting involved with all the Brazilian students and speaking Portuguese. So I was studying Spanish, French, Italian, and now Portuguese. The only romance language I never learned was Romanian; somehow that eluded me.

But my experience at NYU was basically a combination of finding my wings in political science and realizing it wasn't the thing for me, and really getting involved with foreign students. One of the part-time jobs I had was as a foreign student coordinator. That's how I met my first husband. He was a foreign student at NYU.

Q. Where was he from?

Carole: The Netherlands. He was coming here to do his graduate degree in business. That was back in the day when the School of Business was down by Wall Street, on Trinity Place. I took a marketing class down there. The funny thing was though, basically, he wound up pursuing me. I'm not going to go into the romance, but Phyllis didn't like the idea. He just kept following me and he refused to allow me not to go out with him. We were married at NYU at Holy Trinity Chapel. And of course, Koert was born at NYU. Now, Carole's description of her current life:

Carole: I call this stage of my life "back to the future." It's really back to the future. It's really starting to remember that the New York Phil was my first experience with symphonic music and it's connected to my grandmother. It's also remembering that foreign languages and travel were really, really important to me, not only as a girl, but remember, I married a Dutchman whose whole family was in the Netherlands. I was in Europe every other year, sometimes two years in a row. I got him involved in Mexico and Latin America. So we were in Mexico six, seven times. I went to Brazil. I went to Peru.

I traveled internationally for years until my divorce. I haven't been to Europe since the euro, God knows. But this whole job was a "back to the future" job in two senses: both in terms of my love for languages and travel and the fact is I had twenty years to travel and to use my languages. This is the first time I've actually come back to that. So, both the Lincoln Center job and the Relais & Chateau job were tying everything together. It's kind of spooky.

Phyllis H. is experimenting with emerging technologies, and this, as much as her body of work, may be her legacy:

Q. So tell me about the video work and sort of how that emerged. It seems to me that that's played out in a variety of different ways on its way to what it's becoming now.

Phyllis H.: I want to just say—for the benefit of humanity and all women listening— I think I spent a large part of my life in the category called "development and becoming something." A journey towards something. Right now in my life, I am really not doing anything to become anything or to change anything necessarily.

I'm absolutely experiencing doing video work, for example. I love to do it. I love being part of this technological shift that we are in. We're in a huge shift; we're like in the days of the beginning of the television. This is the same period, only bigger and different. Apple has announced that it's it is making a new device ... that it's going to be like the wrist watch and have functions like it's the best part of its cell phone. There are all kinds of changes that are going to occur that I can't even predict.

Having my hand in video technology means I have to keep up with the changes, how people watch things. Right now, everybody's beginning to watch things on devices like iPads or Tablets or phones, so it's forcing me to learn new things on a regular basis. Plus, I love talking to people, as I said earlier in the interview. Now, I just don't talk to, I do biographies of people. I do biographies of unsung people.

Q. What got you started on that?

Phyllis H.: I think what got me started was the fact that there were people I interviewed in television who were far more fascinating, in many cases, than so-called well-known people. Of course, there were brilliant, well-known people too, but it was always the second person on the Nobel Prize or the guy who had a series but didn't get an Academy Award or the attention of his community that were pulling me forward. There was a brain surgeon who maybe didn't get all the attention that everyone else got but who had a cure for dysautonomia and was fascinating.

If you want to have a full life, open as many packages as you can. That's how I do the interview process. I interview as many people as I can who make a difference. Now, thanks to Google, I'll be able to do it more often because they're providing studio space for people like me who do thoughtful content. I can't say that a minute goes by when I don't meet someone that I want to talk to.

Isora is one of many women who carried the theme of service into retirement:

Isora: Recently, I've been very active in the Dominican Republic. I spoke at a conference last November at FUNGLODE, the sister organization of the Global Foundation for Democracy and Development (GFDD), in Santo Domingo, Dominican Republic. The organization was created in 2002 by Dr. Leonel Fernandez, former president of that country and president of both institutions. The conference was titled "Emotions, Dialogue and Action for a Better Coexistence." I spoke about learning together through dialogue for a better coexistence. Since we are living in a diverse society, we have to learn how to live in a peaceful and harmonious fashion.

I see a need for awareness to develop our emotional intelligence and how we generate our stress with our negative thoughts. I also spoke about the role of education in decision-making, and individual responsibility in all sectors of society, and how education must be relevant to the problems and experiences of adults involved in the learning process.

I also offered a workshop on anger management and effective leadership for staff members of Dr. Margarita Cedeño de Fernandez, Vice President of the Dominican Republic. This was organized by the Foundation for Values Development (FUNDE-VAL). I also did a radio program in Santo Domingo about our need to pay attention to the violence we are facing in the world. The main purpose of the workshop was to facilitate individuals' awareness and management of their emotions. We worked on those things we have learned during our early years, but that, in reality, work against us during our adult life; they make us feel angry and are often reflected in automatic and unconscious behaviors. At the end of the workshop, participants had to formulate a critical reflection plan in order to develop empathy and improve communication and better relationships in the workplace.

Elements of Legacy, Creating Meaning, and Having Fun

Having fun consists of knowing what gives you pleasure and incorporating that into your life. Creating meaning consists of reviewing the elements of your life and deciding if they still make sense as you move forward. It means seeing interconnections among aspects and often revisiting your beliefs. Thinking about legacy involves investigating your desire to be remembered. It includes reviewing what you have done, what is important to you, and what you still have to give.

Barbara finds ways to have fun in all aspects of her life. She sought a job that involved her in a continuous round of celebratory activities; she remains active in sports, and loves her volunteer work. Similarly, Sally finds her volunteer work fun. It also gives her a deep sense of fulfillment and of giving back. The orphans she has helped are her legacy. Phoebe's family trips are fun and also a way of building lasting memories with her family. Natalie's career choices all centered on having fun, and she approached each new position with the intent of having fun as well as contributing. Marcia reinterpreted her teaching skills to create a national movement around kindness.

How You Can Develop Meaning and Legacy

- Identify ways that you are currently having fun. Are there things you no longer do that should be added to the list? Things you want to try?
- Take time to identify and list the events most important to you in your life up to this time. How do these contribute to your legacy?
- List people who you admire and identify the accomplishments that you admire. Are there items you would like to add to your list?

Exercise

- Take time to review your life. One way to do this is to imagine what will be said about you at your memorial service or at an event honoring you. How do you want to be remembered? Write this out.
- Now make a list of the elements not currently present in your life. How will you incorporate those things?

Final Thoughts about Legacy

In the end, what is most important is the life that you want for yourself. There are many examples in the book; some that will fit your own dreams and desires, some so far removed that you cannot imagine that life. There are many paths, and we must each find our own. To me, happiness and purpose are the keys to a satisfying life. Each comes in many forms, though. As we age, we spend more time looking for meaning. As we realize that we are closer to the end than the beginning, we hope to be remembered – to leave some legacy.

I think about my great-aunt, Auntie Adelaide. She was the quieter of the two sisters; not the go-getter career woman my grandmother became. As children, we loved spending time in her gentle presence. She had a big heart and an open house. She became a piano tuner and was the first women to be admitted to what is now the National Association of Piano Technicians. In some circles, that distinction has value.

But not in our family: whenever Auntie's name comes up in conversation, a wistful feeling crosses our faces. They aren't thinking about piano tuning. They're thinking about apple pie. As far as any of us is concerned, that's her legacy—she made the best apple pie any of us ever ate.

Resources

THERE are many resources available to you if you would like to make changes in your life. The exercises and questions within each chapter are meant to get you started.

Below are some ideas for further growth. This is by no means a comprehensive book list; rather, these are books that have had a powerful influence on my work and my personal development.

Coaching, Retreats, and Books by the Author

Life Design Blueprint Coaching with Dr. Susan R. Meyer

Coaching, tele-seminars and spa retreats are available through my website, www.SusanRMeyer.com. Use the code FIFTY for a 20% complementary reduction on any tele-seminar, retreat, or your first month of individual coaching.

The Life Design Blueprint Playbook: A Step-By-Step Guide to Your Ideal Life
Dr. Susan R. Meyer
Life-Work Café Press, 2013

Just as you would collaborate with an architect to develop or modify the plan for your home, Dr. Meyer's *Life Blueprint Playbook* will guide you room by room through your life. You will be coached on setting overarching goals and creating a vision for your life and then address important areas including nurturing, meaningful work, surroundings, and creativity. You will then create an action plans for all seven areas of a fulfilling life.

Dr. Susan R. Meyer brings thirty years of experience as a coach and consultant to help you create the future you envision. Be motivated! Be inspired! Be empowered! Find the greatness in your own life.

Midlife and Women's Lives

Women Who Run With the Wolves: Myths and Stories of the Wild Woman Archetype
Clarissa Pinkola Estes
Ballantine Books, 1992
Estes interprets ancient myths and stories about women in a more positive light than you may remember and from these, shows that "wild" really means strong and free. Many of the archetypes she develops will speak to you in a new way. For example, the story of the girl focused on her red shoes morphs from willfulness to persistence

Inventing the Rest of Our Lives: Women in Second Adulthood
Suzanne Braun Levine
Viking, 2005
This is a classic and one of the first books to explore midlife transition specifically for women. It provides a thorough explanation of the bonus years and excellent advice on how to make the best of them.

Passages: Predictable Passages of Adult Life
Gail Sheehy
Penguin Books, 1974

New Passages: Mapping Your Life Across Time
Gail Sheehy
Random House, 1995
For decades, theorists told us that adult development ended at around age thirty. Sheehy explores what adulthood really looks like in *Passages* and, in *New Passages,* extends her research to cover older adults. You will be able to identify your life stage, read about common joys and fears for each, and see the pattern of your own life. These are wonderful books for anyone who feels no one else is where they are in their journey.

Women and the Leadership Q
Shoya Zichy
McGraw-Hill, 2001
Zichy's Color Q system is applied to women's development in this book. Knowing your color helps you understand your own wants and needs and improves your ability to interact successfully with others.

Life Planning

Finding Your Own North Star: Claiming the Life You Were Meant to Live
Martha Beck

Three Rivers Press, 2001

If you are looking for an in-depth exploration of your life that is spirit-centered, this is an excellent book for you. Beck leads you through an inner journey of discovery.

Repacking Your Bags: Lighten Your Load for the Rest of Your Life
Richard J. Leider and David A. Shapiro

Berrett-Koehler, 1994

By midlife, all of us have a lot of baggage. This is the book to help you sort through all that "stuff" in your mind and in your life. You are guided through a process of deciding what to keep and what to shed as you repack your bags for the next leg of the journey.

The Life Audit: A Step-By-Step Guide to Taking Stock, Gaining Control, and Creating the Life You Want ... Now
Caroline Righton

Broadway Books, 2004

If you like lists and charts, this is the book that will give you a system for looking at exactly where you are in life and what you want to change. The book helps you evaluate where you are now and plan a balanced life.

Smart Women Don't Retire–They Break Free
The Transition Network and Gail Rentsch

Springboard Press, 2008

This book embodies the mission of The Transition Network (TTN). It includes interviews with members of TTN and describes how to create and live a full life after leaving formal employment.

About the Author

DR. SUSAN R. MEYER knows how to help people create what they want. Whether you're looking for a totally different life or just a few tweaks, needing guidance on updating your leadership skill set, or planning for retirement, her extensive experience in life, career, and transition coaching will help you see into your crystal ball (that really means taking good look at yourself) and build on what's revealed.

Dr. Meyer has worked in education at every level, from pre-school through grad school and coached and consulted in corporate, non-profit, and government settings. She has coached women returning to work, managers wanting to be happier and more productive, people who felt like failures or had no self-confidence, and successful women who wanted just a little bit more in their lives.

Dr. Meyer holds a Doctorate in Adult Education and Leadership from Teachers College, Columbia University, and Master's degrees in Educational Psychology and Counseling from New York University. She is a past President of the International Association of Coaching (IAC), an IAC Certified Coach and Board-Certified Coach. Her "Women Living for Today and Tomorrow" workshops were featured in The *New York Times*.

She the author of articles and book chapters on midlife, stress, transitions, and transformative learning and has published two books, *Mapping Midlife – Sensational at Sixty* and *The Life Design Blueprint Playbook*. To learn more, visit her website at SusanRMeyer.com

CPSIA information can be obtained at www.ICGtesting.com
Printed in the USA
BVOW04s1333191114

375546BV00004B/8/P